Corporate Cash Management

Techniques and Analysis

Corporate Cash Management

Techniques and Analysis

EDITED BY

Frank J. Fabozzi
Walter E. Hanson / Peat,
Marwick, Mitchell
Professor of Business and
Finance
Lafayette College
and
Leslie N. Masonson

DOW JONES-IRWIN
Homewood, Illinois   60430

F.J.F.'s corner
To Elizabeth and Walter Hanson

L.N.M.'s corner
To my wife, Marilyn
To my son, Daniel
To my daughter, Amy

Preface

Cash management has blossomed into a full-fledged financial profession in the last 10 years. Volatile interest rates, peaking at 21 percent, coupled with the Federal Reserve's aggressive float reduction policies brought about by the passage of the Monetary Control Act of 1980, have emphasized the importance of managing corporate cash more effectively. The demand for cash management expertise has reached the point where the National Corporate Cash Management Association (NCCMA) is sponsoring the development of a certification-program in the discipline. For 10 years one of the only courses available in cash management was provided by the American Management Association. This is no longer the case, as the Cash Management Academy, Duke University, John Leahy, and University Analytics, Inc., and others offer cash management courses. In addition, the cash management seminar business has exploded with specialized offerings from firms such as Bank Administration Institute; NCCMA; White Papers, Inc.; MDS Cash Communications, Inc.; The Corporate Cash Managers Association of New York, Inc.; The World Trade Institute; and the Donoghue Organization, Inc.

Not only has the field of cash management grown in importance but also the job responsibilities of the typical cash manager have expanded. Contemporary cash managers handle bank relationships, investment portfolios, borrowings, and cash forecasts in addition to the more traditional areas of collections, disbursements, funds mobilization, and information. Moreover, the microcomputer has provided modern cash managers with a unique tool to automate the treasury functions of their companies and tie them directly into their accounting systems.

Our objective in preparing this book was to further advance the knowledge of the cash management profession. Less than a handful of books on cash management have been published. This book is unique in that it provides the knowledge of 12 experts in their field rather than one author. Moreover, it covers more sophisticated topics not included in previous texts such as microcomputer applications to cash management, short-term investment opportunities using instruments that are taxable, and tax-exempt, as well as interest rate futures and options. Also, a detailed discussion of handling cash internationally in the same country and across borders is provided, as well as sections on computer models and daily short-term cash forecasting techniques.

We'd like to thank the contributors for their time and effort in advancing the profession of cash management. We offer our gratitude to several individuals for their support: Josephine Iannone for her help in typing sections of the manuscript and Dessa Garlicki for her assistance in reviewing them.

Frank J. Fabozzi
Leslie N. Masonson

Contributors

Frank J. Fabozzi, *Ph.D., C.F.A., C.P.A., Walter E. Hanson/Peat, Marwick, Mitchell Professor of Business and Finance,* Lafayette College

Sylvan G. Feldstein, *Ph.D., Vice President and Manager,* Municipal Research Department, Merrill Lynch, Pierce, Fenner & Smith, Inc.

Andrew R. Gaul, with Capital System Group, Inc.

Andrew D. Kerr, *Vice President,* Global Cash Management Department, Citibank, N.A.

Steven F. Maier, *Ph.D., President,* University Analytics

Helen N. Martin, *Vice President,* Global Cash Management Consulting, Citibank, N.A.

Leslie N. Masonson, *M.B.A., Vice President,* Treasury Management Consulting, Citibank, N.A.

Tom W. Miller, *Ph.D.,* Associate Professor of Business Administration, School of Business Administration, Emory University

Marcia Stigum, *Ph.D.,* Stigum & Associates

Bernell K. Stone, *Ph.D.,* Mills B. Lane Professor of Banking and Finance, College of Management, Georgia Institute of Technology

Norman L. Weinberg, *President,* Norman L. Weinberg Associates

Robert B. Whittredge II, *Assistant Treasurer,* Savin Corporation

Contents

Section III
Forecasting, Models, and Microcomputers

Section IV
Investing Short-Term Funds

Section V
International Cash Management

Corporate Cash Management
Techniques and Analysis

1

Introduction

Leslie N. Masonson
Vice President, Treasury
Management Consulting
Citibank, N.A.

The importance of cash management has grown dramatically over the past 10 years. This is evidenced by the proliferation of cash management publications—magazines, newsletters, and books—and a myriad of seminars and conventions. The formation of at least 40 cash management associations across the United States, coupled with the birth of the National Corporate Cash Management Association in 1979, is further evidence of this explosive trend.

To place the importance of cash management in perspective, consider the opportunity cost of allowing $1 million to sit idle in a bank account overnight. At a 10 percent annual interest rate, the interest lost is $278. When interest rates are 15 percent, as they were in 1980, the overnight opportunity cost rises to $417 per $1 million. Due in large measure to the high interest-rate environment in 1979, 1980, and 1981, corporate cash management sophistication among financial executives increased dramatically. As Exhibit 1 shows, the annual rate of inflation outpaced the average Treasury bill rate from 1977 through 1980 but, since 1981, this trend has reversed. Thus, the effective earnings on investments are worth more in the most recent years, assuming the same corporate tax rate. Moreover, high interest rates result in many companies losing potential bottom-line benefits if their cash management systems are not operating at peak effectiveness.

HISTORICAL BACKGROUND

Kierkegaard, the Danish philosopher and theologian, said: "Life can only be understood backwards, but it must be lived forwards." To gain historical perspective, let us look back at some key cash management events.

Exhibit 1
Interest Rates and Inflation

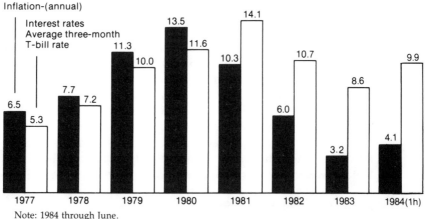

Interest rates and inflation

Inflation-(annual)

Interest rates
Average three-month
T-bill rate

Note: 1984 through June.

In 1931, payable-through-drafts came into existence because bankers wanted to avoid paying the federal stamp tax on checks. This checklike instrument is drawn by a corporate non-bank payer on itself and is payable through a specified bank as indicated on its face. These instruments are still in existence today for paying insurance claims, reimbursing salesmen, and paying freight bills. In essence, the bank acts as a conduit for the checks and verifies neither the signature nor the endorsement since they are the responsibility of the issuing corporation. Each day the bank sends the checks to the corporation for examination and approval to pay. Thus, the corporation retains the final word as to each draft's acceptability.

The first cash collection tool developed was the lockbox concept used by RCA in 1947 through Bankers Trust Company and First National Bank of Chicago. Post-office boxes (lockboxes) were opened in New York City and Chicago to collect large-dollar customer payments. The two banks had RCA's approval to extract the mail from the post-office box, open it, and process the checks, thereby reducing mail time and improving the speed for converting the checks into cash (available funds).

A few remote disbursement accounts were offered in 1967 by Key Bank in Albany and North Carolina National Bank. Since these banks were not located in major Federal Reserve cities, checks took longer to clear back to these locations, thereby providing the issuing corporations with extended float time to invest the funds until the checks actually cleared. Usually, a wire transfer from another bank would be sent to the disbursement bank once the bank notified the issuing corporation of the check-clearings totals early in the morning.

In 1974, the National Automated Clearinghouse Association (NACHA) was formed. Its objective was to replace paper checks with electronic transactions. Currently, there are 30 ACH associations located in the United States that processed 476 million transactions in 1983. Even this number of transactions represents less than 2 percent of all transactions compared to checks.

Also, in the mid-1970s banks and other vendors developed balance reporting systems, whereby the cash manager could obtain his prior day's balance details in his accounts using a terminal in his office that was connected via a phone line to his banks. Moreover, third-party vendors inaugurated deposit reporting services by which a corporation's field offices could call a toll-free number to report their daily bank deposits and their locations. The vendor would then gather the information obtained from all the offices and send it via magnetic tape to the company's concentration bank where the bank would automatically print a depository transfer check for each location and deposit the funds in the concentration account that night.

Beginning in late 1978 and early 1979, the Federal Reserve Board verbally criticized not only banks for offering remote disbursement services to extend float, but also corporations for actively pursuing this service to take advantage of the check depositor who usually received delayed funds availability by his depositing bank. Additionally, the Fed was concerned that certain remote disbursement banks were at risk in the sense that the disbursement dollars flowing through their banks on a daily basis were in some cases larger than their capital base. If a corporate user of this disbursement service went into bankruptcy and did not cover the outstanding checks the same day as they cleared, then the bank could be in serious financial trouble.

Monetary Control Act of 1980

On March 31, 1980, a major piece of financial legislation was passed which has and will continue to have a major impact on the cost of cash management services. Entitled the "Monetary Control Act of 1980," this legislation resulted in the Federal Reserve Board directly pricing its services—checks, wire transfers, ACH transactions, and security transactions—to member banks for the first time since 1918. Also, a plan was put forth to eliminate Fed float (the difference between the availability granted on check deposits to its member banks and the actual time it takes the checks to clear back to the drawee bank) by September 1982. In December 1982, a tremendous controversy developed between the Fed and commercial banks regarding the Fed's intended program to eliminate Fed float by presenting checks later in the day—up to noon. After receiving public comment and having extensive internal meetings, the Fed put in place its Noon Presentment program in a two-phased approach in May 1983 with commercial banks in Fed cities and in April 1984 for commercial banks in non-Fed cities with over $10 million in out-of-zone daily check clearings. This resulted in a further decline in check float and a delay of about one half to one hour in the final notification time.

FUTURE SCAN

The evolving cash management environment in the 1970s can be considered evolutionary compared to the revolutionary changes expected in the 1980s and 1990s. Already a clear trend is developing to automate the treasurer's back office using treasury workstations (microcomputers); to transact business with vendors using electronic payments instead of paper invoices and checks; to reduce check collection float by using state-of-the-art lockbox banks, including those that offer multiple receipt locations; to improve investment yields by knowing early in the day the company's cash position with certainty; and to forecast with a higher degree of accuracy the cash flows on a day-to-day basis.

The most significant change will be the technological revolution. The microcomputer is certainly paramount. From obscurity seven years ago, microcomputers have exploded onto the scene, possibly to a larger extent than the Industrial Revolution. To place the capability of the microcomputers in perspective, one should consider the following comparison from *Software News* (May 1983): A $2,000 microcomputer has more computational capability than a $10 million computer developed 30 years ago. Translating this example into the automobile industry would produce the following comparisons: A Rolls Royce could be purchased today for $2.75, get 3 million miles to the gallon, and would be powerful enough to tow an aircraft carrier.

The explosive surge in microcomputer usage in the last three years has been phenomenal. However, their use in the treasurer's office has been much more restrained. Although cash managers are very interested in purchasing microcomputers for their cash management applications, many companies have been reluctant to purchase them unless a documented cost-benefit analysis has been performed. Additionally, the proliferation of integrated treasury management systems which supply not only the hardware but the software applications as well, has resulted in confusion in the cash manager's eyes as to which vendor to select and which system best meets his needs. A few companies have built and others are building their own treasury management systems because they have not found a comprehensive package to meet all their needs. During the next two to five years, as treasury workstations become easier to use, address the requirements of more corporations by having customized software, become integrated with a company's main-frame computer, and become less costly, the number of companies purchasing these systems will mushroom.

Cash managers will be able to use integrated treasury software to tie together their internal cash management record keeping and external banking data with their accounting records. These transactions will be input on a terminal and automatically update the general ledger, accounts payable, and accounts receivable files. The data from the banks will be captured using an automatic telephone dialer (preprogrammed with the bank telephone numbers) which will call each bank every day and print out at the cash manager's terminal the balance detail in his preferred format before he comes into the office. A few technologically advanced companies will prefer to have a direct computer-to-computer hook-up with the bank's demand deposit accounting system to update their own accounting records. Banks will be reluctant to offer this service until proper internal safeguards have been built to ensure that computer fraud cannot be committed.

Moreover, cash managers will be able to improve their decision-making capabilities by using software that analyzes the raw data and presents the results in summary form with graphic interpretation for ease of understanding. Handling investments will be more automatic since preselected criteria such as risk and maturity levels can be specified beforehand. The microcomputer can then electronically query different investment houses and banks for the best rates and automatically place the order without human intervention.

Another major technological event will be on the retail side—home banking. About 20 banks and vendors are offering consumers the opportunity to bank at home. This usually entails providing balances on accounts, paying bills to vendors, moving funds to different accounts at the same bank, and determining which checks have cleared. Besides these basic banking services, other conveniences offered by some systems are airline schedules, Dow Jones stocks and news, department store shopping, weather, and encyclopedia reference. By the early 1990s, approximately 8 million homes will be using some form of home banking service. Savvy cash managers whose companies deal with these consumers on a retail level should become very interested in this home banking phenomenon to obtain payment via the consumer's terminal rather than by check.

DEFINITION OF CASH MANAGEMENT COMPONENTS

Many financial executives consider the subject of cash management solely from the accounting perspective which considers present value, depreciation, tax implications, and the cash and accrual method of accounting. This book approaches the subject of cash management from a completely different perspective, that is, on an operational basis where the actual management of incoming and outgoing cash on a daily basis is managed effectively. Cash management is composed of five basic elements:

1. *Collections*—speeding up timing of receipts into available funds.
2. *Disbursements*—controlling the release and timing of funds.
3. *Concentration*—inexpensively mobilizing funds from outlying banks to one location for their efficient use.
4. *Investments*—maximizing yield within acceptable levels of risk and maturity.
5. *Information and control*—externally obtaining accurate, timely data on bank balances, bank deposits, lockbox receipts, and internally obtaining data for accurate short-term cash forecasts.

This book treats cash management from all these perspectives. Additional areas addressed include:

- The bank-corporate relationship from the perspective of the banker and corporate cash manager.
- The evolution and current developments in the electronic funds transfer systems, corporate trade payments, and home banking.
- The use of short-term daily cash forecasting models.

- The development of mathematical models for optimizing collection locations, selecting disbursement locations, and determining optimal cash concentration strategies.
- The rapidly developing advancement and use of microcomputers in the treasury function.
- The opportunities to invest short-term cash in numerous instruments such as taxable and tax-exempt instruments and using interest-rate futures and options in managing the portfolio.
- The techniques to handle cross-border international cash management and in-country treasury management.

Cash management is an ever-changing field. Thus, practitioners must keep abreast of the latest developments in the field to remain in the forefront. This can be accomplished by meeting with knowledgeable bank cash management representatives; attending industry seminars; participating in local cash management associations; reading periodic cash management information sources such as magazines, newsletters, and newspapers; and studying books such as this one for new ideas and concepts.

SECTION I

Banking Relationships

2

The Bank-Corporate Relationship from the Banker's Perspective

Leslie N. Masonson
Vice President, Treasury
Management Consulting
Citibank, N.A.

BACKGROUND

The bank-corporate relationship has undergone a significant transition in the last 30 years. During the 1950s and 1960s, most corporations maintained long-term relationships with their banks for credit requirements and basic banking services. Since interest rates and inflation were relatively low compared to the 1970s and 1980s, corporations were not very selective in choosing banks for services. Moreover, the number of banks used by most corporations has shrunk since the early 1970s. The corporate rationale is that better service quality and less administrative control are required with fewer banks. As corporations grew in size, banks began offering new and improved cash management products to meet their demands such as balance reporting systems, depository transfer checks, automated lockbox processing, controlled disbursement, and the automated clearinghouse. Corporations began rearranging their banking relationships to meet not only their credit needs but, more importantly, their service needs. This occurred because of the sharp rise in interest rates and inflation, as well as the expanding needs of the corporation. Thus, as we move through the decade of the 1980s, corporations are critically examining their banking needs and costs, bank service quality, and future credit needs.

Another complicating factor in selecting banks was the passage of the Monetary Control Act of 1980 by Congress and the Noon Presentment (1983) policies of the Federal Reserve Board of Governors. Both of these actions resulted in increased costs to banks for services and the absorption of the cost of Federal Reserve check float by banks and corporations. The banks in turn, reevaluated their internal processing costs and raised prices on the most used bank services, including wire transfers and check processing. Thus, corporations received a double blow—the bank's new pricing which also included the Fed's price passalongs. Since the passage of the Monetary Control Act, bank costs to corporations have increased an estimated 50–150 percent for specific services.

Increased Competition

From the banker's perspective, maintaining existing banking relationships is becoming more difficult because of the increased competition from other domestic banks and a myriad of foreign banks.

Another important factor that will strain existing bank-corporate relationships is the development of keen competition from nonbank entities such as American Express; Sears, Roebuck; Merrill Lynch; and 'Equitable Life. These companies have created banking/financial services without the constraint of being governed by restrictive banking legislation. Examples of these services include the money market accounts (in which a reserve requirement is not necessary), cash management accounts, travelers checks, and loans. A survey by Trans Data indicated that 80 percent of the middle market companies responding to the survey reported that a brokerage house or management consulting firm had approached them to provide cash management services.[1]

Banks must continue to offer innovative services that are competitively priced, in order to increase or maintain their corporate relationships. Thus, money center and regional banks have been spending millions of dollars on developing new products for the corporate marketplace. Not only will innovative product development be important, but the interrelationship of telecommunications and information management will be equally important. Since the banking industry is moving into the "electronic and information" age at an ever increasing pace, corporations will be more inclined to use banks that meet not only their current but also their future needs. For example, Citibank's foray into satellite communications is only the beginning of the electronic future of banking.

In the future, banks will have to incorporate a broader range of services to compete effectively in this marketplace. This trend has already started, with banks acquiring savings and loans as-

---

[1] "Middle-Market Firms Push for Fee Payments to Banks, Survey Finds," *CASHFLOW*, May 1983.

sociations in other states, insurance companies, and discount
brokerages.

Interstate Banking

Furthermore, the eventual passage of interstate banking legislation will further blur the distinction between banks and other
financial organizations. South Dakota, Nebraska, Delaware, and
Maine have begun to offer out-of-state banks the opportunity to
enter their states for banking, insurance, and securities brokerage. Chase Manhattan Bank is using Equitable Life Assurance's
facilities in three cities to collect lockbox receipts for its customers. This means that a Chase customer will need only one
account with Chase in New York City rather than accounts with
four other banks to handle its processing, eliminating the costs
of moving funds and information from four banks and strength-
ening the relationship to Chase. First Bancshares has formed a
network of five banks in five states to offer the same type of
services. Other banks have begun offering similar services. (See
lockbox networking in Chapter 4.)

RELATIONSHIP CONSIDERATIONS

A successful bank-corporate relationship is dependent
upon objective advice, periodic contact, rapid problem resolution, fair compensation, and the bank's operational capabilities.
Let's review each of these areas in more detail.

Objective Advice

Corporations should expect to receive objective advice from
their bankers. This should occur in all areas of the relationship,
from details on the best approach to use in obtaining credit
facilities with the various options to the good and bad points of
using certain bank services. For example, if a corporation is
using a bank's fee-based cash management consulting service,
then it should expect to receive a nonbiased objective report
without mentioning that bank's products and services as solutions to its cash management problems.

On the other hand, the banker wants to receive similar treatment. Negative financial facts on problems being encountered
by the company should be discussed honestly with bankers,
especially when a borrowing situation exists. Neither the corporation nor the banker wants any surprises in their relationship
with each other.

Periodic Contact

In order for a bank-corporate relationship to flourish, there should be periodic contact between both parties. The corporation should frequently call its banker to get the latest trends in banking, the money markets, and recent economic developments in its industry or in foreign countries. An excellent supplement to this personal contact is receiving weekly reports from the bank's economics department, foreign exchange department, and money market desk, among others. Also, attending bank presentations, seminars, or discussions by their experts in areas of interest should be rewarding from the standpoint of knowing what's happening in specific topics, as well as meeting other corporate attendees who have similar interests and problems.

The banker, on the other hand, should visit or call the corporate client when he has a substantive matter to discuss. Negotiating the terms of a loan, providing insight on new tax regulations, discussing money market investment alternatives, or solving an operational problem all fall into this category. A banker should be careful not to bombard the client with all the bank's product specialists since the client may not be interested in many of these offerings. The best relationship occurs when the banker selectively responds to the client's needs and time constraints.

Rapid Problem Resolution

Probably no other factor has soured a corporation's bank relationship more than unresolved operational problems at a bank. Due to the huge volumes of bank transactions, a small percentage of errors occur. Typical errors are debiting an account twice for the same transaction, not stopping a check as instructed, sending a wire transfer to the wrong bank or the wrong beneficiary, and printing new checks with an incorrect account number. The corporate client should expect the bank to research the problem and resolve it within a few days for a simple transaction to a week if it is a more complicated one. The bank should have adequate staffing and knowledgeable personnel to resolve the problem to the client's satisfaction.

A few banks have set up a workstation approach to handle large accounts in which all the customer-related activity (e.g., account reconciliation, funds transfer, check processing, letters of credit, and investigation) are handled by the same individuals daily. This approach provides the client with a quicker response time and a more personal approach to its problems. However, the majority of banks have separate departments that handle specific types of investigations for all the bank's customers.

Fair Compensation

The banker wants a banking relationship with a customer that provides the bank with a fair profit. Typically, the more important the customer in terms of size and account profitability, the greater the attention and service received. Bankers are relationship oriented rather than transaction oriented. This means that the banker is much more interested in dealing with a company which is a customer for the long term and which uses the bank for many services, including credit needs, rather than in a company which maintains just a lockbox account, transfers out all available balances each morning to a concentration bank, and pays by fee. Another reason the banker doesn't prefer to deal with a nontransaction-oriented customer is that the bank may be losing money on these types of customers. Traditionally, banks have had difficulty in determining the true cost of pricing many of their services. For example, even if a bank determines that a service should be priced at $0.50 an item, while the competition is charging only $0.35, the bank may lower its price to $0.40, just breaking even on each transaction in the hope of obtaining more profitable business in the future.

Banks' Operational Capabilities

Banks vary widely in their operational capability. Those with the highest quality service, latest technology, and fairest pricing should be able to attract sufficient customers to be profitable. A corporation can gauge a bank's capability by:

- Designing a detailed questionnaire and sending it to the bank for completion. This approach is typical for assessing a bank's lockbox or disbursement service capabilities.
- Visiting a bank's operational facilities (such as check processing, data center, lockbox processing, money transfer, and money market trading room) and asking pointed questions. Look for the latest in processing equipment, microcomputers, a well-organized and attractive working environment, and the latest telecommunications capabilities. Evaluate attitude, demeanor, and personal contact with the operating personnel.
- Obtaining at least 10 references, 5 who have been using the desired service for the last few years and 5 customers who have been using it for the past three months.
- Reviewing surveys conducted by private firms, such as

Louis Harris, Greenwich Research Associates, Phoenix-Hecht, Inc., and TransData, to determine a bank's ranking and trends. Be particularly careful to determine the methodology used in the survey, as well as the types and numbers of respondents, and especially the exact questions asked in order to arrive at valid conclusions.

- Discussing a bank's capabilities with its competitors. Usually other bankers can offer useful insights into the disadvantages of using another bank's services.
- Contracting with a consulting firm or well-known bank consultant who can objectively assist in designing and analyzing questionnaires, evaluating banks during on-site visits, and developing a custom-designed survey. This is often the most expensive of the five approaches mentioned above but is usually very accurate.

A corporation often neglects to evaluate the quality of the bank's operating personnel. Especially in bank operations departments, the personnel quality has a significant impact on the bank's ability to deliver a high-quality service. Questions should be directed to the managers of the specific departments regarding the number of employees, years of experience of supervisory and clerical staff, turnover rate, productivity standards, quality control standards, and reward system for superior performance. An on-site inspection is particularly useful for assessing these factors firsthand.

State-of-the-Art Services

One of the most important aspects of the bank-corporate relationship is the bank's ability to offer the kinds of high-quality services that corporations need. If banks expect to retain their existing customers' business, as well as to expand their customer bases, they must be able to offer innovative, cost-effective, and practical services with continual product enhancements. From the cash management viewpoint, the following types of services are required in today's marketplace.

1. High-Quality Lockbox Processing. Significant technological changes have occurred in the past 10 years to improve the quality and speed of lockbox processing. High-speed encoding equipment with OCR/MICR read heads have reduced the number of manual processing steps. Banks which have invested in expensive processing technology have been able to capture an increasing share of this competitive market.

2. Controlled Disbursement Capability. About 100 regional and money center banks have developed this disbursement service. The bank is able to notify its customers by 11 A.M. of the exact dollar value of the checks to be cleared that day. This is possible since the bank's disbursement facility is located in a non-Federal Reserve city which receives one or two early-morning check presentments from the local Federal Reserve office. The customer then funds the account either by wire transfer from another bank to cover the transaction or automatically by a transfer from an account at the same bank. Using controlled disbursement, a company does not have to keep excess balances in an account since it has exact knowledge today of the dollar amount of clearings to be debited to the account that night. Additionally, cash forecasting may not be necessary if controlled disbursement is used.

3. Automated Clearinghouse Payments Capability. As the price of checks continues to escalate, corporations are seriously considering the use of electronic alternatives such as the Automated Clearinghouse (ACH) to obtain funds from their retail customers (e.g., obtaining preauthorization to debit a customer's account for the monthly utility or insurance payment) or to concentrate their funds from local depository accounts, replacing paper-based depository transfer checks.

4. Highly Developed Information Reporting Systems. As corporations become more sophisticated and automated in their treasurers' offices, they are demanding more information from their banks. Typically, corporations using terminals in their offices require the following information from their banks:

- Opening available and ledger balances in all their accounts.
- Closing available balance of the prior day.
- One- and two-day float.
- Lockbox deposit totals at all banks.
- Intraday lockbox deposit reporting.
- Real-time information on outgoing and incoming wire transfers.
- Detailed debit and credit data on certain transactions.
- Target balances versus actual balance comparison.
- Wire transfer capability from terminal.
- Investigation and inquiry to bank personnel via the terminal.
- Rates on money market instruments.
- Portfolio tracking.
- Automatic dial-up capability to query other balance reporting systems.

A number of highly sophisticated companies are requesting that their banks provide them with computer-to-computer interface directly into their demand deposit accounting system so that they can determine account activity as it occurs and update their own accounting records. Banks have to be careful in offering this capability because of the potential for computer fraud.

IMPORTANCE OF ACCOUNT ANALYSIS STATEMENTS

A useful tool for measuring bank service costs is the account analysis statement (Exhibit 1). This statement should

Exhibit 1
Typical Account Analysis Statement

ABC NATIONAL BANK
Account Analysis Statement
For Month Ending October 1984
XYZ Instrument Company

Account No. 74367989

Average ledger balance	$ 10,000,000
Less average float	−2,000,000
Average available balance	8,000,000
Less reserve requirement at 12.00%	−960,000
Net available balance	$ 7,040,000
Earnings allowance at 10%	

Monthly Activity

Service	Quantity	Unit Price	Amount
Account maintenance	1	3.00	$ 3.00
Lockbox activity	5,000	0.25	1,250.00
Account reconcilement	3,000	0.04	120.00
Checks paid	3,000	0.14	420.00
Wire transfers	20	5.00	100.00
Total service charges			$ 1,893.00
Balance required to support activity			$ 227,160.00
Balances available to support other services			$6,812,840.00

not be confused with a bank statement, which shows the dates that checks and credits were applied to the account accompanied by a closing ledger balance each day. Rather, it is a statement which indicates the balances necessary to pay for bank services used during the past month. Exhibit 2 reviews the elements of this document.

Exhibit 2
Elements of Account Analysis Statements

Component	Meaning
Average ledger balance	The sum of the daily closing book balance in the account each day divided by the number of calendar days in the month.
Average float	The sum of the face value of each check multiplied by the assigned availability (0, 1, or 2 days depending upon the bank's check availability schedule and deposit cut-off times) each day divided by the number of calendar days in the month. (Note: see separate discussion on float.)
Average available balance	The balance remaining after subtracting the check float.
Required reserves	Bank's deposit of funds at the local Federal Reserve bank to support this demand deposit account. The reserve percentage is fixed by regulation and is dependent upon the bank's size. Banks with over $25 million in net transaction accounts are required to keep 12% reserves effective February, 1984. Most banks subtract the reserve requirement since they feel it is a cost of doing business.
Net available balance	Balances that can be used to pay for services or cover compensating balance requirements.
Earnings allowance (also known as earnings credit rate)	Interest rate (e.g., three-month T-bill) used to value the net available balance.
Monthly activity	A listing of the bank services used during the month. The volume of transactions and the unit price or balance equivalent are provided.
Total service charge	The cost of all services used for the month.
Balance required to support services	This is determined using formula:

$$\frac{\text{Total service charges} \times 12 \text{ (months in year)}}{\text{Earnings allowance}} = \frac{\$1,893 \times 12}{0.10}$$
$$= \$227,160$$

Component	Meaning
Balance available to support other services	The residual balance remaining after service costs and compensating balances for loans have been covered. This number is obtained by subtracting the total services charges from the net available balance. In this case:

$$\begin{array}{r} \$7,040,000 \\ -227,160 \\ \hline \$6,812,840 \end{array}$$

By carefully analyzing his bank account analysis statements, the cash manager can assess whether his balance levels should be adjusted. Typically, most corporations monitor their available balances daily for their more active bank accounts compared to once a week or once a month for their smaller transaction accounts.

Exhibit 3
Typical Questions Asked on Account Analysis Statements

Do all commercial banks provide them?	Almost every money center and regional banks provide them. Smaller banks may or may not offer them depending upon their individual capabilities, corporate demand, and internal policies.
How are they obtained?	Unless the corporation requests it by letter or by oral communication with the corporate account officer banks will not usually provide this statement.
Are they usually computer-generated?	Yes. The degree of automation in compiling the statement varies significantly from bank to bank. Some banks obtain all the input on the bank services from other automated internal systems. Other banks may physically obtain the necessary information from various internal departments and keypunch the data into their systems. Smaller banks usually prepare the statement manually because of the lack of demand.
How much do they cost?	Typically, there is no cost for this statement. However, a few banks have begun charging a nominal fee.
If there are five accounts at one bank, can the bank provide separate statements?	Yes. Also, a composite statement combining all the account activity and balance levels can be obtained if requested.
When do banks normally send out the statement?	Statements are sent out between one to six weeks after the month ends. The norm is about three to four weeks.
Are most statements from different banks in a standard format?	No. Each bank has designed the statement to suit its internal operating requirements. Therefore, the terminology, methodology of calculations, and layout of statement varies among banks. (Exhibits 4–7 show four layouts of the same information.)
How accurate are the statements?	They are as accurate as the bank's methodology and quality control procedures for controlling the data input and verification process. The more automated the input process, the less likely errors will occur.

Typical questions asked on account analysis statements are shown in Exhibit 3.

ACCOUNT ANALYSIS INSIGHTS

Meaning of Availability

Availability is an important factor that should be clearly understood by financial executives. Since availability plays an important part in determining the balances necessary to support services, let's first review the basic concepts.

Availability is assigned by a bank based upon the bank's unique internal operating systems and policies. There are two methods used in assigning availability to corporate check deposits. The most common method is actual availability. In this case, the bank assigns availability of zero (immediate funds or a check drawn on the bank in which it is deposited), one (a bank in the same city or a Federal Reserve city), or two days (all other locations, usually country points and other geographically remote cities) to each check based upon where the check is drawn and the time of day the check is deposited.

A second method is to assign a fixed availability factor to each check that is based upon a prior analysis of the corporation's mix of checks and their drawee bank destination. For example, a bank may assign an availability factor of 1.25 days to all check deposits. From the corporate perspective, the former method is more accurate and thus more desirable. Also, most money center and regional banks offer actual availability.

Banks differ in their assignments of actual availability. Each bank has specific internal deposit deadlines for assigning availability. If this deadline is missed by just one minute, one full day of availability may be lost. Many banks "direct send" checks to the drawee banks or to Federal Reserve offices in other cities to speed up their funds flow. Usually, one day is gained by using these air flights to other cities. Certain banks pass along this improved availability to their corporate customers, while other banks pass along a percentage or none of the gain. Thus, the corporate customer should determine the bank's availability, methodology, deposit deadlines, and direct send passalongs compared to those of other banks in the same city.

Earnings Allowance

The earnings allowance (also known as the earnings credit rate) is calculated by the bank each month. Banks have different rates based upon their selection of the measurement rate and their internal calculations. Rates used include: preceding three-month Treasury bill rate, average of weekly Treasury bill auction rates, bond equivalent yield, and federal funds approximation. Just because a bank has a higher earnings allowance does not necessarily mean that the bank has a lower cost for its services. Three factors must always be taken into account to make this determination: the bank's reserve requirement, earnings allowance, and cost for specific services. An example will clarify this discussion. Let's assume that three banks provide the following information.

Bank	Earnings Allowance	Reserve Requirement	Monthly Service Charges
1	10%	None deducted	$1,000
2	15	13.59%	1,100
3	17	12.00	1,200

Which bank would be the least costly to use assuming that their service quality was equal? The formula to use is as follows:

Available balance required for services
$$= \frac{\text{Monthly service charges} \times 12 \text{ months}}{(1 - \text{Reserve requirement}) \times \text{Earnings allowance}}$$

In our example, the results are as follows:

$$\text{Bank 1} = \frac{1,000 \times 12}{(1 - 0) \times 0.10} = \$120,000$$

$$\text{Bank 2} = \frac{1,100 \times 12}{(1 - 0.1359) \times 0.15} = \$101,840$$

$$\text{Bank 3} = \frac{1,200 \times 12}{(1 - 0.12) \times 0.17} = \$96,257$$

Thus, Bank 3 is the least costly from the standpoint of balances required for services even though it had the highest cost of services. Interestingly, Bank 1 did not deduct a reserve requirement and had the lowest service charge, yet was the most expensive because of the lowest earnings allowance.

Maintain Balances in Noninterest-Bearing Certificate of Deposit

A useful method for a corporation to improve its effective earnings allowance (after subtracting required reserves) is to place its balances in a noninterest-bearing certificate of deposit (CD) instead of a demand deposit account. This is beneficial to both the corporation and the bank since the reserve requirement is 3 percent on the CD compared to at least 12 percent in the checking account. Therefore, the corporation's balance is worth more.

Fees or Balances

The controversy as to whether a corporation should pay for bank services using fees or balances continues to be a lively one. The conclusion of many corporations is that fees are usually preferable to balance compensation. Moreover, a survey by Phoenix-Hecht, Inc., indicated that only 12 percent of a bank's customers are paying by fee.[2] Some banks add a premium (e.g., 25 percent) to the fees if balance compensation is not used. However, each bank has its own policy.

If a corporation prefers to pay in fees, then it should use the following formula to convert balances into fees.

$$\text{Monthly fee} = \frac{\begin{array}{c}\text{Balance required for services} \\ \times \text{ (Earnings allowance)} \\ \times \text{ (1 } - \text{ Reserve requirement)}\end{array}}{\text{Days in the year} \div \text{Days in the month}}$$

The corporation benefits from fees if it is a net investor of funds and can earn a rate of interest on its investments that exceeds the bank's earnings allowance (less reserves). Additionally, if the corporation is short of cash, the maintenance of high balances is costly. When a corporation is required to pay compensating balance according to a loan arrangement, its options are more limited.

Balances are used by some financial executives to pay for bank services such as consulting studies when they don't have the budget for consulting expense. Normally, the balances are increased for a month or two to cover the cost of the study. Another reason for maintaining balances is to build the relationship so that, when the corporation needs a loan or other assistance, the bank will deliver. In actuality, this corporate rationale may

---

[2] 1982 Collection Practices Survey, Phoenix-Hecht, Inc., Chicago, Ill., 1982.

not always work out. Banks evaluate the entire corporate relationship from the standpoint of account profitability, financial strength of the company, honesty, openness, and management strength. All these factors enter into their decision to provide additional funding for future financial needs.

Certain bank services are not necessarily priced to the corporation, but are very useful. Examples of these intangible services include investment advice and reports, credit investigations, economic briefings, meetings with foreign exchange experts, and a home relocation service for the corporation's executives.

Banks generally monitor a corporation's balances on a monthly basis but evaluate the profitability of the relationship every year. Thus, over the course of the year, the average available balance in the account should cover any loan requirements and service charges for activity performed. Excess balances in one month can be used to offset balance shortfalls in other months and vice versa.

A few banks "double count" balances that support credit lines for other service activity. For example, if $100,000 is the available balance required for a loan agreement, the bank will count up to $100,000 in balance-related service activity as well. This practice is not very frequent and is typically provided to customers on an individual negotiated basis or other special arrangement.

Treasury Tax and Loan (TT&L) Credit

Certain banks provide corporations with additional account analysis credit for deposit of Treasury tax and loan checks. Corporations are required by law to make tax payments (e.g., quarterly estimated income tax) by a specific date each quarter. They provide the bank with a check and a TT&L card that identifies the paying corporation. The bank is then required to deposit the check at the local Federal Reserve Board for credit to the bank's TT&L account. On a periodic basis, usually a day or two later, the U.S. government removes the funds. Depending upon the bank's earnings on these deposits, a credit is passed along to the corporation's account analysis statements as compensation for depositing the check with the bank.

Comparing Account Analysis Statements
from Different Banks

As previously pointed out, no standard format is used by banks in preparing their account analysis statements. There are hundreds of variations. Exhibits 4–7 provide varying formats using

Exhibit 4
Account Analysis Variation

ABC NATIONAL BANK
Customer Account Analysis
October 1984
XYZ Instrument Company

Account No. 74367989

Deposit Statistics

	Average Balances for Month
Gross balance	$10,000,000
Check float	2,000,000
Available balance	8,000,000
Balance required for services	227,160
Balances remaining	7,772,840

Services Performed for October

Service	Volume	Price per Unit	Total Price	Balance Required per Unit	Total Balance Required
Account maintenance	1	$3.00	$ 3	$360.00	$ 360
Lockbox activity	5,000	.25	1,250	30.00	150,000
Account reconcilement	3,000	.04	120	4.80	14,400
Checks paid	3,000	.14	420	16.80	50,400
Wire transfers out	20	5.00	100	600.00	12,000
Total			$1,893		$227,160

Note: Earnings allowance is 10 percent (three-month average of T-bill rate). Reserves are not deducted at all.

Exhibit 5
Account Analysis Variation

ABC NATIONAL BANK
Account Analysis
Period Ending October 31, 1984
(days: 31)

For: XYZ Instrument Company
Acct. No. 74367989

Cost Analysis

Account maintenance	1 at	$3.00	=	$ 3.00
Lockbox activity	5,000 at	0.25	=	1,250.00
Account reconciliation	3,000 at	0.04	=	120.00
Checks paid	3,000 at	0.14	=	420.00
Wire transfers out	20 at	5.00	=	100.00
Total service cost				$1,893.00

Balance Analysis

Average ledger balance	$10,000,000
Less: Uncollected funds	2,000,000
Average collected balance	8,000,000
Less: Legal reserves at 12%	960,000
Net funds	$ 7,040,000

Account Summary

Investment earning on net funds at 10%	$ 55,833
Total cost of service	1,893
Net profit	53,940

Exhibit 6
Account Analysis Variation

XYZ Instrument Company
Acct. No. 74367989

ABC NATIONAL BANK
Analysis for Month of October 1984

Average Funds Deposited

Ledger balance	$10,000,000
Less: Uncollected funds	2,000,000
Collected balance	$ 8,000,000
Earning allowance on collected balance = 10%	

Required Collected Balance

Reserve requirement at 12%	$ 960,000
To pay for noncredit services	227,160
Collected balances available to support other services	6,812,840

Analysis of Services for the Month

Services	Volume	Per Unit	Collected Balance per Unit	Total Collected Balance Required
Account maintenance	1	$3.00	$360.00	$ 360
Lockbox activity	5,000	0.25	30.00	150,000
Account reconcilement	3,000	0.04	4.80	14,400
Checks paid	3,000	0.14	16.80	50,400
Wire transfers out	20	5.00	600.00	12,000
Collected balances required to pay for services				$227,160

the same data as shown in Exhibit 1. Some interesting observations comparing these five exhibits are:

1. The bank in Exhibit 4 does not deduct reserves from the average available balances. Thus, the balance available to support other services is 12 percent higher than in Exhibit 1. In essence, the corporate customer can use more bank services for the same level of balances.
2. The banks in Exhibits 4 and 5 equate the service cost to a balance equivalent. This is another way of showing the total service charges.
3. The banks in Exhibits 5 and 7 show the account profitability on a direct service charge basis (e.g., $1,893 in service costs) rather than showing the balance equivalent of the excess funds.

Exhibit 7
Account Analysis Variation

XYZ Instrument Company
Acct. No. 74367989

ABC NATIONAL BANK
Analysis for Month of October 1984

Average Funds Deposited

Analysis of earnings:	
Average ledger balance	$10,000,000
Less: Average uncollected funds	2,000,000
Less: 12% reserve requirement	960,000
Funds available to invest	$ 7,040,000
Value of investable funds at 10%	$ 55,833

Analysis of Service Costs

Service	Volume	Rate	Charges	Balance Required
Account maintenance	1	$3.00	$ 3.00	$ 360
Lockbox activity	5,000	0.25	1,250.00	150,000
Account reconcilement	3,000	0.04	120.00	14,400
Checks paid	3,000	0.14	420.00	50,400
Wire transfers out	20	5.00	100.00	12,000
Cost of services			$1,893.00	$227,160

Analysis Summary

Value of investable funds	$55,833
Less: Cost of services used	1,893
Net gain on account	$53,940

Corporations with over 20 bank relationships would benefit by standardizing the format and terminology for ease of comparison. Currently, a handful of large banks and a few software vendors offer this service to corporate customers. Instead of spending many hours each month analyzing the account analysis statements for all its banks, a corporation can receive printed reports showing for the past 12 months, by bank:

- The average ledger, average float, average available, and target balances for each account.
- Earnings allowance and required reserves.
- Balance required for services, total service charges, and balances available to support other services.
- Per item pricing and volume for all services used.

• Comparison of pricing and ranking of all banks from lowest cost provider of a service to highest cost provider.

SUMMARY

The bank-corporate relationship will continue to undergo changes as electronic banking services, regulatory changes, and technological improvements continue to evolve. The banker is looking for a long-term relationship with his corporate client, while the corporation is looking for a service-related relationship with an innovative, high-quality, and personally attended bank. Both parties to this relationship can receive satisfaction if they understand and respond to each other's needs.

3

The Bank-Corporate Relationship from the Corporate Perspective

Robert B. Whittredge II
Assistant Treasurer
Savin Corporation

In the job description of every Company treasurer, among the primary functions listed are the selection of banks, maintenance of good relations with banks, and management of the company's cash flowing through banks. The life blood of a company is the cash made available by bankers through credit lines, the cash received through banks from customers, and the cash disbursed through banks to vendors, employees, and investors; therefore, the task of choosing the appropriate banks, as well as establishing and maintaining close relationships with them, is critical to the effective operation and growth of any business.

BANK SELECTION

The selection of a company's bankers is an ongoing process. A new treasurer, assistant treasurer, or cash manager will certainly want to review the situation that he has inherited. But the needs of a company also change as its business evolves. So even the experienced cash manager will find that constant review of banking arrangements is necessary. For example, a cash manager may have become dissatisfied with the quality of service being provided by an existing bank or the bank may have ceased offering a necessary service. Perhaps the existing bankers cannot accommodate a company's needs for increased credit availability or don't have expertise in the markets newly established by the company. Or, the cash manager and the banking officer simply don't have the rapport necessary for an effective relationship. In sum, the cash manager must have a clear understanding of his company's requirements, both for credit and for operational services. Then, a review of bank strengths and weaknesses will show if the company and each bank are well matched. Among the important factors in this review are:

Cash management capability.

Credit availability.

Geographic location.

Special expertise.

Bank size.

Number of banks.

Personalities.

Bank cancellation.

Certainly there are other factors of particular interest to individual companies, but this list will be used as an outline for this discussion.

Cash Management Capability

In effect, any bank operating service that handles cash can be considered as a cash management service, although certain services, such as lockbox remittance processing and controlled disbursing, are among the primary ones traditionally thought of as cash management services.[1] A key consideration in selecting a bank to provide cash management services is the bank's commitment to the continued provision of existing services as well as future service development and expansion. During the late 1970s, many major banks were offering a full line of cash management products. But, beginning in the early 1980s, it became apparent that not all these banks could afford to compete in every sector of the market. Some, for example, made abrupt decisions to cease lockbox remittance processing. Their customers had to move quickly to find alternative banks and switch their own customers and receivables processing over to new banks.

Cash management banks in the 1980s clearly are being split into those that will continue a commitment to a full line of cash management services and those that will trim their sails and compete in niches that fit their special markets and capabilities. Accordingly, it is necessary to carefully sound out existing banks as to their strategic plans for cash management services.

---

[1] These techniques of cash management are discussed in greater depth in Chapters 4 and 5.

Then, if their commitment is satisfactory, a contract should be negotiated as tangible evidence of that commitment. Aside from being a good way to clarify the relationship between the parties, the contract may limit price increases to a certain percentage over a certain time and may require some adequate period of notice in case either the company or the bank prefers to cancel a service.

Within the general category of cash management, there are a number of specific services that should be investigated before selecting a cash management bank.

Treasury Information Systems   Interface with the company's treasury information system is one of the most important evidences of a bank's capabilities. Simple balance and transaction reporting via a terminal in the office may be adequate, but many banks, as well as nonbank vendors, are also able to offer more advanced systems that operate on a microcomputer in the company's office.[2] These systems can automatically retrieve balance and transaction data from banks, update investment and borrowing records, as well as short-term cash forecasts, and prepare cash transaction entries in a format suitable for the individual company's general ledger system.

Regardless of whether a bank or nonbank vendor is used, the company's cash management banks must be able to work closely with the company to make such a system effective. Although the logical design of these systems is generally the same, the individual company's specific mode of operation, and even the format of the daily reports, requires selection of a bank that can be flexible; the system should meet the company's needs, not what the bank thinks these needs might be.

Electronic Funds Transfer (EFT)[3]   Any bank can process wire transfers, but each company must determine if it wants the ability to initiate transfers from the office terminal. If so, the bank must be able to process the transfer order in a fully automated fashion and quickly confirm that the funds were in fact transferred. There must also be an adequate level of security over such electronic information. The press is full of stories about unauthorized access to bank computers. Some companies with special concern over this area don't trust even two-level passwords, but have set up arrangements to scramble their EFT orders to their banks. In such cases, the bank must make a

---

[2] The use of microcomputers in cash management is discussed in Chapter 9.

[3] Electronic funds transfer is discussed in Chapter 6.

unique arrangement to accommodate the company's requirements, evidence of the special effort that is the hallmark of a
good cash management bank.

Furthermore, as programs are developed to convert corporate-to-corporate payments from check to electronic transfers,
the ability of a bank to service both the company's needs and
those of its vendors will become more and more important.

Controlled Disbursement[4]   These accounts are now available
from a variety of banks, not only the geographically remote.
Delay of check presentment may still be considered when a
company selects a bank but, as the Federal Reserve continues its
efforts to wring float out of the banking system, the benefit of
"remote" disbursing will become minimal. Nevertheless, the
ability to control cash balances will remain paramount, so banks
should be selected on the basis of their ability to give timely and
accurate reporting of all checks presented each day. A controlled
disbursment bank must also provide a fully automated reconciliation service that meets the needs of the company's accountants. It might be necessary to change a controlled disbursment
bank simply because the controller's staff finds the reconciliation documents to be cumbersome and confusing.

Lockbox Remittance Processing[5]   This is a very specialized service that not all banks are equipped to handle well. Because
today's high-speed computer-controlled check processing systems are so costly, only selected banks are willing to make the
commitment of capital necessary for such an automated service.
If it is necessary to process a large volume of remittances, choose
a bank that has already made such a commitment, as shown by
the installation of the necessary equipment. Such a bank can
also easily transmit the data captured in its computers to each
company's computerized accounts receivable system, thereby
enabling automatic cash application. Of course, if the company's remittances consist of 50 checks a month, each of $100,000
or more, such a sophisticated system is unnecessary. The manual wholesale lockbox service available from many banks will be
entirely adequate.

Consulting   Cash management systems design expertise is
now available from a variety of sources, whereas in the 1970s it
was available primarily from bankers. Now, with ex-cash man-

---

[4] Disbursement control is discussed in Chapter 5.
[5] Lockbox remittance processing is discussed in Chapter 4.

agement bankers setting up their own firms and departments at public auditors, consulting assistance outside of banks is available. But banks are still the primary source of disbursement and collection studies and may well offer very inexpensive fees for running these computerized models. Generally, a low fee is a sign that the bank plans to include its own performance in the results of the study, hoping that there will be an opportunity to sell its own disbursement or remittance service. Only a few banks consciously seek to set up independent consulting groups. Such groups not only perform collection and disbursing studies (at a higher price that reflects the avowed independence from their cash management sales teams), but can also assist in a general review of cash management systems and procedures, both domestic and foreign.

Credit Availability

Few businesses can prosper on the basis of operating cash flow alone; for most, the bank is a necessary source of working capital.

Aside from ensuring that it can handle the desired line of credit, the bank should be in a position to offer funds at competitive rates. This competitive pricing capability is founded on the bank's access to funds at the best rates, based on its own deposit gathering and alternative sourcing capability. As an example, while a major money center bank will generally have access to funds at the best deposit rates, such banks depend heavily on deposits that are very sensitive to price. The bank must pay the market rate at all times, otherwise, investors will place their deposits elsewhere. In contrast, a smaller bank may not be able to command the very best rates, but its deposits may not be as price-sensitive as at the money center banks. Thus, credit lines from smaller banks will tend to be more stable in pricing, while those from money center banks will be more volatile.

Of course, the spread that the bank wants to earn over its cost of funds is likewise very important. This would be affected by the bank's general loan profitability experience, as well as its evaluation of a company's desirability as a credit risk. As a result, banks charge anywhere from a fraction of 1 percent over their deposit costs to full percentage points over prime rate. The prime rate is, in effect, now the maximum rate being charged to creditworthy companies with the very best being offered substantially lower rates.

All other things being equal, some banks will just be hungrier than others to put money to work. In recent years, this has been amply demonstrated by the numerous branches of foreign banks that have often undercut the domestic banks on pricing loans to well-regarded companies.

A farmer wouldn't want to put all his eggs in one basket and neither should a company; a bank might turn against an industry or a specific company. Against that possibility, a company should use more than one bank. In this way, when additional borrowing is necessary, which often occurs rather quickly, the company has resources which are readily available.

Geographic Location

Now that telecommunications has reduced apparent distances, a bank in San Francisco with a New York City client may be at only a very slight disadvantage due to its geographic location. Yet it is certainly true that having the company's banker so near that frequent visits are possible is still one of the important elements in the banking relationship. It is for this very reason that most major banks have established regional loan production offices in cities around the country. Alternatively, it may be necessary to choose a bank not for its nearness to headquarters, but for its proximity to customers, in the case of a remittance processing bank, or nearness to the company's plants, in the case of payroll and other personal banking services for employees.

Geography can also foster different viewpoints among your bankers. In New York City, for example, a variety of differing opinions on both national and world affairs affecting a company can be had simply by contacting the company's U.S., Canadian, French, German, or Japanese bankers. Each will bring to a question a special approach that is a direct result of their different geographic bases.

The trend toward nationwide banking has begun to blur the distinction between "city" and "country" banks. Now local banks are developing broad capabilities to handle specialized services. Thus, even companies located outside of traditional metropolitan business centers can choose a nearby bank that offers many of the services previously available only from the major city banks.

Special Expertise

Aside from credit and cash management services, there are a variety of special services that a company may require from a bank.

Short-Term Investments   These are sold by every bank. The larger ones effectively compete with traditional securities dealers by offering the full range of money market securities, such as secondary certificates of deposit, commercial paper, Eurodollar deposits, and bankers' acceptances. As there are only so many investment sales people from whom a cash manager can receive a telephone call each day, it is wise for the cash manager to do business primarily with those who handle a variety of investments, know his needs and guidelines, and keep very close touch with him during the few hours of each day when investments can be made.

Foreign Exchange   Such expertise is necessary for companies with purchases and sales in foreign currencies. Again, as with short-term investments, the quantity and quality of information are paramount in foreign exchange trading. Maintain competition, but limit the number of foreign exchange contacts so that the business can be spread around in sufficient quantity to encourage close attention to the company's needs.

Foreign Trade and Banking   For multinational companies, a bank's expertise in foreign business and banking practices is likewise important. Whether the objective is to set up or close down a foreign operation, speed up remittances from overseas subsidiaries, or repatriate funds blocked by foreign regulations, banks that have branches or business in countries where the company has an interest are a primary source of help. Successful resolution of these problems requires intimate knowledge of the detailed regulations, as well as personal acquaintance with those officials who are in a position to give the necessary approvals. The company's banker can be an invaluable ally in this process.

Trust Services   Many publicly traded companies hire a bank as registrar and transfer agent. But the cost of the necessary computer systems and special staffing requirements limit the number of banks that can effectively offer this specialized service. As a result, it is quite possible that the company may find itself with a transfer agent that is not part of its credit and cash management banking network.

Other examples of the specialized expertise that can be purchased without requiring credit and cash management services are pension management, trustee, and consulting services. Many major banks are equipped to provide investment management for portfolios, but then so are many investment banking and management firms. The company chooses the one with the investment philosophy that best matches its own. Bankers, however, are especially equipped to function as custodians for investments and as trustees for the beneficiaries of pension plans. The specialized computer systems needed to track investment performance, account for gains and losses, and track participants in the plan tend to limit the field to only the larger banks that are capable of funding the extensive technology required.

Investment Banking Bank deregulation is having an important effect on the ability of banks to provide services traditionally considered the sole province of nonbank investment bankers ever since the passage of the Glass-Steagall Act in 1933. No longer mere underwriters of local municipal securities, banks have underwritten commercial paper programs for industrial and finance companies and are aggressively pursuing corporate finance services, such as mergers and acquisitions and capital structure consulting. While only the largest money center bankers may ultimately compete with the big investment bankers, regional banks will certainly provide an effective alternative to the services previously available only from regional investment houses.

Bank Size

One of the obvious benefits of choosing a large bank is the larger lending limit that is available. A small company may not immediately require a loan for the maximum legal limit available from a large regional or money center bank, but the flexibility to increase borrowing as needs and creditworthiness grow is important. If a company deals only with a local bank with a limit of $10 million, for example, new relationships will have to be sought as working capital requirements exceed the $10 million figure. Likewise, major opportunities, such as acquisitions and large manufacturing contracts, often arise quickly. A large bank has the capacity to make the additional funds available on short notice. A smaller bank, even if it still liked the company's credit at the higher level, could not handle the full amount in-house and would have to syndicate the deal with one or more of its correspondent banks. The company would still get the credit, but only after an uncertain period of delay that might cause the opportunity to be lost. In short, a big bank can accommodate a big credit request more easily than a small bank.

The special services and expertise mentioned earlier are generally available only at larger banks. Most of these services are available separately, are explicitly priced, and so don't need to be acquired only from primary bankers. Still, there are times when the convenience of one-stop shopping is important. It can be better to provide a quick, effective fix to a problem rather than to exhaustively analyze the cost effectiveness of each competing bank vendor. A close relationship with the large bank having many special services is the key to such fast solutions.

Not all is perfect at a big bank, however. If you are a small company and business turns poor, the large bank may prove insensitive to your needs and go only by the book. At a smaller bank, where a company's loans would loom larger as a percentage of that bank's total assets, the company may find a greater willingness to stand by in difficult times. Also, a problem with the big banks is the larger operational organization. This can cause difficulty simply because the volume of transactions is so great that it can be difficult to get a fast solution when things go wrong. Although sophisticated automation has reduced this problem at many larger banks, their cost structure is often higher than that of smaller ones. The people and the real estate allocated to services simply cost more at a big bank because they are generally located in major metropolitan areas where such costs are high.

Number of Banks

Is it best to rely on 1 bank, 2 banks, or 10 banks? Each business will have its needs, but all would certainly find that they are going to get a greater variety of useful information and views from many different banks. Whether a company is seeking information on how to overcome the latest Federal Reserve salvo in its war against float or what will be the trend for the Japanese yen over the coming six months, multiple sources from whom it can solicit opinions will improve the quality of information on which it may base an important decision.

Furthermore, numbers promote competition. As a company adds bankers to its network, not only will it increase the array of products and services from which it can choose, but it will find that pricing begins to drop, sometimes by surprising amounts. A quick survey of pricing from alternate sources can halt, or at least minimize, a bank's proposed increased service fee. And, of course, the same holds true for credit lines; the competition from other banks will certainly lower the rate at which the company will be able to borrow.

However, a pie can be sliced in only so many ways, so the company should control the number of bankers with whom it does business. Each bank should be offered sufficient business so that the company will be seen as an important customer. But, if too many bankers are sitting around the table, it is time-consuming to feed each the needed information. Therefore it is wise to prune back those portions of the company's bank network that have grown unwieldy. Less total time will be spent maintaining relationships with those remaining, yet each relationship will become more fruitful.

Personalities

If any word can sum up the effect of personalities on the banking-corporate relationship it is "rapport." Without a good rapport between the cash management representative of the corporation and the banker as representative of his institution, the useful services that are expected from the bank won't be delivered. This is such an important point that the account officer should be replaced with another if things aren't working out between the bank and the company. Banks look at their account relationship officers as salespeople. They want them to be successful in developing the kind of rapport that is a precedent to successful marketing of bank services. Thus, they appreciate knowing when a relationship is rocky and will often reassign account managers in an effort to improve the situation. So, the problem should be discussed first with the account manager directly and then, if no satisfactory response is seen, with higher levels of bank management.

Aside from personality alone, it is important that a banker have a good problem-solving attitude. He should respond quickly to requests and have the expertise to recommend which of his banking services can solve a given problem. A background in the company's business is very helpful and will certainly enable him to better understand the basis of requests for assistance.

Bank Cancellation

After the banking network has been reviewed, using the elements of bank selection just discussed, some banking relationships may be found wanting. Perhaps there are more banks than needed, or a good new bank has surfaced that the company can't add without eliminating another, or some banks' operations are inferior in quality, or they are becoming too expensive.

This is the time for diplomacy. Discuss the issues openly with the banker. Let him know why the company has come to its conclusions and, if the company seeks a change, tell him what is to be done and by when. If the problem can't be solved, or if the initial decision was final, issues should be discussed in such a way that the banker understands the facts. Keep a bridge in place, if possible. At some future time, the bank may well have a service that the company wants. If the cancellation was businesslike, a new relationship can be developed on a firm basis.

BANK COMPENSATION

After the banks are selected, based primarily on the services they are able to offer, the next step is to decide how the fees are to be paid. Traditionally, banks have charged for services and credit lines by requiring that noninterest-bearing balances be kept on deposit. The banks could put these free balances to work and collect interest that compensated the bank for the cost of providing the service. With increasing competition, "double counting" became prevalent as banks, in effect, discounted their prices by allowing the same balances that were used to provide service compensation to provide credit line compensation also. In the early 1980s, the trend to explicit pricing has continued, so that most major banks will accept compensation for both services and credit through payment of a cash fee rather than through a noninterest-bearing compensating balance.

Service Fees versus Balances

The case for proposing to pay cash fees for services rests on the simple fact that it is cheaper for a corporation to pay a fee than to maintain a compensating balance. Take a look at this example to see why:

Compensating balance $\times$ (1 − Reserve Requirement)
$\times$ Earnings credit rate = Earnings credit

$$\$1,000,000 \times (1 - 0.14) \times 0.0913 = \$78,518$$

This example shows that a typical bank will determine how many dollars of service fees can be supported by a given amount of free compensating balances by first deducting the current Federal Reserve requirements (14 percent in the example) from the total balances on deposit and then multiplying by the bank's earnings credit rate, often the rolling average of the 90-day Treasury bill (9.13 percent in the example). Thus, in the example above, $1 million of balances would support $78,518 of fees.

But what if the corporate cash manager were to take the same $1 million in hand? Not only would he invest the full amount, with no deduction for bank reserves, he would get a higher earnings rate because he would probably invest in commercial paper, Eurodollar deposits, or other securities that would earn more than Treasury bills. The example would then look like this:

$$\text{Cash invested} \times 100\% \times \text{Earnings rate} = \text{Earnings credit}$$

$$\$1,000,000 \times 100\% \times 0.095 = \$95,000$$

Thus, by investing the cash himself, the corporate cash manager could earn $95,000 or $16,482 per year more than the bank was crediting for the same funds kept as compensating balances.

Not only is there the economic benefit of earning a higher rate of interest on the full amount invested, but the true cost of the banking services is made clear when paid in cash and thus can be accounted for more easily within the company. Paying the fee in cash makes the company more accountable because it must be budgeted and, when the bill comes in, it will be scrutinized carefully before it is approved. Balances could also be tracked versus budget, but balances are one step removed from the bottom line, the dollar cost of the services, and are thus somewhat more difficult to deal with. Paying fees gives a clean audit trail. Furthermore, if operating units are charged for services paid for by headquarters, all that is necessary is to take the fee payment for each bank and split it among the units receiving that bank's services. The monthly bank account analysis can be sent to each operating unit as an invoice to support the charge. A side benefit of this procedure is that the operating units can critique their bills and suggest economies in the use of bank services.

The corporate cash manager should be careful, however, not to agree to pay fees that equal the gross total shown on the account analysis. The banks should continue to credit the company with earnings on balances maintained, however small they may be. After all, few cash managers are so good that they can hit zero cash every day. So, keep collected balances very low, but not so low as to cause a deficit, and pay the rest in cash fees, as in this example:

Gross service fee	$1,000
Less: Credit for balances	10
Net cash fee	$ 990

If these charges are allocated to operating units, use a schedule such as this:

$$\text{Unit} \quad \text{A} + \text{B} + \text{C} + \text{D} - \text{Corp} = \text{Total}$$
$$100 + 300 + 400 + 200 - 10 = 990$$

Here each operating unit is charged for the full amount of the gross fees charged by the bank. Then, assuming that the earnings credit of $10 came from miscellaneous cash balances that could not be easily squeezed from the system, corporate treasury takes this earnings credit for its own budget, because all cash in the system can be considered as being under the responsibility of the treasurer.

To keep track of these expenses, compute a running tally sheet each month using the following formula:

Balance × (1 − Reserve requirement) × Earnings credit rate
= Earnings credit − Gross fee
= Net fee − Credit line charges
= Total fee versus budget

A schedule should be maintained for each major bank relationship. It will keep the company up to date as to the total dollars being paid to the bankers and will point out unbudgeted increases in prices and services.

Credit Line Fees versus Balances   The other main class of bank compensation is credit line fees. Compensation for credit lines has, like services, traditionally been in the form of free balances, for example, 10 percent of the total line of credit plus 10 percent of all borrowing under the line of credit. Competition has whittled that down to the point where balances, if used at all, are frequently under 10 percent of the line. In addition, the trend toward compensation on a cash fee basis has affected this area also. The reason, again, is simple economics. If a company kept 10 percent compensating balances to cover a line of credit, it would be paying more than if it paid a fee of one half of 1 percent per year as shown in the following example:

A.
$1,000,000	Credit line	
×0.10	10 percent	
$ 100,000	Compensating balances	
×0.095	Earnings credit rate	
$ 9,500	Effective fee for credit line	

B. $1,000,000 Credit line
                 ×0.005 ½ of 1% flat fee
        $ 5,000 Fee for credit line

The savings in this example are $4,500 per $1 million credit line every year.

NEGOTIATIONS

To get the best deal with the bankers, a company should be prepared with information. The right kind of information will show what similar companies are getting, both in variety and quality of services, and the price. The best source of information is contemporaries in other companies. How can they be reached? Join a local cash management association, as well as the National Corporate Cash Management Association. Subscribe to professional journals and newsletters. This will put the corporate cash manager in a position to negotiate an arrangement that gets the desired service and credit lines at a competitive price, while allowing the bank to make a return that makes it pleased to have the company's business. Don't forget to put the deal in writing. It doesn't have to be a complicated agreement. A simple letter is often satisfactory and will ensure that both sides have a common understanding of the terms.

MANAGING THE RELATIONSHIP

It is tempting to put the new bank agreements away in the file and forget about them. Don't. Keeping open the lines of communication with the bankers is an ongoing process. Keep a file on each bank; record the substance of each contact and/or periodically summarize the company's experiences and satisfaction with the bank's services. This file should reflect regular efforts through meetings, lunches, and social occasions to develop the relationship with the bankers based on knowledge and confidence. Through these efforts, the company's bankers will gain an in-depth knowledge of the company's business, its needs, and the corporate cash manager's personal capability. The company will gain the same knowledge about its bank and banker.

Periodically—at least once a year—the corporate cash manager should make an effort to have a formal visit with each of the bankers. Prepare ahead of time; review the files and make a list of the good and bad dealings and the company's satisfaction, or lack thereof, with the overall relationship. The banker, if informed beforehand, can do likewise. These structured reviews can turn up little problems that may be festering, yet were never identified at the more informal meetings.

In the end, a banking relationship based on such openness and trust will gain the company services and credit lines that fit the company's requirements, keep costs under control through competitive pricing, and promote the corporate cash manager's personal reputation for professionalism.

SECTION II

Techniques for Speeding Cash Receipts and Controlling Disbursements

4

Collection and Concentration Techniques

Norman L. Weinberg
President
Norman L. Weinberg Associates

The acceleration, collection, and concentration of customer remittances are critical cash management functions. This chapter discusses techniques that minimize the elapsed time to process, collect, and concentrate cash for investment purposes or to reduce borrowing needs. Since each corporation has different operating requirements and geographic mix of customers it is incumbent upon the financial executive to analyze his company's needs and the options available for accelerating and concentrating funds. For example, in some cases a single bank would be used for concentrating corporate cash, while in other cases the use of regional concentration banks would be applicable.

The subjects covered in this chapter include check clearing operations, funds availability, lockbox banking, and concentration techniques.

CHECK CLEARING OPERATIONS

Bank Check Processing

The process of receiving, processing, and clearing checks has many components. The process will be examined in detail to point out ways by which a corporation can speed up this process, thereby reducing the time it takes to convert remittances into cash.

The bank receives checks either through a lockbox[1] or by a deposit made at the bank by the corporation. These checks must

---

[1] Lockbox banking is explained later in this chapter.

be transported to the check processing area for processing. The check processing department flow is as follows:

- The deposited items are encoded with the check dollar amount and the check totals are proved to the deposit amount.
- The encoded deposits are prepared for computer processing which sorts and totals the checks by end-point (destination) in accordance with either Federal Reserve or correspondent bank sorting requirements.
- The computer runs are reconciled and the total run proved. This includes the processing and rehandling of rejected (unreadable) items. These items must be reprocessed by either reencoding the check with a new magnetic ink character recognition (MICR) line using a Lundy strip or placing the check in a special envelope called a carrier. The carrier is then encoded with the information contained on the bottom of the check and reprocessed.

If these rejected items are not made machine readable, they are considered "nonmachinable" items and are subject to a three-business-day delay from the Fed. This delay is assigned to all items in this condition even if they are payable at a local clearinghouse or are Treasury checks.

Federal Reserve Check Clearing

Almost half of all checks processed in the United States are cleared by the Federal Reserve check clearing network. Banks receive, process, and sort checks and then send them to a local Federal Reserve Bank. The Fed uses an air courier and ground transportation to transport the checks from the deposit Fed office to the district where the check is drawn. The drawee Fed sorts and presents the check for payment to the drawee banks. All checks presented to the Federal Reserve Banks are physically cleared in one to three days, with the majority in one to two days.

The Federal Reserve System has 12 district banks, 25 branch offices, and 11 regional check processing centers. Table 1 indicates these offices by Fed district.

Local Clearinghouses

In most major cities, the local banks have formed a clearinghouse association where the banks meet to exchange checks drawn on each other. Clearinghouses clear checks in one day and, in some cases, can clear a check on the date it is received in

Table 1
Federal Reserve System Offices

District Number	Head Office	Branch Offices	Regional Check Processing Centers
1	Boston		Lewiston, Windsor Locks
2	New York	Buffalo	Cranford, Jericho, Utica
3	Philadelphia		
4	Cleveland	Cincinnati, Pittsburgh	Columbus
5	Richmond	Baltimore, Charlotte	
6	Atlanta	Nashville, Birmingham, Jacksonville, Miami, New Orleans	Columbia, S.C.
7	Chicago	Detroit	Des Moines, Indianapolis, Milwaukee
8	St. Louis	Little Rock, Louisville, Memphis	Charleston, W.V.
9	Minneapolis	Helena	
10	Kansas City	Denver, Oklahoma City, Omaha	
11	Dallas	El Paso, Houston, San Antonio	
12	San Francisco	Los Angeles, Portland, Salt Lake City, Seattle	

the lockbox. The New York Clearinghouse, for example, meets at 6:00 A.M., 8:00 A.M., and 10:00 A.M. for the exchange of checks among its member banks. Prior to these meeting times, each bank sorts the checks and separates them by bank. A physical exchange then takes place. After the 10:00 A.M. meeting, a net settlement occurs on the books of the Federal Reserve Bank where each bank has an account. This process is shown in Exhibit 1.

Exhibit 1
Check Clearing at the Clearinghouse

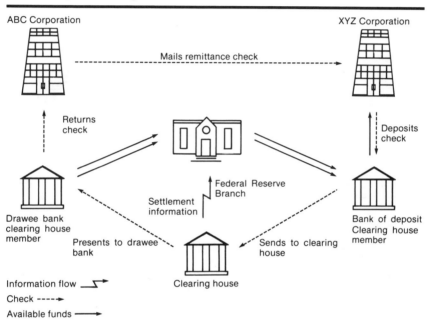

ABC Corporation

Mails remittance check

XYZ Corporation

Returns check

Deposits check

Federal Reserve Branch

Settlement information

Drawee bank clearing house member

Bank of deposit Clearing house member

Presents to drawee bank

Sends to clearing house

Information flow
Check
Available funds

Clearing house

Correspondent Banks

A correspondent bank is a bank that specializes in check clearing services. They are usually located in large cities and have state-of-the-art check processing equipment capable of handling a high volume of checks in a short period of time. They also have established a comprehensive direct send and correspondent bank network in order to offer later deposit deadline and excellent availability schedules. These banks are usually located in cities with frequent airline service to enable them to transport the checks efficiently to most major cities in the country. As a result of their commitment to check clearing services, they receive and process a large number of checks for most major cities, enabling them to establish cost-justified correspondent bank and direct sending relationships. Examples of some of the cities that offer these services are New York, Chicago, Atlanta, Memphis (e.g., Federal Express hub), Philadelphia, Dallas, and Los Angeles.

Many banks will sort checks received by drawee-bank city and send them to a correspondent bank located in that city or a nearby city for clearing. These checks usually clear in one day. This procedure is used where clearing time is faster than that offered by the Fed or the deadline later than that offered by the Fed. This check flow is shown in Exhibit 2.

Exhibit 2
Check Clearing By Correspondent Bank Direct Send

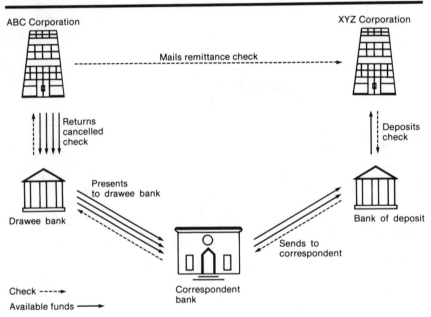

Direct Sends

By using air couriers, a bank can clear checks on the date received for most banks located in major cities in the country. The receiving bank sorts the checks by individual drawee bank. These items are then flown to the drawee-bank city and deposited directly in the drawee bank. This technique provides immediate availability of funds to the depositing bank and to the bank's customers in most cases. Direct sends are used when at least one day is gained in availability compared to the local Fed's availability schedule.

The feasibility analysis of utilizing the direct send technique requires computation of the availability gain offset by the cost of the additional processing, correspondent check charges, courier costs, and the ability to meet the correspondent's deadline as often as possible. If the expectation is that the deadline will be missed 10 percent of the time, the cost of the sending must be increased.

Bank Determination of Optimum Clearing Arrangements

The clearing of checks in the United States is an extremely efficient system. Almost all checks can be presented and paid within two days following the deposit date. The determination by a bank of the specific method to clear checks is a complex decision which includes the following factors.

Proximity to the Federal Reserve Bank   This distance affects the cutoff time for processing checks. The cash letters (package of checks) must be completed and transported to the Fed in order for them to be received for credit on that day. The further the distance, the earlier the checks must leave the sending bank.

Deposit Deadlines   A bank determines its internal cutoff time by taking the Fed deposit deadline, determining the transportation time from the bank to the Fed, and determining the amount of time it takes to encode, process, prove, and prepare the cash letters. This is determined by the volume to be processed, speed, and amount of equipment available for processing and staffing levels. This same type of analysis is performed by the Fed in developing its internal cutoff times.

Check-Sorting Equipment   A bank's ability to process the checks and sort them to the end-points in accordance with the requirement of the Federal Reserve Bank or correspondents is based upon the type of equipment used.

Check Charges   A bank must evaluate the cost of check clearing through its Fed and through correspondents to determine the most cost-effective clearing pattern. The availability gain for the average check amount must be compared to the cost of processing internally and the Fed or correspondent charges to determine the check-clearing network which makes the most sense for each bank.

Transportation Arrangements To effectively utilize correspondents or direct sends, a bank must be able to transport the checks to the banks in specific cities by their deadlines. The availability of commercial airlines or privately owned couriers is essential for utilizing the techniques.

Check Volume To justify using a correspondent or a direct send, a bank must analyze its volume of checks and dollar value to determine if the availability gain justifies the additional cost of processing and transporting these checks. Without sufficient dollar volume, these techniques will not be cost-effective. In addition to the dollar volume, the cost of the courier and the evaluation of the number of times the checks will not arrive on time to get the additional availability must be included in the analysis.

Determination of the optimum clearing mechanism has become even more complicated as a result of the Monetary Control Act of 1980. This legislation required the Fed to price check-clearing services and to charge back to depositing banks the Fed's cost of float. Fed float occurs when the Fed is unable to process, transport, and collect the checks within the time they have published (availability schedule) for the clearing of the checks. As a result, to reduce Fed check charges and Fed float charge-backs, banks have expanded their use of clearinghouses and correspondent networks.

Banks are utilizing sophisticated internal computer models and specialized models offered by vendors to maximize their ability to process checks rapidly at the lowest cost. It is important for a bank to review its sorting and direct send arrangements periodically because of the constant changes. Thus, it is just as important for a corporation to review and analyze its lockbox banks and their availability schedules at least every one to two years.

FUNDS AVAILABILITY

Availability and Collectability of Checks

To understand the process of clearing checks, one must differentiate between the availability and collectability of funds. Although these terms are used interchangeably, they are quite different.

The *availability delay* is the elapsed time for a check to be converted to cash after it has been deposited in the bank. The *collectability delay* is the elapsed time for a check that has been presented for payment at the drawee bank to be dishonored and returned to the depositing bank. The elapsed time for a check to be collected, beginning with the day it was deposited is the *collection period*. It is the total of the availability and collectability delay.

The availability delay on deposited funds can be determined by looking at an availability schedule published by the Federal Reserve Bank, a depositing bank, or a correspondent bank. An example of an availability schedule is shown in Table 2. Notice that it lists the deposit cut-off time, as well as the availability in days.

The collectability delay can be determined by examining the process of returning a check to the depositing bank. As a general rule, the amount of the check has no bearing on the return cycle. However, to reduce the risk of loss, banks will, on occasion, have a longer collection period assigned for larger items. Table 3 indicates the approximate timing for collectability delay. The time for a check to be returned ranges from five to six business days for Fed items and from six to nine days for correspondent bank items. Since this time is measured in business days, the weekends must be added when computing the date an item should be considered as "finally collected."

An illustration of the availability and collectability delays and collection periods for different methods of check clearing follows.

Check-Clearing Method	Availability Delay	Collectability Delay	Collection Period
Local clearinghouse checks deposited before daily exchange	0	2	2
Local clearinghouse checks deposited after daily exchange	1	2	3
Federal Reserve one-day end-points	1	5–6	6–7
Federal Reserve two-day end-points	2	5–6	7–8
Nonmachineable and other low-speed items	3	5–6	8–9

If a correspondent bank is used for clearing, the collection period would be extended by an additional one to three days.

Table 2
Bank Availability Schedule for Selected Cities

Location	Transit Code	Cut-off Time	Availability Time (days)
ALABAMA			
Birmingham	0620	5:00 P.M.	1
Birmingham RCPC	0621, 0622	12:00 Noon	1
New Orleans RCPC	0651	8:00 P.M.	0
ALASKA			
Seattle RCPC	1252	12:00 Noon	1
ARIZONA			
Los Angeles RCPC	1221	8:00 P.M.	0
ARKANSAS			
Little Rock	0820	4:30 A.M.	0
Little Rock RCPC	0829	8:00 P.M.	0
Memphis RCPC	0841	8:00 P.M.	0
CALIFORNIA			
Los Angeles	1220	8:00 P.M.	0
Los Angeles RCPC	1222	8:00 P.M.	0
San Francisco	1210	8:00 P.M.	0
San Francisco RCPC	1211	8:00 P.M.	0
COLORADO			
Denver	1020	4:30 A.M.	0
Denver RCPC	1070	8:00 P.M.	0
Denver Country	1021	4:30 A.M.	1
CONNECTICUT			
Windsor Locks RCPC	0111, 0118, 0119, 0211	12:00 Noon	1

Location	Transit Code	Cut-off Time	Availability Time (days)
INDIANA			
Chicago RCPC	0712, 0719	12:00 Noon	1
Indianapolis	0740	4:00 P.M.	1
Indianapolis RCPC	0749	12:00 Noon	1
Louisville RCPC	0839	12:00 Noon	1
IOWA			
Des Moines	0730	4:00 P.M.	1
Des Moines RCPC	0739	12:00 Noon	1
Omaha RCPC	1049	10:00 A.M.	1
KANSAS			
Kansas City	1010	6:00 P.M.	0
Kansas City Country	1011	4:30 A.M.	1
KENTUCKY			
Cincinnati RCPC	0421	12:00 Noon	1
Louisville	0830	4:00 P.M.	1
Louisville RCPC	0813, 0839, 0863	12:00 Noon	1
LOUISIANA			
New Orleans	0650	4:30 A.M.	0
New Orleans RCPC	0651, 0652, 0654	8:00 P.M.	0
Dallas Country	1111	8:00 P.M.	0
MAINE			
Lewiston RCPC	0112	12:00 Noon	1

Table 3
Collectability Delay

Elapsed Days		Description of Process
0	1.	The check arrives at the drawee bank which has been cleared through the Federal Reserve Bank.
1	2.	The drawee bank has until midnight of the day following the date of presentation to return that item unpaid to the Federal Reserve Bank.
2–3	3.	The Federal Reserve Bank receives, sorts, and prepares a return cash letter for each and every Fed branch in the country for which a return has been received.
3–4	4.	The Federal Reserve Bank, by use of its transportation network, sends the return items directly to the depositing Fed. *Note:* In the case of the correspondent banks, the items would be returned by the Fed to the correspondent who would then have to return it to the depositing bank, then returned to the correspondent who would then have to return it to the depositing bank, then returned to the customer. This may take 1–3 additional days.
4–5	5.	The item is received at the depositing Fed, sorted, and sent to the bank that originally deposited it.
5–6	6.	The item is researched to determine the depositor and the item is then charged back.

Deposit Availability Computation Methods

Every bank computes the availability of funds for each customer deposit. Those factors which influence the clearing time for checks include:

1. Time of check deposit at the bank versus the bank's cutoff time for same-day ledger credit.
2. Processing time necessary to prepare checks for presentation to the Fed, correspondent bank, or local clearinghouse.
3. Sorting requirements for presentation to obtain the best availability.
4. Deadlines for delivering checks to the Fed, correspondent, or clearinghouse.

Deposit availability is assigned using three methods. The first is to assign availability to each check individually and then total the dollar-weighted availability for each deposit. Another method is to analyze a customer's deposits over a period of time (week or month) and determine the average float in a typical deposit. A float factor such as 1.5 days is then assigned to that customer's future deposits until a new analysis is undertaken or requested by the company. A third method is to determine the bank's float for all customer deposits and then compute a float factor which is assigned to all customers. The most accurate method is the individual check float assignment method. Most large money center and regional banks provide availability in this manner.

ACCOUNTS RECEIVABLE FLOAT

A corporation is subject to six time periods when it does not have use of money due from selling goods and services. These time periods are:

1. Invoicing float—elapsed time from the sale until the invoice is prepared and mailed.
2. Invoice mail float—elapsed time for the invoice to reach the customer.
3. Credit term float—the number of days the customer is given before payment is due.
4. Payment mail float—elapsed time for the vendor's check, once drawn, to arrive at the corporation or bank for processing.
5. Payment processing float—elapsed time to process the check and deposit it in the bank for clearing.
6. Availability float—elapsed time from check deposit date until "goods funds" are obtained.

All of these factors comprise the time frame in which funds due the corporation are not available for its use. An analysis of the procedures used in some of the controllable aspects of this process will reduce this period and improve the corporation's cash flow.

Among the techniques that can be used to reduce this float are:

1. Streamlining billing procedures.
2. Ensuring that all invoices are prepared and mailed the same day.
3. Analyzing credit terms and strict enforcement of discounts taken by customers, which may or may not be within the discount time frame.
4. Following up on outstanding receivables in a timely fashion.
5. Using lockboxes to speed receipt, processing, and clearing of the remittances.

The typical time frame for the six components of accounts receivable float are:

Typical Receivable Cycle of a Corporation	Elapsed Days
Invoicing float	1–4
Invoice mail float	1–3
Credit term float	10–30
Payment mail float	1–3
Payment processing float	0–2
Availability float	0–2
	13–44

These ranges do not include weekends, which could add 2–14 additional days. The time frame for the receivables cycle is rather broad. Using more effective procedures and techniques could reduce the cycle considerably, increasing the cash flow of a corporation and providing savings by reducing borrowing needs or increasing income from additional investments. The ability to accelerate the collection cycle has more potential within the corporation then within the banking system.

LOCKBOX BANKING

A lockbox is a bank-offered service that has been in existence since 1947. Customer remittances are addressed to a specified post office box in which a bank has been given prior authority to pick up and process the checks. The lockbox location is selected so that the mail time of checks is minimized. Most banks collect mail from the post office at least three times a day, while some collect from the post office as often as every hour. On average, banks make 40–45 pickups of mail each week. One advantage of a bank lockbox is its ability to pick up mail on weekends. Thus, the funds are deposited as ledger balances on the next business day. Once collected, the bank can immediately begin opening the mail and processing the remittances in order to reduce the time it takes to begin the check-clearing process.

Wholesale and Retail Lockboxes

There are two basic types of lockboxes—wholesale and retail. The difference is that a wholesale lockbox handles small-volume, high-dollar items (e.g., over $1,000), while retail lockboxes process high-volume, low-dollar items (e.g., insurance or utility payments). Determination of the type of payments a company receives is critical in the selection process of the appropriate lockbox cities and the specific bank chosen. This is especially important in the case of retail lockboxes where there are a limited number of banks that provide this service at reasonable cost with the most modern equipment.

If a company has a small volume of high-dollar items, the question of per item processing cost is not as important as the mail time reduction. For example, reducing mail and processing float by three days on a $10,000 check is equivalent to earning $8.33 if the funds were invested at 10 percent overnight for three days. On the other hand, a large volume of small-dollar checks can be expensive if the per item costs are high. Thus, the selection of a specific lockbox bank is very important since costs vary widely among banks.

Internal versus External Processing

Before discussing the options and capabilities of lockboxes, let us review the use of internal versus external remittance processing. Many large retail firms have found it more advantageous to establish an in-house remittance processing facility than using a bank's services. This occurs because a bank must add overhead and profit to its price, while corporations can purchase or lease the same MICR processing equipment at a lower per item transaction cost. In-house processing usually results in faster updating of the accounts receivable files and faster handling of exceptions or special items. The price and processing advantages of an in-house processing operation are offset by the operational headaches that can result if quality control techniques and strong management are not present. If a corporation's customers are primarily local, rather than nationwide, mail delays may not be an important factor and in-house processing may not significantly reduce the time it takes to process and clear local checks. However, the operating costs may be lower than with local banks.

Necessary Steps for Establishing a Lockbox Network

Assuming that a financial executive determines that a lockbox network is necessary, a lockbox analysis should be performed to accurately select the optimal lockbox cities.

Lockbox Model Study   The model analysis determines the optimal cities that minimize mail and availability time from the customer's location to the lockbox city. The optimal number of lockbox cities required is dependent upon the geographic concentration of customers, the dollar value of these concentrations, and the drawee banks used by the customers. The typical number of lockbox locations used by a company is between one and four. Without using a bank's lockbox model, it is difficult to predict the exact number and location of the optimal cities. A simplified approach to determining potential lockbox cities is to manually review the largest customers (top 25 to 50 customers) by dollar volume (75 percent or more of the dollars) to determine their mailing locations and drawee banks. Coupled with the use of mail time data supplied by Phoenix-Hecht, Inc. (provider of periodic mail and clearing time surveys), a financial executive can determine suitable locations, although they may not be the optimal.

Lockbox model studies are performed by most major money center and regional banks, private vendors, and a few accounting firms. Some companies have developed internal programs for this analysis. Although many banks use these models, their study approach, pricing, and depth of analysis vary greatly. A few banks offer free studies, while most banks charge for their analysis. The free studies are offered by banks in cities that usually appear as optimal or near optimal cities. Thus, the bank is hoping to obtain the lockbox business. Lockbox models are described in Chapter 8.

Lockbox Networks

The most recent bank-developed lockbox service is networking. Innovative lockbox banks have developed a nationwide collection system by extending their collection points to other strategically located cities. Their goal is to provide their customers with the ability to collect receipts using one bank relationship, thereby reducing the corporation's processing costs and providing better control since fewer banks are used. Currently, many corporations use three to six lockbox cities in order to minimize mail and availability float. Because of the existing banking laws prohibiting interstate banking, corporations are using a different bank in each city. Now banks have bypassed this obstacle by developing four types of networks.

1. Bank Affiliation

    First Interstate (Los Angeles) and 11 other affiliate banks in the West have offered a service with any one bank as the main concentration bank with the others as lockbox processing banks. The lockbox information and funds are funneled through the concentration bank.

    Four banks—Valley National Bank of Arizona, Wells Fargo, United Banks of Colorado, and Bank of Hawaii—have formed a federation to process wholesale receipts.

Other cities such as New York, Chicago, Dallas, and Atlanta are also being considered to offer a nationwide network.

2. Mail Intercept

Norwest Bank (Minneapolis) offers a 10-city network,
which uses post office boxes to collect remittances that are
emptied and couriered to Minneapolis for same-day processing and crediting to customers' accounts. The cities
include: Minneapolis, Boston, Atlanta, St. Louis, Chicago, New York, Dallas, Denver, Los Angeles, and Toronto.

Northern Trust developed its "TNT Intercept," using Dallas, Atlanta, Miami, Los Angeles, Newark, and two non-
U.S. locations—Toronto and London. The checks are collected in post office boxes and sent to its headquarters in
Chicago for processing.

Continental Bank offers its "Remittance Intercept Service," which collects at 18-city post office boxes and couriers the checks to its main office in Chicago for same-day
ledger credit and processing.

National Bank of Detroit uses a 13-city post office box
network, including Canadian cities (that are collected by
its Canadian bank).

3. Joint Venture

Mellon Bank and Sears, Roebuck joined forces to expand
Mellon's retail lockbox coverage to Boston, Dallas, Columbus, Atlanta, Philadelphia, Jacksonville, and Los
Angeles. These cites complement Mellon's current wholesale lockbox processing facilities in Pittsburgh and Chicago. Sears processes the checks for Mellon's customers,
using its existing check processing equipment. The checks
are deposited locally, while Sears transmits the lockbox
detail to Mellon.

Chase and Equitable Life Assurance Society use a similar
approach to Mellon dubbed "CHEQNET." However,
Chase focuses on wholesale receipts using Equitable's
facilities in Chicago, Atlanta, Dallas, and San Francisco. Chase currently collects receipts in New York and
Newark.

4. De Novo

First Chicago set up its own processing centers in Atlanta,
Dallas, New York, and Pasadena. Checks are deposited
locally with deposit detail transmitted to Chicago (their
main lockbox facility) for aggregation before being sent to
the customer.

Wachovia Bank and Trust Company set up facilities in Atlanta to supplement its premier Charlotte location.

First National Bank of Louisville opened centers in Phoenix in addition to Louisville.

Network Advantages Lockbox networks offer numerous advantages compared to multibank systems. Besides reducing the mail time (usually the more locations, the faster the mail time) resulting in improved cash flow, networks offer a centralized bank for receipt and information processing. This reduces overall banking costs, because charges for account maintenance, wire transfers, deposit reports, lockbox rental charges, and any other fixed charges are eliminated. If the network bank deposits checks locally (e.g., De Novo, affiliates, and joint venture methods), then interregional Federal Reserve check charges may be eliminated since checks can be cleared locally. Another advantage to the corporation of using networks is the bank's ability to send one combined data transmission for accounts receivable updating. Also, the time to handle lockbox inquiries should be minimized, since only one bank is used.

Network Risks Companies should be aware of the potential risks of using mail intercept and De Novo networks. Reduced funds availability may result in both cases. In the former case, the lost time to the processing bank may result in missed internal deadlines, thereby delaying funds availability by one day on checks drawn on that end-point location. In the latter case, the local bank may not offer around-the-clock deposit-taking service, thereby missing its direct send deadlines and delaying funds availability. The De Novo approach may result in premium-priced check charges, since two banks are involved in processing rather than one. The mail intercept technique is heavily tied to delivering checks from distant locations via air couriers. During bad weather conditions in certain cities (e.g., Chicago and Minneapolis), the checks may be late resulting in delayed availability on all the checks on that shipment. Moreover, if that bank experiences any unforeseen problems (e.g., power failure, equipment malfunction, heavy workload), the checks may not be posted to the account with preferential availability. One area to pursue with the De Novo arrangement is who owns the funds. Since the checks may be deposited in a local bank under the name of the lockbox bank, there may be problems in the rare case that funds are frozen because of financial difficulties.

Another major risk of using networks—in particular, bank affiliation, joint venture, and De Novo—is the service quality.

Since other banks or satellite processing facilities are used, the quality of service may not be comparable to the quality of the single city lockbox bank. Careful analysis should be performed in judging the service quality by basing the decision on such characteristics as: use of unique zip codes, number of mail pick-ups at post office, processing hours, deadlines for same-day ledger credit, and processing equipment used. Also, the facilities should be toured to gain firsthand experience on the bank's capabilities.

In summary, lockbox networks are still in their infancy, the number of companies signing up is progressing slowly, and the number of competitors is growing rapidly. The advantages and disadvantages, as well as a carefully prepared cost-benefit analysis, should be prepared before moving ahead.

Selecting a Lockbox Bank   Following the completion of the lockbox study and the selection of the cities to be used for the lockbox network, the financial executive must select the bank to be used. The factors to be considered in this analysis are:

1. *Per item cost.*   This is the cost for processing each item received, expressed in dollars or balances. The financial execution must take into account the bank's "earnings credit rate" and "reserve requirement" when comparing prices at different banks.
2. *Minimum monthly charge.*   Banks will usually have a minimum charge for this service. This might be higher than the monthly volume times the per item cost.
3. *Equipment used and services available.*   In selecting the bank, it is important to determine the type (e.g., image processing) and capacity of the lockbox equipment. It is also necessary to evaluate the type of services offered by the bank. These include:

   Photocopy services—sending copies of the check and/or the remittance document.

   Exception processing—the type and cost of providing special handling or procedures to satisfy a company's unique needs. Many banks will not be able to or will charge extra fees for unusual or difficult special handling requests.

   Data transmission capabilities—the bank's ability to provide computer-to-computer transmission of check information and remittance document information read by either MICR or OCR equipment. The cost of these services must also be evaluated.

Mail pick-up schedule—the number of pickups at the post office each day, including the schedule for Saturday and holiday pickups.

4. *Availability schedule.* The availability times for the principal end-points of a company's major customers should be compared for each of the banks in that city to obtain the best and fastest availability possible.

5. *Current capacity of the operation.* The financial executive should determine how many items the bank could handle with the existing equipment and its plans for future expansion. Do not select a bank that is at or near capacity.

6. *Experience and reputation of the bank and its staff.* A corporation should speak to other clients of the prospective bank to determine its reputation and commitment to the business. The financial executive can also find out about potential problems and pitfalls in setting up the lockbox from those who have already been through the process.

After the initial evaluation of these factors has been completed, the financial executive or a member of his staff should visit the banks and tour their facilities. Arrange the visit during the peak operation time so that a real-life picture of the bank's ability to work under pressure can be evaluated. At the same time, consider analyzing the bank's other cash management products, such as balance reporting and concentration capabilities, to determine whether the bank is a likely provider of the service as a concentration bank.

Types of Lockbox Services Available

There are two types of lockbox services available—manual lockbox and automated lockbox. *Manual lockbox* provides mail pickup at the post office and then opening and processing of remittances manually. Each payment is compared with the invoice, if enclosed. The checks are then processed through the check-clearing department and the remittance photocopies and invoices are packaged together and sent to the company. This type of lockbox is generally used for wholesale (low-volume) processing and usually provides the company with photocopies of the check attached to the envelope. This is called the *photocopy plan.* Two other plans are available. One is the *envelope plan* in which the company receives only the envelopes and invoices with the check amount written on the face of the envelope. The other plan is the *report plan* in which a computer report is generated of each transaction without the inclusion of a photocopy or envelope.

Automated lockbox systems are used mostly for high-volume retail processing. The automated lockbox simultaneously processes payments and invoice documents. The system automatically reads the check MICR line and the invoice detail, and computes the deposit availability. In most cases this information is captured on magnetic tape. These data can then be transmitted computer-to-computer or tape-to-tape from the bank to the company to automatically update the company's accounts receivable file. Automated lockbox is used extensively for retail payments and is usually cost-beneficial if at least 90 percent of the customer checks are accompanied by an invoice. Otherwise, the exception processing costs rise drastically.

There are two principal types of information transmitted. First, each check's MICR line containing the bank's transit-routing number, customer account number, and dollar amount is sent. Since most customers use the same bank on a month-to-month basis for their disbursements, the bank information uniquely identifies each customer. By having this bank information in the customer's file, a financial executive can improve the matching percentage of files updated. Second, turnaround documents (invoices) printed with many different types of print formats can also be transmitted including: OCR-A numeric, OCR-A alpha, OCR-B numeric, Farrington 7B (credit card), Farrington 12F, 1403 (407) numeric, E13B (ABA check format), and 1428 numeric.

Processing equipment with these transmission capabilities provides a more effective and efficient way of processing proving, and updating a company's accounts receivable system than the more traditional manual lockbox. A bank's lockbox operation utilizing automated equipment provides a faster, less costly operation and enhances the bank's capability of processing a large volume of remittances more easily.

Image Processing[2]

Typical lockbox processing is slow, labor intensive, and expensive. A technology to bypass these disadvantages has evolved for retail and wholesale lockbox banks called "image processing." This technique captures video images of checks and the accompanying invoice by digitizing them for storage on computer disk or tape. After this process occurs, the physical documents need not be handled by the operators. Exhibit 3 illustrates

---

[2] This section was based upon materials provided by BancTec, Inc., Dallas, Texas.

Exhibit 3
Conventional Check Processing

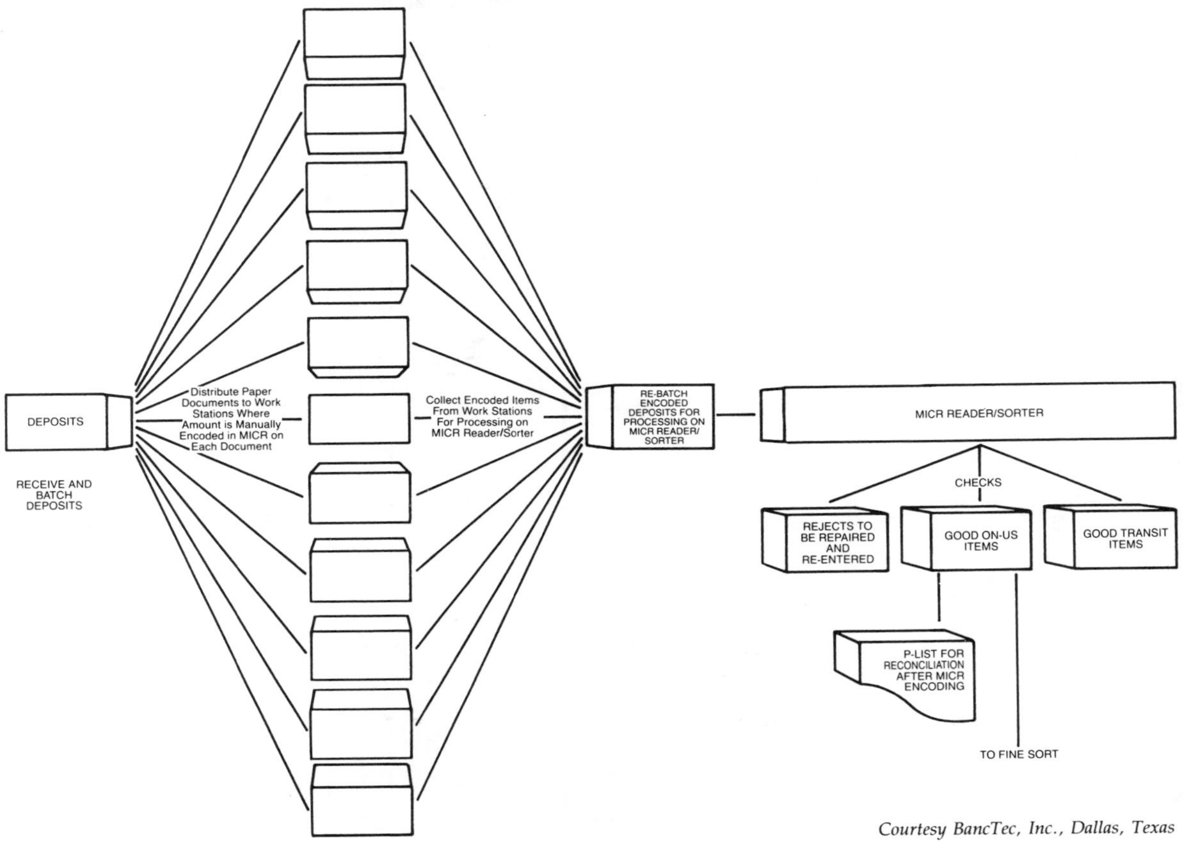

MICR READER/SORTER

CHECKS

GOOD TRANSIT ITEMS

GOOD ON-US ITEMS

REJECTS TO BE REPAIRED AND RE-ENTERED

P-LIST FOR RECONCILIATION AFTER MICR ENCODING

TO FINE SORT

RE BATCH ENCODED DEPOSITS FOR PROCESSING ON MICR READER/ SORTER

Collect Encoded Items From Work Stations For Processing on MICR Reader/Sorter

Distribute Paper Documents to Work Stations Where Amount is Manually Encoded in MICR on Each Document

DEPOSITS

RECEIVE AND BATCH DEPOSITS

Courtesy BancTec, Inc., Dallas, Texas

the conventional method of processing checks at most lockbox banks. This process entails the following steps.

1. Checks and deposit tickets are manually batched for distribution to unit work station operators for MICR dollar amount encoding.
2. The encoded checks are manually batched for processing on high-speed MICR reader/sorters.
3. The equipment reads, endorses, and sorts the documents into the pre-designated sorter pockets for end-point delivery. The typical check categories are on-us items, transit items, and rejects (checks unable to read for a myriad of reasons).
4. The rejects are repaired using various methods (Lundy strip, carrier envelope, CRT entry) and re-entered into the sorter.

Exhibit 4 depicts the steps in image check processing, as performed by BancTec's IMPAC (Image Processing and Archival Control) system, using the following four-phase approach.

Exhibit 4
Image Check Processing

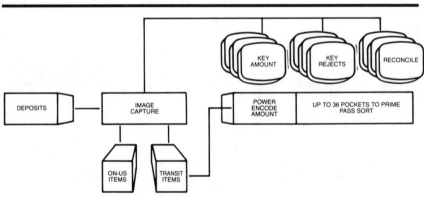

Courtesy BancTec, Inc., Dallas, Texas

Phase I—Unencoded Deposits The system captures and proves unencoded deposits and prepares transit items for dispatch. This is accomplished by capturing the computer image of the check, including the MICR line, comparing it, and sending the images to computer disk storage. The system places an audit trial on each check, while microfilming, endorsing, and sorting checks. Next the images are retrieved on a CRT for dollar amount encoding, reject correction, and computer-assisted balancing. All transit items are power encoded with dollar amount and sorted by end-point destination.

Phase II—Inclearings   The system uses the images to correct any MICR line problems, verify signatures of selected accounts by comparing them to a windowed image on file, and identify return items.

Phase III—Imaged Statements   Banks can provide laser-printed statements, which show full or partial check images of each check paid. The physical checks don't have to be returned. This process eliminates the need for the bank to sort, bulk file, fine sort, statement merge, and stuff checks in envelopes. Exhibit 5 shows a statement with laser images of data written, check amount, and payee.

Phase IV—Archival Storage   The system will use images to replace microfilm for archival storage. This technology provides very high speed searching for specific documents.

CONCENTRATION TECHNIQUES

Having discussed the acceleration and collection of remittances, the next step is to concentrate the funds on deposit in numerous bank locations throughout the country in a central account for efficient usage. There are three methods that are used for concentrating these funds into a bank. They include depository transfer checks (DTCs), automated clearinghouse DTCs (ACHDTCs), and wire transfers.

Depository Transfer Checks

A depository transfer check is a draft, payable to a corporation, which is drawn on the bank account where the funds are on deposit. The check does not require a signature and is usually prepared by and deposited by the concentration bank. The availability on the DTC is in accordance with the bank's availability schedule for that end-point. Checks drawn on major cities are usually available in one day. Otherwise, they are available in two days. The DTC is the most popular concentration

Exhibit 5

TENTH
National Bank of Dallas

T. Q. LeBrun
P.O. Box 64873
Dallas, Texas 75206

CYC	MC	
11	01	116-940-8

STATEMENT PERIOD				
12	16	81	thru	01	82

13	M	00 00	1

Your Balance Was	We Subtracted Checks and Debits	We Added Deposits and Credits	Making Your Present Balance	PRESENT BALANCE
1 943 31	11 1 581 38	2 358 00	719 93	

DEPOSITS, CREDITS, CHECKS, AND DEBITS

		DAILY BALANCES		FROM CHECK IMAGE	
Check Number		Amount	Balance	Date Written	Check Amount	Check Written To
	1216	Prev. Bal.	194331			
123	1221	50000	144331	12/18	500.00	American Airlines
124	1224	32433	111898	12/20	324.33	J.A. Aaron Brown
125	1231	5000	106898	12/25	50.00	Cash
126	0105	10000	96898	12/29	100.00	Visa
127	0105	10000	86898	12/30	100.00	Universal Ins.
CR	0107	5800	92698	1/7	58.00	DEPOSIT
128	0107	15000	77698	1/4	150.00	Thomas Industries
129	0107	10000	67698	1/5	100.00	Cash
130	0111	5000	62698	1/7	50.00	Addison Clinic
CR	0112	30000	92698	1/12	300.00	DEPOSIT
131	0115	10000	82698	1/14	100.00	Esco Ins & Service
133	0106	8705	73993	1/14	87.05	Lone Star Gas
135	0118	2000	71993	1/15	20.00	Martin Pharmacy

Courtesy BancTec, Inc., Dallas, Texas

method and is relatively inexpensive. Costs average $0.35 to
$0.60 an item. The use of a third-party vendor to gather the
deposit data will add another $0.50 to $0.75 per item.

Many companies utilize DTCs to collect funds from distribu-
tors, regional offices, or in the case of retail operations (with
numerous locations) to transfer funds from local depository

Exhibit 6
Depository Transfer Check Flow

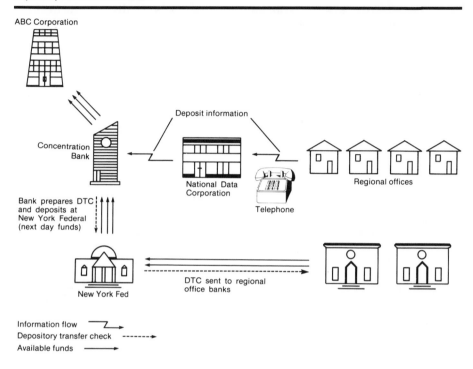

ABC Corporation

Concentration Bank

Deposit information

National Data Corporation

Telephone

Regional offices

Bank prepares DTC and deposits at New York Federal (next day funds)

New York Fed

DTC sent to regional office banks

Information flow
Depository transfer check   - - - - - - - ▶
Available funds

banks to one or more concentration accounts. A typical DTC scenario is illustrated in Exhibit 6.

Automated Clearinghouse Depository Transfers (ACHDT)

This technique is similar to the paper DTC but offers some unique advantages. All ACHDT (also known as Electronic Depository Transfer Checks, EDTCs) transactions are available funds in one day, regardless of the depository bank's location. Any bank in the country which is a member of the National Clearinghouse Association (NACHA) can be used to concentrate funds since clearing time or location is not a factor when utilizing this technique. The use of the ACH is more cost-effective and enables the corporate cash manager to know the exact available cash position for the next day. This technique will generally reduce the situation where funds are on deposit in two locations simultaneously because of Fed Float. However, since

Fed Float will be charged back to the depositing bank, it will also increase the per item deposit cost. The reduction of float in the clearing system is making it more cost-effective to utilize the ACH method instead of the check.

Wire Transfers

The wire transfer method is the most expensive method of concentrating funds. Once the deposited items have become available funds, the corporation can request the depositing bank to transfer these funds to the concentration bank. This method ensures that the transferred funds are immediately usable at the concentration bank. Exhibit 7 indicates the typical flow of a wire transfer transaction.

Exhibit 7
Wire Transfer Funds Concentration

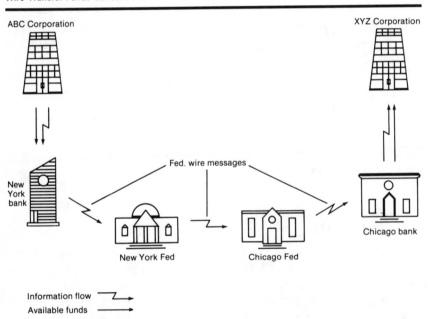

If wire transfers are used, the adoption of the ACHDT method should be considered in its place. To accomplish this, an ACHDT would be generated the day before the funds would become available. The ACHDT will be charged to the depositing bank account on the day the funds become available. This would be a more cost-effective method without the loss of funds availability.

Concentration Bank Selection

The decision to concentrate funds in a single bank or regionally is based on the number of locations that a company has and their geographic distribution. At some corporations, the concentration is done by region, division, or company. This setup would probably best be served by a regional concentration network. In some corporations with highly centralized cash management, functions would concentrate all funds in a single institution.

Determining the optimal concentration bank(s) is sometimes a difficult task for the financial executive. One practical solution is to narrow the choice to two banks and utilize them simultaneously to compare their capabilities, service quality, and responsiveness. The final decision can then be based on the experience gained and can usually be made six months after the account has been opened. Preselecting one concentration bank and then finding its performance to be inadequate results in difficulty in changing banks quickly and efficiently.

The ability to have an effective concentration system can be accomplished only with the ability to receive and utilize timely and accurate deposit information. For this reason, the number of deposit locations and their ability to report timely information is a determining factor in the design of a collection and concentration system. Time-zone problems and remote locations make it more difficult to design an optimal system. It may be necessary to implement the system in phases so that the number of locations can be managed. There are services available which can aid the corporation in receiving and utilizing deposit information to simplify the system implementation and facilitate the control of deposit and receivable information.

Providers of these services include a few banks and third-party vendors of data gathering services such as National Data Corporation, Automatic Data Processing, and Interactive Data Services. These companies will take telephone calls from reporting locations, provide information to the corporation, and electronically transmit the information to a bank to automatically create DTCs or ACH transactions to concentrate funds.

Some corporations have designed and implemented internal information systems rather than utilizing a bank or third-party vendor. They have found that they have better control of their internal information and are able to correct or request additional information from the reporting location. They record the deposit information and then create a tape for the creation of paper DTC or format a tape for ACHDT to be executed by their concentration banks.

SUMMARY

Rapid collection of customer remittances and cost-effective cash concentration strategy are two important cash management objectives. Knowledge of the various methods a bank uses to clear checks is required to understand precisely how banks' operational capabilities in the check processing and lockbox departments differ from one another. The manner in which a bank assigns availability on deposits and their deposit cutoff times have a major impact on a corporation's ability to convert checks into available funds for more productive use. Internally, the financial executive has control over two functions that should be expedited to speed cash flow: the timing of invoice mailing and in-house payment processing. Also, by using strategically placed lockboxes to reduce the mail and availability time and thereby convert customer remittances into cash more rapidly, the financial executive can establish a cost-effective procedure to improve his corporation's cash flow. Additionally, through the use of automated lockbox processing using machine readable invoices and data transmission techniques, he can update his accounts receivable file overnight. An effective strategy to concentrate funds from deposit and lockbox banks using wires, ACH, or DTCs can be developed after careful consideration of the costs involved, timing, and frequency of transfers.

5

Disbursement Practices*

Leslie N. Masonson
*Vice President, Treasury
Management Consulting*
Citibank, N.A.

In contrast to collections, disbursements is one critical cash management area where financial executives have complete control. They can choose the disbursement instrument, payment release date, method of funding the disbursement account, whether to use remote or controlled disbursement, and when to centralize the function.

Disbursement policies vary widely among companies and industry groups. Few companies pay an invoice upon receipt, some pay within the terms of the payment period, while many pay late. A strong connection exists between a company's payment practices, the state of the economy, and the level of interest rates. Especially in a high interest rate environment, many companies will hold on to their payments longer than usual. Moreover, many companies mail payments late in the week to take advantage of the weekend mail float. The most common strategy is to preserve cash by delaying payment until the last possible moment. Then, the finance officer can evaluate any discounts, offered to induce earlier payment, to see if they offer better cash flow advantages than other alternatives, such as paying down a loan or investing funds in overnight instruments at a higher rate.

PAYMENT INSTRUMENT: ZERO BALANCE ACCOUNT

Unsophisticated companies use their corporate checking accounts for deposits as well as disbursements (i.e., payroll,

* Reprinted by permission from *Corporate Accounting*, vol. 1, no. 2 (Spring 1983). Copyright © 1983, Warren, Gorham & Lamont, 210 South St., Boston, Mass. All rights reserved. The contents of this chapter have been updated to reflect the Federal Reserve's High Dollar Group Sort Program.

trade payables, utilities, insurance, and petty cash). Combined deposit/disbursement accounts, however, make it difficult to reconcile different categories of disbursement checks, manage balances to the minimum required level, or forecast disbursement funding requirements each day.

To avoid these problems, many companies use zero balance accounts (ZBAs) for disbursements. With this system, checks presented for payment against each account during the course of the day are automatically totaled by the bank's demand deposit accounting system that evening. Each ZBA is then automatically credited with the exact dollar amount of the debits, bringing the account balance to zero. These credits can be automatically transferred from the corporation's concentration account at the bank.

While most money center and regional banks offer this automatic service, known as a "true" ZBA, others make bookkeeping entries manually the next morning to adjust the balances. In either case, the company does not know until the next morning the exact dollar value of the check clearings—which makes it difficult to manage cash effectively. This ZBA shortcoming, however, is outweighed by its numerous advantages:

- It eliminates the need for maintaining additional balances.
- It indicates exact dollar clearings of each type of disbursement the next morning.
- It provides automatic funding from a concentration account in the same bank.
- A monthly float summary report indicating daily check-clearing patterns over the past month is available from certain banks. This report can be used for future disbursement forecasting and is usually obtainable when an account reconcilement service is provided by the bank.

For ease of reconcilement and accounting purposes, companies normally open separate ZBAs for payroll, trade payables, dividends, and petty cash. Likewise, separate accounts are usually maintained for divisions if separate accounting is required.

Funding ZBA through Concentration Accounts

Most ZBAs are replenished by transferring funds from a concentration account held at the same bank. This is accomplished either automatically the same evening or manually the next morning, depending upon the individual disbursement bank's processing capability. In either case, an automatic overdraft line of credit may have to be established in the event that disbursements exceed the available balance in the concentration account.

Alternatively, disbursement accounts may be funded by transferring available funds from a concentration account at another bank. In this case, the ZBAs are funded by a wire transfer (FedWire) which arrives one day *after* the disbursements have already cleared. Thus, the disbursement bank is in effect lending the company funds overnight to cover the transactions. To compensate for its funds loss, the bank will usually charge the corporation on its monthly account analysis statement. This shows a corporation's average available balance position for the month together with the bank services used and their associated costs, translated into a balance equivalent.

This late funding problem may possibly be avoided by using historical check-clearing patterns to forecast needs and then wiring funds from another bank in anticipation of each day's clearings. Unless vendor payment patterns are very stable, however, this technique is not very reliable.

Funding by Depository Transfer Checks

A funding method used less frequently is to deposit a depository transfer check (DTC) into the disbursement account. The DTC is a check drawn on another bank that does not require a signature. Since it is not drawn on the same bank where it is deposited, funds are usually not immediately available on the deposit date. Therefore, the bank applies an account analysis charge or draws down a prearranged overdraft line of credit. Most banks do not prefer funding via DTCs because of the additional clerical costs and the potential risk if the corporation becomes illiquid and does not have available funds in the drawee bank to cover the checks issued.

Funding by Automated Clearinghouse Payment

The least popular funding method for disbursement accounts is an automated clearinghouse (ACH) payment. This electronic credit transaction is processed through the ACH network and, when generated prior to the ACH deadline, guarantees available funds the next day at any ACH member financial institution. The ACH method could be used in place of the DTC, but is not equivalent to the FedWire because of the one-day lag in availability of funds. Typically, the corporation has to determine the dollar amount of the ACH transaction at least one day in advance of its issuance. Otherwise, any shortfall in available balance will have to be covered by a loan takedown, a backvalue transaction, an adjustment on the account analysis statement, or a direct fee at a predetermined rate.

PAYMENT INSTRUMENT: PAYABLE-THROUGH-DRAFT

Another disbursement instrument with a more limited application is the payable-through-draft. Physically similar to a check, it is drawn by a corporation on itself and is payable through a specific bank, named on its face. The bank is used solely for presentation purposes as a conduit for the checks. After special handling by the bank, the checks are delivered early in the day to the corporation for approval or return that day. The corporation, not the bank, is responsible for checking the signatures, dates, and endorsements. The bank then charges the corporation's demand deposit account that night for the total dollar value of the accepted checks. Since the bank did not debit the corporation's account the previous night, it charges for loss of funds availability.

Payable-through-drafts are commonly used for settling insurance claims by field agents, reimbursing salesmen for expenses, paying dividends to shareholders, and paying employees at geographically isolated locations. The main advantage of using this instrument is that the corporation, rather than one of its representatives, retains the right of final acceptability of the transaction. This is especially useful in the insurance industry, where agents pay insured motorists for damages incurred in accidents. Banks, however, do not usually encourage the use of payable-through-drafts because of the extra processing expenses, potential float loss, and risk of nonpayment. Over the past few years, payable-through-drafts have dropped in popularity compared to other types of instruments.

PAYMENT INSTRUMENT: MONEY MARKET FUND CHECKS

Over the last nine years, the money market fund has been used as another method for making disbursements. Under this arrangement, a corporation can issue checks for $500 or more on its fund account. While the checks clear, the corporation earns interest at the prevailing daily rate. Before using a money market fund, however, financial executives should be aware of the following factors:

- A balance sufficient to cover disbursements must be maintained in the account or the checks will be returned unless other arrangements are made.
- Exact information regarding the checks cleared each day may not be available from the fund's clearing bank the next morning.
- Account reconcilement services or other required ancillary services may not be available.
- The interest rate may be lower than other comparable money market instruments.
- The funds are not insured by the FDIC.

Because of these potential limitations, use of a money market fund is more applicable to small businesses or those companies that are less concerned with same-day disbursement funding or other bank services. A discussion of the use of money funds as an investment vehicle is reviewed in Chapter 12.

FOR THE FUTURE: ELECTRONIC PAYMENT INSTRUMENTS

The least popular disbursement instruments are the wire transfer and the ACH. In the case of the wire transfer, a company will not wire funds to a vendor unless required by contract, verbal agreement, or industry practice because it gives up its available funds immediately upon issuance of the wire.

In using the ACH network for disbursements, the company creates ACH entries with specific value dates instead of sending checks to vendors. Its checking account is then debited, and the vendors' checking accounts credited, with available funds on the appropriate days. Three major problems exist.:

1. The paying corporation gives up float earnings when electronic payments are substituted for paper checks—and most corporations are unwilling to give up float without financial justification.
2. Adequate spacing has only recently become available on the ACH record format for multiple invoice detail in the corporate trade payments program.
3. Vendors have to be notified beforehand that payment is being made to their accounts so that the funds are usable and do not remain idle in the accounts.

In the next few years, the concept of "negotiated settlement," coupled with the Fed's actions to eliminate or charge member banks for check float, will have a major effect on the conversion of payments from paper to electronics. Negotiated settlement involves a compromise between the disburser and the recipient in which they both agree to an explicit payment date in available funds. For example, assuming payment is due on the fifteenth day following the month-end close, if the disburser normally mails a check to the vendor on the twelfth of the month, the vendor usually receives it by the fifteenth. Although the vendor deposits the check in his account on the fifteenth, it may be drawn on a country bank and therefore not become available until the seventeenth. One negotiated settlement option could be for the disburser to send an ACH payment to the vendor value dated the sixteenth. In turn, the vendor can provide the disburser with a discount equivalent to one-half-day's float earnings. In essence, both parties are giving up a half-day's float earnings. The vendor benefits by knowing exactly when he will have available funds; the disburser benefits by using an electronic entry to replace the more expensive paper check. Still, conversion to this technique is likely to be evolutionary rather than revolutionary since most companies appear reluctant to give up their float.

CONTROLLED DISBURSEMENT: AN ALTERNATIVE TO REMOTE DISBURSEMENT

In the 1960s and early 1970s, banks in non-Federal Reserve cities, especially in the South, Southwest, and West began offering "remote disbursement." Under remote disbursement, the geographically remote drawee bank receives a daily check presentment and then calls the corporation each day with that day's check-clearing totals. The corporation, in turn, usually wires funds from another bank to cover the transaction. This enables the organization to maximize check-clearing time by using isolated banks and funding its account as checks clear.

Inefficiencies in the check-clearing transportation network, processing delays, and optimistic availability schedules at the Federal Reserve banks resulted in extra days of float for the paying corporation. During 1979, Fed float averaged $6.7 billion a day, while in mid-1984, it averaged about $0.6 billion a day. Thus, the Fed has been subsidizing the banking system, corporate payers have extended their float, and vendors have received checks for funds which in most cases do not become available for two days. Taking note of this situation, the Federal Reserve Bank issued a directive on remote disbursement in January 1979 in which it requested that banks refrain from offering remote disbursement and, over the past four years, many banks have. One major reason for their refrainment is the development of a viable substitute—controlled disbursement.

Controlled disbursement is a variant of the ZBA. Accounts are opened with a bank which receives early-morning check presentments or magnetic tape transmissions with account number dollar totals from its local Federal Reserve office, branch office, or regional check-processing center. Checks are then sorted by customer account number and customers are notified that morning by telephone, telex, or balance reporting system of the total dollars presented.

The corporation then wires from another bank or transfers from the same bank into the ZBA the exact dollar value of the clearings. Since the disbursement checks will be debited to the corporation's account on the same day the funds are received, the next day's opening balance is zero.

Since controlled disbursement allows a corporation to determine its disbursement funding requirements early in the morning, it can invest any excess funds residing in its concentration account(s) in short-term investment or pay down loans. Banks in the eastern and central time zones can usually notify their East Coast corporate clients between 10:30 and 11:30 A.M. of that day's clearings. The earlier a bank notifies a client, the better the opportunity for the client to obtain the best rates in the short-term money markets.

Controlled disbursement banks also offer ancillary services to the corporation, such as account reconcilement, check truncation, disbursement float summary report; serial check sorts, and microfilm copies of checks. In addition, they provide an opportunity for float extension, compared to banks in Federal Reserve cities. Although controlled disbursement banks are predominantly located in country points and RCPCs, a handful of banks do offer this service from a Fed city because they possess a separate transit routing field or can sort their customers' checks to provide them with 12 noon notification of at least 95 percent of their dollars cleared.

Financial executives should consider using controlled disbursement for large dollar disbursements, such as trade payables, since most banks charge much higher prices for controlled disbursement services compared to ZBAs. Dividend payments, payroll, and petty cash can be handled using a regular ZBA not only because it is less expensive but also because the clearing patterns of these payments are more stable over time, and the transaction size tends to be smaller. Certain controlled disbursement banks, however, will permit companies to disburse dividend and payroll checks.

A survey of 86 banks, conducted by Phoenix-Hecht Inc. of Chicago, indicated that controlled disbursement accounts are priced substantially higher than regular disbursement accounts. (See Exhibit 1.) Interestingly, although 88 percent of the banks

Exhibit 1
Controlled versus Regular Accounts—Average Price Comparison

Service Components	Controlled Disbursement Account	Regular Disbursement Account
Checks paid	$ 0.127	$0.111
Monthly minimum service charge	156.57	5.27
Account maintenance	35.09	5.78

would accept compensation in fees instead of balances, only 22 percent of the customers chose to pay by fee.

The survey also indicated that controlled disbursement accounts are funded in order of frequency as follows: wire transfer, internal transfer from the same bank, DTC, and ACH.

Less frequently used funding methods include selling short-term investments, drawing down on a loan arrangement, and using available funds from lockbox deposits. Some companies use various funding methods depending upon their individual situation.

Noon Presentment Had Minor Impact on Controlled Disbursement Banks

The Federal Reserve Board developed a two-phase program in December 1982 to reduce Federal Reserve float by speeding up the collection of checks presented for payment through the Federal Reserve banks. The first phase of this program, which took effect in May 1983, extended the Fed's check presentation deadlines from 9:00 A.M. to 12 noon to commercial banks in Federal Reserve cities. The Fed estimated that the first phase of the program cleared checks worth $2 billion one day earlier.

The second phase, scheduled for July 1983 implementation, would have included selected non-Federal Reserve city banks that cleared a large dollar volume (i.e., $20 million a day) of daily check disbursements. Because the Fed did not have sufficient time to review the criteria for selecting banks for noon presentment, it decided to ask for public comment through June 1983, thereby postponing its second-phase implementation.

In February 1984 the Federal Reserve Board decided on the criteria for selecting banks for inclusion in the second phase designated as "High Dollar Group Sort" (HDGS). The program's purpose was to collect checks drawn on the non-Federal Reserve city banks at least one day earlier than at present. The selection criteria were as follows:

1. All banks with average daily out-of-zone disbursements exceeding $10 million.
2. Banks with less than $10 million may be included on a case-by-case basis after periodic analysis indicating it is cost-beneficial within three months of its inclusion.

Since most controlled disbursement banks are located in non-Federal Reserve cities, they were affected by this program. One of the corporation's benefits of maintaining a controlled disbursement account is the early-morning notification of check clearings for that day. Early notification is important when a financial executive wants to invest in the money market to obtain the highest rates. As the morning progresses, the rates available on certain instruments may decline by 25–50 basis points.

When the Fed's HDGS program became effective on April 23, 1984, the Fed banks provided account total information between 9:30 A.M. Eastern time and 11:30 A.M. local time. The Fed anticipates that the HDGS will collect $1 billion in checks one day earlier. The methods for providing these data are electronic transmission and telephone advices.

The HDGS program had a varying impact on controlled disbursement banks. On average, about 7–14 percent additional dollars were cleared in the second presentment. The majority of banks on the East Coast that previously notified their customers with the total clearings between 9:00 and 10:00 A.M. EST are now providing two notifications—one at about 9:30 A.M. and the other at about 11:00 A.M. Some banks in the Midwest are notifying their customers between 11:00 A.M. and 12:30 P.M. EST depending upon their location. Interestingly, one Chicago bank has not been impacted at all by the second presentment.

A corporate cash manager should carefully evaluate the impact of the Fed's HDGS program and determine the specific effect on his current and future controlled disbursement banks. At the minimum, he should expect his company's disbursement float to decrease compared to previous years.

WHO BENEFITS FROM A DISBURSEMENT STUDY—AND HOW?

"Uncontrolled" Companies

Companies that do not use controlled disbursement locations for vendor disbursements potentially can gain the most from implementing a study's recommended solution. The study indicates the cost and float benefits of moving its disbursement location to another city compared to its existing system.

"Controlled" Companies

Companies that have been using controlled disbursement for the past five years can benefit from a restudy, since it is likely that their vendor mixes have changed and banks in nearby cities have not been evaluated or their controlled disbursement locations have not been analyzed for effectiveness compared to other banks in their network.

Companies with Big Bills

Usually, the larger the company's monthly vendor disbursements, the larger the potential benefits. For example, typical results of recent studies in which controlled disbursement was not previously used are shown below. In each case the company specified that no remote cities be used in the analysis.

Company	Monthly Vendor Disbursements	Optimal One-Site Solution Annual Benefit at 15 Percent Interest Rate
A	$ 6.7 million	$ 50,000
B	20.0 million	120,000
C	7.1 million	45,000
D	470.0 million	3,400,000

Multiple-Site Disbursement Companies

Unlike lockbox study results, where three, four, or five cities can potentially provide higher benefits, disbursement studies usually indicate that a one- or two-site solution is optimal. However, this is dependent upon the universe of cities selected by the client and his disbursement and banking philosophy. If, for example, the client wants to use not a remote location but a controlled site, this constraint dramatically reduces the potential universe of acceptable cities analyzed.

HOW TO CHOOSE A DISBURSEMENT LOCATION

Set Policy

To determine the best location for disbursing vendor payments, the financial executive must first establish a corporate disbursement policy and philosophy. Unlike the collection process, where the corporate objective is to rapidly convert customer checks into available funds, the disbursement objective is more complicated and risky. Of course, financial executives want to maximize disbursement float. However, there are other critical factors that must be considered when setting disbursement policy. Each is described below.

Corporate Image   Many corporations will not want to risk their high-integrity images by using out-of-state bank checks to extend float to take advantage of their local vendors. Still, some companies are interested only in maximizing disbursement float without regard to vendor reaction. They feel that as long as vendors are paid, their actions are legitimate. Some companies simply adopt a hybrid disbursement philosophy: They pay local vendors with locally drawn checks and all others with checks drawn on geographically diverse locations.

Potential Vendor Reaction   Few vendors respond negatively to remotely drawn checks. The vast majority are satisfied to receive payment and are not concerned with where it is drawn. However, vendors that *are* concerned sometimes react by changing payment terms, eliminating discounts, or complaining. Consider how your particular vendors will react to nonlocal checks.

Current Banking Locations   Do existing banking locations offer feasible disbursement services (e.g., controlled disbursement with the required ancillary services)? If so, then one or two of these banks could be used for corporate disbursements. Note, though, that the corporation still runs a slight risk of affecting its image and receiving negative vendor criticism if the selected disbursement locations extend float over existing arrangements.

Select Optimal Disbursement Cities

Selected money center and regional banks, as well as other vendors, offer a computerized disbursement model that is similar in principle to the lockbox model that banks use to select optimal collection cities (for minimizing mail, processing, and availability float). In essence, the disbursement model maximizes check-clearing float to pinpoint the optimal disbursement cities within the corporation's constraints. To execute the model, the financial executive provides the bank with a representative month of paid vendor disbursement checks. Payroll and dividend payments are usually excluded from this analysis. The data from the sample are extracted, transcribed, and keypunched. They include for each check the issue date, paid date, deposit date, dollar amount, mailing city zip code, deposit city, and vendor name.

The bank executes the model and prepares the analysis for review by the corporation. Typical reports include:

- Current system's mail, check clearing, and availability float.
- Vendor deposit patterns by city, state, and Federal Reserve district.
- Date checks were mailed versus date paid.
- Analysis of depositing vendors' banks' clearing and availability times.
- Optimal and alternative solutions for one-through four-city solutions.
- Cost-benefit analysis (see Exhibit 2).
- Recommended disbursement sites based upon the corporation's constraints.

Like lockbox studies, most disbursement model studies are performed by regional and money center banks using a model developed internally or with outside assistance, or purchased, leased, or used in a time-sharing mode from other vendors.

The price for performing a disbursement study depends upon its complexity, the model used, and the consultant selected. Factors that influence the price include:

- The number of checks to be analyzed, and whether the bank or the corporation will perform the check encoding and key-punching.
- Whether analysis is by division or by the company as a whole.
- Whether a restricted set of cities, such as the existing disbursement cities, or specific cities are used.
- Whether or not the capabilities of specific banks in the optimal cities are analyzed.
- Turnaround time required for completion.
- Cost of executing the computer model.
- Cost of rerunning the model for additional scenarios.

Exhibit 2
Disbursement Study—Cost/Benefit Analysis for One- and Two-Site Solutions

	Presentation Time (Days)	Gain Over Existing System (Days)	Cash Flow Gain	Valued at 15% Opportunity Cost	Cost of Controlled Disbursement System	Annual Net Benefit
Current system	1.26					
Optimal and alternative one-city solution						
Ft. Myers, FL	3.06	1.80	$1,177,147	$176,572	$ 6,060	$170,512
Lewiston, ME	2.97	1.71	1,118,289	167,743	6,060	161,683
Wilmington, DE	2.97	1.71	1,118,289	167,743	6,060	161,683
Harrisburg, PA	2.81	1.55	1,013,654	152,048	6,060	145,988
Scranton, PA	2.80	1.54	1,007,114	151,067	6,060	145,007
Allentown, PA	2.78	1.52	994,035	149,105	6,060	143,045
Trenton, NJ	2.78	1.52	994,035	149,105	6,060	143,045
Bridgeport, CT	2.78	1.52	994,035	149,105	6,060	143,045
Stamford, CT	2.61	1.35	882,860	132,429	6,060	126,369
Augusta, GA	2.60	1.34	876,320	131,448	6,060	125,388
New Bedford, MA	2.59	1.33	869,781	130,467	6,060	124,407
Optimal and alternative two-city solutions						
Ft. Myers, FL Lewiston, ME	3.24	1.98	$1,294,862	$194,229	$10,520	$183,709
Ft. Myers, FL Charleston, WV	3.20	1.94	1,268,703	190,305	10,520	179,785
Ft. Myers, FL Wilmington, DE	3.17	1.91	1,249,084	187,363	10,520	176,843
Wilmington, DE Bridgeport, CT	3.16	1.90	1,242,544	186,382	10,520	175,802
Ft. Myers, FL Trenton, NJ	3.16	1.90	1,242,544	186,382	10,520	175,802

- Cost of man-days for consultant required for analysis.
- Out-of-pocket costs for typing, report preparation, and presentation.

The typical price tag on a standard disbursement study, which encompasses a corporationwide analysis of a month's disbursement checks encoded by the consulting bank, is between $1,500 and $5,000. Larger multidivision studies could cost between $10,000 and $50,000, depending upon the consultant selected.

Banks will normally accept compensation for a study in balances or fees. Selected banks do not charge for these studies, or they perform them as loss leaders in order to strengthen the client relationship, obtain future business, or prove that the bank's controlled disbursement location is comparable to or better than the competition's.

Choose Specific Controlled Disbursement Banks

After determining the most feasible disbursement cities, the company's next step is to select a specific bank. Many banks do not advertise or promote their controlled disbursement services. There are approximately 100 banks that offer this service.

To choose the bank that best suits the needs of the corporation, the following information should be requested from each candidate:

1. Number of current corporate customers and the total item and dollar volume processed per month.
2. Pricing schedule with specific price for services such as account maintenance, checks paid, incoming wire, funding notification, reconcilement, microfilming, check truncation, and float summary report.
3. Reserve requirement and earnings allowance for the past 12 months.
4. The bank's pickup schedule at the local Fed office and its earliest and latest notification time to the client. (East Coast banks usually offer early notification times because of time-zone differences.)
5. Acceptable methods of funding the account—wire transfer, DTC, internal transfer, or ACH—and the charges for nonavailable funds.
6. Name of the bank(s) appearing on the face of the check. (Certain banks use an affiliate or correspondent bank to offer this service with their bank's name appearing on the check. Financial executives may prefer to deal with better-

known banks if they have a conservative banking philosophy and want to minimize potential vendor reaction.)

7. Required method for compensation, i.e., balances or fees.
8. Latest survey of check-clearing times to that bank from
    other cities.
9. Whether or not direct sends are accepted from other banks.
10. Five to 10 references.

SUMMARY

Over the past 10 years, disbursement practices have
evolved from the simple deposit/disbursement account to the
more sophisticated zero balance accounts, remote disbursement
accounts, and, finally, controlled disbursement accounts. This
transition has resulted in the cash manager knowing today's
check clearings early today rather than obtaining this information the next day. This benefits the cash manager because he can
invest excess funds with a high degree of certainty since idle
funds do not have to be maintained to cover disbursements.
Various banks offer different disbursement account funding
methods. These include same-day wire transfer, book transfer
from another account at the same bank, ACH, or DTC. Each
method has different compensation requirements since in the
case of the latter two the deposited funds are not available until
the next day.

Three other techniques a cash manager should consider for
disbursing are payable-through-drafts, money market funds,
and electronic payments (e.g., via the ACH). Each method has
advantages and disadvantages which should be carefully
weighed before a choice is made. Since the Federal Reserve
Board has been successful in reducing check-clearing float since
1980, the cash manager should continually monitor his disbursement patterns and costs to determine if they are optimal based
upon his corporation's disbursement philosophy.

6

Electronic Funds Transfer Systems

Leslie N. Masonson
Vice President, Treasury
Management Consulting
Citibank, N.A.

Electronic funds transfer (EFT) systems handle the majority of all payments in the United States from the standpoint of dollar volume, but with only a small transaction volume processed. The EFT systems include FedWire, BankWire, CHIPS, SWIFT, ACH, POS (Point-of-Sale), and credit and debit cards. (See Table 1, pages 96–97.) Together, these systems account for over 90 percent of the value of all payments in the United States but represent only 1 percent of the transaction volume. Paper-based systems, including checks and U.S. postal money orders account for 9 percent of the value of all payments and 15 percent of the transaction volume. Last, cash accounts for 84 percent of the transaction volume but represents only 1 percent of the value of all payments.[1] Business-to-business check payments account for only 20 percent of all checks written in the United States, but represent 80 percent of the checks written in the $75–$100 category.[2]

Electronic payment usage has greatly expanded in the past 20 years, with tremendous future growth expected in the next decade. The EFT system has numerous advantages over paper-based systems including:

1. Eliminating the time and costs associated with paper checks. These include printing, preparing, mailing, depositing, clearing, reconciling, storing, and retrieving.
2. Reducing personnel.

---

[1] Bureau of Government Financial Operations, "Payments Mechanisms Study," September 1982.

[2] "Business-to-Business Payments: Verging on a Breakthrough?" *Economic Review,* Federal Reserve Bank of Atlanta, October 1983, p. 52.

3. Processing transactions faster with quicker funds availability, in many cases eliminating check float entirely.
4. Improving cash flow by obtaining more reliable and faster information on debits and credits.
5. Providing accurate short-term cash forecasting and higher investment income.

MONETARY CONTROL ACT (MCA) OF 1980

According to Senator William Proxmire, the MCA was the most significant banking legislation since the passage of the Federal Reserve Act of 1913. The MCA is only one part of the Depository Institutions Deregulation and Monetary Control Act of 1980 (Public Law 96-221), which has had a major impact on financial institutions of all types and sizes. The other parts of the legislation cover:

- Eight-year phase-in of reserve requirements for nonmember banks.
- Six-year phase-out of interest rate ceilings (Regulation Q) by March 31, 1986.
- Nationwide N.O.W. accounts that provide interest on checking accounts.
- Expanded powers to federal savings and loan associations.
- Preempts state usury ceilings on first-mortgage loans.
- Requires the disclosure of annual percentage rate to consumers on credit transactions.

Importance of MCA to EFT Growth

The passage of the MCA on March 31, 1980 was the beginning of the era when Fed float would be greatly diminished and the Fed's services to its member banks would be explicitly priced. Thus, the proverbial "free lunch" at the Fed's expense was ending. Without the impetus from the MCA, the growth in usage of the electronic funds transfer services such as the Automated Clearinghouse (ACH) and wire transfer may have been much more restrained. This landmark legislation will continue to have an impact on cash management practices throughout the decade as the Fed continues to raise the price of processing paper checks. The impact of the growth of EFT services will be substantial. ACH usage will continue to grow at the expense of paper checks as different uses for the medium are developed. The financial executive should be knowledgeable about this legislation so that he can understand the reasons for the future trends.

Table 1
Bank-to-Bank Electronic Funds Transfer Systems

System	Origination Date	Daily Dollar Volume	Daily Item Volume	Time of Settlement
FedWire	1970 Switch computerized			
	1977 Computer-to-computer	$586 billion	254,000	Immediate
BankWire I	1952			
BankWire II	1978	$12.6 billion	12,600	End of day
CashWire	1982	$1 billion	1,000	6:00 P.M. EST
SWIFT I	1973 (organized)	—	—	—
	1977 (live)	N.A.	320,000	None
SWIFT II	1985	N.A.	N.A.	None
CHIPS	1970	$278 billion	91,000	End of day
ACH	1972			
	1974 (NACHA formed)	$49 million (gov't.)	893,000 (gov't.)	Value date
		538 million (private)	938,000 (private)	

N.A.–Not available.
TBD–To be determined.
Note: Cost per transaction column is the system's cost to the bank. The bank usually adds a mark-up to its corporate users.

Historical Perspective

From the perspective of the corporate financial executive, the MCA section of the legislation is the most important. A brief history of the reasons for this legislation is necessary to understand its ultimate purpose—to foster an electronic funds transfer environment, to unbundle Fed services, and to eliminate Federal Reserve float. The impetus for the Act were the following factors:

- The volume of checks processed in the United States was estimated at 37 billion in 1980. The cost of printing, mailing, depositing, clearing, reconciling, and storing these paper-based instruments was growing. The Fed, in particular, was experiencing increased handling costs.
- Over 60 percent of the check volume was handled outside the Federal Reserve System by correspondent banks.
- Member banks were leaving the Fed system at an increasing pace. At one point, only 38 percent of all commercial banks were members, which resulted in difficulties for the Fed in managing the monetary policy. Since member banks had to

Cost per Transaction to Bank	Responsible Organization	Member Organizations	Normal Operating Hours
	Federal Reserve Bank Payment & Telecommunications Services Corp.	3,500 banks	9 A.M.–4:30 P.M. EST
$2.00	PATS	170	8 A.M.–10 P.M. EST
$0.30–0.35	PATS	59	8 A.M.–4:45 P.M. EST
—	—	—	—
$0.35	S.W.I.F.T.	1,142	24 hours a day
TBD	S.W.I.F.T.	1,142+	24 hours a day
$0.62 round-trip	NYCHA	130	7:00 A.M.–4:30 P.M.
Varies between $0.005 to $0.035	Federal Reserve Bank NACHA/NY ACH		

maintain noninterest-banking reserves, banks were not willing to give up the earnings lost as interest rates rose to 16 percent.

- Federal Reserve float was approaching $8.0 billion a day in 1978 and was costing the Fed hundreds of millions in dollars in lost earnings as it subsidized the check-clearing process to the benefit of the commercial banks.
- High rates of inflation in the last half of the 1970s were increasing the Fed's processing costs.

Key Features

Based upon all these factors, Congress passed the Act on March 31, 1980. Its key features were:

- For the first time since 1918, the Fed began explicitly pricing its services (check processing, wire transfers and net settlement, ACH, coin and currency handling, and securities safekeeping) to its members.
- The Fed was mandated to eliminate or price out Fed float by year-end 1982.
- For the first time, savings and loans, credit unions, mutual savings banks, and foreign banks were required to keep reserves at the Fed, whether or not they were members.

These institutions were now permitted to borrow from the Fed's discount window for the first time.

- The Fed planned to subsidize below its cost the ACH payments until 1985 to foster the growth of EFTs and minimize the creation of paper checks.
- A four-year phase in reduction in reserve requirements from 16¼ percent to 12 percent as of February 2, 1984. Previously, larger banks were keeping 16¼ percent in reserves in a noninterest-bearing account.

CORPORATE FUNDS TRANSFER SYSTEMS

Funds transfers account for over 85 percent of the dollar volume of all payment transactions. They are large-dollar (e.g., $2 million), low-volume transactions. These transfers typically occur between:

- Corporations to pay each other for goods and services.
- Banks to debit or credit corporate accounts at the request of other corporations or to credit or debit accounts with other banks on their books.
- U.S. Government or Federal Reserve bank with consumers, banks, corporations, or other governmental agencies.

The funds transfer networks are FedWire, BankWire, CashWire, CHIPS (Clearing House Interbank Payments System), SWIFT (Society for Worldwide Interbank Financial Telecommunication), and the ACH (Automated Clearinghouse). Let's examine each network in detail.

FedWire

The U.S. government owns the Federal Reserve Communications System (FRCS), which is also known as FedWire to bankers and financial executives. One of its purposes was to replace the usage of paper checks for large-dollar transactions by electronic transmission of administrative messages and funds transfers over a 40,000-mile communications network. Each day, approximately 254,000 messages valued at $586 billion are sent over the system from more than 3,500 on-line originating banks through the Federal Reserve System to receiving banks. Member banks that are not on-line can phone the local Fed with the wire information or use a correspondent bank. The FedWire is used for funds transfers and for transferring government securities in book-entry format. It is the only network that provides immediately available funds. In New York City, for example, the movement of virtually all U.S. government securities between banks for dealers takes place through FedWire.

Prior to 1970, the growth in wire transfer volume averaged 5 percent per year. However, it has grown at 15–25 percent per year (Table 2) since then, except for the slow down in the past

Table 2
FedWire Growth at Year-end

Year	Annual Transactions (millions)	Percentage Annual Increase	Dollar Value of Transactions (trillions of dollars)	Percentage Annual Increase
1972	9	—	22	—
1973	12	33	29	32
1974	15	25	31	7
1975	17	13	32	3
1976	21	24	39	22
1977	25	19	50	28
1978	29	16	61	22
1979	35	21	64	5
1980	43	23	79	23
1981	54	26	94	19
1982	58	7	121	29
1983	62	7	143	18
1984E	64	3	148	3

Source: Federal Reserve Bank of Philadelphia, "By the Way," May 1980; Federal Reserve Board.

three years. This growth can be attributed to the following factors:

- A reliable computerized system to transfer funds for same-day availability with no settlement risk.
- The increased cash management sophistication of corporate treasurers in moving funds to concentration accounts.
- The tremendous spurt in interest rates from 1974–80, resulting in $1 million in idle balances overnight being worth $438 at 16 percent interest compared to $219 at 8 percent interest.
- Beginning in late 1983, the U.S. government's use of the system for paying certain large-dollar transfers and paying vendors by wire when the payment exceeded $25,000 in value.
- The explosive growth of money market funds and the importance of time value of money.
- The passage of the Monetary Control Act of 1980 granting access to the FedWire to new member organizations.

Transaction Mechanics   Each commercial bank maintains a reserve account with the closest of the Fed's 12 district banks or one of its 25 branches. If Bank of America in San Francisco transfers funds for one of its corporate customers to Citibank in New York, for example, it is actually moving funds from its reserve account at the Fed in San Francisco to the reserve account of Citibank at the New York Fed. This transaction takes place over the FedWire system. Bank of America debits its customer's account for the value of the wire transfer, while Citibank credits its customer's account the same day. This funds transfer is considered final upon Citibank's acceptance.

A cash manager can initiate a FedWire through his bank by a phone call, facsimile transmission, hand-delivered letter, telex, or via in-house terminal connected via a modem to a bank's balance reporting system. The information necessary to make the transfer is:

- Originating corporation's account number.
- Transfer dollar amount.
- Receiving bank's name and address.
- Beneficiary's name and account number.
- Text referencing the payment details.

Repetitive Transfers   Over the past 10 years, there has been a growing trend among cash managers to transfer funds via a bank's balance reporting system. The most common approach to handling repetitive transfers is to setup a predetermined line sheet with the transferring bank. This sheet contains the basic information necessary to send repetitive wires to the same beneficiaries, except for the dollar amount, which varies. For example, a cash manager would provide the bank with a numerical list of the beneficiaries' bank account numbers, bank addresses, transit-routing fields, and text. When the cash manager initiates a payment to any of these beneficiaries, he just provides the line number pertaining to the right beneficiary with the appropriate transfer dollar amount. Since the bank already knows the transaction details, it executes the transaction automatically. Transactions handled by using the line sheet greatly limit the corporation's exposure to internal wire fraud since the ultimate beneficiary is fixed beforehand. The line sheet prevents the corporate employee from sending the funds to his own account at another bank.

Nonrepetitive Transfers   From the fraud standpoint, nonrepetitive or unstructured wire transfers are much more difficult to control by the corporation. In this type of transaction, the beneficiary is different for each wire transfer. Therefore, the corporation has to be extremely cautious in permitting its employees to initiate these transfers. The usual practice is to require at least two authorized signers to verify the transaction accuracy. When using a balance reporting system to input the transaction, a corporation should require that two separate individuals input their unique passwords before the payment can be released. Additionally, certain bank systems provide the wire transfer activity for the day on-line. This can be accessed before the wire deadline to verify the transaction accuracy and possibly reverse the wire the same day.

Some corporations feel that certain balance reporting systems do not offer adequate security against potential wire fraud. Instead, they prefer calling in the transaction detail to a bank representative. In this situation, the corporation should setup stringent written procedures to ensure that no unauthorized employees initiate wires. One recommended method would be to have the bank call back a higher-level corporate employee to verify the transaction prior to its execution.

Pricing   Prior to 1918, the FedWire service was free to Federal Reserve member banks, although they had to maintain reserve requirements without earning any interest. The passage of the Monetary Control Act of 1980 required the Fed to explicitly price its services. Thus, on January 29, 1981, the Fed began pricing FedWire messages at a base price of $0.60 to its member banks. The current pricing is:

Originator	$0.65
Receiver	0.65
Offline (surcharge)	5.50
Telephone advice	3.00

These prices reflect only the Fed charges to the member banks that use the wire transfer service. The banks, in turn, add their overhead and profit margin. Typically, banks charge $5.00–$10.00 for an outgoing wire transfer and $2.00–$5.00 for an incoming transfer.

BankWire   BankWire is a cooperatively owned private organization of 170 member banks. It is operated by PATS (Payment and Telecommunication Services Corporation) and competes directly with the other wire transfer systems. In 1983, approximately 12,600 messages valued at $12.6 billion were transmitted over the system each day. (See Table 3.) BankWire provides U.S. financial institutions with a domestic communications network

Table 3
BankWire Volumes

Year	Annual Transactions (millions)	Percentage Annual Change	Dollar Value of Transactions (trillions)
1978	4.56	—	4.56
1979	4.57	0.1	4.57
1980	4.83	5.8	4.83
1981	4.43	(8.2)	4.43
1982	3.84	(13.6)	3.84
1983	3.15	(18.0)	3.15

Source: BankWire.

that handles funds transfer and administrative messages but does not provide settlement services. Settlement occurs through correspondent bank account transactions. BankWire was upgraded in May 1978 and called the new system BankWire II. The transaction cost per message to member banks is about $2.00; however, the banks' charges to their corporate customers are similar to those of FedWire. Member banks are also assessed an annual allocation based upon the system's expenses.

One of BankWire's unique features is its handling of diverse, financially related administrative messages[3] such as:

- Confirmation of purchases or sale of securities, federal funds, and foreign exchange transactions.
- Securities safekeeping custodial instructions.
- Letter-of-credit details.
- Electronic mail between banks.
- Balance reporting.
- Daily statements.

BankWire does not offer a "true" funds transfer capability. It acts as a transactor of information which results in one bank initiating a transaction to another bank which executes the transaction by debiting and crediting accounts on its books. For example, Bank ABC instructs Bank XYZ, via BankWire II, to

---

[3] Bureau of Government Financial Operations, Payments Mechanism Study-Digest, Payments Mechanics, September 1982.

debit its account on Bank XYZ's books and credit the account of Company B for $100,000.

CashWire   The lack of a same-day settlement feature is one of the reasons why BankWire's growth did not parallel that of FedWire. During the past few years, Bernhard Romberg, President of BankWire until 1983, was continually lobbying the Federal Reserve for the same-day settlement feature. His persistence finally yielded results. In October 1982, the Fed approved the request. CashWire was the name chosen for this application. Each day the CashWire system nets the funds transfer transactions of its member banks and sends a net settlement report to the appropriate Federal Reserve district bank. At the same time a message is sent to the appropriate banks over BankWire indicating the exact debit or credit to their individual reserve accounts.[4] Settlement transactions in 1983 totaled about 100,000. Currently there are about 1,000 transactions a day valued at approximately $1 million each. For the 59 CashWire syndicate members the transaction cost is $0.30 in and out, while other banks pay $0.45 round trip. There are currently 23 settlement system users.[5]

CHIPS

The New York Clearinghouse Interbank Payments Systems (CHIPS) was formed in April 1970. It was one of the first banking systems to use electronic communications facilities to transfer large-dollar payments between New York City banks (and Edge Banks located in New York City) with the purpose of eliminating paper checks. CHIPS is owned by the New York Clearinghouse Association, which also has full operating responsibility for the system including its security. CHIPS competes directly with FedWire, BankWire, and CashWire for domestic payments; the system, however, is used predominantly for handling international transactions. Currently, about 89,000 transactions valued at $273 billion are handled each day (90 percent international, 10 percent domestic) by over 124 member organizations. CHIPS charges its members $0.31 per transmission or $0.62 per round trip.

Settlement occurs the same day. Like BankWire, CHIPS is a transactor of information where funds are moved on the books of the receiving bank from the sending bank to the beneficiary.

---

[4] Ibid.
[5] BankWire letter response, April 13, 1984.

Member banks whose daily position (after taking into account their debits and credits on other member banks) is negative are required to send funds from their reserve accounts to the CHIPS settlement account.[6]

SWIFT

The Society for Worldwide Interbank Financial Telecommunication (SWIFT) was formed in May 1973 in Belgium by 239 of the largest banks in Europe, Canada, and the United States. Its purpose is to provide a secure, reliable, and timely international payments transaction system. SWIFT is the only system that permits banks in foreign countries to send funds transfer messages to each other 24 hours a day, 7 days a week. SWIFT, headquartered in Brussels, is a cooperative nonprofit company that is wholly owned and operated by its 1,142 members (141 U.S. banks[7]) in 53 countries.[8]

SWIFT offers various message types:

- Customer transfers.
- Bank transfers.
- Foreign exchange confirmations.
- Loan/deposit advices and confirmations.
- Collections—advice and acknowledgement of payment.
- Letter of credit.

SWIFT is similar to CHIPS and BankWire II in that it is a transactor of payment information rather than a true funds transfer system like FedWire. Funds are moved by the member banks for their customers or through a central bank. Thus, settlement is the responsibility of each of the participating banks and can vary based upon their arrangements but is typically handled through correspondent bank relationships.

The cost to members of using SWIFT is based upon a cost-recovery principle. Thus, the tariff is composed of a one-time connection charge, direct costs, and message charges. A typical message of less than 325 characters costs members $0.35 each and $0.69 for a higher-priority message.

SWIFT II, which will debut in 1985, will provide greater technological innovation, increased speed and security, and message capacity of 1 million messages a day versus the current

---

[6] Bureau of Government Financial Operations.

[7] "SWIFT Executives and Bankers Model the System's Future," *American Banker,* May 17, 1983.

[8] S.W.I.F.T. Brochure, Brussels, Belgium, 1979.

500,000. The network is also planning to offer domestic and international balance reports, as well as information concerning stock and bond transactions.

Automated Clearinghouse

During the 1960s, check volume increased at a 7 percent rate and financial institutions became interested in replacing manual check handling with an electronic alternative, providing a lower-cost instrument for processing payments and improving the funds clearing process. Therefore, in 1972, the first Automated Clearinghouse was developed in California. Currently, 30 ACHs in the continental United States form an interconnected nationwide network between financial institutions (commercial banks, savings and loans, credit unions, and mutual savings banks) for their corporate and retail customers. New York is the only private ACH.

In 1974, the National Automated Clearing House Association (NACHA) was formed to promote and oversee the system.[9] The current NACHA membership includes 11,563 commercial banks, 4,295 thrift institutions, and 25,394 companies.[10]

In May 1984, 49.8 million transactions flowed through NACHA. The U.S. government credits totaled 21.6 million items. Private sector transactions equalled 17.8 million debits and 10.5 million credits.[11] The Federal Reserve estimates that the ACH will handle 192 million commercial transactions and 225 million in government transactions in 1984.[12]

The mechanics of the ACH are as follows:

1. A corporation prepares ACH-formatted transactions (debits and/or credits) on magnetic tape, data link, diskette, or paper and delivers it physically or via a computer-to-computer interface to an originating financial institution (OFI).
2. The OFI processes the data and strips off the transactions that are drawn on customers of its bank based upon MICR transit-routing field identification and makes the appropriate book transfers.
3. The OFI delivers the tape to its local ACH for processing. The ACH strips off the transactions that pertain to banks in its jurisdiction and electronically transmits the remaining transactions to the other ACHs to perform a similar function.

---

[9] *NACHA Corporate Trade Payments Notebook,* NACHA 1983.

[10] NACHA SurePay Update, June 1984.

[11] Ibid.

[12] *Corporate EFT Report,* September 28, 1983, p. 2.

The most common type of ACH debit and credit transactions are as follows[13]:

Debits	Credits
Utility bills	Social Security
Insurance premiums	Annuities
Mortgage and loan payments	Payroll
Electronic depository transfer checks	Pensions
Dealer/distributor payments	Telephone bill payments
	Dividends
	Corporate trade payments

Pricing   The MCA of 1980 instituted pricing for ACH transactions that became effective in August 1981. This below-rate pricing was based upon a mature volume of 2 to 3 billion items per year as an incentive for companies to substitute the ACH for paper-based checks. By the end of 1985, the Fed is expected to recover its full ACH processing cost. Although the Fed's cost of ACH processing was estimated at $0.055 per item in 1980, the Fed initially priced the service at $0.01 for intradistrict transactions and $0.015 for interdistrict transactions.

In 1983, the Fed's pricing reached 40 percent of the costs and is expected to reach 60 percent of the costs in 1984. The Fed's 1984 pricing for ACH is $0.005 for the intra-ACH originator and $0.015 for the receiver. Inter-ACH costs are $0.005–$0.01 for the originator and $0.025–0.030 for the receiver.

Debit originators pay a premium because they benefit most from the transaction according to the Fed's rationale. Corporations are beginning to assess the cost benefit of ACH versus paper checks as the price of checks keeps escalating, interest rates fall from the double digit level, and check float diminishes. An analysis similar to that presented in Exhibit 1 can be used to assess all the corporate collection factors.

Corporate Trade Payments

Background   In late 1980, NACHA began investigating the feasibility of corporations dealing more efficiently with each other on trade payments through the ACH rather than the more typical paper-based checks. In the past five years, corporations have been automating their back offices, as well as their internal and external communication systems. However, one area that was

---

[13] NACHA Corporate Trade Payments Notebook.

virtually untouched was the electronic transmission of orders, invoices, receiving documents, payments, and cash application through an automated means. The existing ACH formats at that time did not have sufficient capacity to handle all the critical detailed information.

After evaluating the work of the ANSI X12 Committee, which dealt with business data interchange standards, NACHA decided to begin the following three-phase project to study the market potential for electronic corporate trade payments[14]:

Phase I On-site interviews occurred from June through October 1983 with industry groups to review their receivables and payables practices. These companies were American Airlines, Black & Decker, Exxon, Pacific Gas & Electric, Pillsbury, PPG, Proctor & Gamble, Sears, Texas Instruments, Western Electric, and Xerox.

Phase II Committees composed of these companies developed rules for the handling of corporate-to-corporate payments, systems design for the file formats, and an education program for dissemination to corporations and financial institutions.

Phase III Begin implementation of the corporate-to-corporate trade payments program in June 1983, with 10 originating pilot companies who will send transactions up to a maximum of 50 receiving companies. A major feature of this program was the revised file format which held 4,990 addenda records to handle all the invoice information.[15]

Results The pilot project of corporate trade payments resulted in 300 transactions valued at $14.5 million being processed for the 6-month period ending December 1983. Electronic transactions replaced the typical checks, invoices, and bills. Sears, Roebuck & Co. and three of its vendors participated in the project. Westinghouse estimated that potential annual savings would be $2.3 million for all its trade accounts. During the pilot program, payments ranged from $400 to $1 million. Approximately 10 invoices were eliminated and about 3,000 checks were replaced by wire transfers. In addition to the 11 companies mentioned above, other participants were Associates Corporation of North America and Equitable Life Assurance Society. Other companies

---

[14] Ibid.
[15] "Business-to-Business Payments," p. 57.

Exhibit 1
Comparison of ACH to Paper-Based Processing for Collections

Corporate collections cost factors Paper-based	Unit Cost	Corporate collection cost factors ACH Seller Initiated (ACH Debit)	Unit Cost	Customer Initiated (ACH Credit)	Unit Cost
From processing of order until placing related invoice in mail		No change in processing		No change in processing	
Internal		Internal		Internal	
Process:		ODFI and receiving company agreements		R. D. financial institutions and originating company agreements	
Checks received internally		Create prenote		Receive prenote	
Lockbox generated remittance papers		Prepare Input		Receive remittance data tape	
Initiate appropriate accounting entries		Create tape or transmission		Data transmission	
Update accounts receivable manually		Tape costs		Update accounts receivable	
Electronically (lockbox transmission)		Tape delivery		Record cash entries	
Record cash entries		Transmit		Reconcile bank account	
Process returned items		Courier		Administration	
Reconcile bank account		Update accounts receivable		Storage/retrieval	
Receive lockbox remittance papers (internal courier/delivery service, etc.)		Record cash entries			
Administration/overhead (depreciation, interest, equipment, occupancy, supplies)		Process returned items			
Document storage/retrieval		Reconcile bank account			
		Administration/overhead			
		Storage/retrieval			

External

Bank fees
Check deposit   _____
Item charge*   _____
Lockbox processing   _____
Data transmission   _____
Delivery of remittance papers
(banks courier)   _____
Document storage/retrieval   _____

Other

Receivable float   _____
Bad debts   _____

External

Bank fees
Tape charge   _____
Item charge*   _____
Special collection services   _____

Other

Receivable float   _____
Changed terms   _____
Discounts/price   _____
Bad debts   _____

External

Bank fees
Tape charge   _____
Item charge*   _____
Special collection services   _____

Other

Receivable float   _____
Changed terms   _____
Discounts/price   _____
Bad debts   _____

---

* May include Federal Reserve charges.
Source: *NACHA Corporate Trade Payments Notebook*, p. II-4.

that indicated their interest were Sony Corporation, American Hospital Supply Corporation, United McGill Corporation, and Emery Air Freight Corporation.[16] *Corporate EFT Report,* an EFT newsletter, reported that 25 companies participated in the pilot, including U.S. Steel, Exxon, General Electric Information Services, and Mabsco Audio Visual Services. Other companies planning to participate include ITT and Datatronics.[17] The NACHA pilot program found that the typical corporation could save $0.40–$0.45 per disbursement transaction, while the receiving corporation would save about $1.23 per item.[18]

Resistance to Corporate-to-Corporate Trade Payments   Although the NACHA pilot project was successful, there are many financial executives who will not use the ACH for disbursement unless they are forced to. Their reasons encompass the following factors:

1.   The gain in disbursement float far outweighs the benefits from using the ACH, especially for larger average payments. For example, the float earned on a $10,000 check overnight at 10 percent interest is $2.74 compared to the $0.40 gained by eliminating the paper check.
2.   Maintaining two payment methods—ACH for those vendors agreeing to accept those electronic payments, and the paper check for paying other vendors—is cumbersome and not cost-effective.
3.   A large portion of the banking system is neither ready to handle the NACHA format nor is capable of handling the automated computer-to-computer input.
4.   The potential economic loss from discarding a larger quantity of preprinted paper checks is one that many companies aren't willing to absorb. Companies usually order a one- or two-year supply from their printers to take advantage of volume discounts.
5.   There is uncertainty over the legal implications of electronic payments when erroneous transactions or fraud occur. Since EFT systems are not perfectly secure, the corporate executive must be given a written statement on who has responsibility for the potential liability incurred by using this type of payment mechanism.

---

[16] "Electronic Project Slashes Paper Work, 45 Companies Say," *Wall Street Journal,* January 20, 1984.

[17] December 14, 1983 issue, p. 1.

[18] "Business-to-Business Payments," p. 57.

RETAIL FUNDS TRANSFER SYSTEMS

Telephone Bill Paying

In 1973, banks began offering telephone bill paying (TBP) services to retail customers to reduce their check and paper processing costs while increasing their transaction fees. However, the use of TBP has not grown to the degree expected over the past decade. Although over 420 financial institutions offer the service, TBP displaced only 80 million consumer checks valued at $7 billion during 1982.[19] Thirty-eight percent of financial institutions offering the service use their own internal system, 48 percent use a service bureau, and 13 percent use a correspondent bank.[20]

The mechanics of TBP are straightforward. A bank customer dials a specific bank phone number to contact the bank operator, provide his account number and password, the vendor or merchant's code number or name, and the amount to pay. The bank then aggregates all the data from all its customers and prepares one check or an electronic payment to each vendor, listing all the payees and their payments. A touch-tone service, in which no bank human intervention is required, is offered by more automated banks. In this scenario, a customer keys in his information on a touch-tone phone that responds to a computerized voice request for information.[21]

The TBP banks maintain a fixed list of local merchants and vendors that they will pay. They typically include utilities, department stores, banks, real estate companies, and hospitals. Since other merchants, such as dentists, doctors, landlords of small houses, and other small businesses, are not on the bank's system, the usefulness of the services is limited.

Each month the TBP customer receives a monthly descriptive bank statement listing the transaction detail. He benefits from using the service since there are no checks, stamps, or envelopes, and the time saving is also in his favor.

The reasons that TBP growth has not exploded are as follows:

- Consumers' concern about the privacy of information about their buying habits.
- Consumers' apprehension about billing errors that may be difficult to resolve.

---

[19] "Telephone Bill Paying Continues to Expand, but Not at Wild Pace," *American Banker*, January 5, 1983, p. 8.

[20] Ibid.

[21] "Paying Bills by Telephone," *New York Times*, October 10, 1983.

- Consumers' desire to receive their paper checks as evidence of payment if a dispute occurs in the future.
- The inconvenience of paying many smaller businesses by check because the bank has not listed them as one of its payees.
- The lack of aggressive marketing and follow-up by banks in advertising and promoting the positive features of the product.

A survey of 229 banks by the Direct Marketing Association indicated the following results regarding telephone bill paying[22]:

Profitability	Percent of Banks	TBP Plans	Percent of Banks
Currently profitable	1	Currently provide service	14
Currently not profitable	21	Plan to provide service	23
Will be profitable	24	No plans to provide service	55
Within 1 year	1		
1–5 years	13		
More than 5 years	10		
Don't know	63		

Home Banking

European countries and England were the initiators of two-way home information services technology known as Videotex. The development of equipment and software for home banking began in the United States in the late 1970s. Because of the increasing volume and cost of consumer transactions, banks and software company vendors began developing electronic alternatives. The market for two-way home banking services is expected to expand to 8 million houses by 1990.[23] In mid-1981, John F. Fisher at Banc One Corp. said, "Home banking represents the most significant change in banking delivery systems, and the greatest opportunity to be responsive to market needs and to impact the economies of delivery bank services."[24] Most experts believe that home banking systems cannot successfully evolve by just concentrating on bank services alone. Therefore, many nonbank entrants have emerged, such as Knight-Ridder, AT&T, Automatic Data Processing, CompuServ Corporation, American Express, IBM, Sears, Roebuck & Co., Radio Shack, and CBS among others. An example of this trend toward ex-

---

[22] *BankLetter*, January 30, 1984, p. 6.

[23] "Home Banking Moves off the Drawing Board," *Business Week*, September 20, 1982.

[24] *Bank Automation Newsletter*, Warren, Gorham & Lamont, August 1981.

panded home services was an ad in the *Miami Herald* (December 6, 1983) indicating the following services available at home (TV set, phone lines, and terminal) called Viewtron (offered by Knight-Ridder):

- Banking—checking, savings, funds transfer, bill paying, loans.
- Shopping—selecting merchandise at Burdines.
- News—headlines in newspaper.
- Education—Grolier's American Encyclopedia, Scholastic Aptitude Tests.
- Sports—scores.
- Stock market—closing prices.
- Travel—cruise information, airline schedules.
- Electronic mail—send to friends.
- Weather forecasts.
- Restaurant guide.
- Consumer reports—rating of products.

Early pilot projects in the home information/banking field included:

- *Channel 2000*—joint venture between Banc One Corp. and OCLC, a library service company. Services provided to consumers included banking and information retrieval (video encyclopedia, educational programs).[25]
- *Chase Manhattan*—developed a telephone bill paying service for which a consumer needs a telephone-type terminal with a numeric keypunch. The customer can store up to 20 bills with value dates.[26]
- *Cox Cable Communications, Inc.*—began experiment in 200 San Diego households in May 1981 using five banks, including Security Pacific and United California Bank to provide home banking and bill-paying services to consumers.[27]
- *Express Information*—joint venture of United American Service Corp. (12 banks) and CompuServ Corporation and Radio Shack.[28]
- *Home Banking Interchange*—Automatic Data Processing began a research pilot in mid-1981 to determine the feasibility and applications to be pursued.[29]

---

[25] Ibid.

[26] *Bank Systems and Equipment,* September 1981, p. 36.

[27] "Cable Firm Plans Home Banking Systems in Omaha, New Orleans," *American Banker,* March 2, 1981.

[28] "Money Market Fund Available through Home Computer," *American Banker,* December 17, 1982.

[29] "ADP Starts Home Banking Pilot," *American Banker,* September 5, 1981.

- *Home Base*—Citibank began testing its home banking system in mid-1981 with a limited base of test customers provided with a small portable terminal. Services provided include on-line transfer of funds to another account in the bank, balance information on different Citibank accounts, stop checks, obtain travelers checks, pay any bill with a value ate.[30]
- *Liquid Green Trust*—this $160 million money market mutual fund began using the CompuServ Information Service network on September 23, 1982. Investors can display their account information, institute their own sweeps, and transfer money to any of the 11,000 ACH member banks to their accounts.[31]

The more recent home banking developments involve the following:

CBS Inc. and American Telephone At the end of January 1983, 100 consumers in Ridgewood, New Jersey were added to a test group. Three New Jersey banks (Fidelity Union Bank, Newark; Citizens First National Bank of New Jersey, Ridgewood; and Independence Bank of New Jersey, Allendale) were participating in the project. Besides the basic banking services of account inquiry, funds transfer, and bill payments, the other services offered include television listings, shopper's guide, stock portfolio of 12 securities, and an electronic reminder feature.[32]

VideoFinancial Services A joint venture of Banc One Corp. (Columbus), Southeast Banking Corp. (Miami), Wachovia Corp., and Security Pacific Bank was providing banking services in southern Florida in September 1983. These banks will use only telephone lines and TV sets and not the more costly home computers.[33]

Pronto Chemical Bank began marketing its "Pronto" home banking service to other banks by January 1984. The system required 3 years to develop and was tested on 200 New York City households. Pilot consumers can review and pay credit card payments, pay recurring bills automatically to 250 mer-

---

[30] "Home Banking at Citibank: Testing Consumer Wants—And More," *American Banker*, July 10, 1981, p. 10.

[31] "Money Fund Offered via Home Computer," *American Banker*, December 17, 1982, p. 1.

[32] "CBS-Bell Videotex Network Tests Home Banking," *American Banker*, February 2, 1983.

[33] "Home Banking Network Due in Florida in September but Cost May Limit Appeal," *The Wall Street Journal*, February 23, 1983, p. 12.

chants, prepare budgets, and send or receive messages to other "Pronto" subscribers.[34]

Home Banking Interchange   Twenty banks with combined assets of $153 billion are participating with Automatic Data Processing to test home banking and videotex services in early 1984 with 2,000 consumers nationwide. The Times Mirror Co. and Informat of Canada provide the nonbanking data.[35]

CBS-IBM-Sears Joint Venture   In February 1984, three well-known corporations joined resources to develop a home videotex service. Financial services will be provided not only from commercial banks, but from savings and loans, insurance, and brokerage houses. The system will use a wide variety of personal computers, information services, and merchandisers. The service will not be available for a few years because of the extensive hardware and software development and technical specifications.[36]

American Express Joins Times Mirror and Knight-Ridder Amexco announced, in February 1984, that it joined forces with Knight-Ridder and the Times Mirror Videotex Service. This service will provide:

- American Express cardholders with the ability to review their account transactions for the last six months and query any transactions using electronic mail.
- Travel and information services, including reservations.
- Shopping and ordering through Amexco catalog.
- Investment services through Shearson/American Express.
- Insurance advice from Fireman's Fund.
- Other services including banking, news, restaurant reviews, shopping, and theatre tickets.[37]

Implications for Cash Managers   The increased emphasis on home banking and videotex application by a myriad of participants including banks, communications companies, software vendors, and others should be viewed as a positive step in the evolution of electronic banking. Consumers have become accus-

---

[34] *Business Week*, September 20, 1982, p. 39.

[35] "Consortium Will Test Home Banking," *American Banker*, May 19, 1983, p. 3.

[36] "CBS, IBM, Sears Team Up to Offer Videotex," *American Banker*, February 15, 1984, p. 1.

[37] "American Express Offering Services Through Videotex," *American Banker*, February 22, 1984, p. 1.

tomed to the advancing technology through the use of bank telephone bill paying and automated teller machine services.

Corporations that receive a large portion of their payments from consumers should benefit by the home banking revolution. Retailers, utilities, insurance companies, local merchants, and other companies can reduce their overall banking costs and improve their cash collection forecasts by receiving payments through home banking devices. For instance, in the retail environment a consumer can order merchandise at home via his home banking/videotex service by simply viewing the latest offerings and making his selections. The bank would create the appropriate audit trail by creating an electronic invoice with the consumer's store account number, method of payment (ACH, credit card), and timing of payment, and send the data electronically to the retailer for execution. Payment would be made to the retailer's account on the value date.

Corporate cash managers, in consumer-dependent companies, should become familiar with the developments in home banking and work with the appropriate departments in their companies that may be participants in a home banking pilot to ensure that not only are the retail sales expanded but also that the cash management impact is considered and managed effectively.

SUMMARY

Electronic funds transfer systems are continuing to overshadow the paper-based systems from the perspective of dollar volume, but they still lag far behind as far as transaction volume. However, this latter trend is being dramatically impacted by the tremendous surge in EFT volume in the past five years and the expected growth in the future. Since 1980, with the impact of the Monetary Control Act on float reduction and higher prices for paper checks, financial executives have been weighing the advantages and disadvantages of using EFT to replace paper checks for paying their customers. The corporate trade payments pilot project to replace paper invoices and paper checks was successful, although the number of transactions was small. On the retail EFT side, banks and other vendors are concentrating on home banking as one way to increase their consumer business, while at the same time providing an electronic mechanism for them to pay bills. Based upon past experience, the development of the EFT systems will be more evolutionary than revolutionary.

SECTION III

Forecasting, Models, and Microcomputers

7

Daily Cash Forecasting*

Bernell K. Stone, Ph.D.
Mills B. Lane Professor of Banking and Finance
College of Management
Georgia Institute of Technology

Tom W. Miller, Ph.D.
Associate Professor of Business Administration
School of Business Administration
Emory University

From a manager's perspective, cash forecasting success requires a framework for viewing and organizing the problem of daily cash forecasting and a means for structuring the activities of staff and/or external assistance, e.g., assistance from statisticians, programmers, and systems analysts. This chapter presents a framework for structuring and organizing daily cash management.

This chapter does not treat statistical techniques per se[1] but rather deals with the organization of cash forecasting activities necessary to use statistical and other methodologies.

TYPES AND USES OF DAILY CASH FORECASTS

There are a variety of daily cash forecasting problems and forecast concerns. Exhibit 1 lists some of the major concerns.

The most common objective in daily cash forecasting is probably a forecast of the net cash flow before investment-borrowing flows, which is often treated as the net flow at the concentration

---

[1] The following books discuss statistical techniques for forecasting: George E. Box and Gwilym Jenkins, *Time Series Analysis, Forecasting & Control* (San Francisco: Holden Day, Inc.), 1976; Brown, R. G., *Smoothing, Forecasting, and Prediction of Discrete Time Series* (Englewood Cliffs, N.J.: Prentice-Hall, 1963); N. R. Draper, and H. Smith, *Applied Regression Analysis* (New York: John Wiley and Sons, 1966); and J. Johnston, *Econometric Methods*, 2d ed. (New York: McGraw-Hill, 1972).

Exhibit 1
Major Types of Daily Cash Forecasting Problems

Problem	Concern
Net flow at concentration bank	1. Net daily flow • Net inflow • Net outflow 2. Big flows
Lockbox deposits	1. Amount deposited by lockbox 2. Availability 3. Amount misdirected
Field deposits	1. Amount deposited, availability 2. DTC clearing time 3. Amount available at concentration bank 4. Control data, e.g., deviation from past behavior
Disbursement clearing	1. Amount disbursed 2. Clearing time distribution 3. Amount predicted to clear

bank. This provides information on future cash surpluses or deficiencies and is thus input to a company's investment-borrowing decisions. Such information can provide a higher return than without any forecast by allowing investment in nonmarketable (less marketable) instruments, by allowing longer maturities (when appropriate), by enhancing ability to ride the yield curve,[2] and possibly by enhancing use of interest-rate hedges.[3] Even more important, a company can avoid "wash investments" and "wash borrowing," i.e., the practice of investing at one point only to have to borrow an off-setting amount later or vice versa. Given substantial improvements in investment yield and/or a reduction in net borrowing cost, there is an obvious incentive to develop a forecast of net daily cash flow over some time horizon, e.g., 30 to 60 days and possibly as long as 90 days.

While the net daily cash flow is an obvious forecast concern, there are many others dealing with components of the cash flow. For instance, companies with large field deposit systems (e.g., retailers, fast food companies, retail oil companies, consumer finance companies, and brokerage firms) have more cash in field deposit banks than necessary for compensating balances. *Anticipation* (initiating a transfer before notification of deposit) can usually accelerate flow and reduce or eliminate excess

---

[2] For a discussion of this investment strategy, see Chapter 12.

[3] For a discussion of interest rate hedge strategies, see Chapter 13.

field balances. A daily forecast by field unit and/or by field deposit bank is the crux of good anticipation. Such a forecast may also have significant control value.

Another common forecast concern pertains to disbursement funding.[4] Conventional practice today is to rely on some kind of information report to trigger funding, e.g., the conventional controlled disbursement service with daily wire funding. Alternatives can reduce balance reporting, money transfer, and administrative costs while giving a company more control over its day-to-day balance fluctuations.[5]

Besides a forecast of the daily cash flow and/or its components, information on matters impacting the cash flow can have management value, especially in identifying float improvement opportunities. For instance, it is desirable to identify remote disbursers in a lockbox collection system as well as incorrectly directed items. Field deposit availability and DTC clearing times are inputs to cash concentration management that can favorably accelerate cash movement and increase favorable DTC float.

Control

Besides providing information to support cash management activities, daily cash forecasts are useful for control. Variations in overall noncredit sales, a slow-down in payments on credit sales, shifts in deposits from field units, and changes in check-clearing times are examples of departures from expected behavior that indicate a possible problem and a situation that may require corrective action.

The essence of control is comparing differences between expected (or desired) behavior and actual behavior. "Large" differences indicate a problem requiring management attention. Putting control on a management-by-exception basis requires exception reports whenever the deviation between actual and expected results exceeds a critical level—the monitoring control limit. As forecast quality improves, tighter control becomes possible without incurring the cost of false alarms and/or unnecessary investigations. Thus, there is a direct correspondence between daily forecast accuracy and the quality and cost of the control activities based on daily cash forecasts.

While the impetus for daily cash forecasting generally arises from cash management needs, especially aggregate cash posi-

---

[4] See Chapter 5 for a discussion of disbursement funding.

[5] These alternatives are discussed in detail in: B. K. Stone and T. W. Miller, "Forecasting Disbursement Funding Requirements: The Clearing Pattern Approach," *Journal of Cash Management*, 3, no. 5, October/November 1983, pp. 67–78.

tion management and cash concentration, the need for accuracy generally is dictated by the control uses to which the forecast is applied.

FORECASTING FRAMEWORK

There are four steps involved in an organized, systematic approach to daily cash forecasting—problem structuring, approach selection, measurement modeling, and technique-tool selection and use. Exhibit 2 lists and briefly defines each. The

Exhibit 2
The Four Key Steps of Daily Cash Forecasting

Step	Brief Description
Problem structuring	Breaking the problem into subproblems and identifying available data as forecast input and/or as the basis for forecast model parameterization.
Approach selection	Deciding for each forecast subproblem whether to use standard statistical projection, distribution, information transformation, or an appropriate combination.
Measurement modeling	*Forecast modeling* (relating the quantity or quantities to be forecast to the forecast input) and *estimation modeling* (developing an expression or expressions relating forecast parameters to available data).
Statistical technique/tool selection	Choosing (when appropriate) a statistical estimation technique and the way to use the technique and/or designing information transformation procedures.

next four sections develop these steps into a systematic framework for daily cash forecasting.

Step 1: Problem Structuring

Problem structuring means working from a cash management and/or cash control problem to the information required to support decision making. This information then indicates what should be forecast and how much forecast precision (accuracy) is required. Once desired information is identified, one works from available (or at least theoretically attainable) data to required information. Forecasting arises as part of the transformation of available (attainable) data into the desired information.

It is crucial to recognize explicitly a common forecast fallacy— the seemingly logical (but incorrect) view that the desired cash flow information (e.g., net daily flow at the concentration bank) is the logical forecast focus. In fact the opposite is usually true.

Rarely is the desired cash flow information the logical forecast focus in the conventional sense of applying conventional statistical techniques to past values of the desired cash flow information.

After recognizing the fallacy of making the desired cash flow stream the forecast focus, it is logical to ask how a focus should be selected. Problem structuring involves considerable art (as opposed to science). Yet several principles can aid the art of deciding what should be forecast. Exhibit 3 summarizes some of these principles and the rest of this section discusses them.

Exhibit 3
A Summary of Problem Structuring Principles

Principle	Summary Statement
Major versus nonmajor	Major flows (such as taxes, bond interest, sinking fund payments, lease payments, insurance payments, large rentals, dividends, benefit payments, payroll, major receipts, etc.) should be separated from other small payments.
Component focus	The cash flow should be broken into logical components. The objective should be statistical stability in the case of direct statistical estimation in distribution and either a common data source or transformation equation for the case of scheduling.
Time sequencing	The cash flow can be divided into time stages when there is an opportunity to observe or predict an intermediate flow. Multiple stages can improve forecast quality by allowing alternative forecast approaches, models, or estimation techniques at each stage. They can also serve control functions by giving advance warning of a departure from an earlier forecast or another aspect of intended behavior.

Major versus Nonmajor Flows   Analysis of most cash forecasting problems reveals that much of the cash flow is known. Major outflows such as the timing and amount of tax payments, bond interest, bond sinking fund payments, lease payments, major rentals, and dividends are almost always known at least 60 days in advance. Even though payroll and benefit payments consist of many small items, they may also be treated as "major items" since these payments are initiated at discrete times for large amounts that are generally known accurately in terms of timing and total payment.[6]

---

[6] The key point here is that large payroll, benefit payments, dividends, and any other periodic payments should be separated from other payment streams. Generally the forecast task here is a prediction of the clearing distribution.

A number of large contractual receipts are also frequently known in both amount and timing. The amount of other major receipts may be known, with receipt timing being contingent on satisfactory delivery or other performance requirements plus the uncertainty of mail time and other payment delays.

It would be foolish to use statistical techniques to estimate these major flows. First, as noted already, most are known in amount or timing and require no statistical estimate to specify their occurrence. Second, those major flows that are not known, such as payments or receipts subject to delivery or performance conditions, are generally not amenable to conventional statistical techniques. They are, moreover, usually offset by a single financial transaction. Third, and most important, including major flows in a sample for statistical estimation would generally prevent any forecast success using statistical estimation because the major flows represent neither extrapolatable trends nor periodic patterns. Moreover, because the major flows are very large, they obscure any trends or patterns in the remainder of the cash flow.

Any cash flow that is not a major flow will be called a *nonmajor flow* here. The first principle of good problem structuring is to separate all major flows from the nonmajor flows. This immediately handles a significant portion of the total flow without any need for statistical estimation. It reduces the rest of the forecast task to treating the nonmajor flows. Because these consist of many small payments or receipts it is these flows that are potentially amenable to statistical estimation.

Thus, separating the major flows from nonmajor flows can be viewed as a necessary step to prepare for any statistical estimation that may be conducted.

Cash Flow Components   Forecast success can usually be enhanced by breaking the nonmajor flow into components. At a minimum, inflows should be separated from outflows, but even more detail is usually desired. For instance, inflows are logically broken into flows from credit sales and noncredit sales. Credit sales might be organized by credit terms and flows from divisions, territories, product lines, and other logical subunits of the company.

In payments, payroll and benefit payments (if not already separated as a major flow) clearly should be separated from vendor disbursements. In turn, vendor disbursements might be separated into payments to companies and individuals. They are generally classified by the location of the payee and the bank upon which the checks are to be written.

The problem situation, the available data, and the desired accuracy will indicate the logical division of the cash flow into components. The key point is the need to focus on logical component identification as a critically important part of problem structuring.

Guidelines can be given for component identification, but these are best presented after discussion of approach selection and measurement modeling.

Sequence Detail: Stages in Cash Flow Prediction   Given that the nonmajor cash flows are divided into appropriate components, another structuring question concerns how the cash flow stream should be tracked over time. Frequently, it is desirable to use two or more information conversion stages in converting data pertinent to a cash flow component into the prediction of the cash flow component.

1. Disbursement Clearings.   For the case of predicting clearings at disbursement banks, one could focus directly on the amount cleared at each disbursement bank. Alternatively, one could take the conventional two-stage approach of first predicting the schedule of checks to be written by bank location and then measuring the time distribution of clearings.

2. Credit Receipts.   In predicting receipts from credit sales, it is usual to predict credit sales first and then use knowledge of payment delays to convert the predicted credit sales into a schedule of cash flow predictions from credit sales.

Multiple stages make possible different forecast approaches or techniques at each stage. Multiple stages can also provide control benefits by giving more information and/or an earlier warning of problems. However, multiple stages usually mean more forecast effort and an information system able to handle the intermediate flow data.

While two or more stages may be desirable, a company is often forced to use a single stage in initial forecast efforts until the necessary data gathering and information support systems can be obtained. Preference for one stage versus two or more stages generally depends on the situation, the available data, and required accuracy.

Information Systems   The ability to isolate major from nonmajor flows, to break the nonmajor flow into components, and to handle time sequencing depends on a company's information system. In the short run, a forecaster must usually accept the current information system and the various limitations that it may entail. However, in the longer run, defining an appropriate information system to capture, organize, and make accessible the necessary data is the crux of successful daily cash forecasting and control. The ideas developed in the rest of the chapter should convince the reader that good daily cash forecasting is usually more an information system problem than a statistical estimation task even though it is very common to view the problem as primarily an issue of statistical estimation technique.

A key part of the information system can be handled by clever use of the banking system. Creating zero-balance subaccounts to handle logical components of the cash flow means that the banking system is organizing key data in computer-readable form. Moreover, much of the effort for managing the information collection is transferred to the banking system as part of its normal data processing.

Step 2: Approach Selection

It is common to talk of a "receipts and disbursements" approach, a "sources and uses" approach, and an "adjusted income" approach.[7] In fact, these are really alternative ways to structure the problem by identifying components of the net flow in the context of the company's accounting system. Thus, they should be viewed more as problem structuring (deciding what should be forecast and breaking the forecast into components) rather than as approaches in the sense of a generic method for converting available data into its cash flow implications.

We identify several approaches: (1) statistical projections from past flows (trend extrapolation and/or seasonality), (2) scheduling, and (3) distribution. In this chapter, emphasis is placed on scheduling and distribution. Many daily cash forecasts logically use one or a combination of these two approaches.

Trend Extrapolation A standard forecast technique is to extrapolate a past trend into the future. Moving averages, exponential smoothing, growth-rate forecasts, and some regression and Bayesian revision models convert past data trends into forecasts under the assumption that past behavior will continue.

Seasonality Variation with time of year is common to economic time series. Seasonality adjustments scale levels up or

---

[7] For a discussion of these and related financial statement structuring methods in the context of cash budgeting, see W. E. Mitchell, "Cash Forecasting: The Four Methods Compared," *The Controller*, 28, April 1960, pp. 162–66 and 194.

down on the basis of past seasonal variations. Some of the more sophisticated forecast techniques such as Box-Jenkins[8] deal with seasonal and other cyclical patterns and their resolution from trends in very general ways.

Scheduling   *Scheduling* is the transformation of information into cash flow implications. To provide a very simple illustration, consider the cash outflows associated with vendor payables in a company that buys all materials, supplies, and services on terms of net 30 and always pays on time by check but never pays early. A schedule of disbursements for vendor payments over the next 30 days can be constructed from invoices received and approved for payment. Knowledge of company payment policy is used to transform the invoice data into a payment schedule. In this case, invoice data and payment scheduling policy enable construction of the payment schedule for the next 30 days without the use of any statistical estimation. This example is purely a situation of data capture and transformation using the known time delay between invoice receipt and payment initiation.

Because no statistical estimation is involved, this example is a case of pure scheduling. In practice, pure scheduling is rare aside from major items and some payment streams. Usually, there is a combination of scheduling (transforming information) and statistical estimation (using past data to predict unknown values). For instance, going beyond 30 days in the scheduling framework above would require a prediction of the invoice amounts to be transformed, e.g., by using purchase authorizations and order placements. Moreover, even for the 30-day payment period, some fraction of invoices might not have been received and processed so that statistically predicting the amount from invoices yet to be received and processed could also be necessary.

Distribution   *Distribution* is spreading a total flow for a time period over the days comprising the time period.[9] For instance, total nonmajor cash receipts taken from a cash budget may be spread over the days of the month in accord with an estimate of the proportion normally received on each day. Or payments made on a particular day may be transformed into a pattern of

[8] George E. Box and Gwilym Jenkins, *Time Series Analysis, Forecasting & Control* (San Francisco: Holden-Day, Inc.), 1976.

[9] This definition is in terms of daily forecasts. A total may be distributed over periods longer than a day. For instance, in the three articles cited in footnotes 10–12, each uses distribution of credit sales in a month over subsequent months to deal with month-to-month forecasts of accounts receivable and payments.

clearings at the disbursement bank in subsequent days. Or credit sales over a particular time period (day, week, month) may be transformed into a schedule of daily payments over subsequent days using a daily version of the payment-pattern technique developed by Lewellen and Johnson,[10] Lewellen and Edmister,[11] and Stone.[12]

The key attribute of distribution is spreading a total over days. The forecast input is the total (which may itself require forecasting). The required parameter is the proportion for each day over the distribution period. Measuring these proportions is typically tantamount to finding a probability distribution for the total. Hence, the term "distribution" is used to characterize this approach.

There are two major benefits of distribution. First, seasonality and trends can often be incorporated in the total to be spread rather than the distribution proportions. Second, it can facilitate time staging where distribution is one of the stages.

For instance, as already noted, it is common in treating disbursements to first forecast the total payment by disbursement bank by day and then use distribution to convert each day's payments into schedules of check clearings at each disbursement bank.

Combination Approaches In the pure scheduling example, all that was scheduled was payment initiation (check writing). The cash management concern is usually the schedule of check clearings at each disbursement bank. The standard technique to obtain disbursement clearings is distribution of each day's payments in accord with a pattern of check-clearing times using methods described by Stone and Miller.[13] Hence, forecasting check clearings by the disbursement bank involves a combination of scheduling and distribution in a two-stage process in which the first stage uses scheduling and the second uses distribution.

1. Disbursement Scheduling. A schedule of planned payments is obtained by transforming invoice and other payment data into a planned payment schedule using credit-term information and company payment policy. If necessary, the schedule

[10] W. G. Lewellen and R. W. Johnson, "Better Way to Monitor Accounts Receivable," *Harvard Business Review*, 50, May–June 1972, pp. 101–109.

[11] W. G. Lewellen and R. O. Edmister, "A General Model for Accounts Receivable Analysis and Control," *Journal of Financial and Quantitative Analysis*, 8, March 1973, pp. 195–206.

[12] B. K. Stone, "The Payments-Pattern Approach to the Forecasting and Control of Accounts Receivable," *Financial Management*, 5, Fall 1976, pp. 61–78.

[13] Stone and Miller, "Forecasting Disbursement Funding Requirements."

is scaled up statistically in accord with the usual level of late invoices, short-term invoices (e.g., discounts), and no-invoice payments.

2. Payment Distribution. The amount paid each day is distributed in accordance with an estimate of the proportion clearing on subsequent days. The forecast of total clearings for each future day are the amounts for that day from the series of preceding payments.

Approach Synthesis Trend extrapolation and seasonality are common ways to approach a forecast task. Distribution is less common but particularly suited to daily cash forecasting. Scheduling (information transformation) is often implicit in forecast models but rarely given explicit attention.

In most daily cash forecasting problems, the usually neglected approaches of distribution and scheduling tend to be the most pertinent. Understanding them and giving them explicit attention is crucial, especially for managers interfacing with systems analysts and statisticians, since the latter do not generally think in terms of these approaches.

It is particularly important to recognize information transformation (scheduling) as an alternative to direct statistical projection in some cases and as a way to structure it in others, especially in combination approaches using multiple-stage forecasts. It is generally preferable not to estimate statistically the information that is obtainable via data transformation. Using data transformation generally brings to bear more information and, therefore, improves forecast quality. Moreover, data transformation does not rely on projecting past behavior into the future and is, therefore, more robust than purely statistical projections.

Step 3: Measurement Modeling

Problem-structuring action (separating major from nonmajor cash flows, breaking the cash flow into components, and time sequencing the components), plus approach selection for the various component sequences, encompasses much of what would normally be called "forecast modeling," namely, organizing the forecasting task by breaking it into subproblems and making decisions about data transformation and statistical estimation. Thus, the problem-structuring techniques and approach classification can be viewed as a framework for organizing preliminary modeling.

Once the preliminary modeling has taken place, measurement modeling is the next logical step. It involves forecast and estimation modeling.

1. Forecast Modeling. The forecast model relates the forecast input data to the quantity (or quantities) to be forecast. For instance, in the example to be presented, nonmajor components of the cash flow on workday t of the month are modeled as a proportion of the monthly total obtained from the cash budget. Thus, if CF_t denotes the cash flow on workday t of the month, the forecast equation is

$$CF_t = (\text{Proportion})_t(\text{Total})$$

Given that the monthly total is input data obtained from the cash budget, the measurement task is to obtain the proportion appropriate for each workday of the month.

2. Estimation Modeling. The parameters of the forecast equation may be estimated directly from it. However, it is often necessary to develop an estimation equation to estimate the forecast parameters efficiently.

A failure to distinguish between the forecast model and the estimation model is another common failing of much contemporary practice in daily cash forecasting.

Step 4: Statistical Techniques and Tools

In the case of a deterministic scheduling approach, no statistical estimation is necessary. In the more common case of a statistical or a combination approach, the right techniques and tools are generally implied by the estimation equation(s) of the measurement modeling step. Thus, once the crucial steps of problem structuring, approach selection, and measurement modeling are accomplished, the step of selecting the pertinent statistical techniques[14] and tools is generally straightforward.

The four-step framework is designed to work backward from the forecast problem and the company situation to the selection of forecast techniques and tools. Thus, what is frequently the starting step ("We will use regression." or "Box-Jenkins will do the job.") is logically the last of the four steps in the framework advocated here.

---

[14] Here "technique" is used to refer to a generic approach to statistical estimation, e.g., moving averages, regression, Box-Jenkins, etc. "Tool" refers to a particular package or method for using a technique.

A benefit of this four-step framework is that proper structuring often means that fairly simple estimation techniques are adequate. And in the special case of deterministic scheduling, no statistical estimation at all is required. Relative to the very sophisticated techniques, the standard simple estimation procedures have the merits of being (1) understandable, (2) robust, and (3) easy to use. *Robust* refers to tolerance for a breakdown in estimation assumptions and general insensitivity to errors. *Easy to use* refers to availability in standard computer packages, amount of effort to implement, the availability of required data, and overall effort to estimate and maintain.

Example: An Illustration of the Four-Step Framework

A major forest products company wanted a forecast of the net daily flow at its concentration bank to facilitate the management of the overall cash position.[15] In addition, a prediction of the net inflow and outflow was desirable, especially since discretion on release of checks for vendor payments could handle small temporary excesses of outflows over normal inflows.

Step 1: Problem Structuring   Given the objective of predicting the net daily flow at the concentration bank, the fundamental structuring question is: What data are available? First, the company had daily flow data at the concentration bank for all deposits, all checks, and all transfers between other banks. Second, the company generated monthly cash budgets in considerable detail.

1. Major versus Nonmajor.   Major flows were identified and separated from nonmajor flows. The primary forecast task was reduced to predicting nonmajor flows.

2. Components.   The overall flow was broken into nonmajor outflow (vendor payments and some payroll) and nonmajor inflow. The nonmajor inflow was further divided into "regular deposits" (deposits at the concentration bank from the company's own receivable processing at company headquarters) and "transfer deposits" (all transfers from lockbox and other depository banks). The reason for this division was evidence from preliminary analysis that company deposits from headquarters

---

[15] This example case is presented in more detail in B. K. Stone and R. A. Wood, "Daily Cash Forecasting: A Simple Method for Implementing the Distribution Approach," along with more detail in distribution and some of the other ideas mentioned here. We acknowledge Robert A. Wood for influencing our thinking about daily cash forecasting, especially the use of dummy-variable regression as a way to resolve monthly and weekly patterns.

and transfer deposits had different statistical properties, especially a different day-of-week pattern.

3. Time Sequencing.   A one-stage procedure for all nonmajor components was selected. The primary reason was expediency. The daily flows at the concentration bank were readily available in computer-readable form. In contrast, intermediate flows required accounting data that were not readily available in computer-readable form. Many of the intermediate accounting data were available only from company subunits (e.g., divisions) and not at corporate headquarters. Moreover, in some cases the intermediate data were not complete, especially in terms of precise daily timing.

Step 2: Approach Selection.   A distribution approach was selected for all nonmajor components. It followed logically from the fact that month-to-month cash budget data was the assumed "input" to the forecast procedure. Hence, the crux of the forecast task was to spread the total value of nonmajor disbursements, regular deposits, and transfer deposits obtained from the cash budget over the workdays of the month.

Step 3: Measurement Modeling

1. Forecast Equation.   Once it is determined that monthly totals for each nonmajor component are the primary forecast input, the implied forecast procedure is to take an appropriate proportion of each total for each workday. If the workdays of the month are indexed by t, then this equation is

$$\text{Flow}_t = (\text{Proportion})_t(\text{Monthly Total})$$

Such an equation holds for each nonmajor component. To the extent that the patterns are different, each component will have a different set of day-of-month proportions. Within the framework of this particular distribution equation, having different proportions is the reason for division into components.

2. Estimation Equation.   Using the distribution approach means that the set of proportions is the primary measurement task. These proportions must be estimated statistically. If the only issue were a day-of-month effect such as that depicted in Exhibit 4, the proportion could be estimated as a simple average of past values of the proportion occurring on each particular workday in past months. However, in this particular case, there

Exhibit 4
An Illustrative Day-of-Month Pattern

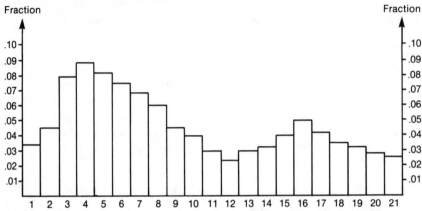

Source: *Financial Management*, 6, Fall 1977, p. 42, and *Journal of Cash Management*, 1, October 1981, p. 45.

was also a strong weekly subcycle like that shown in Exhibit 5 as well as the basic day-of-month pattern.

The occurrence of both a monthly pattern and day-of-week disturbance means that the estimation task was more complex than taking an average proportion on each workday in the sam-

Exhibit 5
An Illustrative Day-of-Week Pattern

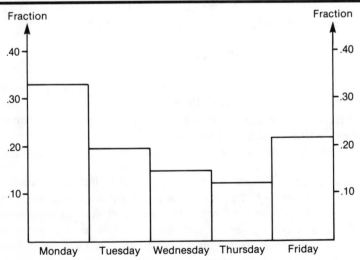

Source: *Financial Management*, 6, Fall 1977, p. 43, and *Journal of Cash Management*, 1, October 1981, p. 46.

ple. For instance, if there were more Mondays on the first work-day in the sample with the above-average Monday flow depicted in Exhibit 5, then there would be an overstatement of the true proportion for the first workday. Likewise, a predominance of Wednesdays with their below-average flow would cause an understatement. Moreover, in putting together the prediction for a particular workday, an adjustment should be made to reflect the day-of-week effect. For instance, the normal flow for a particular workday, such as the tenth, should be increased if the tenth is a Monday and decreased if it is a Wednesday. In summary, it was necessary in both estimation and forecasting to reflect both the basic day-of-month effect and the day-of-week disturbance in creating the forecast.

To handle this estimation task, it was assumed that the proportion on a particular workday could be modeled as a basic day-of-month proportion plus a measure of the day-of-week disturbance.

To express this model of day-of-month and day-of-week effects, let t and w be indices for workdays and weekdays. Let a_t denote the proportion of the monthly total that would occur on workday t if there were no day-of-week disturbance. Thus, if 5 percent of the flow occurred on workday eight, then a_8 would be 0.05. Let b_w be the day-of-week correction. Assume that Monday is day 1 ($w = 1$) and Friday is day 5 ($w = 5$). With this notation, the proportion on workday t and weekday w is represented as

$$\text{Proportion}_{tw} = a_t + b_w$$

A w subscript has been added to the left side to reflect the fact that the proportion depends on the day-of-week as well as the workday.

Example of Day-of-Week Adjustment   Assume that $(b_1, b_2, b_3, b_4, b_5)$ is $(0.03, -0.01, -0.02, -0.01, 0.01)$. If the proportion of the total that would occur on workday 12 in the absence of any day-of-week effect were 0.07, then the proportion for workday 12 when it is a Monday is 0.10 (i.e., $a_{12} + b_1 = 0.07 + 0.03 = 0.10$). But when workday 12 is on a Wednesday, the proportion is 0.05 (i.e., $a_{12} + b_3 = 0.07 - 0.02 = 0.05$).

Step 4: Statistical Estimation   This example shows how the basic monthly pattern can be adjusted to reflect day-of-week effects given values of the a_t's and the b_w's. Obtaining appropriate values for the a_t's and the b_w's is the task of statistical estimation.

Readers familiar with statistical estimation probably recognize least-squares regression as an appropriate technique for estimating the a_t's and b_w's from past cash flow data. The particular type of regression called for is dummy-variable regression. The tool implied is a standard regression package, ideally one that can handle constrained regression.

The objective of this chapter is not to discuss statistical technique per se but rather to illustrate how the four-step framework organizes the problem faced by a particular company concerned with the net daily flow.[16] Exhibit 6 shows the forecast and actual flows for each nonmajor component for August. In general, the actual flow tracks the forecast reasonably well for such a simple model, although there are some large daily errors.

Comments on Forecast Example It is clear from inspection that the three nonmajor components have different patterns. Trying to forecast these three components as a single flow would mean combining different patterns. Since the relative amounts of these three components vary over time, there would be no pattern stability and hence very limited ability to forecast.

It is particularly interesting to look at the two components of inflows—regular deposits and transfer deposits. Regular deposits have a weekly cycle with a peak on Monday similar to that depicted in Exhibit 5. Transfer deposits have a similar weekly cycle but with a peak on Tuesday. The shift in both the peak and the overall pattern reflects a one-day delay in moving money from deposit banks into the concentration bank. In initial attempts to develop this forecast, there were only two components—inflows and outflows at the concentration bank. The forecast of inflows was very poor. There appeared to be no stable pattern despite a *prior* belief that inflows had considerable stability, probably more than outflows. Analysis of forecast failure leads to recognition that transfers from other banks involved a delay and shift in both the day-of-month and day-of-week pattern. Hence, the need for breaking deposits into at least two components was indicated by the failure of a one-component treatment of inflows and the analysis it generated.

---

[16] A word of caution is in order for readers thinking of using the additive model and dummy-variable regression to treat day-of-month and day-of-week effects. First, there are alternatives to the additive model used in this case such as multiplicative and mixed-effect treatments of the day-of-week disturbances. Second, there are some estimation issues. Miller and Stone update the treatment in Stone and Wood by noting a number of pitfalls and estimation problems and presenting a variety of ways to deal with them. (T. W. Miller and B. K. Stone, "Daily Cash Forecasting and Seasonal Resolution: Alternative Models," *Journal of Financial and Quantitative Analysis* [forthcoming 1985].)

Exhibit 6
Actual versus Forecast for Nonmajor Cash Flows

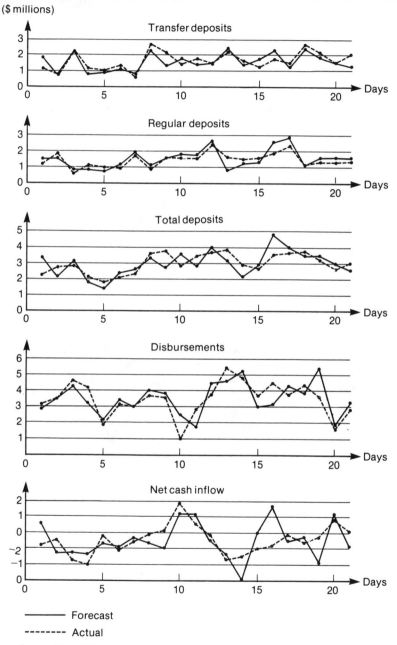

Forecast

-------- Actual

Source: *Financial Management*, 6, Fall 1977, p. 45, and *Journal of Cash Management*, 1, October 1981, p. 47.

There were other refinements during the initial development of the forecast procedure. Preliminary efforts to use calendar days to characterize the day-of-month pattern with Saturday and Sunday flows shifted to Monday did not work well. Therefore, workdays were tried and used when workday-based forecasting performed better.[17] Also, initial forecast efforts showed very large irregular payments despite efforts to identify and remove major flows. The definition of "major" was not complete and some big, irregular items were being incorrectly placed in the nonmajor flow.[18] All payments over $100,000 were reviewed and a tighter and more comprehensive definition of major was imposed.

With the refinements of (1) two inflow classes, (2) a workday rather than calendar-day characterization of the day-of-month pattern, and (3) the tighter definition of major payment, the forecast model performed satisfactorily for managing the overall cash position. Thus, even though further breakdown into components had been planned, the forecast procedure was used without more component detail.

Synthesizing Points   These comments highlight several points on the four-step framework.

1. Major versus Nonmajor.   The separation of all major, irregular flows is crucial to the success of statistical estimation. For the forest products company, even the smaller major flows caused total breakdown of statistical estimation efforts. The reason is that these large irregular flows are interpreted as big errors. A statistical method such as least-squares error minimization gives the big errors (major flows) great weight and is distorted by them. Hence, there is a false indication of no useful statistical stability even when appropriately defined nonmajor components have much stability.

2. Framework Logic.   Each step of the forecast framework sets up the next by indicating the type of decisions that should be made. In this example, the forecast input (monthly cash budget projections) and the available historical data (daily balances at the concentration bank) indicated the approach (distribution). In

---

[17] The fact that workdays performed better in this particular forecast effort for this particular company is not intended to suggest a general superiority of workdays over calendar days. In several subsequent forecast efforts, we have found that calendar days perform better.

[18] With the pattern model used here, big payments per se were not a problem. Payments occurring for the same amount on the same day each month could be handled. Rather it was big and irregular that was the problem.

turn, the approach implied the forecast equation. Given both day-of-month and day-of-week patterns, an estimation equation in turn led to the use of dummy-variable regression. The point here is that the four-step framework (even though not expressed as such at the time this forecast procedure was developed) makes sense here in that problem structuring implies approach, which in turn indicates appropriate measurement modeling, which then suggests the appropriate statistical technique.

3. Trial-and-Error Refinement. Having noted that the problem conforms to the four-step framework, it is important to note also that it is not a simple step-to-step sequence. There is always trial-and-error refinement. In this case, the refinements included a tighter definition of major disbursements, a further breakdown of nonmajor inflows into components not initially envisioned, and a shift to workdays from calendar days. Encountering problems at one step often meant a need to go back and refine or redo a previous step. Thus, one or more of the four logical steps are generally repeated either as problems arise in subsequent steps or as new information becomes available. However, the four-step framework organizes the trial-and-error problem discovery and learning. By structuring both "getting started" and "making refinements," the four-step framework tends to reduce "wheel spinning" that is characteristic of many forecast efforts and other ill-structured problems. Likewise, it tends to reduce the likelihood of incorrectly reaching the false conclusion of "no ability to forecast" since it identifies and treats most of the usual errors.

THE EVOLUTION OF DAILY
FORECASTING SYSTEMS

A company's daily cash forecasting system is never static. It must adapt to changes in the environment and the company. Moreover, as in most system development efforts, initial versions of the system are a compromise between the desired system and the need to have a system able to function in a company's existing information system environment. Thus, most forecasting systems are designed with evolution in mind.

Because of changes in the environment and the company and because of planned changes, daily cash forecasting systems give the appearance of being in a constant state of flux. In order to have orderly change, it is crucial to plan for evolution of the system and the associated information support system.

The four-step framework of this chapter facilitates the design and management of an evolutionary system in which change and refinement can proceed in an organized, structured manner. First, the focus on components leads to modular designs. Modularity is the key to change management since it enables change in one component without change in the entire system. Second, the required information is at the core of the approach. Hence, a modular, component-focused hierarchical information system is a natural consequence of this procedure. Most importantly, the four-step procedure is a planning framework so that specifying both an immediate system and ways to evolve toward future systems are an integral part of the process.

SYNTHESIS

Much of the daily cash forecasting is art rather than science. The art pertains especially to problem structuring and the identification of meaningful subproblems and to system planning. The reduction of the overall forecast task to well-structured subproblems is the crux of successful use in either statistical projection, distribution, or information-based scheduling approaches. The framework developed in this article is designed to organize the art side of daily cash forecasting.

Problem structuring involves the reduction to subproblems by separating major from nonmajor flows, breaking the nonmajor flows into appropriate components (subproblems), and possibly identifying stages of a component for time sequencing (more detailed subproblem definition).

Approach selection is the choice of a generic way to relate input data to quantities to be forecast. In addition to conventional projection and seasonal resolution techniques, the two primary alternatives are information-based scheduling using time lags between information sequences and statistics-based distribution of a total amount over days in accord with an estimate of the daily proportions, the distribution pattern.

Measurement modeling involves two activities—relating forecast input to the quantity being forecast and, in the case of any statistical estimation, relating parameters of the forecast equation to available estimation data.

Statistical technique enters in formulating the estimation equation, selecting methods for measuring its parameters, adapting existing programs to the estimation task, and interpreting the resulting measurements.

Benefits

An obvious benefit of the four-part framework is an organized, systematic way to deal with daily cash forecasting, especially those parts of the problem that are often neglected.

Another benefit pertains to treasury information systems, especially when efforts are made to use scheduling by transforming data. It is common to find that the desired input data are not available, at least not in an organized, computer-readable, timely way. While the initial consequence of this discovery is the frustration of not being able to use the most desirable approach to best advantage, the ancillary benefit is a good definition of desired data and how they should be organized. In effect, the framework leads to working from the desired forecast information to the implied information system requirements and thus the logical design for part of the treasury information system. Moreover, because the most effective data gathering is often achieved via the use of appropriate bank subaccounts with appropriate data capture from checks and invoices, the information system requirements also provide input to the design of a company's banking system.

Finally, the framework usually has significant control benefits. Besides the value of forecast accuracy, the component detail and data tracking, especially via information transformation, lead naturally to procedures and reports to convey control information.

While we have stressed the benefits of the four-part framework, it is not a forecast panacea. At best, daily cash forecasting is a difficult problem with much that is specific to a particular company. However, an organized framework like that developed here increases the chance of success in practicing the art of forecasting and helps treasury management interface to and better manage technical support.

8

Models in Cash Management

Steven F. Maier, Ph.D.
President
University Analytics

The growth in the use of models in cash management has been nothing short of explosive during the last 10 years. Perhaps this is as much a statement about the discipline itself as anything else. Cash management has clearly matured from when it was a back-of-the envelope type of calculation. In the early days, banks were chosen based on the lowest prices offered. Today, the complexity of dealing with as many as several hundred different banks, each of whom can provide a multitude of different services, has forced cash managers to resort to computer models in order to make reasonable economic choices.

Models in cash management may be conveniently divided into two basic categories: those used for planning and those used in an operational capacity. The planning models are characterized by periodic, but infrequent, use. In some instances this may be quarterly, but more typically on a one- to three-year cycle as changes in the system or environment take place. On the other hand, the operational models are used either daily or perhaps weekly. Another distinction between these two classes of models is that the planning models are almost always used in a consulting capacity by a bank or other outside vendor, while the operational models are used directly by a corporate financial officer. Finally, planning models appear to have entered the cash management scene earlier than the operational models, with the earliest applications in this area dating to the mid-1960s.

In the remainder of this chapter we will introduce a sampling of the various applications for models in both planning and operations. Because of space constraints, purely information gathering systems, such as balance reporting systems, are not within our definition of a model. A definition for our purposes is that a model provides a means of choosing between alternative scenarios in a systematic fashion. Usually, this will involve optimization, although the degree of optimization will vary greatly from one application to another.

LOCKBOX LOCATION MODEL

Ferdinand Levy[1] provided the first of what was to be many contributions to the lockbox problem.[2] A recent study of the Fortune 1000 companies continues to show this problem as being the most widely solved planning problem in cash management. Most corporations today review their lockbox systems on a two- to four-year cycle utilizing a lockbox location model.

The basic problem that these models attack is rather simple: Choose an appropriate set of commercial banks to use as lockbox sites and assign customers to the banks in such a way as to minimize mail and availability float. In order to perform a lockbox study, it is necessary that the corporation collect a sample of its receivable data for one month. This sample is used to determine from where the customer base is mailing its checks and on which banks they are drawing them.

The original concern of the academic literature was how the lockbox selection optimization procedure could be made more efficient. It was recognized rather early that the problem was complex and required an integer programming approach. In a series of articles it was ultimately determined that variations on what are known as branch-and-bound algorithms could solve the problem efficiently. In an excellent article, Mavrides[3] showed that the problem could be solved efficiently by a technique known as LaGrangian Relaxation. This is the technique used in the most sophisticated of the lockbox systems.

Although optimization algorithms have received much attention in the academic literature, other issues appear to dominate the application of this technology. The data required to optimize lockbox sites includes the mail times from various sending loca-

---

[1] F. K. Levy, "An Application of Heuristic Problem Solving to Accounts Receivable Management," *Management Science*, 12, no. 6, February 1966, pp. 236–44.

[2] A lockbox is nothing more than a post office box maintained in the corporate name but emptied on a regular basis by a commercial bank or other agent. The bank further provides the service of opening the envelopes, photocopying the contents, and depositing the checks. See Chapter 4.

[3] L. P. Mavrides, "An Indirect Method for the Generalized k-Median Problem Applied to Lock-Box Location," *Management Science*, October 1979, pp. 990–96.

tions to lockbox sites and the availability granted by the lockbox banks once the deposit is made. In the beginning only mail times were considered in the lockbox problem, since availability schedules were difficult to obtain. This was followed by a period during which Federal Reserve bank availability schedules were added to the mail times and finally, in 1979, Phoenix-Hecht Incorporated and University Analytics developed the first standardized data base of bank availability schedules. The use of a combined data base of mail times and bank availability schedules has greatly improved the accuracy of lockbox analysis. Maier and Vander Weide described the application of this technology.[4]

In late 1983, University Analytics introduced its newest version of the lockbox location system. The measurement of both mail and availability times was changed to conform better to actual payment collection experience. The mail survey was expanded in size by over 50 percent and integrated into a common data base containing both mail and availability times. Lockbox networks (a single bank offering multiple collection sites) and deposit schedules (the use of multiple deposits to speed processing) were included in the model. University Analytics has estimated that these improvements would cause changes in the preference for one lockbox bank over another as great as when availability was first considered in lockbox selection.

As should be readily apparent, lockbox models tend to locate lockbox sites in the regions in which there are large customer concentrations. Typical cities chosen include Philadelphia and Pittsburgh in the East; Atlanta, Charlotte, and Dallas in the South; Chicago and St. Louis in the Central states; and San Francisco and Los Angeles in the West. Interestingly, costs are usually not much concern in this problem. This arises because: (1) the float benefits derived from reducing mail and availability times tend to dominate cost differences between banks, and (2) lockbox services tend to be extremely competitively priced with little variation within the same city and even between cities. In some applications, such as retail lockbox systems (consumer payments), the average check size is small and the volume going through the lockbox is large. Here the cost and operational compatibility with corporate requirements dominate float issues. Sample output for a typical lockbox system showing customer assignment to lockbox sites (Exhibit 1) and the output from the optimization process (Exhibit 2) are shown for illustrative purposes.

[4] S. F. Maier, and J. H. Vander Weide, "What Lockbox and Disbursement Models Really Do," *Journal of Finance*, 28, no. 2, May 1983, pp. 361–71.

Exhibit 1
Example Corporation Lock-Box Study
September 1984 (Optimized System
Analysis Destination Directory For a Three
Lock-Box System)

CUSTOMER AREA			SEND TO LOCK-BOX		
NO.	NAME		NO.	NAME	
1	SPRINGFIELD	MA	35	PITTSBURGH	F
2	BOSTON	MA	35	PITTSBURGH	F
3	NEW HAMPSHIRE		35	PITTSBURGH	F
4	MAINE		35	PITTSBURGH	F
5	VERMONT		35	PITTSBURGH	F
6	CONNECTICUT		35	PITTSBURGH	F
7	NEWARK	NJ	35	PITTSBURGH	F
8	TRENTON	NJ	35	PITTSBURGH	F
10	NEW YORK	NY	35	PITTSBURGH	F
11	BROOKLYN	NY	35	PITTSBURGH	F
12	ALBANY	NY	35	PITTSBURGH	F
13	SYRACUSE	NY	35	PITTSBURGH	F
14	BUFFALO	NY	35	PITTSBURGH	F
15	PITTSBURGH	PA	35	PITTSBURGH	F
16	ERIE	PA	35	PITTSBURGH	F
17	HARRISBURG	PA	35	PITTSBURGH	F
18	SCRANTON	PA	35	PITTSBURGH	F
19	PHILADELPHIA	PA	35	PITTSBURGH	F
20	WASHINGTON	DC	35	PITTSBURGH	F
21	MARYLAND		35	PITTSBURGH	F
22	FALLS CHURCH	VA	35	PITTSBURGH	F
23	RICHMOND	VA	35	PITTSBURGH	F
24	ROANOKE	VA	35	PITTSBURGH	F
25	CHARLESTON	WV	35	PITTSBURGH	F
26	WHEELING	WV	35	PITTSBURGH	F
27	RALEIGH	NC	35	PITTSBURGH	F
28	CHARLOTTE	NC	35	PITTSBURGH	F
29	SOUTH CAROLINA		35	PITTSBURGH	F
30	ATLANTA	GA	35	PITTSBURGH	F
31	SAVANNAH	GA	35	PITTSBURGH	F
32	JACKSONVILLE	FL	7	CHICAGO	F
33	MIAMI	FL	35	PITTSBURGH	F
35	BIRMINGHAM	AL	7	CHICAGO	F
36	MONTGOMERY	AL	7	CHICAGO	F

Source: Lock-Box Release 4.0, Copyright
1984, University Analytics, Inc.

One final aspect of lockbox modeling deserves mention. Traditionally, some banks have provided consulting services, including the use of their lockbox models, for prices that do not fully reflect their costs. The logic behind this is at the core of what is known as "relationship banking." A bank knows that if it does a consulting study using its lockbox model and the study shows that it is an appropriate lockbox site, then it will not only gain some potential lockbox business but, much more importantly, it will likely gain a credit relationship. This occurs because lockboxes create large fund inflows, some of which cannot be transferred out on a daily basis as soon as the funds become available. These collected balances, as they are known, can be used to compensate the bank for credit services. This in turn has made certain banks very aggressive in their consulting activities with regard to lockbox studies.

The reaction of many corporations to this tie-in between credit and lockbox analysis is to view with some skepticism the lockbox analyses done by some banks. Many times corporations will

Exhibit 2
Example Corporation Lock-Box Study, September 1984 (Summary of Optimization Runs)

RUN NO.	NO.OPEN SITES	SOL'N RANK	SITES IN SOLUTION NO. NAME			SOLUTION VALUE DOLLARS/DAY	DAYS
CURNT SYST.	3	SCHED.	38 RICHMOND	F	MAIL FLOAT	$19,193,550.08	2.50
			17 INDIANAPOLIS	F	CLEARING FLOAT	22,749,509.52	3.07
			1 ATLANTA	F	COMPENSATING BAL	112,950.68	0.02
					TOTAL FLOAT	$42,056,010.27	5.68
1	2	OPTIMAL	7 CHICAGO	F	MAIL FLOAT	$11,439,333.26	1.55
			35 PITTSBURGH	F	CLEARING FLOAT	19,649,578.46	2.65
					COMPENSATING BAL	96,587.04	0.01
					TOTAL FLOAT	$31,185,498.75	4.21
1	2	1	7 CHICAGO	F	MAIL FLOAT	$12,123,070.42	1.64
			48 KANSAS CITY	F	CLEARING FLOAT	19,485,733.69	2.63
					COMPENSATING BAL	96,587.04	0.01
					TOTAL FLOAT	$31,705,391.16	4.28
1	2	2	7 CHICAGO	F	MAIL FLOAT	$12,123,070.42	1.64
			18 KANSAS CITY	F	CLEARING FLOAT	19,485,733.69	2.63
					COMPENSATING BAL	96,587.04	0.01
					TOTAL FLOAT	$31,705,391.16	4.28
1	2	3	13 DETROIT	F	MAIL FLOAT	$12,255,232.30	1.66
			35 PITTSBURGH	F	CLEARING FLOAT	19,509,893.53	2.64
					COMPENSATING BAL	96,587.04	0.01
					TOTAL FLOAT	$31,861,712.87	4.30
1	2	4	35 PITTSBURGH	F	MAIL FLOAT	$12,194,333.72	1.65
			48 KANSAS CITY	F	CLEARING FLOAT	19,666,096.17	2.66
					COMPENSATING BAL	96,587.04	0.01
					TOTAL FLOAT	$31,957,006.93	4.32
1	2	5	18 KANSAS CITY	F	MAIL FLOAT	$12,194,333.72	1.65
			35 PITTSBURGH	F	CLEARING FLOAT	19,666,086.17	2.66
					COMPENSATING BAL	96,587.04	0.01
					TOTAL FLOAT	$31,957,006.93	4.32

Source: Lock-Box Release 4.0, Copyright 1984, University Analytics, Inc.

choose to have more than one lockbox study performed or to have noncredit-line banks perform the study in order to keep the lockbox banks "honest." Given that the banks tend to underprice this consulting service, this way of guaranteeing honesty tends to be cost-effective for corporations. Although corporate skepticism is healthy, there is little evidence of bias in the studies performed by banks. This is especially true where the consulting function has been separated from the marketing and credit departments of the bank.

DISBURSEMENT LOCATION MODELS

In the early 1970s, corporations discovered that the float benefits they could obtain from optimizing their collection systems through lockboxes could also be gained on their disbursement systems. However, the modeling objective turned out to be reversed. Instead of trying to minimize float, disbursement location models attempted to maximize check clearing and/or mail float. This in turn gave rise to a practice known as remote disbursing, which was not particularly appreciated by the corporations on the receiving end (vendors) nor the Federal Reserve System. For instance, on January 11, 1979, the Federal Reserve Board issued a statement which said in part, "The Board believes the banking industry has a public responsibility not to design, offer, promote or otherwise encourage the use of a service expressly intended to delay final settlement and which exposes recipients to greater than ordinary risks. The Board is calling on the nation's banks to join in the effort to eliminate remote disbursement practices intended to obtain extended float."

Notwithstanding this Fed criticism, models to analyze disbursement scenarios have evolved remarkably in the past few years. For instance, risk has entered this problem as a dimension for consideration because the cities that tend to produce maximum float advantage also tend to be rather unstable. For example, in order to maximize float it is usually necessary to choose a small bank, although it may be affiliated with a much larger bank, located in a remote part of the country. It is also necessary that the checks be presented in both a very predictable fashion and meet requirements for information reporting. Because the bank is usually small, the issue arises as to whether very large corporations which have significantly daily disbursements can use such banks without being at risk should the bank fail. If a delayed funding mechanism is used, such as a DTC or ACH transfer, then the issue also arises of risk to the bank should the corporation fail. This latter risk is the one the Fed brought up in the 1979 statement quoted above. There is also the issue of whether the Federal Reserve Board will attempt to thwart banks from being actively used as disbursing sites, given that they tend to slow down the payment process and exacerbate the Fed's difficulties in meeting the availability schedules it has promised the depositing banks. In fact, the Federal Reserve Board has actively attempted to discourage remote disbursement practices through changes in the way it presents checks. Finally, there is a problem with regard to the quality of the data used in measuring check-clearing times. This latter issue deserves additional attention since it is a problem that arises in many other optimization applications.

In this mathematical modeling problem, as in the case of the lockbox problem, the optimization algorithm is constructed to select the configuration that will optimize the value of a mathematical equation called an objective function. In the disbursement case, one objective is to maximize float and do so by selecting an appropriate set of disbursing banks and vendor assignments to these banks. Unfortunately, if the data contain sampling errors, the model is likely to select a disbursing bank not because it produces outstandingly good disbursement times, but rather because of unusually large data observations. For example, it may turn out that a city's actual clearing time is usually three days, but because of weather problems the data collected showed the clearing time to be four days. The model seeing four days clearing time would find this site to be particularly attractive and select it. Of course if there had been no aberration in the clearing-time observation, the site would not have been unusual and the model would not have seized the "opportunity." With more than 20,000 individual point-to-point clearing times being observed, there are many opportunities for such aberrations to occur.

The issue of risk became even more important in 1983 because of changes implemented by the Federal Reserve Board. Much of the value of controlled disbursing to corporations comes not just from float extension, but from the information they are able to obtain about the daily amounts of disbursements they must fund. This information is very valuable in that it minimizes and in many cases eliminates idle balances that would otherwise have to be kept in the disbursing account. However, the Federal Reserve System cannot easily distinguish between the practice of obtaining such information, called controlled disbursing, and remote disbursing, even though it believes the former to be acceptable and the latter to be unacceptable. (For instance, in the January 11, 1979 policy statement cited earlier, the Fed also said "there is no intention to discourage corporate disbursement arrangements with banks that provide for improved control over daily cash requirements.") The Fed's current position is that whenever it sees large daily volumes being drawn on small banks outside of major cities it assumes that this is remote disbursing and it attempts to eliminate the practice. When it moves on a remote disbursing site it many times causes the corporation to abandon that bank and move its disbursing activity to another bank. As one might surmise, this is not without some considerable cost to both the banks and corporations involved.

Sample output from a typical disbursement model is shown in Exhibits 3 and 4. Exhibit 3 again shows a destination directory. Notice that both the mailing location and the disbursing bank must be assigned for each vendor city. Moreover, these are usu-

Exhibit 3
Example Reports Disbursement Location System June 1982 (Optimized
System Analysis Directory For a Two Mail Point. Two Disbursement
Bank System)

VENDOR AREA		MAILED FROM		DISBURSED FROM	
NO.	NAME	NO.	NAME	NO.	NAME
2	ABILENE TX	2	ABILENE TX	76	BALTIMORE CNTRY
5	AKRON OH	2	ABILENE TX	76	BALTIMORE CNTRY
15	ALBANY NY	2	ABILENE TX	25	ALLENTOWN PA
20	ALBUQUERQUE NM	20	ALBUQUERQUE NM	76	BALTIMORE CNTRY
25	ALLENTOWN PA	2	ABILENE TX	25	ALLENTOWN PA
48	ASHEVILLE NC	2	ABILENE TX	76	BALTIMORE CNTRY
49	ASHTABULA OH	2	ABILENE TX	25	ALLENTOWN PA
50	ATLANTA GA	2	ABILENE TX	76	BALTIMORE CNTRY
60	AUGUSTA GA	2	ABILENE TX	76	BALTIMORE CNTRY
75	BALTIMORE MD	2	ABILENE TX	76	BALTIMORE CNTRY
76	BALTIMORE CNTRY	2	ABILENE TX	76	BALTIMORE CNTRY
80	BATON ROUGE LA	2	ABILENE TX	76	BALTIMORE CNTRY
83	BEDFORD VA	2	ABILENE TX	76	BALTIMORE CNTRY
100	BIRMINGHAM AL	2	ABILENE TX	76	BALTIMORE CNTRY
105	BOISE ID	20	ALBUQUERQUE NM	25	ALLENTOWN PA
110	BOSTON MA	2	ABILENE TX	25	ALLENTOWN PA
115	BRIDGEPORT CT	2	ABILENE TX	25	ALLENTOWN PA
117	BRIDGETON NJ	2	ABILENE TX	76	BALTIMORE CNTRY
121	BROWNSVILLE TX	2	ABILENE TX	76	BALTIMORE CNTRY
122	BROWNWOOD TX	2	ABILENE TX	76	BALTIMORE CNTRY
125	BUFFALO NY	2	ABILENE TX	25	ALLENTOWN PA
133	CAMDEN TN	2	ABILENE TX	76	BALTIMORE CNTRY
137	CARROLLTON TX	2	ABILENE TX	76	BALTIMORE CNTRY
150	CHARLESTON SC	2	ABILENE TX	76	BALTIMORE CNTRY
155	CHARLESTON WV	2	ABILENE TX	76	BALTIMORE CNTRY
160	CHARLOTTE NC	2	ABILENE TX	76	BALTIMORE CNTRY
161	CHARLOTTESVILLE	2	ABILENE TX	76	BALTIMORE CNTRY
165	CHATTANOOGA TN	2	ABILENE TX	76	BALTIMORE CNTRY
170	CHEYENNE WY	20	ALBUQUERQUE NM	76	BALTIMORE CNTRY
175	CHICAGO IL	2	ABILENE TX	25	ALLENTOWN PA
180	CINCINNATI OH	2	ABILENE TX	76	BALTIMORE CNTRY
185	CLEVELAND OH	2	ABILENE TX	25	ALLENTOWN PA
195	COLUMBIA SC	2	ABILENE TX	76	BALTIMORE CNTRY
205	COLUMBUS OH	2	ABILENE TX	76	BALTIMORE CNTRY
210	CONCORD NH	2	ABILENE TX	25	ALLENTOWN PA
212	CONROE TX	2	ABILENE TX	76	BALTIMORE CNTRY
215	CORPUS CHRISTI	2	ABILENE TX	76	BALTIMORE CNTRY
220	DALLAS TX	2	ABILENE TX	76	BALTIMORE CNTRY
230	DAYTON OH	2	ABILENE TX	76	BALTIMORE CNTRY
237	DEARBORN MI	2	ABILENE TX	25	ALLENTOWN PA
238	DE KALB CTY GA	2	ABILENE TX	76	BALTIMORE CNTRY
240	DENVER CO	20	ALBUQUERQUE NM	76	BALTIMORE CNTRY
245	DES MOINES IA	2	ABILENE TX	76	BALTIMORE CNTRY
250	DETROIT MI	2	ABILENE TX	25	ALLENTOWN PA
255	DULUTH MN	2	ABILENE TX	25	ALLENTOWN PA

Source: Disbursement Release 3.0 Copyright 1981, University Analytics,
Inc.

ally different because of the differences in mail and clearing
times and because of company restrictions on office and bank
locations. Exhibit 4 shows the optimum solution and a set of
alternatives. Notice how close the optimum and the next best
five solutions are. If the solution involves two or more sites, the
alternatives will usually be within 5 percent of the optimum.

CONCENTRATION MODELS

This is the newest planning model area in cash management. Currently, only Citibank, Mellon Bank, and the First Na-

Exhibit 4
Example Reports, Disbursement Location System June 1982 (Alternative Solutions Found)

RANK	NO.	- SITES IN SOLUTION - NAME	- -MAIL FLOAT- - DOLLARS/DAY	DAYS	PRESENTATION FLOAT DOLLARS/DAY	DAYS	- -TOTAL FLOAT- - DOLLARS/DAY	DAYS
OPTIMUM	25	ALLENTOWN PA			$ 228,124	2.57		
	76	BALTIMORE CNTRY			107,471	2.61		
		TOTAL	$ 274,861	2.11	$ 335,594	2.58	$ 529,378	4.07
1	60	AUGUSTA GA			$ 61,709	2.31		
	76	BALTIMORE CNTRY			262,443	2.54		
		TOTAL	$ 274,861	2.11	$ 324,152	2.49	$ 517,936	3.98
2	15	ALBANY NY			$ 212,493	2.59		
	60	AUGUSTA GA			111,569	2.33		
		TOTAL	$ 274,861	2.11	$ 324,062	2.49	$ 517,846	3.98
3	25	ALLENTOWN PA			$ 255,912	2.53		
	60	AUGUSTA GA			68,088	2.35		
		TOTAL	$ 274,861	2.11	$ 324,000	2.49	$ 517,783	3.98
4	48	ASHEVILLE NC			$ 100,044	2.14		
	83	BEDFORD VA			222,865	2.68		
		TOTAL	$ 274,861	2.11	$ 322,909	2.48	$ 516,693	3.98
5	48	ASHEVILLE NC			$ 109,019	2.17		
	76	BALTIMORE CNTRY			211,068	2.65		
		TOTAL	$ 274,861	2.11	$ 320,086	2.46	$ 513,870	3.95

Source: Disbursement Release 3.0 Copyright 1981, University Analytics, Inc.

tional Bank of Chicago have sophisticated models that can actually optimize the design of concentration systems. The basic problems addressed in concentration models are three-fold:

1. *Select an appropriate concentration mechanism.* This means that the model will determine if it is most beneficial to the company to concentrate by wire transfer, depository transfer check (DTC), or through the automated clearinghouse system (ACH).

2. *Determine an optimal transfer schedule.* This involves setting up rules for the transfers to take place. A simple rule might be to transfer the deposit as soon as it is known to management. Usually this means that a transfer of today's deposit will occur tomorrow morning, with the actual money moving the following day since the two most popular means of transfer, the DTC and ACH, have a one-day delay built in.

3. *Select an optimal set of concentration banks.* The concentration function is usually spread over multiple banks. In most cases this is done to reduce the time involved in the transfer of funds. This occurs because a two-day DTC transfer is reduced to one day, or because a branch banking system can concentrate money with no delay at all.

The trade-offs involved in instrument selection are straight-forward. The wire transfer is the most costly of the instruments, with a total cost of approximately $15. The wire transfer, how-ever, also provides for immediate movement of the money on the same day that the instructions are received. However, the wire transfer must be initiated prior to the close of the wire transfer system, which is late in the afternoon.

The DTC is relatively inexpensive ($0.35 to $0.50), especially when compared to the wire transfer. Moreover, the DTC may be initiated later in the business day than the wire transfer. The drawback of the DTC is that it takes a minimum of one day for it to become available funds. In some cases it takes two days if the point on which the DTC is drawn is remote.

The principal advantages of the ACH are that it guarantees one-day availability to all banks on whom checks are drawn who are members of the ACH system and its costs are somewhat lower than the DTC. The principal disadvantage of the ACH is that not all banks are members of the Automated Clearinghouse system, thus resulting in either a need to switch bank relation-ships or a dual system in which both DTCs and ACH transfers are used. Another disadvantage of the ACH is that slippage is less likely to occur using this system than is the case with the DTC.

The issue of slippage is an important one in concentration design. Slippage is the difference between the availability granted the corporation by its concentration bank and the actual time for the check or ACH item to reach the depository bank. In a paper-based money movement system, such as with DTC con-centration, there is usually some small level of slippage. If the money movements are large enough in amount, this slippage can prove very valuable. Then the corporation could make use of the money at both bank locations simultaneously. In fact, in many cases the value of slippage can more than offset the costs involved in the actual transfer process.

The optimization of slippage is one of the issues that needs to be addressed in the transfer scheduling problem. The objective function in this problem is to minimize excess balances at the depository bank, while simultaneously maximizing the level of slippage. Mathematically, this is equivalent to maximizing the level of investable balances at the concentration bank.

The transfer scheduling problem has been formulated as a linear programming model by Bernell Stone.[5] The model takes

---

[5] See, for example, B. K. Stone, and N. C. Hill, "Alternative Cash Transfer Mechanisms and Methods: Evaluation Frameworks," *Journal of Bank Research*, Spring 1982, pp. 7–16.

advantage of the corporation's ability to anticipate deposits in
the design of the transfer schedule. Where slippage is an important factor, transfers tend to be lumped together on Thursday,
since this day provides for the maximum slippage value within
the system. Where slippage is not a factor, the model's policy
recommendations have the characteristic of being anticipatory
in nature. Exhibit 5 shows a typical transfer policy. Notice that

Exhibit 5
University Analytics, Inc. Concentration Model (Current System
[Optimized] Transfer Policy Summary)

ACCOUNT NUMBER 0712-0009/01	CONCENTRATION BANK	0710-0012
ACCOUNT NAME DOWNTOWN STORE	NAME	MAIN LINE BANK
	INSTRUMENT TYPE	DTC
DEPOSIT BANK 0712-0009	INITIATION TIME	4:00PM
NAME CENTRAL NATIONAL BK	DEPOSITS KNOWN	40%

DAY	WEEK	POLICY DESCRIPTION
MONDAY	1 OF 1	TRANSFER SUM OF 92% OF TODAY'S REPORTED DEPOSIT (37% OF TOTAL DEPOSIT) 56% OF LAST FRIDAY'S REPORTED DEPOSIT ALL OF LAST FRIDAY'S PREVIOUSLY UNREPORTED DEPOSIT ALL OF WEEKEND DEPOSITS (IF ANY) LESS $ 4,162
TUESDAY	1 OF 1	TRANSFER SUM OF 61% OF TODAY'S REPORTED DEPOSIT (24% OF TOTAL DEPOSIT) 8% OF YESTERDAY'S REPORTED DEPOSIT ALL OF YESTERDAY'S PREVIOUSLY UNREPORTED DEPOSIT LESS $ 12,522
WEDNESDAY	1 OF 1	TRANSFER SUM OF 46% OF TODAY'S REPORTED DEPOSIT (18% OF TOTAL DEPOSIT) 39% OF YESTERDAY'S REPORTED DEPOSIT ALL OF YESTERDAY'S PREVIOUSLY UNREPORTED DEPOSIT LESS $ 29,944 LESS 24% OF YESTERDAY'S TOTAL DEPOSIT
THURSDAY	1 OF 1	TRANSFER $ 30,354 PLUS ALL OF TODAY'S REPORTED DEPOSIT (40% OF TOTAL DEPOSIT) 54% OF YESTERDAY'S REPORTED DEPOSIT ALL OF YESTERDAY'S PREVIOUSLY UNREPORTED DEPOSIT 24% OF THE TOTAL REPORTED DEPOSIT FOR LAST TUESDAY
FRIDAY	1 OF 1	TRANSFER $ 16,274 PLUS 44% OF TODAY'S REPORTED DEPOSIT (17% OF TOTAL DEPOSIT) ALL OF YESTERDAY'S PREVIOUSLY UNREPORTED DEPOSIT

Source: Concentration 1.00 5/82, Copyright 1982, University Analytics, Inc.

Thursday's transfer includes $30,354 in anticipated deposits as
well as a cleanup of yesterday's deposits which were made too
late to make the reporting deadline.

The third area to which concentration models address themselves is that of the selection of the actual set of concentration
banks to be used by the corporation. Many companies utilize a
multibank concentration system, especially if they concentrate
with DTCs. This is because, by locating the concentration banks
around the country, they can eliminate all or almost all the two-
day DTC collection points. In some instances the system is set
up so that the initial concentration takes place by DTC and the
money is then moved to a central bank by wire transfer.

The design of concentration systems is of great interest to the
banking community. This is because a bank's selection as a concentration bank almost always ensures it a portion of the credit

relationship. At a minimum, it makes the bank a critical link in the corporation's money movement operations. Thus the incentives to design concentration systems are similar to the incentives to design lockbox systems. The selection of concentration sites is not, however, easy to model. The principal difficulty is that there is no data base that can support a systematic selection of concentration banks. Moreover, as pointed out by Stone and Hill,[6] it is necessary to solve a transfer scheduling problem for each additional concentration bank that is considered, thus yielding a very complex model structure.

The use of concentration model technology has been hampered by another drawback as well. In order to implement a sophisticated concentration policy, utilizing, for example, anticipation, it is necessary that the bank have a model that can appropriately forecast deposit amounts. This model, called the transfer scheduler, is not yet readily available. Nonetheless, it is expected that the use of concentration models will increase significantly over the next several years, although it will never reach the level of usage of either the lockbox or the disbursement models. The concentration problem by its very nature is of interest only to corporations who have to manage a large number of bank relationships. It is most applicable to the retail sales industry and fast food franchisers.

BANK RELATIONSHIP DESIGN MODELS

In a famous book, written as a master's thesis, Rudolph Calman[7] described the use of linear programming to design the bank relationship. He addressed the issue of selecting a set of banks to provide transaction services and credit commitments and how these relationships should be optimally assigned. His approach was based on first assigning the credit commitments and, second, assigning transaction services to various banks. His approach took advantage of the phenomenon known as double-counting in which banks who provide credit and require balances for compensating for this commitment also permit those same balances to be used as payment for noncredit services. Stone reports that this model was very actively used during the early 1970s.[8] However, current use of this model appears to have fallen off to the point where it is almost nonexistent. Sev-

---

[6] "Alternative Cash Transfer Mechanisms and Methods: Evaluation Frameworks."

[7] R. Calman, *Linear Programming and Cash Management: CASH ALPHA,* MIT Press, Cambridge, Mass., 1968.

[8] B. K. Stone, "The Design of a Company's Banking System," *Journal of Finance,* 38, no. 2, May 1983, pp. 373–89.

eral changes in the banking system appear to be the cause of this decline.

First, the phenomenon of double-counting is rapidly fading. A few banks still do permit their corporate clients to double count, but it is now a very small minority as opposed to the vast majority, as was the case when Calman designed his model. Second, it has been recognized by the practitioners of cash management that the float issues, as described in the three problems previously mentioned in this chapter, dominate cost considerations. Usually the corporation will wish to assign its noncredit services so as to optimize its float opportunities with costs being only a secondary consideration. Credit services are usually layered on top of this cash management system, being assigned to those banks where significant operational capabilities are required. In summary, the model, although rich in history, has little application in today's cash management environment.

OPERATIONAL MODELS IN CASH MANAGEMENT

At this point we make the transition to models that can be used by corporations on either a daily or weekly basis. As will be discussed below, such models tend to use statistical techniques as opposed to optimization techniques such as linear or integer programming. A more detailed discussion of cash forecasting is presented in Chapter 7.

Short-Term Disbursement Forecasting

Many corporations face a problem when it comes to funding checks they have written. In some cases, they can address this need by the use of controlled disbursing, which entails early-morning notification of the actual presentment amount. In other instances this can prove infeasible or inadequate. The most common problem is that the corporation wants more than just the dollar value of today's presentment. For example, it wants to know the daily presentments for the next week or month. In this case, the company usually turns to forecasting. The most successful approach to this problem is derived from a statistical technique known as the clearing-pattern approach. This idea, which was originally applied by Stone to the problem of predicting receivables[9] and later to the disbursement problem,[10] at-

---

[9] B. K. Stone, "The Payment-Pattern Approach to the Forecasting and Control of Accounts Receivable," *Financial Management*, Autumn 1976, pp. 65–82.

[10] B. K. Stone and T. W. Miller, "Forecasting Disbursement Funding Requirements: The Clearing Pattern Approach," *Journal of Cash Management*, 3, no. 5, October/November 1983, pp. 67–78.

tempts to relate information on when the check was written to when the check will be received for payment at the disbursing bank. This approach, which was also investigated by Maier, Robinson, and Vander Weide[11] provides greater accuracy than has been reported for other methods.

An example of the use of this technique is shown in Exhibit 6. The forecast shown is for the next 10 business days. Notice that

Exhibit 6
Disbursement Forecast for Example Corporation

	Expected Values		Conservative Estimate	
Date	Daily Disbursement	Cumulative Disbursement	Daily Disbursement	Cumulative Disbursement
3/02/77	$ 6,861.	$ 6,861.	$ 12,991.	$ 12,991.
3/03/77	14,286.	21,147.	65,171.	78,162.
3/04/77	39,112.	60,259.	87,713.	165,875.
3/07/77	237,508.	297,767.	270,103.	435,978.
3/08/77	111,730.	409,497.	114,910.	550,888.
3/09/77	118,873.	528,370.	114,983.	665,871.
3/10/77	120,970.	649,340.	120,422.	786,293.
3/11/77	120,287.	769,627.	130,866.	917,159.
3/14/77	382,304.	1,151,931.	321,835.	1,238,994.
3/15/77	110,833.	1,262,764.	116,666.	1,355,660.

both a best guess and a more conservative estimate are computed. The conservative estimate is computed so that only 1 out of 20 forecasts will be less than the actual presentment, which means that only about once each month would the company be in a position of having underfunded its disbursement needs and therefore require a short-term bank loan or other adjustment.

The limitation of the use of the clearing-pattern approach to forecasting is that one can forecast into the future for only a very short period of time. Assuming one knows only the checks that have already been written, then the ability to forecast check presentments is limited to 5 or perhaps at most 10 days. Even if information on checks that will be written can be obtained from the accounts payable system, the approach is still limited to no more than 30 days.

As is true of many statistical applications, there is a certain type of firm for which this forecast procedure will prove ideal. A company which disburses only a very few checks will find it difficult to forecast check presentments. On the other hand, a

---

[11] S. F. Maier, D. W. Robinson, and J. H. Vander Weide, "A Short-Term Disbursement Forecasting Model," *Financial Management*, 10, no. 1, Spring 1981, pp. 9–20.

company which disburses a great number of items, all of which are small relative to the total, can forecast daily disbursement with only the simplest of models, or perhaps no model at all. The application of a sophisticated statistical model is useful for companies that fall between these two extremes.

Currently the number of companies applying statistical techniques to forecasting is small. For example, at the September 1983, Duke University program on cash management, only 29 percent of the over 90 companies attending indicated that they used statistics-based forecasting. Given that this conference attracts a rather senior audience, the overall industry percentage use of statistical forecasting is no doubt much smaller. One important factor leading to the growth of forecasting models may be the Federal Reserve's efforts to eliminate remote disbursing. This is because, as previously discussed, the Federal Reserve is making it increasingly difficult to provide the early-morning notification used for same-day funding. Faced with the loss of the traditional controlled disbursing system, many companies could be forced to turn to forecasting as the only reasonable alternative.

Collection Forecasting

The usual technique for forecasting the daily amount of collections is based on the statistical method called the distribution approach. In this method the company forecasts its total monthly collections and uses historical data to distribute this over the business days of the month. Stone and Hill[12] and Stone and Miller[13] have done pioneering work in the development of this technique.

The technique capitalizes on the repetitive nature of cash flows. For most companies, Monday is the biggest collection day of the week, because checks mailed on Thursday and Friday are received on Monday. Some weeks during the month tend to be better than others. Also certain days, such as just after the 10th and 25th, usually show heavy cash inflow. The distribution approach examines the firm's historical data to isolate where the cash collection peaks and valleys occur.

From a statistical standpoint, the problem is very difficult. In order to calculate a reasonable forecast one must take into account the impact of weekends, holidays, months of differing

---

[12] "Alternative Cash Transfer Mechanisms and Methods: Evaluation Frameworks."

[13] B. K. Stone and T. W. Miller, "Daily Cash Forecasting with Dummy-Variable Regression Using Multiplicative and Mixed-Effect Models for Measuring Cash Flow Cycles," Working Paper MS–79–18, Georgia Institute of Technology, College of Industrial Management, Atlanta, Georgia, December 1979, 21 pages.

length, and the positioning within the month of key days such as the 10th. Usually a change in the 10th falling on a Friday versus a Wednesday can cause a major shift in the pattern. The solution is usually to collect more data, but then the underlying pattern may shift because of changes in the customer base. In practice, the pattern must be estimated using no more than 12 to 24 months of daily data.

Target Balance Management

Almost all mid- to large-sized corporations subscribe to balance reporting systems which provide a daily status report on the amount of funds maintained in various accounts. Most corporations will have a certain level of balances they are trying to maintain at each bank in order to compensate the banks for services provided and/or credit commitments. Normally, the corporation's target will be expressed as either an annual level of balances or a monthly average balance level. Accordingly, the corporation will usually choose to manage its balance levels around this target, keeping in mind what its previous historical average has been and also the seasonality patterns it is likely to encounter during the remainder of the year.

Some work has been done in trying to model this problem and there are some very simple statistical models in place in the balance reporting systems provided by the major commercial banks. The problem becomes more interesting when the firm has an annual compensation target, since this permits the integration of bank compensation with annual cash forecasting.

In the case where a company borrows during part of the year and invests during another part, there exists an incentive to undercompensate during borrowing periods and make up for this during investment periods. This, of course, is due to the differential between borrowing costs and investment rates. Some enterprising corporations even play this game during each monthly cycle. They deliberately undercompensate during the early part of the month and overcompensate during the latter part. Because of the time value of money, this is less costly than compensating uniformly during the month.[14]

Short-Term Financial Planning

A very sophisticated model used by a few corporations is related to the management of their short-term investment or borrowing

---

[14] See B. K. Stone, "The Design of a Company's Banking System," for a discussion of some of the other issues involved.

portfolios. This has traditionally been an area in which the majority of corporations use little or no modeling. For example, Julie Connelly[15] cites a number of examples of corporations which accumulated large portfolios of investment assets while managing them very passively. The usual approach has been to keep the portfolio very short in terms of average maturity and minimizing risk by investing in only the safest of the money market instruments. Little has been done to take advantage of changing interest rates or various opportunities afforded by different investment instruments or lengthening maturities. Moreover, the cash manager has traditionally followed the policy of buy and hold, showing little inclination to actively trade a short-term investment portfolio.

In 1980 a model was produced and is currently licensed through the Bank of Montreal called CALCULINE. This model provides a cash manager the ability, through linear programming, to optimize either an investment or borrowing portfolio. The methodology takes into account the current yields on a variety of investment/borrowing instruments as well as predicted changes in this yield as derived from an interest-rate forecast. In addition, the model looks at forecast cash requirements and integrates them with a decision as to when to invest or borrow funds. General Telephone reports that this technology helped it refine its own investment strategy with regard to the selling of commercial paper.[16] It permitted it to do a "what if"-type analysis on varying interest-rate scenarios. It also found the CALCULINE technology useful in teaching its new cash managers about the intricacies of managing a commercial paper portfolio.

Exhibits 7 and 8 show some sample output using the CALCULINE model. Exhibit 7 shows the investment and borrowing instruments recommended by the model. In some instances, the optimization process will recommend simultaneous borrowing and investing. In the example in Exhibit 7 this occurs on the first day of the planning horizon. This phenomenon is usually caused by the form of the slope of the yield curve or expected changes in interest rates. With a steeply upward-sloping yield curve, the model invests as long as possible, even though it may incur some short-term borrowing.

Exhibit 8 is a risk-control report. The model can be instructed to maintain a weighted average maturity level for both its invest-

---

[15] *Institutional Investor*, May 1978, pp. 45–50.

[16] J. Austin, S. F. Maier, and J. H. Vander Weide, "General Telephone's Experience with a Short-Run Financial Planning Model," *Cash Management Forum*, 6, no. 1, June 1980, pp. 3–6.

Exhibit 7
The Optimal Short-Term Financial Plan Action Summary

Date	Instrument	Act	Amount	Mature Date	Maturity Value	Yield
3/28	CREDIT LINE	B	$1,730,716.74	3/30	$1,732,439.96	18.171%
3/28	CM PAPER	B	1,570,004.33	4/27	1,593,252.44	18.016
3/28	90-DAY CD	I	1,000,721.07	6/22	1,036,177.78	15.038
3/30	CREDIT LINE	B	1,072,431.42	4/06	1,076,170.64	18.180
3/30	60-DAY CD	I	1,439,991.46	5/25	1,472,686.18	14.799
4/06	CM PAPER	B	2,457,496.13	5/11	2,500,000.00	18.037
4/06	DAILY REPO	I	81,325.49	4/13	81,528.89	13.024
4/13	CREDIT LINE	B	4,027,500.45	4/27	4,055,674.57	18.203
4/13	90-DAY CD	I	64,435.40	7/17	67,044.51	15.557
4/27	30-DAY CD	I	114,457.60	5/25	115,836.10	15.700
5/25	30-DAY CD	I	4,688,522.28	6/22	4,752,521.93	17.794
6/22	CREDIT LINE	B	5,719,173.31	7/20	5,799,852.28	18.285
6/22	CM PAPER	B	5,719,173.31	8/01	5,826,662.43	17.150
6/22	30-DAY CD	I	6,838,078.94	7/20	6,934,336.61	18.350
6/22	60-DAY CD	I	5,188,967.40	8/17	5,338,244.24	18.751
7/17	REPO	I	67,044.51	7/20	67,116.83	13.119
7/20	REPO	I	5,801,601.16	8/01	5,826,662.43	13.117

Exhibit 8
The Optimal Short-Term Financial Plan Risk Summary

	Investments		Borrowing	
Date	Total Dollars Outstanding	Weighted Average Maturities	Total Dollars Outstanding	Weighted Average Maturities
3/28	$ 4,634,776.69	33.459	$ 4,818,810.44	17.096
3/30	6,078,592.14	37.273	4,163,569.33	19.292
4/06	6,177,388.42	29.966	5,559,288.76	24.709
4/13	5,650,734.72	26.542	9,605,944.72	16.154
4/27	2,648,706.01	40.007	2,482,998.45	14.000
5/11	2,663,725.47	26.007	0.00	0.0
5/25	5,778,744.93	28.284	0.00	0.0
6/22	12,093,404.24	39.998	11,438,346.62	34.000
7/20	11,065,206.98	19.611	5,794,415.69	12.000

ment and borrowing portfolios. This prevents the model from going too far out on the yield curve. In situations in which interest rates are very uncertain, reducing the maximum weighted average maturity reduces the company's risk.

Treasury Information Systems

The emergence of the microcomputer as an important cash management tool has introduced the spread sheet program to cash management.[17] This program, which is epitomized by such specific software products as VisiCalc and Lotus 1-2-3, has made it possible to do "what if"-type planning in financial situations which previously could be handled only by large-scale modeling. Usually these models are used to do cash flow forecasting, although not with any statistical basis. In this regard they differ from the disbursement application using the clearing-pattern approach and the collection application using the distribution approach. Nonetheless, the techniques are very powerful because the microcomputer environment can analyze a number of different scenarios in a matter of minutes.

Treasury information systems are the natural evolution of spread sheets. They represent a leading edge product for cash managers. In late 1983 a number of banks announced their availability, including Citibank, Bank of Boston, First Chicago, and Manufacturers Hanover. These systems join the ranks of others introduced by Bank of America and nonbank providers such as Future Technologies and Wismer Associates.

Each of these systems has at its core a balance management module which, in the case of many of the bank-designed systems, can extract data which would normally be received through a terminal as part of the bank's balance reporting and automated wire transfer initiation systems. Some of the more advanced systems have integrated investment and debt management modules, as well as cash forecasting capabilities.

The microcomputer environment offers a number of advantages over either a time-sharing environment or a main-frame computer for these models, including:

Reduced Cost   A full-scale professional microcomputer with letter quality printer, hard disk, and 512K of memory costs less than $10,000. This system can eliminate the majority of a firm's time-sharing and outside vendor computer charges. Moreover, the cost is one-time, not recurring. Especially attractive is the ability to store large amounts of data without incurring storage charges.

Greater Security   Since the data are on your computer, you have control. Of course security is still required to prevent the unauthorized use of private data by your own people.

Fast Turnaround   If the system is on your desk, the answer you want can be obtained in minutes instead of days. Elimination of

---

[17] For a more detailed discussion of the use of microcomputers for cash management, see Chapter 9.

the computer specialist as the interface between you and the computer shortens turnaround time dramatically. The cash manager no longer has to worry what position he occupies in the computer specialist's queue.

Software Availability Because the use of microcomputers is exploding, a great number of software applications have been developed. Three areas of particular interest are spread sheets, word processing, and data management. Moreover, these very sophisticated programs are dirt cheap when judged against main-frame systems. The best-selling and most sophisticated of these general-purpose packages rarely costs more than $500.

For all of these reasons we anticipate growth in modeling using microcomputers. Just as today no cash manager could be without a balance reporting system, by 1985 at the latest no cash manager will be without a microcomputer.

SUMMARY

In summary, several key points can be made about the kind of models currently used in cash management.

1. The sophistication of planning models tends to be greater than the sophistication of operational models.
2. Data base requirements (mail, availability, clearing) are very important in planning models, but tend to be rather unimportant in operational models.
3. There is a strong trend to develop models today for use on microcomputers and to minimize the use of time-sharing services.
4. Since the entire field of cash management is still rather new, with a national association of cash managers having been in place for only four years, there are likely to be many more modeling applications in this field over the coming years.

In conclusion, models in cash management should continue to grow in importance over at least the next 5 or 10 years.

9

Microcomputers in the Treasurer's Office

Andrew R. Gaul with
Capital Systems Group, Inc.

Automation in the treasurer's office is entering a new era in the 1980s. Although most treasury operations have used many forms of automation to enhance their operational efficiency, the tools were never really designed for their particular needs. With the advent of the low-cost, high-performance microcomputer and software written specifically for the treasurer, the time of the automated treasury operation is here. Most automated treasury operations will be similar, in that their focus will be on people productivity, yet different, in that the various sizes and types of firms will automate different aspects of their operations.

HISTORICAL PERSPECTIVE

The 1970s introduced a new era in the delivery of electronic corporate cash management services. Banks and time-sharing vendors joined forces to provide a broad array of data collection and information processing capabilities. Computer power was combined with high-speed telecommunications and specialized software to enhance the flow of time-critical cash management data between banks and the corporate treasurer.

Automation of the cash management function gained quick acceptance in the corporate treasury marketplace. Cash managers were provided with direct access to their bank balances, detailed deposit data, and in some cases the latest money market rates. Additional online services were offered to streamline the wire transfer process and to facilitate portfolio and debt management.

162

Both corporate cash managers and bankers reacted favorably to the new technology (see Exhibit 1). Competition quickly escalated as more and more money center and regional banks entered the automated services arena. Over time, products were

Exhibit 1
Market Growth in Cash Management Services

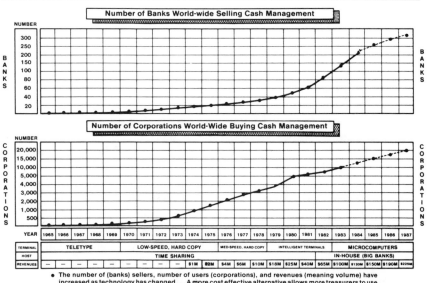

enhanced and some new applications added; however, as the products matured, so too did the needs of the corporate cash manager.

Automation brought forth new management challenges. The availability of current financial data fulfilled a real need, but access to multiple bank and time-sharing systems had to occur with precise timing to be effective. Most systems addressed specific functions but few provided the capabilities needed to integrate data for analysis and planning. While automated systems provided more data than ever before, standardized reporting formats often did not relate to the needs of the cash manager. Customization was the answer but this was not always practical nor cost-effective.

Recent advances in microcomputer technology have made

possible a new era in cash management. By combining the performance and processing power of microcomputers with generalized and specialized software, cash managers are able to perform multiple treasury functions on a single low-cost system. Operations that were previously performed manually or on a main-frame computer can now be done with increased speed and efficiency on a microcomputer-based treasury management system.

Treasury automation can be defined in two categories. The first category is "automated treasury management systems," which are very specialized software systems designed exclusively to satisfy the needs of corporate treasurers. These systems are usually made up of many "programs" or "packages" which are integrated to perform multiple tasks and to function as a unit. The second automation type involves the use of general software programs tailored to satisfy a specific function in the treasurer's office. This type is usually a single "package" that allows treasurers to automate one or more of their activities. The most common packages are "spread-sheets" which perform row and column financial manipulations. The major focus of this chapter will be on the fully automated treasury management systems.

Today's dynamic economic environment has initiated the development of automated treasury management systems. The investment market requires that strategic decisions be made within a narrow time frame. Corporate cash managers, juggling relationships with numerous banks, must manage a large volume of information to make timely decisions. Automating the treasury function allows the time-critical nature of this operation to become more manageable.

The primary benefit of an automated system is a significant improvement in data management. Records can be retained in a more accurate and organized form, and information can be received and manipulated on a more timely basis. Secondary to this, the automation of treasury functions allows the reallocation of previously committed people resources.

The treasury function most frequently automated is the retrieval of balance information, data-basing of selected balances, and the formatting/calculation of these data into a company's daily cash position. In this type of automated function, balance information is retrieved each morning for all banking relationships. This information is processed and the net investing/borrowing position calculated. Often, all this can be accomplished without any manual intervention via an "intelligent" modem (one that automatically dials the appropriate number at an established time and retrieves the information).

Companies are searching for ways to expand the automated interface with their banks to applications beyond balance reporting. Customers are requiring that banks have the capability to accept wire transfers, stop payments, and check inquiries initiated from terminals in the company's offices. Inquiries are frequently made regarding the transmission of account reconcilement information directly to the customer's accounts payable system.

A microcomputer-based corporate treasury management system creates a cost-effective and yet responsive solution to the cash planning and control process. Since the hardware and software needed to operate this system are contained in a single stand-alone unit, many of the current time-sharing costs associated with treasury operations can be reduced or eliminated. As a result, a microcomputer-based corporate treasury management system not only expands the information storage, processing, and analysis capabilities of the treasury staff, but it also reduces the costs associated with using outside sources.

Today's treasury manager faces greater challenges and more intense performance criteria than ever before. By utilizing a microcomputer combined with specialized software capabilities, the treasury operation will increase productivity and compete more effectively in an ever-changing financial environment.

DEFINITIONS

Before we go any further, it is appropriate to define the terms and context of treasury management systems (Exhibit 2). A treasury operation is a very broad and diverse entity and in this context we want to focus on only one major component.

COMPONENTS OF A CORPORATE TREASURER'S SYSTEM

The microcomputer in the treasurer's office normally replaces the manual activities with electronic tools. These tools are intended to retrieve information, store and manage data, analyze data, produce reports and graphs of the data, and generally aid in the decision-making process. Exhibit 3 illustrates the components typically found in an automated treasury management system.

Exhibit 2
Cash Management Definitions

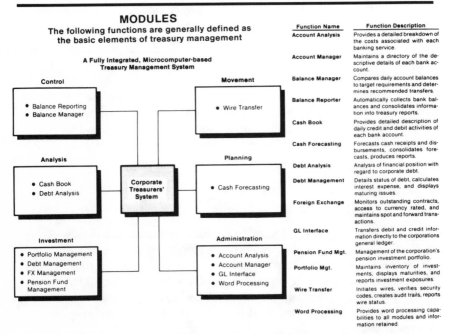

DEFINITIONS

Cash Management
The employment of management techniques, banking services, and communications systems to maximize the productive use of corporate funds and minimize cost of corporate funds.

Treasury Management
The management of a corporation's debt, equity, receivables, payables, banking relationships, and daily cash positions in such a way as to maximize the financial "health" of a corporation.

Corporate Treasurer's System
Electronic tools that allow the treasury operation of a corporation to implement the goals of the cash manager and treasury manager, and to function as the primary link between the sources of financial data (banks) and the ultimate users of that data (corporate operations).

Exhibit 3

MODULES
The following functions are generally defined as the basic elements of treasury management

A Fully Integrated, Microcomputer-based Treasury Management System

Control
- Balance Reporting
- Balance Manager

Movement
- Wire Transfer

Analysis
- Cash Book
- Debt Analysis

Planning
- Cash Forecasting

Corporate Treasurers' System

Investment
- Portfolio Management
- Debt Management
- FX Management
- Pension Fund Management

Administration
- Account Analysis
- Account Manager
- GL Interface
- Word Processing

Function Name	Function Description
Account Analysis	Provides a detailed breakdown of the costs associated with each banking service.
Account Manager	Maintains a directory of the descriptive details of each bank account.
Balance Manager	Compares daily account balances to target requirements and determines recommended transfers.
Balance Reporter	Automatically collects bank balances and consolidates information into treasury reports.
Cash Book	Provides detailed description of daily credit and debit activities of each bank account.
Cash Forecasting	Forecasts cash receipts and disbursements, consolidates forecasts, produces reports.
Debt Analysis	Analysis of financial position with regard to corporate debt.
Debt Management	Details status of debt, calculates interest expense, and displays maturing issues.
Foreign Exchange	Monitors outstanding contracts, access to currency rated, and maintains spot and forward transactions.
GL Interface	Transfers debit and credit information directly to the corporations general ledger.
Pension Fund Mgt.	Management of the corporation's pension investment portfolio.
Portfolio Mgt.	Maintains inventory of investments, displays maturities, and reports investment exposures.
Wire Transfer	Initiates wires, verifies security codes, creates audit trails, reports wire status.
Word Processing	Provides word processing capabilities to all modules and information retained.

THE AUTOMATED CORPORATE TREASURY
SYSTEM MARKETPLACE

Automation in the treasurer's office can benefit both very large and very small firms alike. The deciding factor in adopting treasury automation is the cost of the solution for the value received. Some automation can benefit all firms in terms of people productivity or the better utilization of funds. Therefore, the marketplace could be defined as the top 400,000 corporations in the United States.

The market for automated treasury management systems outside the United States is now emerging. As the European and Asian markets expand their balance reporting and wire transfer systems, the need to provide these additional tools will create additional markets. The speed with which these markets will offer this new technology could rival the U.S. markets. Many European and Asian banks have recently gotten on the automated balance reporting "bandwagon" and have aggressively marketed these products to their clients. One would expect that these same banks would also aggressively market an automated treasury management system to their clients.

More realistically, the number of firms that have the capacity to purchase the hardware and software that make up an automated corporate treasury system is much smaller. The ability to pay and the value received are two limiting criteria. A firm needs to have sufficient volume (number of accounts, loans, investments) and velocity (cash turnover) to justify the expense of a system and to receive reasonable value. Typically, firms ranked 1 to 40,000 fit the above criteria and are generally considered to be the primary users (Exhibit 4).

The other side of the marketplace comprises the sellers of corporate treasury management systems. Banks are the primary sellers and servicers of automated balance reporting and wire transfer systems, and therefore have established a special working relationship with corporate clients. It follows then that banks are also the primary sales focus of automated treasury management systems. However, because of the complexity and support requirements of these automated treasury systems, a new "partnership" has formed between software firms and banks to sell and distribute these kinds of products (Exhibit 4). Because of the dynamics of the market, an exact listing of sellers and buyers would be dated the instant it was written. Instead, a history and forecast of buyers and sellers will illustrate the dynamics of the market.

Costs are another factor that has an influence on and is influ-

Exhibit 4

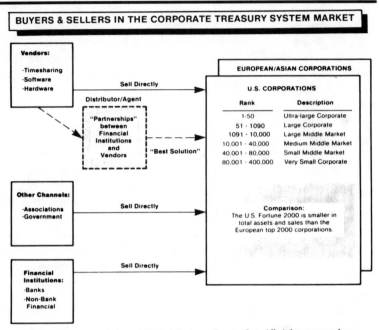

BUYERS & SELLERS IN THE CORPORATE TREASURY SYSTEM MARKET

Vendors:
- Timesharing
- Software
- Hardware

Sell Directly

Distributor/Agent

"Partnerships" between Financial Institutions and Vendors

"Best Solution"

EUROPEAN/ASIAN CORPORATIONS

U.S. CORPORATIONS

Rank	Description
1-50	Ultra-large Corporate
51 - 1090	Large Corporate
1091 - 10,000	Large Middle Market
10,001 - 40,000	Medium Middle Market
40,001 - 80,000	Small Middle Market
80,001 - 400,000	Very Small Corporate

Other Channels:
- Associations
- Government

Sell Directly

Comparison:
The U.S. Fortune 2000 is smaller in total assets and sales than the European top 2000 corporations.

Financial Institutions:
- Banks
- Non-Bank Financial

Sell Directly

enced by this dynamic marketplace. Purchasers prior to 1983 could expect to pay more than $25,000 for a system. For that price, they would receive a reasonably comprehensive software package, training, and some tailoring to an individual treasurer's operation. After 1983, the market for low-cost, "off-the-shelf" treasury management systems emerged. Complete systems were offered for $6,000, and pieces of systems were offered for as little as $2,000. For those prices, the treasurer received one or more modules and documentation. One of the more interesting phenomena that have emerged is the concept of leasing treasury software. A treasurer is able to obtain a comprehensive system for a monthly lease of less than $200. For this amount, the treasurer receives the software, documentation, and training. Most important in the lease concept are the free updates to the software that are provided as part of the package. Treasury management, as an automated discipline, is in its infancy and will undergo dramatic changes. By leasing software, the user has an insurance policy against obsolescence. This could become one of the more important criteria in making the automation decision and in choosing the vendor/bank. The final factor influencing the market is the unbundling of costs. Many systems bundle all costs of software, training, and support into one package. The emergence of totally unbundled pricing, along with multiple levels of service, can provide treasurers with the flexibility needed to obtain a system at a price that fits their requirements.

The number of buyers and sellers of automated corporate treasurers systems should show the same rapid measure (Exhibit 5) in units and revenues that the market experienced with balance reporting systems (Exhibit 1). The speed with which the market accepts automated treasury management systems will potentially be faster than balance reporting because of the proliferation of personal computers and the close relationship between these systems and balance reporting systems.

Exhibit 5

ESTIMATED NUMBER OF PARTICIPANTS IN THE AUTOMATED TREASURY MANAGEMENT MARKET

		1980	1981	1982	1983	1984	1985	1986	1987
BANKS	1-10	2	2	3	5	10	10	10	10
	11-30	0	0	0	3	15	20	20	20
	31-75	0	0	0	2	20	30	35	45
	76-150	0	0	0	0	30	40	45	50
	151+	0	0	0	0	5	10	35	50
	VENDORS	1	1	2	8	15	25	18	10
CORPS.	1-50	5	10	15	25	30	40	45	50
	51-1090	1	5	10	50	300	700	800	900
	1091-10,000	0	0	5	25	200	1,500	2,500	4,000
	10,001-40,000	0	0	0	0	15	50	2,000	6,000
	40,001-80,000	0	0	0	0	0	5	100	500
	80,001-400,000	0	0	0	0	0	0	15	100

Reprinted with permission of Capital Systems Group, Inc. All rights reserved.

TYPICAL HARDWARE COMPONENTS

The introduction of low-cost microcomputer hardware was one of the more important factors in creating a market for automated treasury management systems. Also as important was the emergence of a relative "standard" in hardware and operating systems. IBM's introduction of its personal computer provided the market focus necessary to create this standard. The most common hardware used on treasury operations is the IBM personal computer and XT computers. A typical treasury configuration is shown in Exhibit 6.

Exhibit 6

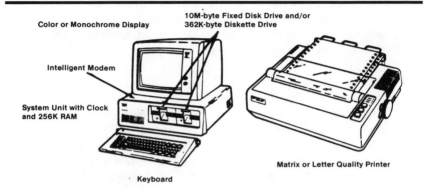

The cost of such a system would be between $4,000 and $9,000, depending on the components contained in the unit.

Example of a Typical System

There are many automated treasury systems available from banks and vendors. Which one is "best" for an individual treasurer must be handled on a case-by-case basis. The following description is of a typical system designed for the middle range of the market (corporations with sales of $25 million to $1 billion).

Exhibit 7

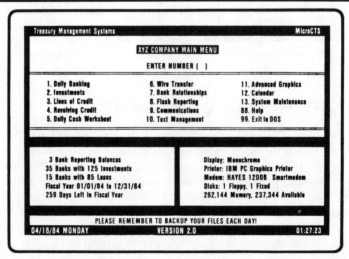

The heart of a corporate treasury system is usually the Main menu. All functions (modules) within the system are managed by this menu.

In this example, there are 13 modules described; each performs separate functions that are interrelated through common data bases. Exhibits 8 through 20 illustrate the details typically found in the modules of an automated treasury management system. The focus is on functionality of a typical system. Other available systems could have more or less functionality or features.

1. The **Daily Banking Module** (Exhibit 8) is the basic element of the system. It keeps track of the cash balances, investments, lines of credit, revolving credit participation, and compensating balance requirements for each key relationship bank entered in the system. In other words, your primary banking relationships can be totally managed by this module.

2. The **Investments Module** (Exhibit 9) helps to manage the investment portfolio by keeping track of individual investments, grouped by bank. It provides a wide range of management reports. These reports include information on accrued interest and interest income which will support a general ledger journal entry, provide the information required for financial disclosure by companies subject to SEC reporting requirements, and help in managing banking relationships.

    Eliminating as many clerical functions as possible is an important objective of this and other modules. It will write a confirmation letter summarizing each day's investment activity for any bank on the system. These letters are completely tailored to the company's relationship for that bank.

    This module calculates daily total investment balances and average interest rates. It automatically updates the investment history report for the key relationship banks set up under daily banking.

3. The **Loans Module** (Exhibit 10) helps to manage the loan portfolio by keeping track of individual loans, grouped by bank. It provides a wide range of management reports. These reports include information on accrued interest and interest expense which will support a general ledger journal entry, provide the information required for financial disclosure by companies subject to SEC reporting requirements, and help in managing banking relationships.

4. The **Revolving Credit Module** (Exhibit 11) operates in much the same manner as the investments and loans modules. There are some differences, however. A revolving credit transaction involves a predetermined group of banks, acting through a single agent bank. Therefore, the user has no discretion regarding with whom to place the loan. The user simply records a revolver loan in the portfolio.

  Each transaction is shared by several banks. The percentage each bank is allocated depends upon the participation entered in the banking module. Note that the data for this module are shared by several other modules.

5. The **Daily Cash Worksheet Module** (Exhibit 12) is designed to provide a spread-sheet mechanism for managing the firm's cash inflows and outflows.

  The daily cash worksheet function offers a highly responsive tool for cash management and financial planning. The worksheet provides an early-morning summary of the corporation's investable funds position, including estimated inputs to project the end-of-day cash position. This allows the treasurer the ability to make several "what-if" projections of receipts and disbursements to determine that day's best use of funds.

  This worksheet is for those accounts or bank relationships that are tracked on a daily basis (key relationship banks). Summary balance information—ledger, available, or opening available, as designated, and any float categories—is transmitted or key-entered to the files and then posted to the daily cash worksheet. Yesterday's projected closing position is posted and the variance between yesterday's actual and projected closing is then calculated. As another aid in determining today's cash management decisions, the required balances necessary to meet the current month's target are posted from today's target balance analysis.

  After all of the above information has been posted to the daily cash worksheet, the treasurer can key-enter projected receipts and disbursements for various categories that are expected to occur that day. Based on these estimates, the projected ending cash position for those accounts and/or banks is calculated. Now a decision can be made to move funds as necessary. The dollar amounts or transfers to be executed are key-entered into the row titled "Today's Wire Decisions." A subsequent recalculation of the projected cash position is obtained.

6. The **Wire Transfer Module** (Exhibit 13) is designed to provide an automated mechanism for preparing wire transfer initiation requests on the microcomputer and then communicating these instructions electronically to a financial institution for further disposition. This module focuses on repetitive, free form, DTC, and ACH transfers. The wire transfer module works directly with the communication module in order to execute a transaction. The repetitive transfers are stored in files and contain the basic instructions necessary to execute the transaction, such as payee, transfer bank, account numbers, etc. The instructions, called "line sheets," are set up by the user and called into use whenever a repetitive transfer is to take place. The date and amount to transfer are added interactively just before the wire instruction is forwarded to the bank. With the completed line sheet(s) ready, the communications module is invoked and the bank(s) automatically called. The instructions are sent to the bank, and the sequence number that is returned by the bank is stored in a file on the microcomputer for further use.

7. The **Bank Relationship Module** (Exhibit 14) provides a control point for the key relationship banks that have been entered. This module is useful for providing fast, easy access to the specified individual's accounts at each bank, as well as providing a summary report recapping the total relationship with each bank.

   The bank relationships module is tied closely to the daily banking module through the sharing of common data-base files. Balances, interest rates, etc., are captured by daily banking. All other nonfinancial elements may be entered or changed using bank relationships.

8. The **Flash Report Module** (Exhibit 15) is a multipurpose module, providing a one-page summary of significant facts about a company and its financial structure. Its target audience is top management. It is a summary of all of the financial data accumulated over time by the other modules, as well as the stock and production statistics.

   The flash report is most useful when tailored for a company's particular business. For example, a manufacturer may be interested in shipments, bookings, backlog, pricing, revenues, product mix by commodity lines, production rates, etc. A retailer would have completely different needs. A service-oriented business would have still others, such as billed and unbilled hours.

   This is a comparative report. Information is displayed

for the current day (generally the day preceding the morning the report is prepared). Key company statistics are accumulated to present a gross month-to-month volume, which is compared with the daily average for the current month. This current month average is then compared with the average per day for the entire preceding month, and the month prior to that one. The treasury/ financial data include interest rates and balances. The current day's balances are compared with the preceding day's, and with balances from one and two months ago. If the prior months' dates happen to fall on a weekend, the flash report will drop back and display the balances from the Friday before the weekend date. The comparison of stock prices works the same way. Interest rates and stock volumes are not compared with prior dates.

The flash report also provides the capability to add comments to the bottom of the report and to elaborate on significant factors or events that are not obvious from the numbers. Examples include a change in interest rates, plant production problems, significant new contracts or labor problems—anything that directly affects the company and that the target audience should be aware of.

9. The **Communications Module** (Exhibit 16) is designed to provide an electronic link between the user's computer and any other computer. Its primary function is to communicate with the various bank automated balance reporting services and the bank wire transfer initiation services. It performs the communications, retrieval, and storage of information in an automated fashion that can save time and reduce errors. This module can also communicate with nonbalance reporting/wire transfer systems to retrieve other data needed by the treasury operation.

10. The **Text Management Module** (Exhibit 17) is designed to provide an easy-to-use, page-oriented word processor. It is intended to handle short memos and letters, to input and maintain the confirmation letters, and to edit output reports from the system.

11. The **Advanced Graphics Module** (Exhibit 18) provides an easy-to-use method of graphing treasury-oriented data. Line and bar charts are the most common form used.

12. The **Calendar Module** (Exhibit 19) provides a mechanism to search all of the investment, loan, and revolving credit portfolios, and lists all current maturities as a bold re-

minder. Besides maturities, there are other events which are extremely important and which could spell disaster if overlooked: scheduled long-term debt service, periodic reporting required by long-term debt covenants, SEC filing deadlines, and other similar events. Calendar stores these upcoming events and lists them along with the maturing loans and investments. In addition, the user can maintain a personal calendar of appointments, called "events," that will be sorted by time of day within dates.

13. The **System Maintenance Module** (Exhibit 20) is designed to provide an overall control point for the system. From managing the attributes of the hardware and peripherals connected to the computer through backup copies of the data, this module provides a simplified approach to system maintenance.

Exhibit 8

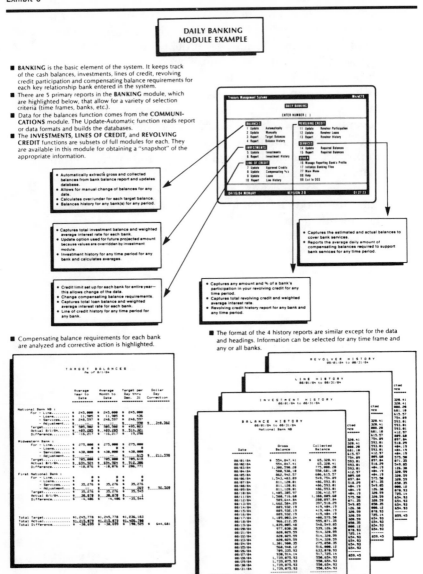

**DAILY BANKING
MODULE EXAMPLE**

- **BANKING** is the basic element of the system. It keeps track of the cash balances, investments, lines of credit, revolving credit participation and compensating balance requirements for each key relationship bank entered in the system.
- There are 5 primary reports in the **BANKING** module, which are highlighted below, that allow for a variety of selection criteria (time frames, banks, etc.).
- Data for the balances function comes from the **COMMUNICATIONS** module. The Update-Automatic function reads report or data formats and builds the databases.
- The **INVESTMENTS**, **LINES OF CREDIT**, and **REVOLVING CREDIT** functions are subsets of full modules for each. They are available in this module for obtaining a "snapshot" of the appropriate information.

- Automatically extracts gross and collected balances from bank balance report and updates database.
- Allows for manual change of balances for any date.
- Calculates over/under for each target balance.
- Balances history for any bank(s) for any period.

- Captures total investment balance and weighted average interest rate for each bank.
- Update option used for future projected amount because values are overridden by investment module.
- Investment history for any time period for any bank and calculates averages.

- Captures the estimated and actual balances to cover bank services.
- Reports the average daily amount of compensating balances required to support bank services for any time period.

- Credit limit set up for each bank for entire year—this allows change of the data.
- Change compensating balance requirements.
- Captures total loan balance and weighted average interest rate for each bank.
- Line of credit history for any time period for any bank.

- Captures any amount and % of a bank's participation in your revolving credit for any time period.
- Captures total revolving credit and weighted average interest rate.
- Revolving credit history report for any bank and any time period.

- Compensating balance requirements for each bank are analyzed and corrective action is highlighted.

- The format of the 4 history reports are similar except for the data and headings. Information can be selected for any time frame and any or all banks.

Exhibit 9

INVESTMENTS MODULE EXAMPLE

- ■ **INVESTMENTS** provides a control point for all non-equity investments made by the corporation. The investments tracked can be of any size and can be placed with key banks, tracked in **BANKING**, or with any financial institution.

- ■ There is no limit to the number of investments that may be tracked, nor a limit on the number of institutions with which you have investments.

- ■ Investments are tracked by individual investment, grouped by bank.

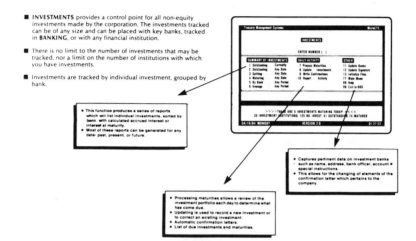

- ● This function produces a series of reports which will list individual investments, sorted by bank, with calculated accrued interest or interest at maturity.
- ● Most of these reports can be generated for any date- past, present, or future.

- ● Captures pertinent data on investment banks such as name, address, bank officer, account # special instructions.
- ● This allows for the changing of elements of the confirmation letter which pertains to the company.

- ● Processing maturities allows a review of the investment portfolio each day to determine what has come due.
- ● Updating is used to record a new investment or to correct an existing investment.
- ● Automatic confirmation letters.
- ● List of due investments and maturities.

- ■ The 6 reports below all have the same basic format with the difference between reports being the selection and sequence of information (banks, time frames, etc.).

- ■ Average investments can be displayed for any time frame for any investment institution or summarized by all institutions.
- ■ Confirmation letters are automatically generated for new and maturing investments.

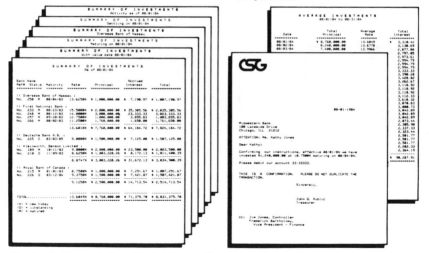

Reprinted with permission of Capital Systems Group, Inc. All rights reserved.

Exhibit 10

**LINES OF CREDIT
MODULE EXAMPLE**

■ **LOANS** provides a control point for all credit relationships (except revolving credits) made by the corporation. The loans tracked can be of any size and can be with key banks, tracked in **BANKING**, or with any financial institution.

■ There is no limit to the number of loans that may be tracked, nor a limit on the number of institutions with which you have loans.

■ Loans are tracked by individual loan, grouped by bank.

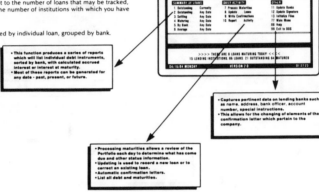

■ The 6 reports below all have the same basic format with the difference between reports being the selection and sequence of information (banks, time frames, etc.).

■ Average loans can be displayed for any time frame for any lending institution or summarized by all institutions.
■ Confirmation letters are automatically generated for new or maturing loans.

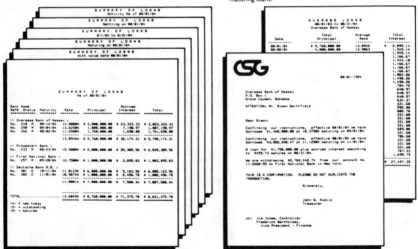

Exhibit 11

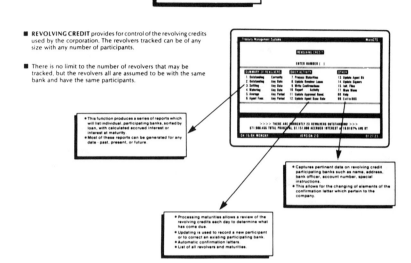

- **REVOLVING CREDIT** provides for control of the revolving credits used by the corporation. The revolvers tracked can be of any size with any number of participants.

- There is no limit to the number of revolvers that may be tracked, but the revolvers all are assumed to be with the same bank and have the same participants.

- The 6 reports below all have the same basic format with the difference between the reports being the selection and sequence of information.

- Average revolvers can be displayed for any time frame.
- Confirmation letters are automatically generated for new or maturing revolvers.

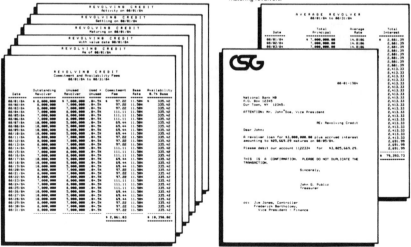

Reprinted with permission of Capital Systems Group, Inc. All rights reserved.

Exhibit 12

DAILY CASH WORKSHEET
MODULE EXAMPLE

■ **CASH WORKSHEET** provides a 'calc' oriented capability integrated into the system. This module functions in a similar way to the most popular spreadsheet packages, the difference being its ability to read selected databases.

■ The primary function of this module is to provide a mechanism for easily verifying yesterday's cash position at all of the key reporting banks and to forecast today's position at those same institutions.

■ The other functions within the worksheet are designed to perform simplified analysis and reporting capabilities.

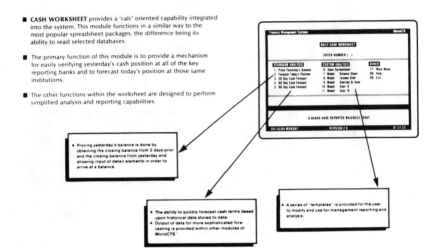

● Proving yesterday's balance is done by obtaining the closing balance from 2 days prior and the closing balance from yesterday and allowing input of detail elements in order to arrive at a balance.

● The ability to quickly forecast cash terms based upon historical data stored to date.
● Output of data for more sophisticated forecasting is provided within other modules of MicroCTS.

● A series of "templates" is provided for the user to modify and use for management reporting and analysis.

■ The **CASH WORKSHEET** has the ability to handle 1200 "cells" or 24 columns by 50 rows. The arrow keys move the cursor throughout the matrix.

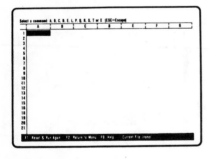

■ The 22 commands provided in the **CASH WORKSHEET** enable the computation of simple as well as complex values:

A	Average of a row or column
B	Blank out current cell
C	Compute (+, -, *, /) any 2 cells
D	Clear any area of the matrix
E	Equation input routine
L	Load or overlay a model and/or data
P	Print any area of the matrix
Q	Equate/recalculate entire matrix
R	Replicate value, data, calculations, labels
S	Save a model and/or data
T	Total any row/column & store in any location
X	Explain the above commands
XXX ...	A series of built-in financial functions
>	Go to any location in matrix
INS ...	Insert a new row or column
DEL ...	Delete an existing row or column
ESC ...	Escape from current action
F1	Erase current matrix & start again
F2	Go back to menu
F9	Help
PgUp ..	Move down 22 lines from current position
PgDn ..	Move up 22 lines from current position

■ The **CASH WORKSHEET** provides the capability to merge one or more models as well as combine data from multiple files into a single model.

■ The replicate command allows for the duplication of a value or calculation over a range with the option to adjust all calculations/equations or not.

Reprinted with permission of Capital Systems Group, Inc. All rights reserved.

Exhibit 13

**WIRE TRANSFER
MODULE EXAMPLE**

■ **WIRE TRANSFER** is designed to provide an automated mechanism for preparing wire transfer requests on your microcomputer and then using **COMMUNICATIONS** to electronically transmit these instructions to a financial institution for further disposition.

■ Only Repetitive Transfers are captured here. Free Form transfers are handled directly by the **COMMUNICATIONS** module.

■ **WIRE TRANSFER** is a highly secured module with a password required to gain access to the module, creation of a line sheet, and creation of a wire transfer file.

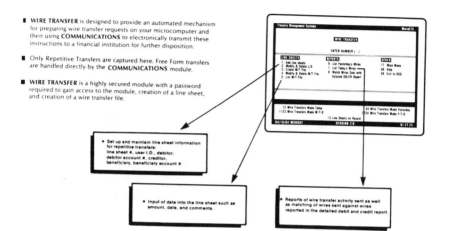

- Set up and maintain line sheet information for repetitive transfers: line sheet #, user I.D., debtor, debtor account #, creditor, beneficiary, beneficiary account #

- Input of data into the line sheet such as amount, date, and comments.

- Reports of wire transfer activity sent as well as matching of wires sent against wires reported in the detailed debit and credit report.

■ 3 reports are provided to track outgoing wire transfer initiation requests.

■ **WIRE TRANSFER** module prepares a repetitive transfer in 2 parts. First a line sheet is set up and second the detailed instructions are entered.

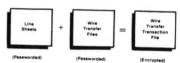

Line Sheets (Passworded) + Wire Transfer Files (Passworded) = Wire Transfer Transaction File (Encrypted)

■ Passwords and file encryption are used to secure the sensitive information.

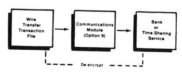

Wire Transfer Transaction File → Communications Module (Option 9) → Bank or Time Sharing Service

De-encrypt

Exhibit 14

**RELATIONSHIP
MANAGEMENT
MODULE EXAMPLE**

- **BANK RELATIONSHIPS** is designed to be the information focal point of each key banking relationship.
- The data captured is useful in day to day dealings with the banks as well as for top management reporting.

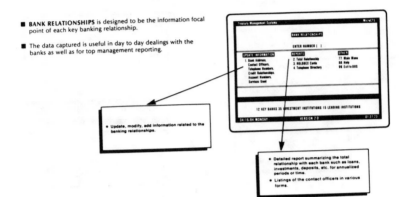

- Update, modify, add information related to the banking relationships.

- Detailed report summarizing the total relationship with each bank such as loans, investments, deposits, etc. for annualized periods of time.
- Listings of the contact officers in various forms.

- The **RELATIONSHIP** report is designed to provide a total snapshot of a key banking relationship. This report is useful to top management and in dealing with the bank calling officers.

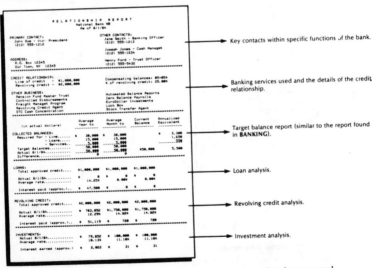

Key contacts within specific functions of the bank.

Banking services used and the details of the credit relationship.

Target balance report (similar to the report found in BANKING).

Loan analysis.

Revolving credit analysis.

Investment analysis.

Exhibit 15

FLASH REPORT
MODULE EXAMPLE

■ **FLASH REPORT** is a multi-purpose module, providing a one-page summary of significant facts about the company and its financial structure.

■ The data contained in this module is a summary of all of the financial data accumulated by the other modules of the system.

■ This is a top management oriented report that can summarize the entire firm at any point in time.

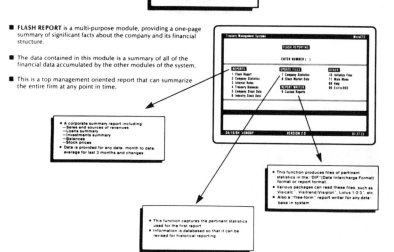

■ Comparative report. Information is displayed for the current day, gross month-to-date volumes which are compared to the daily averages for the previous months, and current month averages per day compared to the previous months.

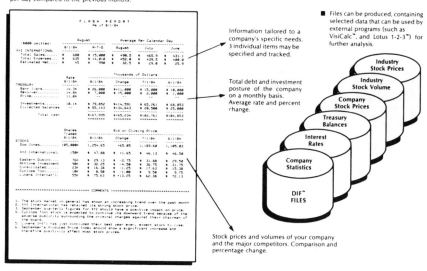

Reprinted with permission of Capital Systems Group, Inc. All rights reserved.

Exhibit 16

> **COMMUNICATIONS MODULE EXAMPLE**

■ **COMMUNICATIONS** provides for the electronic link between the user and any ASC II - based system.

- BALANCE REPORTING SERVICES
- WIRE TRANSFER SERVICES
- TIME-SHARING SERVICES
- IN-HOUSE MAINFRAME COMPUTERS
- OTHER MICROCOMPUTERS

Pull Information Down / Move Information Up

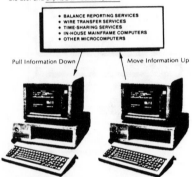

■ **COMMUNICATIONS** requires the use of any 'intelligent' modem - one which is capable of receiving instructions from the computer. Speed is 300 or 1200 baud.

■ Built-in **COMMUNICATIONS** capabilities designed to simplify and streamline the treasurer's communication process include:

DAILY CALL SEQUENCE
- Will call a series of predefined banks or services, one after the other, and execute the commands stored for that bank or service in a totally unattended mode.
- If a service is unavailable or the communications sequence abnormally terminates then the next bank or service in the sequence is automatically called.

AUTOMATIC DIALING
- Will call a single bank or service and execute the commands stored for that bank or service in a totally unattended mode.
- Useful for recalling a bank previously unavailable under daily call sequence.
- Particulary helpful in transmitting wire transfer instructions to the bank.

FREE-FORM DIALING
- Turns the computer into an 'intelligent' terminal.
- All communications parameters are set up for the user.
- Commands are typed into the keyboard in a real-time environment.

■ Unlimited number of banks or services that you can communicate with.

■ One time set-up of data necessary for automatic communications:

■ A communications "Language" provides for complete flexibility in performing the communications steps neded by the treasurer. When encountered during automatic **COMMUNICATION** the following designated activity will occur:

CONTROL COMMANDS (Designated by the * sign)
* COMMAND: ### - Sends any single ASC II code over the communication line (useful for characters that can't be generated by the keyboard)
* PROMPT: ### - Looks for this prompt character sent by host that is used key the transmission of the next command in the sequence.
* SETWAIT: ## - Number of seconds to wait before sending the next command in the sequence if no prompt character is sent.
* FILE: ###### - Transmit the designated file to a receiving computer.
* ########## - Any command that will be accepted by an 'intelligent' modem.

DEVICE COMMANDS¹ (Designated by the % sign)
%F1 = Stop communications, run this process again
%F2 = Stop communications, return to menu
%F3 = Turn screen on
%F4 = Turn screen off
%F5 = Turn printer on
%F6 = Turn printer off
%F7 = Turn on file to store communication session
%F8 = Turn off file storing communication session
%F9 = Display help commands at any time
%F10 = Suspends automatic command processing and allows keyboard input until F10 is hit again, when sequence continues.

¹ F3 thru F10 can be activated automatically during any session.

Exhibit 17

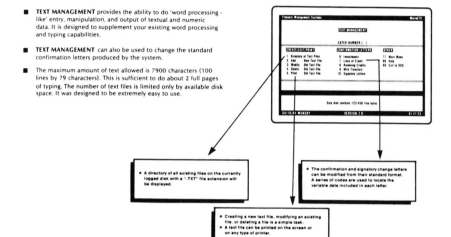

TEXT MANAGEMENT MODULE EXAMPLE

- **TEXT MANAGEMENT** provides the ability to do 'word processing - like' entry, manipulation, and output of textual and numeric data. It is designed to supplement your existing word processing and typing capabilities.

- **TEXT MANAGEMENT** can also be used to change the standard confirmation letters produced by the system.

- The maximum amount of text allowed is 7900 characters (100 lines by 79 characters). This is sufficient to do about 2 full pages of typing. The number of text files is limited only by available disk space. It was designed to be extremely easy to use.

- A directory of all existing files on the currently logged disk with a ".TXT" file extension will be displayed.

- The confirmation and signatory change letters can be modified from their standard format. A series of codes are used to locate the variable data included in each letter.

- Creating a new text file, modifying an existing file, or deleting a file is a simple task.
- A text file can be printed on the screen or on any type of printer.

- The **TEXT MANAGEMENT** module has the ability to handle 5 screen pages of text. Input and editing is straightforward and easy to use.

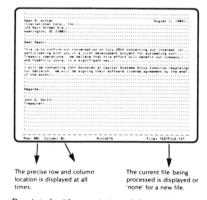

The precise row and column location is displayed at all times.

The current file being processed is displayed or 'none' for a new file.

- The 15 commands provided in the **TEXT MANAGEMENT** module enable you to perform a variety of text and tabular manipulations:

F1	Erase current page(s) and start again
F2	Go back to menu
F3	Load an existing document
F4	Save the current document
F5	Mark a block of text (begin)
F6	Mark a block of text (end)
F7	Justify (right & left) text
F8	Go to END or BEGINNING of document
F9	Help
INS . . .	Insert any amount of text at the current cursor location
DEL . . .	Delete any amount of text starting at the current location and ending when you hit DEL again
PgUp . .	Move up one page (23 lines) of text
PgDn . .	Move down one page (23 lines) of text
HOME .	Move to upper left corner of screen
END . . .	Move to lower right corner of screen

Reprinted with permission of Capital Systems Group, Inc. All rights reserved.

Exhibit 18

> ### ADVANCED GRAPHICS
> ### MODULE EXAMPLE

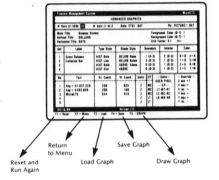

- **ADVANCED GRAPHICS** provides for an easy-to-use method of presenting treasury oriented data in a visual format.

- Line and bar charts in single elements or clusters are available.

- Requires a color graphics adapter card. System uses all standard IBM graphics calls.

- Output to printer is possible through the 'Print Screen' function.

- Graph can be made up of dots, lines, dots & lines, and histograms. Shading can be done above or below each group of elements.

- Up to 4 additional labels can be placed anywhere on the graph.

- Horizontal & vertical grids can be engaged.

- Up to 8 colors.

| | Return to Menu | Save Graph |
| Reset and Run Again | Load Graph | Draw Graph |

- Example of **ADVANCED GRAPHICS** output:

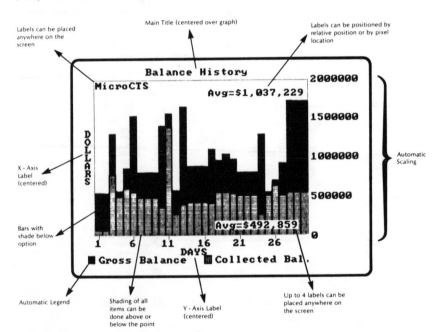

Labels can be placed anywhere on the screen

Main Title (centered over graph)

Labels can be positioned by relative position or by pixel location

X - Axis Label (centered)

Bars with shade below option

Automatic Scaling

Automatic Legend

Shading of all items can be done above or below the point

Y - Axis Label (centered)

Up to 4 labels can be placed anywhere on the screen

Exhibit 19

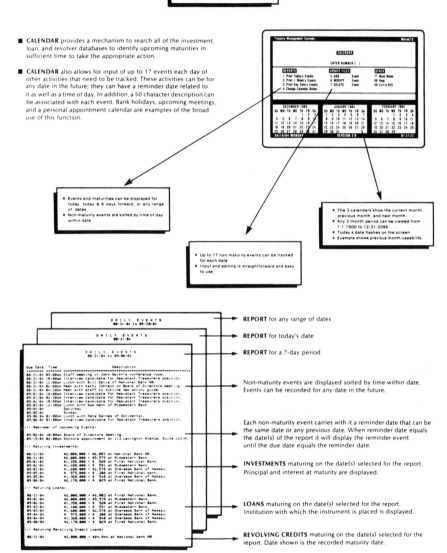

Reprinted with permission of Capital Systems Group, Inc. All rights reserved.

Exhibit 20

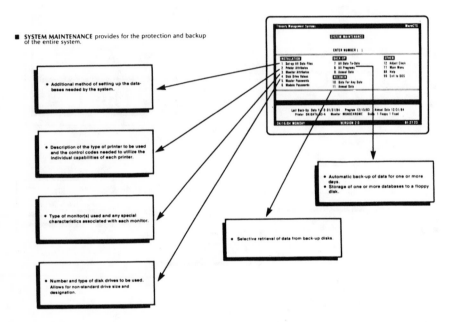

SYSTEM MAINTENANCE MODULE EXAMPLE

■ **SYSTEM MAINTENANCE** provides for the protection and backup of the entire system.

- Additional method of setting up the databases needed by the system.

- Description of the type of printer to be used and the control codes needed to utilize the individual capabilities of each printer.

- Automatic back-up of data for one or more days.
- Storage of one or more databases to a floppy disk.

- Type of monitor(s) used and any special characteristics associated with each monitor.

- Selective retrieval of data from back-up disks.

- Number and type of disk drives to be used. Allows for non-standard drive size and designation.

■ Security is a fundamental element of MicroCTS™

(R) Required (O) Optional (N) Not Required	SIGN-ON	1 DAILY BANKING MODULE	2 INVEST-MENT MODULE	3 LOANS MODULE	4 REVOLV-ING CREDIT MODULE	5 CASH WORK-SHEET MODULE	6 WIRE TRANS-FER MODULE	7 RELA-TIONSHIP MODULE	8 FLASH REPORT MODULE	9 COMMU-NICA-TIONS MODULE	10 TEXT MGMT. MODULE	11 GRAPHICS MODULE	12 CALEN-DAR MODULE	13 MAIN-TENANCE MODULE
PRIMARY PASSWORD	O	O	O	O	O	O	R	O	O	O	O	O	O	R
SECONDARY PASSWORD	N	N	N	N	N	N	R	N	N	O	N	N	N	R
TERTIARY PASSWORD	N	N	N	N	N	N	O	N	N	N	N	N	N	O
FILE ENCRYPTION	N	N	N	N	N	N	R	N	N	N	N	N	N	R

Reprinted with permission of Capital Systems Group, Inc. All rights reserved.

Support Services

Because of the complexity of most automated treasury management systems, there is a strong need for support services. Exhibit 21 shows the kind of components needed by the purchaser of an automated corporate treasury management system. These services are usually provided by a combination of bank and vendor activities.

Exhibit 21

COMPONENTS OF A COMPREHENSIVE SUPPORT PROGRAM

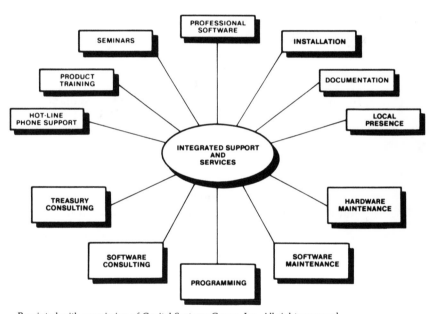

Reprinted with permission of Capital Systems Group, Inc. All rights reserved.

How to Choose an Automated Treasury Management System

Most automated treasury systems seem to offer generally the same features. How then do you go about choosing the system that is right for your corporation?

Here's what you should do:

1. **Define your treasury's needs.** Start by enumerating what your operation does on a daily basis. From this list of tasks or activities, select those that you feel could be done better or faster and those that are most important to you. From this reduced list, describe what you think is the solution or method of handling this task: people, computerization, etc. Segregate them as to "critical today" and "not as critical." You now should have a list of tasks that you perform which could potentially benefit from some type of automated treasury management system.

2. **Identify potential systems.** There are a great number of systems available from a variety of sources. Several publications provide listings of available software and functional descriptions on a regular basis. Compare your list against those publications' lists to determine the systems that will meet your minimum "critical today" needs. Contact those vendors or banks and ask for a detailed description of their systems. Do a further comparison against your list of needs and eliminate those systems that are inappropriate; now you should have a second list of "qualified" systems.

3. **Review potential systems.** Obtain a detailed presentation of each "qualified" system. Ensure that the presentation covers your "needs" list defined earlier. Look beyond the "quality" of the presentation to the actual functionality of the system and how it will satisfy your "needs" list. Eliminate from your "qualified" list any systems that fall short of your "needs."

4. **Operational considerations.** From the list of systems, determine how they will work in your particular environment:

   - Can they communicate with your: PC hardware, modem, balance reporting banks, wire transfer banks, and other services?
   - Can they transmit and accept your forms of information: balance data, wire transfer data, other data forms?
   - Can they automatically "parse" all forms of information received and database it?
   - Can they allow manipulation of the databased information in a variety of ways?
   - How are other data entered into the system?
   - Where will support and service come from? How long will it take to get assistance?

5. **Balance criteria.** You should obtain the exact cost of all systems to: obtain, install, support, and enhance. What are the payment options: cash, balances, lease, etc.? Insist upon

some trial period for use of the software or some other mechanism so you are not locked in.

6. **References.** Contact at least one corporation that is using the systems you are considering. Ascertain their success with implementing the system.

7. **Decide on a system and then buy it!** If you have followed the above recommendations, you will have identified the appropriate system for your needs. Automation of your treasury operation can yield benefits to you only after you have started.

CONCLUSION

Microcomputers in the treasurer's office can provide a substantial benefit in people productivity and enhancing the timing and quality of decision making. These benefits can be realized by the vast majority of treasury operations, large and small. Some type of automation should be "standard" in most treasury operations by the latter part of the 1980s.

Automated treasury management systems will continuously evolve as hardware and software technology changes.

SECTION IV

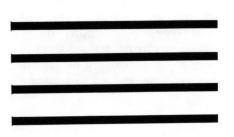

Investing Short-Term Funds

10

Taxable Money Market Instruments

Marcia Stigum, Ph.D.
Stigum & Associates

In the previous three sections of this book, techniques for cash collection, concentration, and disbursement were discussed. In the four chapters of Section IV of this book, we focus on the investment of excess cash in short-term instruments.

In this chapter, taxable money market instruments that would be appropriate for a corporate short-term portfolio are described. In the next chapter, tax-exempt short-term obligations are described. Techniques for managing a corporate short-term portfolio are discussed in Chapter 12. Chapter 13 explains how interest-rate futures and options can be utilized by the manager of a corporate short-term portfolio.

OVERVIEW OF THE MONEY MARKET

The U.S. money market is a huge and significant part of the nation's financial system in which banks and other participants trade hundreds of billions of dollars every working day. Where those billions go and the prices at which they are traded affect how the U.S. government finances its debt, how business finances its expansion, and how consumers choose to spend or save.

The money market is a wholesale market for low-risk, highly liquid, short-term IOUs. It is a market for various sorts of debt securities rather than equities. The stock in trade of the market includes a large chunk of the U.S. Treasury's debt and billions of dollars worth of federal agency securities, negotiable bank certificates of

194

deposit, bankers' acceptances, municipal notes, and commercial paper. Within the confines of the money market each day, banks—both domestic and foreign—actively trade in multimillion-dollar blocks billions of dollars of federal funds and Eurodollars, and banks and nonbank dealers are each day the recipients of billions of dollars of secured loans through what is called the "repo market." State and municipal governments also finance part of their activities in this market.

TREASURY BILLS

Treasury bills (known more familiarly as T bills or bills) represent about 40 percent of the total marketable securities issued by the Treasury. These securities are held widely by financial business firms, nonfinancial corporations, and, to some extent, by individuals. Nevertheless, despite their huge volume and wide distribution among different investor groups, T bills were relatively unknown to the average investor until the late 1960s, when the growing disparity between bill yields and savings deposit rates began drawing small investors into the bill market.

All T bills are negotiable, noninterest-bearing securities with an original maturity of 1 year or less—usually 13, 26, or 52 weeks. Bills are currently offered by the Treasury in denominations of $10,000, $15,000, $50,000, $100,000, $500,000, and $1 million. Bills used to be issued by the Treasury in the form of *bearer certificates.* Accordingly, to prove ownership of a bill, the owner had to produce it. The Treasury and the Federal Reserve System then made it possible to hold bills in *book-entry form.* Since 1977 the Treasury has offered bills *only* in book-entry form.

Bills are always issued at a discount from face value, and the amount of the discount is determined in bill auctions held by the Fed each time the Treasury issues new bills. At maturity, bills are redeemed by the Treasury for full face value. Thus investors in bills earn returns because they receive more for the bills at maturity than they paid for them at issue. This return is treated for federal tax purposes as ordinary interest income and, as such, is subject to full federal taxation at ordinary rates; it is, however, specifically *exempt* from state and local taxation.

In addition to normal bill issues, the Treasury periodically issues *tax-anticipation bills.* TABs, as they are called, are special-issue T bills that mature on corporate quarterly income tax payment dates and can be used at face value by corporations to pay their tax liabilities.

Determining the Yield on Bills

Bill dealers measure yield on a *bank discount basis;* that is, they quote yield as the percentage amount of the discount on an annualized basis. As an illustration, consider an investor who buys a bill maturing in one year at a price of $9,300 for each $10,000 of face value. The discount on this bill is $700, so yield on a bank discount basis works out to be 7 percent ($700/ $10,000). In general, the formula for the yield on a bank discount basis for a bill *maturing in one year* is as follows.[1]

$$d = \frac{D}{F}$$

where

d = yield on a bank discount basis
F = face value in dollars
D = discount from face value in dollars

Alternatively, if the price in dollars is known, d can be calculated as follows:

$$d = \left(1 - \frac{P}{F}\right)$$

where

P = price in dollars

On a bill maturing in less than one year, the discount is earned more quickly. So to get the correct annualized yield on a bank discount basis, the two general formulas above are modified as follows:

$$d = \left(\frac{D}{F}\right)\frac{360}{t_{sm}} \text{ or } \left(1 - \frac{P}{F}\right)\frac{360}{t_{sm}}$$

where

t_{sm} = number of days from settlement to maturity

Thus, if the bill selling at $9,300 had 300 days from settlement to maturity, the annual yield on a bank discount basis would be 8.4 percent, found as follows:

$$d = \left(\frac{\$700}{\$10,000}\right)\frac{360}{300} = 8.4 \text{ percent}$$

---

[1] The formulas presented in this section are derived in Marcia Stigum, *Money Market Calculations: Yields, Break-Evens, and Arbitrage* (Homewood, Ill.: Dow Jones-Irwin, 1981).

or equivalently,

$$d = \left(\frac{\$9,300}{1 - \$10,000}\right) \frac{360}{300} = 8.4 \text{ percent}$$

The simple annual interest rate that an investor earns by buying a bill is found as follows:

$$i = \left(\frac{D}{P}\right) \frac{365}{t_{sm}}$$

where

i = equivalent simple interest yield

For example, the bill with 300 days from settlement to maturity and which can be purchased for $9,300 for each $10,000 of face value would have an equivalent simple interest yield of 9.16 percent, as shown below:

$$i = \left(\frac{\$700}{\$9,300}\right) \frac{365}{300} = 9.16 \text{ percent}$$

Alternatively, given the yield on a bank discount basis (d), the equivalent simple interest yield can be computed using the following formula:

$$i = \frac{365d}{360 - dt_{sm}}$$

Applying this formula to our example and recalling that the yield on a bank discount basis is 8.4 percent, we find

$$i = \frac{365\,(0.084)}{360 - 0.084\,(300)} = 9.16 \text{ percent}$$

Notice that the yield on a bank discount basis understates the equivalent simple interest rate that an investor would realize by holding a bill. This holds for all securities offered on a discounted basis. Moreover, as Exhibit 1 shows, the discrepancy between the two rates is greater the higher the rate of discount (i.e., higher the yield on a bank discount basis) and the longer the time to maturity.

In the secondary market, bids for and offerings of coupon securities are quoted not in terms of yields (as in the case of

Exhibit 1
Comparisons at Different Rates and Maturities
between Rates of Discount and the Equivalent
Simple Interest Rates on a 365-Day-Year Basis

Rate of Discount (Percent)	Equivalent Simple Interest (Percent)		
	30-Day Maturity	182-Day Maturity	364-Day Maturity
4	4.07	4.14	4.23
6	6.11	6.27	6.48
8	8.17	8.45	8.82
10	10.22	10.68	11.27
12	12.29	12.95	13.84
14	14.36	15.28	16.53
16	16.44	17.65	19.35

discount securities) but in terms of dollar prices.[2] On a coupon quote sheet, however, there is always a number for each security stating what its yield to maturity would be if it were purchased at the quoted asked or offered price. However, the yield to maturity figure on a quote sheet for coupon securities *understates* the effective yield to maturity because it ignores the fact that interest is paid *semiannually*; that is, whatever investors do with coupon interest, it is worth something to them to get semiannual interest payments rather than a single year-end interest payment.

In converting the yield on a discount security to an add-on interest rate, various approaches are possible. One is to convert to an equivalent simple interest rate as explained above. However, in putting together quote sheets, "the street" takes a slightly different tack. *It restates yields on discount securities on a basis that makes them comparable to the yield to maturity quoted on coupon securities.* A rate so computed is called a *coupon yield equivalent* or *equivalent bond yield*.

"The street's" decision to restate bill yields on a coupon yield equivalent basis creates a need to distinguish between discount securities that have 6 months (182 days) or less to run and those that have more than 6 months to run. When a coupon security is on its last leg (i.e., when it will mature on the next coupon date and thus offers no opportunity for further compounding), its stated yield to maturity equals its yield on a simple interest basis. For this reason, *on discount securities with 6 months or less to run, equivalent bond yield is taken to be the equivalent simple interest rate offered by the instrument.* Letting d_b equal the equivalent bond

---

[2] An exception is municipal bonds.

yield, then d_b can be found from the rate of discount (d), or the yield on a bank discount basis, by the following formula:

$$d_b = \frac{365d}{360 - dt_{sm}}$$

However, when a discount security has more than six months to maturity, the equivalent bond yield, denoted d_b', is computed by the following formula:

$$d_b' = \frac{\left(\dfrac{-2t_{sm}}{365}\right) + 2 \sqrt{\left(\dfrac{t_{sm}}{365}\right)^2 - \left(\dfrac{2t_{sm}}{365} - 1\right)\left(1 - \dfrac{1}{P}\right)}}{\dfrac{2t_{sm}}{365} - 1}$$

where

P = price per $1 of face value

To illustrate how to use the foregoing formula for a bill with more than 6 months to run, consider a bill with an asked price of 95.0653 percent of face value and 190 days to run. The equivalent bond yield is 9.95 percent as shown below:

$$d_b' = \frac{\left[\dfrac{-2(190)}{365}\right] + 2 \sqrt{\left(\dfrac{190}{365}\right)^2 - \left(\dfrac{2(190)}{365} - 1\right)\left(1 - \dfrac{1}{0.950653}\right)}}{\dfrac{2(190)}{365} - 1}$$

= 9.95 percent

Bill Quotes

Exhibit 2 reproduces Discount Corporation's T bill quote sheet for Friday, April 6, 1979. Notice that the quotes are closing rates on Thursday, April 5, and the assumed settlement date is regular settlement on Monday, April 9. The bid and asked price are quoted in terms of a "rate of discount," which is the same as the yield on a bank discount basis discussed earlier. The coupon equivalent yield (or bond equivalent yield) for each bill is also shown on the quote sheet.

Of particular interest on the quote sheet is the column "Value of 0.01 Per M." Investors and dealers in bills would like to know how much the price of a given bill would fluctuate if its yield changes by one basis point. The column shows the change in the price of the bill for a one-basis-point change per $1 million of

Exhibit 2
Bill Quotes from a Dealer's Quote Sheet for Use on April 6, 1979

DISCOUNT CORPORATION OF NEW YORK

58 Pine Street, New York, N.Y. 10005
Telephone 212-248-8900 • WUI Telex 620863 Discorp • WU Telex 125675 Discorp - NYK

QUOTATIONS FOR U.S. TREASURY SECURITIES	
Closing	APR. 5, 1979
Ylds. for Dely.	APR. 9, 1979

U. S. TREASURY BILLS(1)

Issue	Days to Mat.	Rate of Discount Bid	Asked	Chge.	Coupon Yield Equiv.	Value of .01 Per M	Amount of Issue ($ millions)
4/12/79	3	9.85	9.75	---	9.89	.83	6201
4/19/79	10	9.85	9.75	---	9.91	2.78	14200
4/26/79	17	9.85	9.75	---	9.93	4.72	12205
5/01/79	22	9.55	9.45	+ .05	9.64	6.11	3022
5/03/79	24	9.50	9.40	---	9.59	6.67	6300
5/10/79	31	9.60	9.50	- .05	9.71	8.61	6207
5/17/79	38	9.65	9.55	---	9.78	10.56	6200
5/24/79	45	9.65	9.55	---	9.80	12.50	5900
5/29/79	50	9.65	9.55	---	9.81	13.89	2477
5/31/79	52	9.65	9.55	---	9.82	14.44	5900
6/07/79	59	9.65	9.55	+ .05	9.84	16.39	5800
6/14/79	66	9.65	9.55	+ .05	9.86	18.33	5900
6/21/79	73	9.65	9.55	---	9.87	20.28	5800
6/26/79	78	9.65	9.55	---	9.89	21.67	2781
6/28/79	80	9.50	9.40	---	9.73	22.22	5900
7/05/79 ##	87	9.50	9.46	- .01	9.82	24.17	5900
7/12/79	94	9.54	9.50	- .01	9.88	26.11	2900
7/19/79	101	9.54	9.50	- .02	9.90	28.06	2900
7/24/79	106	9.57	9.53	- .05	9.94	29.44	3377
7/26/79	108	9.56	9.52	+ .02	9.94	30.00	3000

Issue	Days to Mat.	Rate of Discount Bid	Asked	Chge.	Coupon Yield Equiv.	Value of .01 Per M	Amount of Issue ($ millions)
8/02/79	115	9.49	9.45	---	9.88	31.94	3000
8/09/79	122	9.52	9.48	+ .03	9.93	33.89	3000
8/16/79	129	9.50	9.46	+ .01	9.93	35.83	2900
8/21/79	134	9.48	9.44	- .02	9.92	37.22	3539
8/23/79	136	9.50	9.46	---	9.95	37.78	3001
8/30/79	143	9.48	9.44	- .02	9.94	39.72	4001
9/06/79	150	9.45	9.41	- .01	9.93	41.67	3001
9/13/79	157	9.46	9.42	---	9.96	43.61	3000
9/18/79	162	9.44	9.40	- .01	9.95	45.00	3348
9/20/79	164	9.45	9.41	---	9.97	45.56	3001
9/27/79	171	9.43	9.39	- .02	9.96	47.50	3000
10/04/79 ##	178	9.40	9.36	- .01	9.95	49.44	3003
10/16/79	190	9.39	9.35	- .02	9.95	52.78	3469
11/13/79	218	9.38	9.34	---	9.96	60.56	3893
12/11/79	246	9.34	9.30	- .02	9.94	68.33	4023
1/08/80	274	9.29	9.25	- .02	9.92	76.11	3698
2/05/80	302	9.28	9.24	- .02	9.96	83.89	3536
3/04/80	330	9.18	9.14	- .02	9.90	91.67	3320
4/01/80 ##	358	9.18	9.14	---	9.95	99.44	3343

Source: Marcia Stigum, *Money Market Calculations: Yields, Break-Evens, and Arbitrage* (Homewood, Ill.: Dow Jones-Irwin, 1981), p. 30.

face value of bills. Exhibit 3 gives these values for discount securities that mature from 1 to 365 days.[3]

FEDERAL AGENCY DISCOUNT NOTES

From time to time Congress becomes concerned about the volume of credit that is available to various sectors of the economy and the terms on which that credit is available. Its usual response is to set up a federal agency to provide credit to that sector. Thus, for example, there is the Federal Home Loan Bank System, which lends to the nation's savings and loan associations as well as regulates them; the Government National Mortgage Association, which funnels money into the mortgage market; the Banks for Cooperatives, which make seasonal and term loans to farm cooperatives; the Federal Land Banks, which give mortgages on farm properties; the Federal Intermediate Credit Banks, which provide short-term financing for producers of crops and livestock; and a host of other agencies.

In addition to selling coupon securities, the Federal Home Loan Bank, the farm credit agencies, and Fannie Mae all borrow short term by issuing noninterest-bearing discount notes, which resemble Treasury bills.

These notes are sold through dealers who get an 05 for their efforts. An agency selling notes will decide what rate to offer on its notes after conferring with dealers in its selling group about market conditions. Some post rates all the time but post competitive rates only when they want to sell. Agencies invest any excess funds they raise through the sale of discount notes in repurchase agreements (RP or repos). That's a negative carry for them so they are careful not to raise more short-term money than they need.

Outstanding agency discount paper is traded less actively than bills are, and it is somewhat less liquid than bills. When the agencies are writing a lot of new paper, the dealers will bid for old paper to get customers to swap into new paper, and activity in the secondary market for such paper picks up. At other times, when the agencies are not writing, activity dries up. A dealer will always give retail a bid on old paper but getting an offer out of a dealer may be more difficult because, to supply old paper, a

---

[3] The formula used to find the "value of an 0.01 per $1 million" face value on a discount security is

$$V_{0.01} = 0.0001(1,000,000) \left(\frac{t_{sm}}{360} \right)$$

Exhibit 3
Value of an 01 (0.01 Percent) per $1 Million

Days to mat.	.01% equiv.	Days to mat.	.01% equiv.	Days to mat.	.01% equiv.	Days to mat.	.01% equiv.	Days to mat.	.01% equiv.	Days to mat.	.01% equiv.
1	$ .28	31	$8.61	61	$16.94	91	$25.28	121	$33.61	151	$41.94
2	.56	32	8.89	62	17.22	92	25.56	122	33.89	152	42.22
3	.83	33	9.17	63	17.50	93	25.83	123	34.17	153	42.50
4	1.11	34	9.44	64	17.78	94	26.11	124	34.44	154	42.78
5	1.39	35	9.72	65	18.06	95	26.39	125	34.72	155	43.06
6	1.67	36	10.00	66	18.33	96	26.67	126	35.00	156	43.33
7	1.94	37	10.28	67	18.61	97	26.94	127	35.28	157	43.61
8	2.22	38	10.56	68	18.89	98	27.22	128	35.56	158	43.89
9	2.50	39	10.83	69	19.17	99	27.50	129	35.83	159	44.17
10	2.78	40	11.11	70	19.44	100	27.78	130	36.11	160	44.44
11	3.06	41	11.39	71	19.72	101	28.06	131	36.39	161	44.72
12	3.33	42	11.67	72	20.00	102	28.33	132	36.67	162	45.00
13	3.61	43	11.94	73	20.28	103	28.61	133	36.94	163	45.28
14	3.89	44	12.22	74	20.56	104	28.89	134	37.22	164	45.56
15	4.17	45	12.50	75	20.83	105	29.17	135	37.50	165	45.83
16	4.44	46	12.78	76	21.11	106	29.44	136	37.78	166	46.11
17	4.72	47	13.06	77	21.39	107	29.72	137	38.06	167	46.39
18	5.00	48	13.33	78	21.67	108	30.00	138	38.33	168	46.67
19	5.28	49	13.61	79	21.94	109	30.28	139	38.61	169	46.94
20	5.56	50	13.89	80	22.22	110	30.56	140	38.89	170	47.22
21	5.83	51	14.17	81	22.50	111	30.83	141	39.17	171	47.50
22	6.11	52	14.44	82	22.78	112	31.11	142	39.44	172	47.78
23	6.39	53	14.72	83	23.06	113	31.39	143	39.72	173	48.06
24	6.67	54	15.00	84	23.33	114	31.67	144	40.00	174	48.33
25	6.94	55	15.28	85	23.61	115	31.94	145	40.28	175	48.61
26	7.22	56	15.56	86	23.89	116	32.22	146	40.56	176	48.89
27	7.50	57	15.83	87	24.17	117	32.50	147	40.83	177	49.17
28	7.78	58	16.11	88	24.44	118	32.78	148	41.11	178	49.44
29	8.06	59	16.39	89	24.72	119	33.06	149	41.39	179	49.72
30	8.33	60	16.67	90	25.00	120	33.33	150	41.67	180	50.00

Value of an 01 per $1 million $= \left(\dfrac{0.01\% \times t}{360}\right)$ $1 million

where t = days to maturity

Source: Marcia Stigum, *Money Market Calculations: Yields, Break-Evens, and Arbitrage* (Homewood, Ill.: Dow Jones-Irwin, 1981).

dealer must go out to an account that has the paper and try to bid it away.

Agency discount notes trade at a spread over bills. This spread, which can be anything from 5 to 100 basis points, tends to rise when agencies write a lot of paper and when money tightens.

COMMERCIAL PAPER

Commercial paper, whoever the issuer and whatever the precise form it takes, is an unsecured promissory note with a

Days to mat.	.01% equiv.	Days to mat	.01% equiv.	Days to mat.	.01% equiv.	Days to mat.	.01% equiv.	Days to mat.	.01% equiv.	Days to mat.	.01% equiv.
181	$50.28	212	$58.89	243	$67.50	274	$76.11	305	$84.72	336	$93.33
182	50.56	213	59.17	244	67.78	275	76.39	306	85.00	337	93.61
183	50.83	214	59.44	245	68.06	276	76.67	307	85.28	338	93.89
184	51.11	215	59.72	246	68.33	277	76.94	308	85.56	339	94.17
185	51.39	216	60.00	247	68.61	278	77.22	309	85.83	340	94.44
186	51.67	217	60.28	248	68.89	279	77.50	310	86.11	341	94.72
187	51.94	218	60.56	249	69.17	280	77.78	311	86.39	342	95.00
188	52.22	219	60.83	250	69.44	281	78.06	312	86.67	343	95.28
189	52.50	220	61.11	251	69.72	282	78.33	313	86.94	344	95.56
190	52.78	221	61.39	252	70.00	283	78.61	314	87.22	345	95.83
191	53.06	222	61.67	253	70.28	284	78.89	315	87.50	346	96.11
192	53.33	223	61.94	254	70.56	285	79.17	316	87.78	347	96.39
193	53.61	224	62.22	255	70.83	286	79.44	317	88.06	348	96.67
194	53.89	225	62.50	256	71.11	287	79.72	318	88.33	349	96.94
195	54.17	226	62.78	257	71.39	288	80.00	319	88.61	350	97.22
196	54.44	227	63.06	258	71.67	289	80.28	320	88.89	351	97.50
197	54.72	228	63.33	259	71.94	290	80.56	321	89.17	352	97.78
198	55.00	229	63.61	260	72.22	291	80.83	322	89.44	353	98.06
199	55.28	230	63.89	261	72.50	292	81.11	323	89.72	354	98.33
200	55.56	231	64.17	262	72.78	293	81.39	324	90.00	355	98.61
201	55.83	232	64.44	263	73.06	294	81.67	325	90.28	356	98.89
202	56.11	233	64.72	264	73.33	295	81.94	326	90.56	357	99.17
203	56.39	234	65.00	265	73.61	296	82.22	327	90.83	358	99.44
204	56.67	235	65.28	266	73.89	297	82.50	328	91.11	359	99.72
205	56.94	236	65.56	267	74.17	298	82.78	329	91.39	360	100.00
206	57.22	237	65.83	268	74.44	299	83.06	330	91.67	361	100.28
207	57.50	238	66.11	269	74.72	300	83.33	331	91.94	362	100.56
208	57.78	239	66.39	270	75.00	301	83.61	332	92.22	363	100.83
209	58.06	240	66.67	271	75.28	302	83.89	333	92.50	364	101.11
210	58.33	241	66.94	272	75.56	303	84.17	334	92.78	365	101.39
211	58.61	242	67.22	273	75.83	304	84.44	335	93.06	366	101.67

fixed maturity. In plain English, the issuer of commercial paper (the borrower) promises to pay the buyer (the lender) some fixed amount on some future date. But issuers pledge no assets—only liquidity and established earning power—to guarantee that they will make good on their promises to pay. Traditionally, commercial paper resembled in form a Treasury bill; it was a negotiable, noninterest-bearing note issued at a discount from face value and redeemed at maturity for full face value. Today, however, a lot of paper is interest bearing. For the investor the major difference between bills and paper is that paper carries some small risk of default because the issuer is a private firm, whereas the risk of default on bills is zero for all intents and purposes.

Firms selling commercial paper frequently expect to roll over their paper as it matures; that is, they plan to get money to pay off maturing paper by issuing new paper. Since there is always the danger that an adverse turn in the paper market might make doing so difficult or inordinately expensive, most paper issuers back their outstanding paper with *bank lines of credit;* they get a promise from a bank or banks to lend them at any time an amount equal to their outstanding paper. Issuers normally pay for this service in one of several ways: by holding at their line banks compensating deposit balances equal to some percentage of their total credit lines; by paying an annual fee equal to some small percentage of their outstanding lines; or through some mix of balances and fees.

Issuers of Paper

The large open market for commercial paper that exists in the United States is a unique feature of the U.S. money market. Its origins trace back to the early 19th century, when firms in need of working capital began using the sale of open-market paper as a substitute for bank loans. Their need to do so resulted largely from the unit banking system adopted in the United States. Elsewhere, it was common for banks to operate branches nationwide, which meant that seasonal demands for credit in one part of the country, perhaps due to the movement of a crop to market, could be met by a transfer of surplus funds from other areas to that area. In the United States, where banks were restricted to a single state and more often to a single location, this was difficult. Thus firms in credit-scarce, high-interest-rate areas started raising funds by selling commercial paper in New York City and other distant financial centers.

For the first 100 years or so, borrowers in the commercial paper market were all nonfinancial business firms: textile mills, wholesale jobbers, railroads, and tobacco companies, to name a few. Most of their paper was placed for a small fee by dealers, and the principal buyers of paper were banks. Then in the 1920s the character of the market began to change. The introduction of autos and other consumer durables vastly increased consumers' demands for short-term credit, and that in turn led to the creation and rapid growth of consumer finance companies.

One of the first large consumer finance companies was the General Motors Acceptance Corporation (GMAC), which financed consumer purchases of General Motors autos. To obtain funds, GMAC ("Gee Mack," in Wall Street argot) began borrowing in the paper market, a practice that other finance companies followed. Another innovation by GMAC was to short-circuit paper dealers and place paper directly with investors, a practice that made sense because GMAC borrowed such large amounts that it could save money by setting up in-house facilities to distribute its paper.

Despite the advent of finance company paper, the paper market shrank during the 1920s, stagnated during the 1930s, and then slumped again during World War II, with the result that by 1945 paper was a relatively unimportant instrument. Since then the volume of commercial paper outstanding has grown steadily and rapidly due both to the tremendous postwar increase in sales of consumer durables and to the long-term upward trend in interest rates. After 1968, when the Federal Reserve began pursuing tight money on a severe and prolonged basis, the growth of commercial paper became nothing short of spectacular.

Today, nonfinancial firms—everything from public utilities to manufacturers to retailers—still issue paper, and their paper, which is referred to as industrial paper, accounts for about 32 percent of all paper outstanding. Such paper is issued, as in the past, to meet seasonal needs for funds and also as a means of interim financing (i.e., to obtain funds to start investment projects that are later permanently funded through the sale of long-term bonds). In contrast to industrial borrowers, finance companies have a continuing need for short-term funds throughout the year; they are now the biggest borrowers in the commercial paper market, accounting for roughly 48 percent of all paper.

In the recent years of tight money, bank holding companies have also joined finance companies as borrowers in the commercial paper market. Many banks are owned by a holding company, an arrangement offering the advantage that the holding company can engage in activities in which the bank itself is not permitted. Commercial paper is sold by bank holding companies primarily to finance their nonbank activities in leasing, real estate, and other lines. However, funds raised through the sale of such paper can also be funneled into the holding company's bank, if the latter is pinched for funds, through various devices, such as the sale of bank assets to the holding company.

Issuing Techniques

All industrial paper is issued through paper dealers. Currently there are eight major paper dealers in the country; their main offices are in financial centers—New York, Chicago, and Boston—but they have branches throughout the country. Also there are a number of smaller regional dealers. Typically, dealers buy up new paper issues directly from the borrower, mark them up, and then resell them to investors. The current going rate of markup is very small, an eighth of 1 percent per annum. Generally, paper issues are for very large amounts, and the minimum round lot in which most dealers sell is $250,000. Thus the dealer market for commercial paper is a meeting ground for big corporate borrowers and for large investors (the latter including financial corporations, nonfinancial corporations, and pension funds).

Finance companies and banks occasionally place their paper through dealers, but most such paper (more than 80 percent) is placed directly by the issuer with investors. A big finance company, for example, might place $1 million or more of paper with an insurance company or with a big industrial firm that had a temporary surplus of funds. In addition to these large-volume transactions, some finance companies and banks also sell paper in relatively small denominations directly to small business firms and individual investors, as will be discussed later in this section.

Paper Maturities

Maturities on commercial paper are generally very short—one to three months being the most common on dealer-placed paper. Generally, dealers prefer not to handle paper with a maturity of less than 30 to 45 days because, on paper of such short maturity, their markup (which is figured on a percent per annum basis) barely covers costs. However, to accommodate established borrowers, they will do so. Paper with a maturity of more than 270 days is rare because issues of such long maturity have to be registered with the SEC.

Finance companies that place their paper directly with large investors generally offer a wide range of maturities—3 to 270 days. Also, they are willing to tailor maturities to the needs of investors and will often accept funds for very short periods, for example, for a weekend. Finance companies that sell low-denomination paper to individual investors generally offer maturities ranging from 30 to 270 days on such paper. These companies also issue longer-maturity short-term notes that have been registered with the SEC.

Paper Yields

Some paper bears interest, but much does not. Investors who buy noninterest-bearing paper get returns on their money because they buy their paper at a discount from face value, whereas the issuer redeems the paper at maturity for full face value. Yields on paper are generally quoted in eighths of 1 percent, for example, at 7⅛ percent per annum. Paper rates, whether the paper is interest-bearing or not, are quoted on a *bank discount basis,* as in the case of bills.

Bill rates vary over time, rising if business demand for credit increases or if the Fed tightens credit, falling in the opposite cases. The yields offered by paper issuers follow much the same pattern of bill yields except that paper yields are, if anything, even more volatile than bill yields.

The reason paper rates fluctuate up and down in step with the yields on bills and other money market securities is simple. Paper competes with these other instruments for investors' dollars. Therefore, as yields on bills and other money market securities rise, paper issuers must offer higher rates in order to sell their paper. In contrast, if bill yields and other short-term rates decline, paper issuers can and do ease the rates they offer.

The volatility of paper rates has important consequences for the investor. First, it means that the attractiveness of paper as an investment medium for short-term funds varies over the interest-rate cycle. It also means that the rate you get on paper bought today tells you relatively little about what rate you would get if you were to roll over that paper at maturity. Paper yields offered in the future may be substantially higher or lower than today's rates, depending on whether money is tightening or easing.

Risk and Ratings

The corporate short-term portfolio manager thinking of buying paper should consider not only the *return* it yields, but also whether there is any *risk* that the issuer will not make timely payment on the paper when it matures. Basically there are two situations in which an issuing company might fail to pay off its maturing paper: (1) It is solvent but lacks cash, and (2) it is insolvent. How great are the chances that either situation will occur?

Since the early 1930s, the default record on commercial paper has been excellent. In the case of dealer paper, one reason is that after the 1920s the many little borrowers who had populated the paper market were replaced by a much smaller number of large, well-established firms. This gave dealers, who were naturally extremely careful about whose paper they handled, the opportunity to examine much more thoroughly the financial condition of each issuer with whom they dealt.

Since 1965 the number of firms issuing at any time a significant quantity of paper to a wide market has increased from 450 to 1,200; of these about 130 are currently non-U.S. borrowers. Only five issuers of commercial paper have failed over the last decade. Three of these five were small domestic finance companies that got caught by tight money; in each case the losses to paper buyers were small, $2–$4 million. The fourth firm that failed was a Canadian finance company that had sold paper in the U.S. market; losses on its paper totaled $35 million. The fifth failure, one that shook the market, was that of the Penn Central, which at the time it went under had $82 million of paper outstanding.

Although the payments record on paper is good, the losses that have occurred make it clear that an individual putting money into paper has the right—more strongly, the responsibility—to ask: How good is the company whose paper I am buying? Because of the investor's very real need for an answer, and because of the considerable time and money involved in obtaining one, rating services have naturally developed. Today a large proportion of dealer and direct paper is rated by one or more of three companies: Standard & Poor's, Moody's, and Fitch.

Paper issuers willingly pay the rating services to examine them and rate their paper, since a good rating makes it easier and cheaper for them to borrow in the paper market. The rating companies, despite the fact that they receive their income from issuers, basically have the interests of the investor at heart for one simple reason: The value of their ratings to investors and thereby their ability to sell rating services to issuers depend on their accuracy. The worth to an issuer of a top rating is the track record of borrowers who have held that rating.

Each rating company sets its own rating standards, but their approaches are similar. Every rating is based on an evaluation of the borrowing company's management and on a detailed study of its earnings record and balance sheet. Just what a rating company looks for depends in part on the borrower's line of business; the optimal balance sheet for a publishing company would look quite different from that of a finance company. Nonetheless, one can say in general that the criteria for a top rating are strong management, a good position in a well-established industry, an upward trend in earnings, adequate liquidity, and the ability to borrow to meet both anticipated and unexpected cash needs.

Since companies seeking a paper rating are rarely in imminent danger of insolvency, the principal focus in rating paper is on *liquidity*—can the borrower come up with cash to pay off the maturing paper? Here what the rating company looks for is ability to borrow elsewhere than in the paper market and especially the ability to borrow short term from banks. Today, for a company to get a paper rating, its paper must be backed by bank lines of credit.

Different rating firms grade borrowers according to different classifications. Standard & Poor's, for example, rates companies from A for highest quality to D for lowest. It also subdivides A-rated companies into three groups according to relative strength, A–1 down to A–3. Fitch rates firms F–1 for highest grade to F–4 for lowest grade. Moody's uses P–1, P–2, and P–3, with P–1 being their highest rating.

What factors separate differently rated borrowers? The answer is suggested by the following requirements a company must meet to get Standard & Poor's ratings

A rating

1. Liquidity ratios are adequate to meet cash requirements.
2. Long-term senior debt rating is A or better; in some instances BBB credits may be allowed if other factors outweigh the BBB.
3. The issuer has access to at least two additional channels of borrowing.
4. Basic earnings and cash flow have an upward trend with allowances made for unusual circumstances.
5. Typically, the issuer's industry is well established, and the issuer should have a strong position within its industry.
6. The reliability and quality of management are unquestioned.

B rating

1. Liquidity ratios are good but not necessarily as high as in the A category.
2. Long-term senior debt rating is no less than BB.

C rating

1. There would be wide swings in liquidity ratios from year to year.
2. Long-term senior debt rating would not be of investment quality.

D rating

Every indication is that the company will shortly be in default.[4]

---

[4] "Corporate Bonds, Commercial Paper, and S&P's Ratings," a talk given by Brenton W. Harries, President, Standard & Poor's Corporation, on May 6, 1971, in Philadelphia, Pennsylvania.

Standard & Poor's has phrased the meanings of its ratings in less formal terms as follows:

"A-1" to us means a company that is overwhelming—a Sears, a Shell Oil, a Union Carbide, GMAC, or an IAC. . . . An "A-2" is a very good credit and basically has no weaknesses. It has a good operating record and is a long-time company; however, it just isn't overwhelming. . . . An "A-3" to us and our department of professional skeptics is a good credit, but generally has one weakness which can range from a company that is growing too fast and constantly needs money to a company that has temporary earnings problems. . . . Our "B" rating . . . is reserved for companies who are relatively young or old and are mediocre to fair credit risks and should use the commercial paper market only during periods of relative easy money. Our "C" rating is reserved for companies who are in serious financial difficulties.[5]

From the above quotes it is clear that a company has to be in top financial shape to get any sort of A rating from Standard & Poor and the same is true of a P (for prime) rating from Moody. Commercial paper investors are, however, a conservative lot—disinclined to take extra risk to earn an extra ⅛; many of them will buy only A-1 and P-1 paper. Paper rated A-3 and P-3 is salable only to a very few investors. These include some insurance companies that, because they hold large bond portfolios, track on an ongoing basis the earnings and condition of a wide range of firms.

Rates and Tiering

In the early 1960s, when the commercial paper market was small, all issuers paid similar rates to borrow there. Then, after the Penn Central's failure and periods of extremely tight money, investors became very credit conscious; they wanted top names, and rate tiering developed in the market. That tiering today is a function not only of issuers' commercial paper ratings but of their long-term bond ratings. The market distinguishes between A-1 issuers with a triple-A bond rating and those with only a double-A bond rating. Many investors want to buy only unimpeachable credits; looking up an issuer's bond rating is a quick way for an investor to check the credit of an issuer with whom he is unfamiliar.

The spread at which A-1, P-1 paper trades to A-2, P-2 paper varies depending on economic conditions. When money is tight and people are more concerned than normal about risk in general and credit risk in particular, they may drive the yield on A-2

---

[5] Speech by Brenton W. Harries, President of Standard & Poor's.

paper 200 point basis points above that on A-1 paper; this occurred in the summer of 1982. When—after a period of tight
money—rates begin to fall, investors, seeking to maintain past
portfolios yields, tend to become yield buyers; they switch out
of lower-yielding, top-rated paper into higher-yielding, second-
tier paper. As they do, they drive down the spread between A-1
and A-2 paper so that, by the time money eases, it may be only
⅜ or even ¼. Whether money is easy or tight, no institutional
investors will buy P-3 paper from dealers.

Commercial paper, as Exhibit 4 shows, yields slightly more
than Treasury bills of comparable maturity, the spread being

Exhibit 4
Commercial Paper Consistently Yields a Somewhat Higher Rate than Treasury Bills of
the Same Maturity

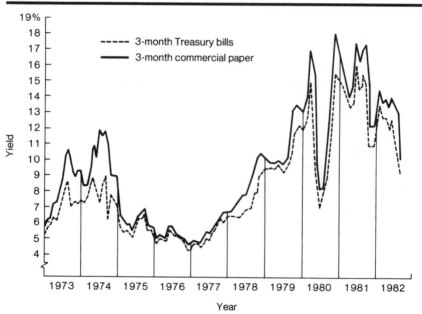

Source: *Federal Reserve Bulletin.*

widest when money is tight. There are two reasons. First, paper
exposes the investor to a small credit risk. Second, commercial
paper is much less liquid than bills because there is no active
secondary market in it.

Dealer Paper

Close to 40 percent of all commercial paper is issued
through dealers. Most of the paper placed through dealers is

industrial paper, but some of it is issued by smaller finance companies, bank holding companies, and muni borrowers.

The two largest dealers in commercial paper are Goldman Sachs and A. G. Becker. Lehman Brothers, Salomon Brothers, First Boston Corporation, and Merrill Lynch are also important; in addition there are a number of fringe dealers.

Issuers who sell through dealers tell the dealer each day how much they want to sell and in what maturities. The dealer's sales force, in turn, tells the firm's retail customers what names and maturities are available and what rates are.

The standard fee dealers charge issuers of commercial paper who sell through them is ⅛ of 1%, which works out to $3.47 per 1 million per day. In exchange for this fee, the dealer assumes several responsibilities vis à vis both issuers and investors. First, every dealer carefully checks the credit of each firm that sells paper through him. The dealer has a fiduciary responsibility to do this. He also wants to ensure that he does not tarnish his own good name in the eyes of either issuers or investors by selling paper of an issuer who goes bankrupt. A second responsibility of a dealer is to introduce the name of a new issuer to investors. He does this by having his sales force constantly show the name to investors and explain to them who the issuer is and what its credit is.

Some sophisticated issuers will themselves set the scale of rates to be offered on their paper in different maturities ranges. And if they do not want money badly, they may post rates slightly off the market in an attempt to pick up some cheap money. Most issuers, however, rely on the dealer to determine what rates should be posted on their paper. Dealers all compete with each other for issuers, and for this reason they all try to post the lowest rates at which it is possible to sell whatever quantity of paper an issuer who sells through them wants sold.

If an issuer permits a dealer to decide what rates will be offered on his paper, the dealer in turn assumes an obligation to position at these rates any of that issuer's paper that goes unsold. Normally a dealer finances paper thus acquired through dealer loans. Such financing is expensive, and carry is sometimes negative; dealers prefer to position as little paper as possible. Said one dealer, "Over the last 4 or 5 years, when we have had to take into position paper that we could not sell, we have actually made money on doing so despite the inverted yield curve. We are not, however, in business to make money that way. Every day I come to work, I would be thrilled if we just broke even on carry. If you make it, fine. If you don't, it is a cost of doing business."

On longer-term, higher-rate paper, a dealer's carry might be positive, especially if he finances in the RP market. Most dealers, however, are loath to position paper to earn carry profits or to speculate; they believe they should reserve their capacity to borrow for financing the paper—in amounts that cannot be predicted—that they might have to position as an obligation to their issuers. Also, some dealers think that, if positioning long paper that an issuer wants to sell seems an attractive speculation because they expect rates to fall, it is their responsibility to advise the issuer that he would be better off issuing short paper.

Dealers don't like to sell very short-dated paper because their transactions costs can easily exceed the fee they earn selling such paper. But to avoid positioning paper, they will occasionally sell even one-day paper. Also, at times they will, if necessary, *break rates* to get paper sold; that is, offer rates above those they have posted.

Secondary Market

Every dealer who sells commercial paper stands ready to buy back paper sold through him at the going market rate for paper of that grade and current maturity plus $1/8$ or so. Also, if an investor wants paper of an issuer who is not selling on a particular day, a dealer will attempt to find an investor who holds that issuer's paper and swap him out of it to generate supply.

Thus there is some secondary trading in dealer-issued commercial paper; such paper is, however, nowhere near as liquid as other money market instruments. An investor who holds commercial paper cannot really count on getting a bid on it from more than one dealer, and an $1/8$ bid above the market is a wide spread.

The failure for an active secondary market to develop in commercial paper has several causes. Commercial paper outstanding is even more heterogeneous than bank CDs outstanding and thus more difficult to trade actively in the secondary market. Also, many buyers of commercial paper are hold-to-maturity investors, so the demands made on dealers to take back paper are minimal. One major dealer estimated that "buy backs" at his shop run to only 1 to $1\frac{1}{2}$ percent of the paper they place.

Foreign Issuers

While the commercial paper market is primarily a domestic market, an increasing number of foreign companies borrow large sums in it. The first to do so was Electricité de France, the nationalized French electric company, which began in 1974 to issue commercial paper through Goldman Sachs to finance oil imports that it pays for with dollars. EDFs' commercial paper borrowings are now approaching $2 billion.

Most of the Fortune 500 are either cash-rich firms, such as IBM, or firms that already issue commercial paper through dealers or directly. Thus the richest potential source of growth for dealers lies in introducing more foreign borrowers to the U.S. commercial paper market—to sell, for example, commercial paper issued by multinational corporations that could profit by taking advantage of the lower short-term rates prevailing in the U.S. paper market. Some such companies already borrow long term in the U.S. market; for others who do not, starting a paper program can provide an entrée to managers of insurance company, pension fund, and bank trust department portfolios. These investors can later be approached—once a relationship is established—to buy the foreign issuer's bonds and equities.

Initially, domestic investors were leery, to say the least, about taking foreign names. This, however, is changing rapidly. In 1978 foreign issuers had to pay a rate 20 to 35 basis points above the 7 percent rate top domestic issuers were paying. Four years later, when these same U.S. issuers were paying 14 percent, the premium commanded for foreign paper had dropped to 20 to 30 points.

LOC Paper

Some smaller or less well-known domestic firms and a number of foreign firms borrow in the commercial paper market by issuing LOC (line of credit) paper. This paper is backed by normal bank lines *plus* a letter of credit from a bank stating that the bank will pay off the paper at maturity if the borrower does not. Such paper is also referred to as *documented discount notes*.

Obtaining a letter of credit to back its paper may permit an issuer to get a P-1 rating on LOC paper, whereas on its own paper it would get only a P-3 rating or no rating. Documented discount notes, which represent only a small fraction of commercial paper outstanding, have been issued by firms that sell nuclear fuel or energy derived from it, leasing companies, REITs, mortgage companies, U.S. subsidiaries of Japanese trading companies, and a number of foreign companies.

Borrowers who get a LOC could not get into the market without it. It is not that they are not creditworthy. Some are foreign companies who do not care to disclose all their financials to the general public but do not mind disclosing them to their dealers or to the rating agencies. Other LOC borrowers are just not large enough to get a rating. U.S. subsidiaries of Japanese companies make extensive use of LOC paper because they are not sufficiently big and self-sufficient to get a rating: The parent company could guarantee the subsidiary's paper but prefers to have the subsidiary get a LOC to back it. The cost of a letter of credit runs anywhere from ½ to ¾, whereas the cost of normal lines is more like ¼.

Direct Issue Paper

About 50 percent of all commercial paper outstanding is placed directly by the issuer with investors. Firms issuing their paper direct—less than 80 do so—are mostly large finance companies and bank holding companies. Some of these finance companies, such as GMAC, Sears, Roebuck Acceptance Corporation, and Ford Motor Credit, are captive finance companies that borrow primarily to finance the credit sales of the parent industrial company. Others, such as Household Finance, Beneficial Finance, and Associates Corporation of North America, are independent finance companies.

The major incentive for an issuer to go direct is that, by doing so, it escapes the dealer's ⅛ commission. For a firm with $200 million of commercial paper outstanding, this would amount to a savings of $250,000 a year. However, the direct issuer has to set up its own sales organization. A firm with a top credit rating can sell a huge amount of commercial paper through a small sales force—three to six people. Thus, for such a firm, it pays to go direct when the average amount of paper it has outstanding climbs to around $200 to $250 million. A few issuers who are big borrowers in the paper market continue to use a dealer either because they anticipate selling long-term debt to reduce their short-term borrowing or because the amount of paper they have outstanding varies sharply during the year.

Direct issuers determine each day how much they need to borrow, what maturities they want, and what rates they will post. Then they communicate their offerings to investors in three ways. All of the big directs post their rates on Telerate. In addition, their sales representatives call various investors. As one such representative noted, "There are a large number of A-1, P-1 issuers who are posting the same rates. So the sales representative's job is partly to develop personal relationships that will distinguish his firm in investors' eyes from the crowd."

The third way that the top direct issuers sell their paper is by posting their rates on bank money desks. Banks are forbidden by Glass-Steagall from acting as dealers in commercial paper, but they can and do post rates for issuers and arrange sales of their paper to investors.[6] The banks do this partly to service clients who use them to invest surplus funds. By posting paper rates, the banks can offer such clients a full menu of money market instruments. Also, direct issuers typically purchase large backup lines from banks that post their paper rates.

The rates that a direct issuer has to pay are a function of its name, credit rating, and use of the market. A nonprime borrower that uses the market extensively will have to pay up.

Once a direct issuer posts rates, it carefully monitors sales throughout the day by its own sales force and on bank money desks. When money market conditions are volatile, an issuer may change its posted rates several times a day to ensure that it gets whatever amount it set out to borrow. Also, if an issuer achieves that goal early in the day, it will typically lower its rates to make its paper unattractive to investors and thereby stem any further inflow of funds.

Most issuers will break rates for a large investor if they want money. Some, when they are just entering the market, will also consistently offer selected large investors rates slightly above their posted rates. The prevalence of rate breaking tends to increase when money is tight and to decrease when it is easy.

An issuer who fails to borrow as much as it had intended to can always fall back on its bank lines. Also, when money is easy and the demand for bank loans is slack, some banks will position short-term paper at a rate equal to the Fed funds rate plus a small markup; this is a way of giving the issuer a cut-rate loan.

A more recent development is the offering by banks to commercial paper issuers and other borrowers of short-term money, fixed-rate advances priced off money market rates. The availability of such loans is likely to be particularly helpful to big direct issuers who on a given day may find themselves $100 or 200 million short.

Prepayments

The big direct issuers of commercial paper will all prepay on paper they have issued if the investor needs money before the paper he has purchased matures. Some issuers do this at no penalty. Others will give the investor who requests prepayment the rate that he would have gotten on the day he purchased his paper if he had bought paper for the period he actually held it.

---

[6] Glass-Steagall does not preclude banks from dealing in muni commercial paper, but so far at least, it is nonbank dealers who have developed this market and have a lock on it.

The no-penalty system would seem to invite abuse—to encourage investors to buy, whenever the yield curve is upward sloping, paper of a longer maturity than that for which they intend to invest in order to get a higher rate. Issuers, however, figure that game out quickly and don't let an investor get away with it for long.

One reason issuers are so willing to prepay is that most do not want investors to sell their paper to a dealer for fear that the dealer's later resale of that paper might interfere with their own sales. Still a few of the largest issuers, GMAC in particular, will occasionally sell longer-term paper to dealers who position it for carry profits and as a speculation.

Master Notes

Bank trust departments have many small sums to invest short term. To provide them with a convenient way to do so, the major direct issuers of commercial paper offer bank trust departments what are called *master notes*. A master note is a variable-rate demand note on which the issuer typically pays the rate he is posting for 180-day money, that rate plus ¼, or some similar formula rate.

A bank trust department with whom an issuer has opened a master note invests monies from various trust accounts in it. Then each day the bank advises the issuer what change, if any, has occurred in the total amount invested in the note. From a trust department's point of view, a master note provides such a convenient way for investing small sums to any date that it typically keeps the balance in any note issued to it close to the limit imposed by the issuer on the size of the note; daily variations in the size of a large master note—say, one for $15 million—might be no more than $100,000.

For the issuer, master notes provide a dependable source of funds and reduce bookkeeping costs. Money obtained through a master note, however, is expensive for the issuer because the rate paid is based on the 180-day rate; most issuers limit the amount of master notes they issue to some percentage—typically well below half—of their total outstandings.

A and B notes   Because bank trust departments keep master notes filled up most of the time, some direct issuers said to them, "Look, you have a master note for *x* million, and most of the time you have it 90 percent full. Let's call the top half of that note an *A note*; you can take money out of it on demand. The bottom half of the note we will call a *B note;* on that part you have to give us a 13-month notice to withdraw funds."

The advantage to the issuer of this arrangement, which is now common among direct issuers, is that the issuer gets cheap money that he can record on his balance sheet as *long-term* debt. From the trust department's point of view, the arrangement provides a high rate on what is really short-term money because different monies are constantly being shifted into and out of the overall note.

Issuers of B notes argue that such debt is not commercial paper but rather a private placement. Still such debt is recorded in money market statistics as commercial paper. A few issuers who do not offer B notes fear that by doing so they would be making an offering that, due to its term and the lack of a prospectus, would not comply with SEC regulations. Because of the attraction of B notes to the issuer, many issuers who offer master notes to bank trust departments will not issue an A note unless they also get a B note.

Prior to its getting into serious financial difficulties, W. T. Grant had a number of master notes outstanding with bank trust departments. While it had closed them out before its bankruptcy, that event did cause a number of bank trust departments to question whether they should not invest cash balances in trust accounts in an institutional money fund rather than in a master note. An institutional money fund offers a bank trust department the same convenient subaccounting that a master note does and a comparable yield. In addition an institutional money fund has the advantage over a master note that it offers, instead of exposure to a single credit risk, *diversity of credit risk.*

Secondary Market

Secondary market trading, uncommon in dealer-issued paper, occurs with increasing frequency in direct-issue paper. Big finance companies, such as GMAC, and big bank holding companies, such as Citicorp, have huge amounts of paper outstanding, some of which has been issued in large blocks that mature on a given day.[7] Money market dealers, who trade BAs and CDs, sometimes position such paper as a rate play.

This practice has become so common that at least one broker of money markets, Garvin, has started to broker blocks of commercial paper among dealers.

---

[7] Taking its cue from the Treasury, Citi's holding company auctions $150 million of its commercial paper every Wednesday.

BANKERS' ACCEPTANCES

The *banker's acceptance (BA)* is an unknown instrument outside the confines of the money market. Moreover, explaining BAs isn't easy because they arise in a variety of ways out of a variety transactions. The best approach is to use an example.

Suppose a U.S. importer wants to buy shoes in Brazil and pay for them four months later, after she has had time to sell them in the United States. One approach would be for the importer to simply borrow from her bank; however, short-term rates may be lower in the open market. If they are, and if the importer is too small to go into the open market on her own, then she can go the bankers' acceptance route.

In that case she has her bank write a letter of credit for the amount of the sale and then sends this letter to the Brazilian exporter. Upon export of the shoes, the Brazilian firm, using this letter of credit, draws a time draft on the importer's U.S. bank and discounts this draft at its local bank, thereby obtaining immediate payment for its goods. The Brazilian bank in turn sends the time draft to the importer's U.S. bank, which then stamps "accepted" on the draft; that is, the bank guarantees payment on the draft and thereby creates an *acceptance*. Once this is done, the draft becomes an irrevocable primary obligation of the accepting bank. At this point, if the Brazilian bank did not want cash immediately, the U.S. bank would return the draft to that bank, which would hold it as an investment and then present it to the U.S. bank for payment at maturity. If, on the other hand, the Brazilian bank wanted cash immediately, the U.S. bank would pay it and then either hold the acceptance itself or sell it to an investor. Whoever ended up holding the acceptance, it would be the importer's responsibility to provide her U.S. bank with sufficient funds to pay off the acceptance at maturity. If the importer should fail for any reason, her bank would still be responsible for making payment at maturity.

Our example illustrates how an acceptance can arise out of a U.S. import transaction. Acceptances also arise in connection with U.S. export sales, trade between third countries (e.g., Japanese imports of oil from the Middle East), the domestic shipment of goods, and domestic or foreign storage of readily marketable staples. Currently most BAs arise out of foreign trade; the latter may be in manufactured goods, but more typically is in bulk commodities, such as cocoa, cotton, coffee, or crude oil, to name a few. Because of the complex nature of acceptance operations, only large banks that have well-staffed foreign departments act as accepting banks.

Bankers' acceptances closely resemble commercial paper in form. They are short-term (270 days or less), noninterest-bearing notes sold at a discount and redeemed by the accepting bank at maturity for full face value. The major difference between bankers' acceptances and paper is that payment on paper is guaranteed by the issuing company only, but payment on bankers' acceptances is also guaranteed by the accepting bank. Thus bankers' acceptances carry slightly less risk than commercial paper. The very low risk on acceptances is indicated by the fact that to date no investor in acceptances has ever suffered a loss.

Yields on bankers' acceptances are quoted on a bank discount basis, as in the case of commercial paper. Yields on bankers' acceptances closely parallel yields on paper. Also, both rates are highly volatile, rising sharply when money is tight and falling in an equally dramatic fashion when conditions ease. This means that when money is tight, yields on bankers' acceptances are very attractive.

The big banks through which bankers' acceptances originate generally keep some portion of the acceptances they create as investments. The rest are sold to investors through dealers or directly by the bank itself. Major investors in bankers' acceptances are other banks, foreign central banks, and Federal Reserve banks.

Many bankers' acceptances are written for very large amounts and are obviously out of the range of the small investor; certainly this includes all acceptances that pass through the hands of dealers. However, acceptances in amounts as low as $5,000 or even $500 are not uncommon. Some accepting banks offer these low-denomination acceptances to their customers as investments. An individual investing in a $25,000 acceptance may in fact be buying a single small acceptance arising out of one transaction, or be buying a bundle of even smaller acceptances that have been packaged together to form a round-dollar amount. Frequently, bankers' acceptances are available in still smaller odd-dollar amounts. The investor who puts money into an odd-dollar acceptance should be prepared to experience some difficulty in rolling over the funds. Also the availability of bankers' acceptances varies both seasonally and over the cycle. Generally, availability is greatest when money is tight and banks prefer not to tie up funds in acceptances.

The rates offered on bankers' acceptances, like those on paper, vary from day to day. Also they may vary slightly on a given day from one accepting bank to another. Thus a few calls to shop for rates are in order if a decision is made to invest in acceptances.

Since payment on acceptances is guaranteed by both the accepting bank and the ultimate borrower, investing in acceptances exposes the investor to minimal risk. For small acceptances, as for paper, there is no secondary market. Thus an investor who needs cash cannot sell a bankers' acceptance to another investor but can use it as collateral for a bank loan. Also, if the investor's need for cash is really pressing, chances are that the accepting bank will be willing to buy back the acceptance early.

To sum up, bankers' acceptances are a little known, but at times very attractive, investment.

NEGOTIABLE CERTIFICATES OF DEPOSIT

In the early post-World War II period, when interest rates were low, bankers were not inclined to accept corporate time deposits on which they would have to pay interest. However, in the late 1950s and early 1960s, things changed for several reasons. First, corporate treasurers, who had customarily met their liquidity needs by holding large balances of noninterest-bearing demand deposits, began to manage their money in a more sophisticated manner as short-term rates rose; they switched funds where possible out of demand deposits into liquid, income-yielding, money market instruments, such as T bills and commercial paper. Second, the large New York money market banks, who had historically enjoyed a dominant position on the national banking scene, found that their competitive position was eroding. As a result of industrial decentralization and the rapid growth of population outside the Northeast, their share of total deposits had declined by almost 50 percent between 1940 and 1960.

In response to these trends, the First National City Bank of New York announced in 1961 that it would issue large-denomination *negotiable certificates of deposit* and that a large, well-known government securities dealer, The First Boston Corporation, had agreed to create a secondary market (act as a dealer) in these securities. *A negotiable CD is simply a receipt from a bank for funds deposited at that bank for some specified period of time at some specified rate of return.*

Negotiable CDs were not a new instrument in 1961; they had been around in small volume for a long time. What made First National City's announcement the beginning of a phenomenal expansion in outstanding CDs was not its willingness to issue this instrument, but rather First Boston's intent to act as a dealer in CDs. To the corporate treasurer looking for liquidity, what is important is not *negotiability* per se, but rather *marketability*. The marketability of an instrument, which is measured in degrees, depends on the existence of a secondary market for that instrument and on the level of activity in that market. Bills and paper are both negotiable, but bills have high marketability, whereas paper does not. Thus, corporations typically use bills to provide first-line liquidity, and they use paper and other less liquid instruments to provide second-line liquidity.

Once First National City made its announcement, the other major banks quickly followed suit, and a number of other dealers joined The First Boston Corporation in the secondary market. From essentially a zero base in 1961, the volume of negotiable CDs outstanding grew rapidly. Today, the major issuers of negotiable CDs are large, nationally known money market banks, principally in New York and Chicago. In addition to these prime borrowers, there are also a number of less well known regional banks that issue CDs.

Since some investors in Eurodollars wanted liquidity, banks that accepted time deposits in London began to issue Eurodollar CDs. A *Eurodollar CD* resembles a domestic CD except that instead of being the liability of a domestic bank, it is the liability of the London branch of a domestic bank or of a British bank or some other foreign bank with a branch in London. Although many of the Eurodollar CDs issued in London are purchased by other banks operating in the Euromarket, a large portion of the remainder are sold to U.S. corporations and other domestic institutional investors. Many Euro CDs are issued through dealers and brokers who maintain secondary markets in these securities.

The Euro CD market is younger and smaller than the market for domestic CDs, but it has grown rapidly since its inception. The most recent development in the "Eurodollar" CD market is that some large banks have begun offering such CDs through their Caribbean branches.[8]

Foreign banks issue dollar-denominated CDs not only in the Euromarket, but also in the domestic market through branches established there. CDs of the latter sort are frequently referred to as Yankee CDs; the name is derived from Yankee bonds, which are bonds issued in the domestic market by foreign borrowers.

CDs can have any maturity longer than 30 days, and some 5- and 7-year CDs have been sold (these pay interest semiannu-

---

[8] A CD issued, for example, in Nassau, is technically a Euro CD because the deposit is held in a branch outside the United States.

ally). Most CDs, however, have an *original maturity* of one to three months. Generally the CD buyer, who may be attempting to fund a predictable cash need—say, provide for a tax or dividend payment—can select his or her own maturity date when making the deposit.

Until May 1973, the Fed, under Regulation Q, imposed lids on the rates that banks could pay on large-denomination CDs of different maturities. Today these lids are past history, and the general level of yields on negotiable CDs is determined by conditions of demand and supply in the money market. Since holding a CD exposes the investor to a small risk of capital loss (the issuing bank might fail), prime-name negotiable CDs, in order to sell, have to be offered at rates approximately one eighth of a point above the rate on T bills of comparable maturity. Of course, in actual practice there is no one CD rate prevailing at any one time. Each issuing bank sets a range of rates for different maturities, normally with an upward-sloping yield curve. On a given day a bank at which loan demand is especially strong, and which therefore needs money, may set rates slightly more attractive than those posted by other banks. Posted rates are not fixed rates; big investors can and do haggle with banks over the rate paid.

Generally prime-name banks can attract funds more cheaply than other banks, the rate differential being one percentage point or less. Foreign banks pay still higher CD rates. In comparing CD rates with yields on other money market instruments, note that CDs are *not* issued at a discount. It takes $1 million of deposits to get a CD with a $1 million face value. CDs typically pay interest at maturity. Thus rates quoted on CDs correspond to yield in the terms in which the investor normally thinks— what we call equivalent bond yield.

Recently banks have introduced on a small scale a new type of negotiable CD, *variable-rate CDs.* The two most prevalent types are six-month CDs with a 30-day *roll* (on each roll date, accrued interest is paid and a new coupon is set) and one-year paper with a 3-month roll. The coupon established on a variable-rate CD at issue and on subsequent roll dates is set at some amount (12.5 to 30 basis points, depending on the name of the issuer and the maturity) above the average rate (as indicated by the composite rate published by the Fed) that banks are paying on new CDs with an original maturity equal to the length of the roll period.

We can sum up our discussion of risk, liquidity, and return on negotiable CDs by saying that CDs are slightly riskier than T bills. They are also slightly less liquid, since the spread between bid and asked prices is narrower in the bill market than in the secondary CD market; the reason for this difference is that in the bill market the commodity traded is homogeneous and buying and selling occur in greater volume.

CDs, however, compensate for these failings by yielding a somewhat higher return than do bills. Euro CDs offer a higher return than do domestic CDs. The offsetting disadvantages are that they are less liquid and expose the investor to some extra risk because they are issued outside the United States. Yankee CDs expose the investor to the extra (if only in perception) risk of a foreign name, and they are also less liquid than domestic CDs. Consequently Yankee CDs trade at yields close to those on Euro CDs. Although variable-rate CDs offer the investor some interest-rate protection, they have the offsetting disadvantage of illiquidity because they trade at a concession to the market. During their last *leg* (roll period) variable-rate CDs trade like regular CDs of similar name and maturity.

Computing the Yield of a CD, Given Its Price

Almost all CDs issued in the domestic market have a maturity at issue of less than one year and pay simple interest on a 360-day basis.[9] The rate of interest paid is the coupon rate, and interest is paid at maturity. In the formulas presented for CDs, the following convention will be adopted. *Price P is always taken to be price per $1 of face value, with accrued interest, if any, included.*[10]

CDs are always quoted, at issue and in the secondary market, in terms of yield on a simple interest basis. The following formula is for the rate of return that a CD offered at a price P will yield an investor.

$$y = \left(\frac{1 + c\,\dfrac{t_{im}}{360}}{P} - 1 \right) \frac{360}{t_{sm}}$$

where

y = yield on the CD
c = coupon rate
t_{sm} = days from settlement to maturity
t_{im} = days from issue to maturity

---

[9] As noted above, the exceptions are variable-rate CDs and a few long-term issues that have been floated at various times.

[10] The formulas presented in this section are derived in M. Stigum, *Money Market Calculations*, pp. 71–80.

For example, suppose that an investor buys a CD that carries a coupon rate of 10 percent and has an original maturity of 90 days and a current maturity of 60 days. If the price P is 1.009024, the yield is 9.5 percent as shown below.

$$y = \left(\frac{1 + 0.100 \, \dfrac{90}{360}}{1.009024} - 1 \right) \frac{360}{60} = 0.095$$

There are two points to note about the formula for computing the yield on a CD. First, if a CD is bought on its issue date, then $P = 1$, and the expression for the yield reduces to the coupon rate (c), as would be expected. Second, the fact that CDs pay interest on the basis of a 360-day year should not be forgotten when CD yields are compared with those on other interest-bearing securities, such as government notes and bonds, that pay interest on a 365-day basis. To convert from a 365- to a 360-day basis, the yield on a CD must be multiplied by 1.014.[11] Therefore, getting a year's interest over 360 days is worth 1.4 extra basis points for every 1 percent interest.

Computing Price, Given Yield

Using the formula for the yield on a CD, a formula for the price at which a CD will trade in the secondary market if it is offered at a yield y can be determined. Solving, we have

$$P = \left(\frac{1 + c \, \dfrac{t_{im}}{360}}{1 + y \, \dfrac{t_{sm}}{360}} \right)$$

Let's use the CD from the yield formula example, given the price, to show how the foregoing formula is applied. The price P is 1.009024, as shown below:

$$P = \left(\frac{1 + 0.100 \, \dfrac{90}{360}}{1 + 0.095 \, \dfrac{60}{360}} \right) = 1.009024$$

---

[11] The conversion factor is found by dividing 365 by 360.

Breaking Out Accrued Interest

Separating the price P paid for a CD into principal and interest is easily done. Let

a_i = accrued interest
t_{is} = days from issue to settlement

On a CD accrued interest is given by the expression

$$a_i = c \, \frac{t_{is}}{360}$$

and

$$\text{Principal per \$1 of face value} = P - c \, \frac{t_{is}}{360}$$

Applying these formulas to the preceding example, we find that

$$a_i = 0.10 \, \frac{30}{360} = 0.083333$$

and

$$\begin{aligned} \text{Principal} &= 1.009024 - 0.083333 \\ &= 1.000691 \end{aligned}$$

Notice that the CD in our example is selling at a premium. This is to be expected since it was traded at a *yield well below* its coupon.

Holding Period Yield

Intuition, which seems to be invariably wrong in money market calculations, suggests that an investor who bought a CD at 10 percent and sold it before maturity at the same rate would earn 10 percent over the holding period. In fact, the investor would earn *less*. The reason is due to compounding. This is because interest is not paid by the issuer on the CD until some period after the investor sells it; the CD is priced at sale, however, so that the buyer will earn the offered yield on an amount equal to the principal paid *plus* accrued interest.

Consider first a CD that is bought by an investor at issue and later sold before maturity. The rate of simple interest (i) earned by the investor over the holding period is

$$i = \left(\frac{1 + c\, \dfrac{t_{im}}{360}}{1 + y\, \dfrac{t_{sm}}{360}} - 1 \right) \frac{360}{t_{is}}$$

where

t_{is} = days from issue to settlement on the sale
y = rate at which the CD is sold

For example, suppose an investor buys a 90-day CD carrying a 10 percent coupon at issue and sells it 30 days later at a 10 percent yield. The return earned is not 10 percent but a lower figure, 9.83 percent. The calculation is:

$$i = \left(\frac{1 + 0.10\, \dfrac{90}{360}}{1 + 0.10\, \dfrac{60}{360}} - 1 \right) \frac{360}{60} = 9.83 \text{ percent}$$

The yield on a CD purchased in the secondary market and sold before maturity can be calculated using a similar but slightly more complex formula shown below:

$$i = \left(\frac{1 + y_1\, \dfrac{t_1}{360}}{1 + y_2\, \dfrac{t_2}{360}} - 1 \right) \frac{360}{t_1 - t_2}$$

where

y_1 = purchase rate
y_2 = sale rate
t_1 = days from purchase to maturity
t_2 = days from sale to maturity

Sensitivity of Return to Sale Rate and Length of Holding Period

The figures in Exhibit 5, show what return (i) an investor would earn by selling a six-month CD purchased at 9 percent after various holding periods and at various rates. Notice first the column labeled 9 percent. It shows that if the investor resells the CD at the purchase rate, the return earned will be higher the longer the holding period is (that is, the closer the sale date is to

Exhibit 5
The Rate of Return (*i*) Earned by an Investor on a 9
Percent, Six-Month CD when Sold at Various Rates after
Various Holding Periods

Holding Period (Days)	Sale Rate, y				
	11%	10%	9%	8%	7%
30	−0.96	3.84	8.67	13.55	18.46
60	4.82	7.77	8.74	10.71	12.70
90	6.81	7.80	8.80	9.80	10.81
120	7.86	8.36	8.87	9.38	9.88
150	8.59	8.73	8.93	9.14	9.35
179	8.99	8.99	9.00	9.00	9.01

the date on which the CD matures and accrued interest is paid out).

Suppose an investor sells a CD at a rate below the rate at which he bought it. He will receive a capital gain and earn over the holding period a return higher than the yield at which he bought the CD. As the columns labeled 8 percent and 7 percent show, this effect becomes smaller the longer the holding period. If, conversely, the investor sells the CD at a rate *above* that at which he purchased it, the effect is the opposite and also decreases as the holding period is lengthened.

The reason the impact of the sale rate on the return earned by the investor diminishes as the holding period increases is: The longer the holding period, the shorter the time in which the buyer of the CD will earn the rate at which he or she buys the CD, and therefore the smaller will be the impact of that rate on the principal amount the investor pays for the CD.

Compounding

We have noted that selling a CD before maturity tends to reduce the yield earned by the investor over the holding period. If the investor *fully* reinvests the proceeds (principal *plus* accrued interest) from the sale of the CD, this effect will be offset by the opportunity for compounding of interest earnings created by the sale and subsequent repurchase.

To illustrate, an investor who purchased at issue a 182-day CD at 9 percent and sold it 91 days later at 9 percent would earn a yield of 8.80 percent over that period. If the investor immediately fully reinvested the sale proceeds ($1.022750 per $1 of face value) in a 9 percent, 91-day CD, total earnings over the 182-day investment period would be identical with what would have been earned by holding to maturity the 182-day, 9 percent CD originally bought.

SUMMARY

The corporate cash manager must be familiar with the alternative investments in which excess cash may be invested and the return and risk characteristics of each instrument. In this chapter, the investment characteristics of five money market instruments are discussed—U.S. Treasury bills, Federal agency issues, commercial paper, bankers' acceptances, and negotiable certificates of deposit. In addition to describing the investment characteristics of each instrument, procedures for converting the quoted yields to yields that can be used to compare investment returns among money market instruments are discussed.

11

Tax-Exempt Short-Term Investments

Sylvan G. Feldstein, Ph.D.
Vice President and Manager
Municipal Research Department
Merrill Lynch, Pierce, Fenner & Smith, Inc.

Frank J. Fabozzi, Ph.D., C.F.A.
Walter E. Hanson/Peat, Marwick
Mitchell Professor of Business
and Finance
Lafayette College

The purpose of this chapter is to describe the various types of tax-exempt short-term investments currently available to the manager of a corporate short-term portfolio and to provide the basic framework for analyzing the credit risks involved with each. The tax-exempt investments we shall focus on in this chapter are those issued by state and local governments. These obligations are commonly referred to as *municipal* obligations. Since the attractive feature of the short-term investments discussed in this chapter is their favorable tax treatment, we begin with a discussion of the tax treatment and its implications for managing a corporate short-term portfolio.

TAX TREATMENT AND ITS PORTFOLIO IMPLICATIONS

Section 103(a) of the Internal Revenue Code of 1954 specifically exempts interest income from obligations of the following issuers from federal income taxes: a state and its political subdivisions, a territory or possession of the United States (Guam, Puerto Rico, and the Virgin Islands), the District of Columbia, and certain local and urban agencies operating under the auspices of the Department of Housing and Urban Development. The exemption applies only to that portion of income from holding a fixed-income obligation that represents interest income; that portion which represents a capital gain is taxable.

230

There are three points to note about the tax treatment of these tax-exempt obligations. First, because of the tax-exempt feature, these obligations offer lower market yields than otherwise comparable taxable obligations. Second, the tax treatment of municipal interest income varies from state to state. *Usually* a state exempts the interest income from obligations issued by the state, its agencies, and its political subdivisions from its state and local income taxes; however, a state generally taxes the interest income from obligations of other states and political subdivisions. Interest income from obligations issued by territories, the District of Columbia, and certain local and urban agencies financially supported by the Department of Housing and Urban Development are exempt from *all* state and local taxes. Third, although as a general rule a corporation is entitled to deduct all interest paid or accrued on indebtedness during the taxable year, interest paid or accrued on indebtedness incurred or continued in order to purchase tax-exempt obligations is not tax-deductible. Consequently, the manager of a corporate short-term portfolio must recognize that portfolio decisions may have implications for interest deductibility.

Measuring Taxable Equivalent Yields

In the previous chapter it was explained why yields on money market instruments had to be converted to an equivalent yield standard so that alternative investments could be compared. The same is true in the case of tax-exempt short-term investments. The formula for determining the taxable equivalent yield of a tax-exempt obligation is:

$$\text{Taxable equivalent yield} = \frac{\text{Tax-exempt yield}}{(1 - \text{effective marginal tax rate})}$$

For example, if a corporation whose marginal effective tax rate is 46 percent purchases a tax-exempt note offering a 5.4 percent tax-exempt yield, the taxable equivalent yield is 10 percent as shown below:

$$\text{Taxable equivalent yield} = \frac{0.054}{(1 - 0.46)}$$
$$= 0.10 \text{ or } 10 \text{ percent}$$

Consequently, if a portfolio manager can invest in either a taxable obligation offering a yield that is less than 10 percent or a tax-exempt yield of 5.4 percent, then the tax-exempt obligation offers the higher yield.

State and Local Income Taxes[1]

There are four basic ways that a municipal obligation may be taxed at the state and local level: (1) income tax on interest, (2) income tax on capital gains, (3) property tax on value, and (4) tax on the purchase or sale of an obligation such as a transfer tax. In the computation of the taxable equivalent yield, the effective marginal tax rate must be determined. This depends on three factors: (1) federal marginal tax rate, (2) state and local marginal tax rate, and (3) deductibility of state and federal taxes for purposes of computing state and local taxes. The effective marginal state and local tax rate is the enacted (or nominal) marginal rate adjusted for factor (3).

To illustrate the importance of the deductibility of state and local taxes on the effective marginal tax rate, consider a state in which federal taxes are not deductible for purposes of computing state and local taxable income. The Internal Revenue Code, however, allows state and local taxes as a deductible item. In such instances, if a corporation's effective federal marginal tax rate is 46 percent and state and local taxes are 10 percent, then each $100 of tax-exempt interest will increase state and local taxes by $10. Since this tax is deductible at the federal level, this reduces federal taxable income by $10 and results in a reduction of federal income taxes by $4.60. Therefore, the effective cost of a state and local income tax of $10 is $5.40 or 5.4 percent.

An investigation of state and local tax laws indicates that there are basically four different state and federal tax procedures regarding deductions. These are (1) one-way deductible states, (2) cross-deductible states, (3) cross-deductible with add-back states, and (4) piggyback tax states. Each is described below.

One-Way Deductible States   State and local income taxes paid are deductible for computing federal income taxes. However, federal income taxes paid are not deductible for computing state and local income taxes. That is, there is only one-way deductibility.

Cross-Deductible States   In some states, federal income taxes paid are deductible in computing state and local income taxes. Since state and local taxes are deductible for computing federal income taxes, this situation is referred to as cross-deductibility.

---

[1] For a more detailed discussion of state and local taxes and formulas for computing effective state and local tax rates, see Steven J. Hueglin. "State and Local Tax Treatment of Municipal Bonds," Chapter 4 in *The Municipal Bond Handbook, Volume I,* ed. Frank J. Fabozzi, Sylvan G. Feldstein, Irving M. Pollack, and Frank G. Zarb (Homewood, Ill: Dow Jones-Irwin, 1983).

Cross-Deductible with Add-Back States As in the case of cross-deductible states, states with this procedure also allow deduction of federal taxes for purposes of computing state and local taxes. The difference is that all state and local taxes that are deducted to determine federal taxable income must be added back to determine state and local taxable income.

Piggyback Tax States In some states, the state income tax is a percentage of federal income taxes. Since state and local taxes are deductible for purposes of determining federal income tax liability, these taxes are therefore effectively deductible from state and local taxes.

Deductibility of Interest Expense Incurred to Acquire or Carry Tax-Exempt Obligation

As a general rule, a corporation is entitled to deduct all interest paid or accrued on indebtedness during the taxable year.[2] However, interest paid or accrued on "indebtedness incurred or continued to purchase or carry obligations the interest of which is wholly exempt from taxes" is not tax-deductible.[3]

In the absence of direct evidence that the purpose of the indebtedness was to purchase or carry tax-exempt obligations, the rule is generally *not* applicable where a taxpayer's investment is "insubstantial." For a nondealer corporation, an insubstantial investment will be presumed to exist if in the taxable year the average amount of the tax-exempt obligations is not in excess of 2 percent of the average total assets held in the active conduct of the corporate taxpayer's trade or business.[4]

When there is no direct evidence linking the debt incurred to the tax-exempt obligations purchased or carried by a nondealer corporation, the IRS will generally not presume an indirect link unless there is evidence that the amount borrowed is in excess of the amount the corporation needs to carry on its business. One indication of excess borrowing is when "the taxpayer in-

---

[2] Section 103(c) of the IRC.

[3] Section 163(a) of the IRC. There are special rules for banks and certain other financial institutions which are not discussed in this chapter.

To understand why interest related to debt incurred to purchase or carry tax-exempt obligations is disallowed as a deduction, consider the following example. Suppose a corporate taxpayer in the 46 percent marginal tax bracket borrows $100,000 at an annual interest cost of 12 percent, or $12,000. The proceeds are then used to acquire $100,000 of municipal bonds at par with a coupon rate of 8 percent, or $8,000 interest per year. If the $12,000 interest expense is allowed as a tax deductible expense, the aftertax cost of the interest expense would be $6,480. Since the interest received from holding the municipal bonds is $8,000, the taxpayer would benefit by $1,520 after taxes.

[4] Revenue Procedure 72–18.

vests a disproportionally large portion of its liquid assets in tax-exempt obligations and there are no facts indicating that such investment is related to the reasonable needs of the taxpayer's business. . . ."[5] The acquisition of short-term, tax-exempt obligations that are frequently liquidated in order to provide funds for use in a corporate taxpayer's operations would generally not be inferred by the IRS to be indirectly linked to indebtedness incurred by the taxpayer. However, the IRS may make an inference of an indirect link "with respect to indebtedness which is itself short-term and is incurred other than in the normal course of the taxpayer's trade or business."[6]

The question of the purpose of incurring indebtedness when there is no direct link depends upon the underlying facts. For example, in one case a nondealer corporate taxpayer used municipal bonds as collateral for a short-term loan. The proceeds of the short-term loan were used to satisfy the taxpayer's current operating expenses. The interest deduction on the short-term loan was denied by the court because it was felt that at the time the municipal bonds were acquired, the taxpayer should have anticipated the need for additional financing to meet current operating expenses.[7] Yet, the interest on indebtedness incurred by the same corporate taxpayer in order to finance the construction of a new plant was allowed by the court. The court justified the deduction on the grounds that the corporate taxpayer's liquidity would be threatened if it was required to dispose of the municipal bonds.[8]

Other cases have established that even though a corporate taxpayer continues to carry tax-exempt securities after borrowing funds, the interest deduction would be allowed if there is a good business reason for doing so rather than disposing of the securities.[9] However, even though there may be a good business reason, the deduction would be denied if the dominant reason for borrowing funds is to hold the securities.[10]

---

[5] Revenue Procedure 72–18.

[6] Revenue Procedure 72–18.

[7] *Wisconsin Cheeseman* v. *United States*, 388 F. 2d 420 (1968).

[8] Ibid.

[9] For example, in *R. B. George Machinery Co.*, 26 B.T.A. 594 (1932) (Acquiesced C.B. XI-2, 4), the nondealer corporate taxpayer acquired nonnegotiable obligations in the course of business operations as payment for its services to the tax-exempt entity. In yet another case, a nondealer taxpayer was required to hold such obligations as a condition to providing a service or product to a state or local government. (*Commissioner* v. *Bagley & Sewall Co.*, 221 F. 2d 944 (1955).)

[10] *Illinois Terminal Railroad Co.* v. *United States*.

TAX-EXEMPT SHORT-TERM
OBLIGATIONS AVAILABLE

Tax-exempt debt issued for periods ranging not beyond three years are usually considered to be short term in nature. Below are descriptions of some of these debt instruments.

Tax, Revenue, Grant and Bond Anticipation Notes (TANs, RANs, GANs, and BANs)

These are temporary borrowings by states, local governments, and special jurisdictions. Usually, notes are issued for a period of 12 months, though it is not uncommon for notes to be issued for periods of as short as 3 months and for as long as 3 years. TANs and RANs (also known as TRANs) are issued in anticipation of the collection of taxes or other expected revenues. These are borrowings to even out the cash flows caused by the irregular flows of income into the treasuries of the states and local units of government. BANs are issued in anticipation of the sale of long-term bonds.

Construction Loan Notes (CLNs)

CLNs are usually issued for periods up to three years to provide short-term construction financing for multifamily housing projects. The CLNs generally are repaid by the proceeds of long-term bonds, which are provided after the housing projects are completed.

Tax-Exempt Commercial Paper

This short-term borrowing instrument is used for periods ranging from 1 to 270 days. Generally the tax-exempt commercial paper has backstop commercial bank agreements, which can include an irrevocable letter of credit, a revolving credit agreement, or a line of credit.

Variable Rate Demand Notes

Similar to tax-exempt commercial paper, tax-exempt variable rate demand notes usually can be "put" to the issuer at par monthly, weekly, or even daily. The security backup includes (or should include) an irrevocable letter of credit or municipal bond insurance, or should be collateralized with highly marketable securities.

Project Notes of Local Housing Authorities (PNs)

Project notes are secured by a contractual pledge from the United States Department of Housing and Urban Development. Monies from Washington are paid directly to the paying agent for the PNs, and the noteholders are given specific legal rights to enforce the pledge. These notes are the safest short-term tax-exempt investments available.

More information about each of these obligations is discussed at the end of this chapter where a framework for analyzing their credit worthiness is provided.

CREDIT RISK AND COMMERCIAL RATING COMPANIES

Credit risk is defined as the degree of uncertainty that the issuer will fail to meet its obligations with respect to interest payment and/or principal repayment. Commercial rating companies such as Standard & Poor's, Moody's, and Fitch Investors Service furnish, for fees paid by the issuers, credit ratings for tax-exempt short-term obligations. However, many of the large institutional buyers now perform their own credit-risk analysis. The final market yield is composed of the assigned credit ratings and adjustments made by market participants to reflect their own perceptions of credit worthiness and marketability. In this section, we shall first describe the rating system of the two largest commercial rating companies, Standard & Poor's and Moody's. In the next section, we provide reasons why market participants have reexamined their reliance on the ratings given by these companies and we provide a framework for analyzing the credit worthiness of the various tax-exempt short-term obligations.

The Ratings of the Commercial Rating Companies

Moody's[11] The municipal note rating system used by Moody's is designated by four investment-grade categories known as Moody's Investment Grade, or MIG, as shown in Exhibit 1.

Moody's also provides credit ratings for tax-exempt commercial paper. These are promissory obligations not having an original maturity in excess of nine months and are backed by commercial banks. Moody's uses three designations, all considered

---

[11] Data are derived from various Moody's publications such as the *Bond Record* and the *Bond Survey*.

Exhibit 1
Moody's Municipal Note Ratings

Rating	Definition
MIG 1	*Best* quality
MIG 2	*High* quality
MIG 3	*Favorable* quality
MIG 4	*Adequate* quality

to be of investment grade, for indicating the relative repayment capacity of the rated issues. They are shown in Exhibit 2.

Standard & Poor's[12]   The municipal note rating system used by Standard & Poor's grades the investment quality of municipal

Exhibit 2
Moody's Tax-Exempt Commercial Paper Ratings

Rating	Definition
Prime 1 (P-1)	*Superior capacity* for repayment
Prime 2 (P-2)	*Strong capacity* for repayment
Prime 3 (P-3)	*Acceptable capacity* for repayment

notes in a 4-symbol system that ranges from the highest investment quality, SP-1$^+$, to the lowest credit rating, SP-3. Notes within the top three categories (i.e., SP-1$^+$, SP-1, and SP-2) are considered by Standard & Poor's as being of investment-grade quality. The respective ratings and summarized definitions are given in Exhibit 3.

Exhibit 3
Standard & Poor's Municipal Note Ratings

Rating	Definition
SP-1	Very strong or strong capacity to pay principal and interest. Those issues determined to possess overwhelming safety characteristics will be given a plus (+) designation.
SP-2	Satisfactory capacity to pay principal and interest.
SP-3	Speculative capacity to pay principal and interest.

Standard & Poor's rates tax-exempt commercial paper in the same seven categories as it does taxable commercial paper. The seven tax-exempt commercial paper rating categories are given in Exhibit 4.

---

[12] Data are derived from various Standard & Poor's publications such as *Bond Guide* and *Credit Week*.

Exhibit 4
Standard & Poor's Tax-Exempt Commercial
Paper Ratings

Rating	Definition
A–1+	*Overwhelming* degree of safety
A–1	*Very strong* degree of safety
A–2	*Strong degree* of safety
A–3	*Satisfactory* degree of safety
B	*Only adequate* capacity for payment
C	*Doubtful* capacity for payment
D	*Defaulted* or expected to be in default

DETERMINING THE CREDIT WORTHINESS OF SHORT-TERM TAX-EXEMPT OBLIGATIONS

While the ability of commercial rating companies to assess the credit worthiness of short-term tax-exempt obligations has evolved to a level of general industry acceptance and respectability and in the large majority of instances they adequately describe the financial condition of the issuers and identify the credit-risk factors, a small but significant number of instances have caused market participants to reexamine their reliance on these commercial ratings.

In fact, since 1975 all of the major municipal note defaults initially had been given high investment-grade ratings by the commercial rating companies. As some examples, the notes of the Urban Development Corporation that defaulted in 1975 had been rated MIG-2 by Moody's. Moody's also had given New York City's notes that defaulted its MIG-1 and MIG-2 ratings. The construction loan notes of the Oklahoma Housing Finance Agency, at the time of their default on June 1. 1982, were still rated MIG-1 by Moody's and had the highest note rating also of Standard & Poor's. This last default highlights the concern of sophisticated investors that the rating companies may not closely monitor their ratings once they are assigned.

Near defaults should also be mentioned. The notes of the Chicago Board of Education, which were on the brink of default in 1980, at issuance had been given investment-grade ratings by Moody's. Also, in 1982 many of the numerous construction loan notes secured by "repos" with the bankrupt arbitraging and trading firm of Lombard-Wall, Inc. had high investment-grade ratings by both Standard & Poor's and Moody's. While the investor may not have lost a single coupon payment, if the corporate treasurer bought the securities when they had high investment-grade ratings and had to sell them prior to maturity and after their ratings had been suspended or lowered, he would realize a substantial capital loss. Unlike 20 years ago, when the commercial rating companies would not rate many kinds of start-up and project financings, today they seem to view themselves as assisting in the capital formation process.[13] This is of particular concern since the commercial rating companies now receive sometimes very substantial fees for their ratings. The major companies are part of large, growth-oriented conglomerates. Moody's is an operating unit of the Dun & Bradstreet Corporation, and Standard & Poor's is part of the McGraw-Hill Corporation. By the 1980s, Moody's charged fees as high as $67,500 per sale, and Standard & Poor's charged up to $25,000.

Also, it should be noted that the timely review of ratings outstanding is believed to be one of the largest difficulties facing investors and the rating agencies. A commercial rating company may have as many as 20,000 ratings outstanding. For the seller, for the buyer, and for the trader of tax-exempt debt the possibility that ratings may be outdated, and therefore of questionable reliability, is distressful.

Tax Anticipation, Revenue Anticipation, Grant Anticipation, and Bond Anticipation Notes

These notes are temporary borrowings by states, local governments, and special jurisdictions to finance a variety of activities. Usually, notes are issued for a period of 12 months, though it is not uncommon for notes to be issued for periods as short as 3 months and for as long as 3 years. There are two general purposes for which notes are issued—to even out cash flows and to temporarily finance capital improvements. Each reason is explained below.

Many states, cities, towns, counties, and school districts, as well as special jurisdictions, sometimes borrow temporarily in anticipation of the collection of taxes or other expected revenues. Their need to borrow occurs because, while payrolls, bills, and other commitments have to be paid starting at the beginning of the fiscal years, property taxes and other revenues such as intergovernmental grants are due and payable after the beginning of the fiscal years. These notes, identified as either "Tax Anticipation Notes" ("TANs"), "Revenue Anticipation Notes" ("RANs"), or "Grant Anticipation Notes" ("GANs"), are usu-

---

[13] See Victor F. Zonana and Daniel Hertzberg, "Moody's Dominance in Municipals Market is Slowly Being Eroded," *The Wall Street Journal*, November 1, 1981, pp. 1, 23; and Peter Brimelow, "Shock Waves from Whoops Roll East," *Fortune*, July 25, 1983, pp. 46–48.

ally used to even out the cash flows which are necessitated by the irregular flows of income into the treasuries of the states and local units of government. In some instances, combination Tax and Revenue Anticipation Notes ("TRANs") are issued, which usually are payable from two sources. An example would be the TRANs issued by the state of New York.

The second general purpose for which notes are issued is in anticipation of the sale of long-term bonds. Such notes are known as "Bond Anticipation Notes" ("BANs"). There are three major reasons why capital improvements are initially financed with BANs.

First, because the initial cost estimates for a large construction project can vary from the construction bids actually submitted, and since better terms are sometimes obtained on a major construction project if the state or local government pays the various contractors as soon as the work begins, BANs are often used as the initial financing instrument. Once the capital improvement is completed, the bills paid, and the total costs determined, the BANs can be retired with the proceeds of a final bond sale.

Second, issuers such as states and cities that have large, diverse, and ongoing capital construction programs will initially issue BANs, and later retire them with the proceeds of a single long-term bond sale. In this instance, the use of BANs allows the issuer to consolidate various, unrelated financing needs into one bond sale.

The third reason why BANs are sometimes issued is related to market conditions. By temporarily financing capital improvements with BANs, the issuer has greater flexibility in determining the timing of its long-term bond sale, and possibly avoiding unfavorable market conditions.

The Security Behind Tax, Revenue, and Grant Anticipation Notes   Tax Anticipation Notes (TANs) are usually secured by the taxes for which they were issued. For counties, cities, towns, and school districts, TANs are usually issued for expected property taxes. Some governmental units go so far as to establish escrow accounts for receiving the taxes, and use the escrowed monies to pay the noteholders.

Revenue Anticipation Notes (RANs) or Grant Anticipation Notes (GANs) are also usually, but not always, secured by the revenues for which they were issued. These revenues can include intergovernmental capital construction grants and aid as well as local taxes other than property taxes.

In one extreme case, and as the result of the New York City note default in 1975, RANs issued by New York City for expected educational aid from the state of New York provide for the noteholder to go directly to the State comptroller and get the state aid monies before they are sent to the City's treasury, if that is necessary to remedy a default. Most RANs just require the issuer, itself, to use the expected monies to pay the noteholders once they are in hand.

Additionally, it must be noted that most TANs, RANs, and GANs issued by states, counties, cities, towns, and school districts are also secured by the "General Obligation Pledge," which is discussed later in this chapter.

Information Needed Before Buying Tax, Revenue, or Grant Anticipation Notes   Before purchasing a TAN, RAN or GAN, the manager of a corporate short-term portfolio should obtain information in five areas. These are in addition to what is required if long-term bonds were being considered for purchase. The five areas are:

1. Determining the reliability of the expected taxes, revenues, or grants.
2. Determining the degree of dependency of the note issuers on the expected monies.
3. Determining the soundness of the issuers' budgetary operations.
4. Determining the problem of "roll-overs."
5. Determining the historic and projected cash flows by month.

Each area is discussed below.

If a TAN is issued in anticipation of property taxes, a question to ask is: What were the tax collection rates over the previous five years? Tax collection rates below 90 percent usually indicate serious tax collection problems. Additionally, if the issuer is budgeting 100 percent of the tax levy while collecting substantially less, serious problems can be expected.

If a RAN or GAN is issued in anticipation of state or federal grant monies, the first question to ask is if the grant has been legislatively authorized and committed by the state or federal government. Some RAN issuers, which included New York City prior to its RAN defaults in 1975, would issue RANs without having all the anticipated grants committed by the higher levels of government. This practice may still be done by other local governments that are hard-pressed to balance their budgets and obtain quick cash through the sales of RANs. A safeguard against this is to see if the issuer has in its possession a fully signed grant agreement prior to the RAN or GAN sale.

One measure of the credit worthiness of the TAN or RAN issuer is the degree of dependency of the issuer on the temporarily borrowed monies. As examples, some jurisdictions limit the amount of TANs that can be issued in anticipation of property taxes to a percentage of the prior year's levy that was actually collected. The state of New Jersey, which has one of the more fiscally conservative local government regulatory codes in the country, limits the annual sale of TANs and RANs by local governments to no more than 30 percent of the property taxes and various other revenues actually collected in the previous year. Many other states are more permissive and allow local governments to issue TANs and RANs up to 75–100 percent of the monies previously collected, or even expected to be received in the current fiscal year.

Another critical element of the TAN or RAN issuer's credit worthiness concerns determining whether or not the issuer has a history of overall prudent and disciplined financial management. One way to do this is to determine how well the issuer maintained end-of-year fund balances in its major operating funds over the previous five fiscal years.

Key indications of fiscal problems are revealed when issuers either retire their TANs and RANs with the proceeds of new issues, or issue TANs and RANs to be retired in a fiscal year following the one in which they were originally issued. Such practices are known as "roll-overs," and are sometimes used by hard-pressed issuers to disguise chronic operating budget deficits. To leave no doubt as to the soundness of their budgetary operations, many states, local governments, and special jurisdictions, either by statute or by administrative policy, have established that all TANs and RANs issued in one fiscal year must be retired before the end of that fiscal year. While such a policy reduces the flexibility of the issuer to deal with unexpected emergencies that may occur, it does help provide protection to the noteholders against TANs and RANs ever being used for hidden deficit financing. It should be noted that in some circumstances RANs and GANs can be properly issued for periods greater than 12 months, provided that the granting agency has established a reimbursement schedule which matches the maturity of the RANs or GANs.

The last area for investigation is the TAN, RAN, or GAN issuer's cash flow history and projections. Initially, what is required here is a monthly accounting going back over the previous fiscal year which shows the beginning fund balances, revenues, expenditures, and end-of-month fund balances. In the analysis of this actual cash flow the investor should determine how well the issuer has met its fiscal goals by maintaining at least a balanced budget and meeting all liabilities, including debt service payments.

The second cash flow table to review is the one on the projected monthly cash flows for the fiscal year in which the TANs or RANs are to be issued. Here, the investor should look to see if the issuer has included in the projections sufficient revenues to retire the TANs, RANs, or GANs, and if the estimated revenues and expenditures amounts are realistic in light of the prior fiscal year's experience.

The Security behind Bond Anticipation Notes BANs are secured principally by the ability of the issuers to have future access to the municipal bond market so as to retire the outstanding BANs with the proceeds of long-term bond sales. Additionally, it must be noted that most BANs issued by states, counties, cities, towns, and school districts are also secured by the General Obligation pledge, which is discussed later in this chapter.

Information Needed Before Buying Bond Anticipation Notes Two factors determine the ability of the issuers to gain market access. Therefore, the BAN investors should obtain information in these two areas. They are:

1. The credit worthiness of the issuers.
2. Expected future market conditions and the flexibility of the issuers.

Each is discussed below.

Since the outstanding BANs are to be retired with the proceeds of long-term bond sales, the credit worthiness of the BANs are directly related to the credit worthiness of the underlying bond issuers. Therefore, the investor must obtain the same credit information on the BANs that he would if long-term bonds were being issued. In general, the stronger the bond credit quality, the greater are the abilities of the BAN issuer to successfully complete their respective long-term bond sales. Besides determining the credit quality of the underlying bonds, the investor should also make a determination as to the probable market access and acceptance of the BAN issuer.

That is, in the past how well have the bonds of the issuer been received in the marketplace? Has the issuer had to pay interest costs substantially higher than other bond issuers that had similar credit ratings? Answers to these questions will determine the credit risks involved when purchasing the BANs.

While it is not possible for the BAN investor to know in advance the future condition of the market when his BANs come due, it is safe to conclude that if the issuer's credit worthiness is at least of investment-grade quality there should usually be a market for that issuer's bonds. Of course, the weaker the credit quality, and the larger the amount of BANs to be retired, the higher the rate of interest would have to be.

If the BANs come due at a time when the municipal bond market is experiencing rising interest rates, the BAN issuer should have the flexibility to retire the maturing BANs with a new BAN issue instead of issuing long-term bonds. Most state and local government finance regulations recognize this need by allowing BANs to be retired from new BAN issues. Also, the ability of the issuer to refund in the municipal market the maturing BANs with new BANs is directly related to the credit quality of the issuer. It should also be noted that, unlike most TANs, RANs, and GANs, BANs can be refunded, i.e., rolled over into new BANs. However, prudent issuers usually are limited by local laws to having their BANs outstanding for no longer than five to eight years. If there is no limit as to how long the BANs can be outstanding, the temptation is great for the BAN issuer to avoid funding-out the BANs with a bond issue.

The Security behind the "General Obligation" Pledge   Many TANs, RANs, and GANs issued by states, cities, towns, counties, and school districts are secured by the General Obligation pledge. What this means is that the issuers are legally obligated to use, if necessary, their full taxing powers and available revenues to pay the noteholders. Therefore, if a tax anticipation note is issued by a city which is secured by property taxes as well as by the General Obligation pledge, and if the city's property tax collection rate that particular year does not generate sufficient taxes to pay the noteholder, the city must use other resources to make the noteholder whole, including available monies in its General Fund. Of course, the importance of the General Obligation pledge is directly related to the diversification of the issuer's revenue base and lack of dependence on note sales, as well as on the soundness of its budgetary operations. Many BANs are also secured by the General Obligation pledge of the issuer. If the overall credit quality, revenue structure, and market image of the underlying General Obligation issuer are stronger than those of the agency or department that has issued the BANs, then the General Obligation pledge would be a positive factor since it would strengthen market access for either rolling over the BANs or retiring them with the proceeds of a long-term bond sale.

In conclusion, while the credit analysis of TANs, RANs, GANs, and BANs has certain similarities to the analysis of long-term bonds, note analysis presents for the investor some additional challenges. In the above discussion, the more important areas of concern are identified. They should be explored in detail for determining the degree of insulation from adversity of any particular note.

Construction Loan Notes

Construction Loan Notes (CLNs) are usually issued for periods up to three years to provide short-term construction financing for multifamily housing projects. The CLNs generally are repaid by the proceeds of long-term bonds, which are provided after the housing projects are completed. There are five major credit risk areas that the manager of a corporate short-term portfolio should investigate when attempting to determine the degree of insulation from adversity of CLNs. Each is discussed below.

Determining if Federal Insurance Already Is in Place during Construction   Before the CLNs are issued, an investor should determine if there is Federal Housing Administration (FHA) mortgage insurance already in place. FHA insurance covers construction loan advances regardless of whether or not the project is completed. This provides comfort to the noteholders should the developer default on his interest or principal payments prior to the maturity of the notes.

Determining if Permanent Financing Is Escrowed or Committed   Another key element in the determination of the credit quality of a CLN is whether or not there is an approved permanent financing plan to take out the construction loan notes. There are generally two plans possible.

In one type of financing plan, bonds are originally sold at the same time as the notes. The bond proceeds are placed in escrow pending project completion, cost certification, and final endorsement for FHA insurance. Then, once these three events occur, the bond proceed monies can be released and used to pay the noteholders. Bonds that are sold simultaneously with construction loan notes are usually done so under HUD's Section 8-11(b) program, which is primarily for local issuers.

In the second type of note take-out plan, the Government

National Mortgage Agency (GNMA) is committed to provide cash which—along with other required monies such as contributions by the developer—is used to retire the construction loan notes. For the GNMA take-out to occur, the project must be completed, be cost certified, and have received final endorsement for FHA insurance.

Determining if There Is Adequate Cash Flow Protection   Still another concern is to determine how well designed are the cash flow projections. For CLNs where bond proceeds are escrowed, and for GNMA issues, temporary investment earnings, interest payments by the developers, and construction payment drawdowns of the CLN proceeds should be based on worst-case assumptions so as to meet all CLN interest payment dates. The cash flow projections should be presented in a format that shows by month the total expected income and expenses. Additionally, the cashflow projections should show worst-case scenarios covering periods when mortgage insurance payments and other backup security features or liquidity enhancements may have to be depended upon. Of course, the combination of the investment earnings and interest payments which the developer makes on advanced monies should be the basis for the financing, though the note trustee should have immediate access to the other security structures as well.

There are additional concerns in the case of CLNs where a GNMA take-out is planned. Since the GNMA take-out provides only 97½ percent of the amount needed to retire the construction loan notes, the gap must be provided for in advance. An investor should make sure that expected investment earnings, together with cash contributions by the developer, are sufficient. Additionally, since the GNMA take-out could occur months before the actual maturity of the construction loan notes, an investor should check to see that investment agreements are in place for the temporary investment of the GNMA monies, or if there is a provision to call the notes following the GNMA take-out.

Determining if There Are Adequate Construction and Certification Periods   Because of possible construction delays and the time required by FHA/GNMA for the processing of the final mortgage documents, ample time should be allowed between the expected completion date of the project construction and the construction loan note maturity date. Generally, a six-month or less lag between targeted construction completion and note maturity is not sufficient. While there may not be a default by the mortgagor on the FHA-insured mortgage loan, a delay in construction or final FHA endorsement could have a negative impact on note security by preventing the timely release of permanent financing funds. Therefore, the CLN issuer's budget must include a minimum period of approximately eight months between the expected construction completion date and the maturity of the construction loan note.

Determining How Reliable Are the CLN Investment Agreements Because many local issuers have limited backup resources available, and the projected investment earnings on the unspent note proceeds play a crucial role in the financing plan, the investment agreement is also of concern in the credit risk analysis. If the investment agreement is in the form of a contract with a commercial bank, the bank should be well capitalized. If the investment agreement takes the form of a repurchase or "repo" agreement, an investor must examine certain other factors which are discussed in the next section.

Repurchase Agreements

A repurchase agreement (or "repo") is a contractual agreement between a municipal issuer (or its bank trustee) and a commercial bank, brokerage firm, or other government bond dealer. In the transaction, the repo issuer (such as a government bond dealer) receives cash and, in turn, should provide interest-bearing high quality securities to a municipal issuer as collateral for the cash, for an agreed upon time period. At the end of this period the repo issuer returns the cash plus interest on the funds and reacquires the securities that had been provided as collateral. Often, construction loan note proceeds, and even cash flow revenues, are invested through repos until the money is needed to pay either debt service or construction expenses associated with the specific projects. Over the years, investment bankers and municipal issuers have found repos to be attractive short-term investment vehicles since they can match the maturity of the repo to their specific cash flow needs.

Repos were not generally recognized as pressing credit concerns until the summer of 1982 when a few modestly capitalized government bond dealers that had repos outstanding experienced severe financial stress. These firms were Drysdale Securities Corporation, Comark Securities, Inc., and Lombard-Wall, Inc. On August 12, 1982, Lombard-Wall filed for court protection under the Federal Bankruptcy Code. Under the automatic-stay provisions of section 362 (a) of the code, as well as a temporary restraining order issued on August 17 by the judge at the request of Lombard-Wall, no note trustee could sell the collateral securing a Lombard-Wall repo without court approval. In effect, the collateral was frozen.

As an example of the severity of this freeze on individual credit worthiness, one hospital bond issuer had $43.34 million, or 37 percent of its bond proceeds, invested with Lombard-Wall. Another issuer had its total debt reserve fund invested with Lombard under a 30-year repo. Several construction loan note issuers also had whole note issue proceeds invested with Lombard-Wall.

The credit risks for the holders of the notes involved were substantially increased because:

1. The bankruptcy court's restraining order on August 17 prevented the sale or disposition of securities received from Lombard-Wall under repurchase or investment agreements without court approval.
2. Several of the note issuers were dependent upon these securities to finance construction and related activities.
3. Future court actions in these areas were unsettled.[14]

Additionally, in an oral opinion by the bankruptcy judge in September 1982 concerning the Dauphin County Hospital Authority of Harrisburg, Pennsylvania, it was held that the repo collateral belonged to Lombard-Wall.[15] That is, the court considered the repo transactions to be "secured loans" to Lombard-Wall and *not* "sales-repurchase contracts." Before the collateral could be liquidated, the judge would have to agree on the terms of the liquidation and who was to receive the proceeds. It should be noted that on July 10, 1984, the President signed into law the Amendments Bankruptcy Act which exempt repos with a maturity of one year or less or on demand from the automatic stay provisions of the U.S. Bankruptcy Code. This law, in effect, removed most of the risks highlighted by the Lombard-Wall bankruptcy.

The Third Party Risk   In the Lombard-Wall case, the judge also refused to release the collateral which had been borrowed by Lombard-Wall from a third party. At least three Texas bond issuers—the Lubbock Housing Finance Corporation, the Abilene Housing Finance Corporation, and the Baytown Housing

---

[14] This is based upon observations, at the time of the court proceedings, as well as upon interviews with various lawyers involved in the litigations.

[15] "Sale Barred of Lombard-Wall Bonds Used in Repo for Hospital Authority," *American Banker*, September 20, 1982, p. 2. According to the counsel for Dauphin, before the Judge's oral decision was typed and signed, the parties involved settled their dispute. Interview with James A. Moyer, Esq., of LeBoeuf, Lamb, Leiby & Macrae, October 4, 1982.

Finance Corporation—received approval to sell only two thirds of their collateral, as the other third had been borrowed by Lombard-Wall from a third party.

It should be noted that after the court's decision, the trustee for the three bond issues—the First Interstate Bank of California—decided to use its own resources to remedy the losses resulting from the Lombard-Wall investments.[16]

Evaluating Repo Agreement While the great bull bond markets of August 1982 helped to bail out Lombard-Wall, at the time over 50 municipal note issuers faced serious financial problems as the result of the bankruptcy. Therefore, if repos are used in financial transactions, the investor should consider the following factors:

1. Are construction funds, any other proceeds, or project enterprise revenues invested through repos? If so, to what extent is the note issuer dependent on the repo monies? Clearly, construction loan note proceeds, debt reserve funds, mortgage loan repayments, and grant receipts invested in repos are of greater concern than are idle funds.

2. Are the repos with large, investment banking firms, established government bond dealers, and major capitalized banks? Repos should not be entered into with small undercapitalized trading firms. Inclusion on a list of the Federal Reserve Bank is not automatically adequate evidence of credit worthiness.

3. Are the repos fully secured with collateral delivered and held by a third party? Are the bank trustees identified in the repo agreements as having a "perfected interest" in the securities they hold as collateral? Title to the collateral should at all times be with them.

4. The collateral should include only:

a. Direct general obligations of, or obligations the payment of the principal and interest of which are unconditionally guaranteed by, the United States of America.

b. Bonds, debentures, or notes issued by any of the following federal agencies: Federal Home Loan Banks, Federal Land Banks, Bank for Cooperatives, Federal Financing Bank, or Federal Home Loan Mortgage Corporation (including participation certificates).

c. Public housing bonds, temporary notes, or preliminary loan notes fully secured by contracts with the United States of America.

---

[16] "3 Texas Agencies Will Be Repaid Lombard Funds," *The Bond Buyer*, September 9, 1982, p. 3. It should also be noted that it was reported that the third party involved was the trust department of Bankers Trust, in *The Bond Buyer*, September 7, 1982, p. 1.

5.   Because the vagaries of the taxable bond markets impose the risk that the fair market value of the collateral may substantially decline at any time, the collateral should be valued at least weekly and preferably daily. The fair market value of the securities, as stated in the repo agreements, should mean the bid prices (principal price *plus accrued interest*) as they appear in the "Composite Closing Quotations for Government Securities," published by the Federal Reserve Bank of New York.

6.   If the value of the collateral decreases below the levels agreed upon under the repurchase agreements and is not replenished immediately upon notification, then the note trustees should have the right to sell the respective securities. Similarly, if the repo issuer defaults in an interest or principal payment, there should be the right to sell immediately.

7.   The repo agreements should state who the principal parties in the transactions are and that the collateral is free of all liens.

Tax-Exempt Commercial Paper[17]

This short-term tax-exempt borrowing instrument is used for periods ranging from 30 to 270 days. Generally, tax-exempt commercial paper has backstop commercial bank agreements, which can include an irrevocable letter of credit, a revolving credit agreement, or a line of credit. If the security does not include a credit "backstop" for the benefit of the investor, the credit risk analysis would follow the guidelines discussed above in regard to tax, revenue, grant, and bond anticipation notes.

Most tax-exempt commercial paper includes a commercial bank backstop such as an irrevocable letter of credit, a revolving credit agreement, or a line of credit. The irrevocable letter of credit is the strongest type of investor comfort. It requires the bank to pay necessary amounts to the limits of the letter. Of course, the investor should review the terms of the agreement carefully, so as to determine, among others, whether the letter of credit extends only to defaulted note principal or also includes principal and interest through the date of default on the note. A revolving credit agreement could have the same credit worthiness as does the irrevocable letter of credit. However, the investor must examine the agreement to see if there are circumstances under which the bank may be released from responsibility. A line of credit agreement is generally the weakest

---

[17] This discussion is drawn from James J. Goodwin II. "Tax-Exempt Commercial Paper," Chapter 34 in *The Municipal Bond Handbook, Volume II*. ed. Sylvan G. Feldstein, Frank J. Fabozzi, and Irving M. Pollack (Homewood, Ill: Dow Jones-Irwin, 1983).

backstop since it usually has a number of release clauses which may allow a bank to avoid providing funds when required. Usually, in all of the commercial bank supports, the monies are provided as a remedy for a default. The investor or trustees must present a claim after the default in order to benefit from the backstop.

The Preference Problem   Under current bankruptcy law there is a question as to whether a paper holder could be forced to repay the trustee if the tax-exempt commercial paper issuer files in bankruptcy and the holder had had a maturity of 90 days or less from such a filing and was "paid" via a roll-over of the paper. This could occur even though the investor did not know of the impending bankruptcy of the paper issuer. Needless to say, the underlying credit worthiness of the tax-exempt commercial paper issuer should also be determined by the investor in addition to the commercial bank credit support.

SUMMARY

The manager of a corporate short-term portfolio may select from a variety of tax-exempt obligations. In this chapter, we have described the general characteristics of these obligations; their federal, state, and local tax treatment; their credit risks; and an analytical framework for evaluating their credit worthiness.

12

Managing a Corporate Short-Term Portfolio

Marcia Stigum, Ph.D.
Stigum & Associates

One might expect most corporate portfolios to be managed with considerable sophistication, but "the startling thing you would find, if you were to wander around the country talking to short-term portfolio managers [bank and corporate], is the basic underutilization of the portfolio." These are the words of the sales manager of the government department in one of the nation's top banks. Another dealer described portfolio management practices similarly but in slightly different terms, "Most portfolio managers would describe themselves as 'conservative,' by which they mean that the correct way to manage a portfolio is to look to your accounting risk and reduce that to zero. The opportunities thereby forgone are either ignored or more frequently not even perceived." Most short-term portfolios are poorly managed, many are not managed at all. Before we talk about that, let's look first at how a liquidity portfolio should be managed.

THE PARAMETERS

A liquidity is always managed within certain investment *parameters* that establish limits with respect to: (1) the types of instruments the portfolio may buy; (2) the percentage of the portfolio that may be invested in any one of these instruments (in Treasury bills the limit might be 100 percent, whereas in Certificates of Deposits (CDs), which are less liquid, it might be much lower); (3) the kind of exposure to names and credit risk the portfolio may assume (which banks' CDs and which issuers' commercial paper it may buy and how much of each name it

252

may buy); (4) whether the portfolio may invest in Euros and foreign names; (5) how far out on the maturity spectrum the portfolio may extend; (6) whether the portfolio may short securities or repo securities; and (7) whether the portfolio may use futures and options.

The investment parameters within which every liquidity portfolio operates are set by top management (treasurer, senior vice president finance). Because senior management delineates the portfolio manager's playing field and thereby the kinds of winnings—return on investment—that he can seek to earn through managing the portfolio, it is important that management take time to learn what the game is about before establishing such guidelines. Another input in this decision should be an evaluation of the kind of money that the firm is likely to have to invest short term: How big is it likely to be? How variable will it be? A third important input is the firm's management style. There are swinging corporations and there are very conservative corporations, and that difference should be reflected in their styles of portfolio management. A fourth factor is the caliber of the personnel the firm hires to manage its short-term portfolio. Investment parameters are meant to limit the portfolio manager's freedom of judgment, and inevitably they will at times prevent him from pursuing strategies that he correctly believes would increase return. For example, tight restrictions on the amount a portfolio manager could invest in bankers acceptances (BAs) might prevent him, when BAs were trading at an attractive spread to bills, from making a profitable swap out of bills into BAs. The more qualified the personnel the firm anticipates hiring to run its liquidity portfolio, the wider guidelines should be set and the greater the latitude the portfolio manager should be given to exercise judgment.

MANAGING A LIQUIDITY PORTFOLIO

In large corporations, a portfolio manager (cash manager or assistant treasurer) is often given several portfolios to manage—one for the firm itself, another for its financing sub, still others for self-insurance funds, and so forth. With respect to each portfolio, the manager has to ask: What are the size, variability, and predictability of the money I am investing? The answer obviously depends in part on the purpose for which the funds are held. For example, the short-term portfolio of a manufacturing firm that experiences big seasonal fluctuations in cash flows, as auto firms and food packers do, will be more variable and less predictable in size than a portfolio supporting a self-insurance fund. A second element in the portfolio manager's evaluation of the sort of money he is investing is the cash forecasts the firm gives him—their frequency, the periods for which they are available (these might be tomorrow, the next week, the next month, and the current quarter), and the confidence that experience suggests he can place in these forecasts. The portfolio manager's assessment of the sort of money he is investing tells him how long he is likely to be able to hold securities he buys and thus the planning horizon—30 days, 90 days, 1 year, or longer—upon which he should base investment decisions.

Relative Value

Once he has determined his planning horizon, the portfolio manager asks: *Where is relative value?* Answering this question requires knowledge, experience, and feel for the market.

On a purely technical level, the portfolio manager first has to face the problem that yields on money market instruments are not quoted on comparable bases.[1] The problem is not just that yields on discount securities are quoted on a discount basis, whereas yields on interest-bearing instruments are quoted on another basis. There are also all sorts of other anomalies with respect to how interest accrues, how often it is paid, whether the security is U.S. or Canadian (Canadian CDs trade on a 365-day-year basis, domestic CDs on a 360-day-year basis), whether it is a leap year, whether a security happens to mature on a holiday, and other factors. These anomalies, moreover, are *not* reflected in the yield to maturity figures on dealers' quote sheets.[2]

A number of portfolio managers, who run such large sums of money that the cost is justified, have developed sophisticated computer programs that permit them to calculate yields on a wide range of securities on a comparable basis. One such portfolio manager noted, "I developed a program that incorporated a day algorithm which I got from a mathematician. I wanted the computer to know when a weekend occurs and to skip it in evaluating yield on a Friday trade I do for regular settlement. I also wanted the computer to recognize that in agencies July 31 is a nonday [in terms of interest accrued], that February 29 exists whether or not it actually does, and so too does February 30;

---

[1] See Chapter 10 for a discussion of how the yields on various money market instruments are quoted.

[2] See Marcia Stigum and John Mann, *Money Market Calculations: Yields, Break-evens, and Arbitrage* (Homewood, Ill.: Dow Jones-Irwin, 1981).

there's an arbitrage from February 28 to March 1 in agencies, and I want the computer to recognize this. The computer also knows a Canadian security from a U.S. security."

In evaluating the relative value of different instruments, being able to calculate their yields on a comparable basis is just a starting point. In addition, the portfolio manager has to have a good feel for the *liquidity* of different instruments, under both prevailing market conditions and those he foresees might occur. This can involve subtle distinctions. The manager of a large portfolio commented, "I buy only direct issue [commercial] paper that I know I can sell to the dealers—GMAC but not Pru-lease. It's a question of liquidity, not quality. Also I buy paper from dealers only if they are ready to take it back."

To determine relative value among different instruments, the portfolio manager must also have a good feel for *yield spreads:* what they are, and how and why they change. This too involves subtleties. Here's an example given by one investor, "Lately the six-month bill has been trading above Fed funds. I ask, 'Why?' The technical condition of the market has been excellent with little supply on the street [in dealers' hands]. So the six-month bill should have done better, but it didn't. The reason is that we've got a pure dealer market. The retail buyer, who is scared and going short, is simply not there."

Finally, to determine where relative value lies among different *maturity* sectors of the market, the portfolio manager must explicitly predict interest rates *and* the slope of the yield curve over at least the time span of his planning horizon. Such predictions will be based on a wide range of factors, including a careful tracking of the Fed's stated objectives and whether it is currently achieving these objectives.

Relative value, in addition to depending on all the factors we have enumerated, may also depend partly on the temperament of the portfolio manager—whether he has the psychology of a trader, as a number of top portfolio managers do, or is more inclined to make a reasoned bet and let it stand for some time, an attitude characteristic of other successful portfolio managers. As one investor noted, it makes a difference, "The nine-month bill will, except in very tight markets, trade at yield levels close to the corresponding long issue, which is the one-year bill. So if you are looking for the most return for your dollar on a buy-and-hold strategy, you buy the nine-month bill and ride it for three months. If, however, you want to trade the portfolio—to buy something with the idea that its price will rise—you are better off staying in the active issue, which would be the current year bill."

Credit Risk

Most companies, when they have money and are trying to increase yield, will start reaching out on the credit spectrum—buying A-2 or P-2 paper.[3] A few do so in an intelligent and reasoned way, devoting considerable resources to searching out companies that are candidates for an upgrading of their credit rating to A-1 or P-1 and whose paper thus offers more relative value than that of A-1 and P-1 issuers.

The average firm, however, would probably be well advised not to take this route. As the sales manager of one dealership noted, "We tell a company doing this, 'It's the wrong thing for you to do because you do not know how to do it. You have no ability to track these companies. Also their financial statements are not worth much, and you of all people should know this because you know what you do to your own.' They sort of look at us with jaundiced eyes, and say 'Oh, yes, I guess that's so.' "

The ablest portfolio managers tend as a group to steer clear of credit analysis. As one of the sharpest commented, "We are not interested in owning anything that does not have unimpeachable credit because, on an instrument that does not, credit will tend to dominate the performance of the instrument more than interest rates. Also, I am a one-man band, and I simply do not have time to evaluate credit risk."

Maturity Choice

While a good portfolio manager can, as many do, refuse to get into credit analysis, he *cannot* avoid making explicit interest rate predictions and basing his maturity choices upon them. As one portfolio manager pointed out, "The mistake many people make is to think that they do not have to make a forecast. But buying a 90-day bill and holding it to maturity *is* making a forecast. If you think that rates are going to move up sharply and soon, you should be sitting in overnight RP; and then when rates move up, you buy the 90-day bill."

Making rate predictions is important not only because an implicit rate prediction underlies every maturity choice a portfolio manager makes, but because good portfolio managers feel as a group that the way yield on a large portfolio can most effectively be increased is by positioning correctly along the maturity spectrum—by recognizing which maturity sectors of the market are cheap (have relative value), which are expensive, and by buying or selling accordingly.

---

[3] Commercial paper, as noted in Chapter 10, is rated by several rating services. A-2 and P-2 paper are a grade off top-rated A-1 or P-1 paper.

Riding the Yield Curve   The best way to illustrate the kind of dividends yielded by maturity choices based on an explicit prediction of how interest rates might move is with a few concrete examples. Let's start by illustrating how a technique commonly used to raise return—namely, *riding the yield curve*—must be based on an explicit prediction of how short-term rates might change.

The yield curve graphically portrays the relationship between yield and current maturity. Normally, the yield curve is positively or upward sloped, indicating that the longer the time to maturity, the higher the yield. The idea of riding the yield curve is to increase return, when the yield curve is positively sloped, by buying a security out on the shoulder of the yield curve and holding that security until it can be sold at a gain because its current maturity has fallen and the yield at which it is currently trading has consequently decreased. Note that the main threats to the success of such a strategy are that short-term rates might rise across the board or that the yield curve might invert at the very short end.

Assume that an investor has funds to invest for three months. The 6-month (180-day) bill is trading at 7.90, and the 3-month (90-day) bill is trading at 7.50 (Exhibit 1). The alternatives the

Exhibit 1
Yield Curve in an Example of Riding the Yield Curve

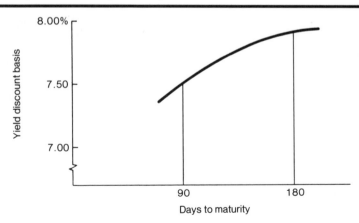

investor is choosing between are: (1) to buy the 90-day bill and mature it and (2) to buy the 6-month bill and sell it 3 months hence. To assess the relative merits of these two strategies, the investor does a *break-even analysis.*

On $1 million of bills, a 90-day basis point (a basis point earned for 90 days) is worth $25.[4] If the investor bought the 6-month bill, he would earn 40 basis points more than if he bought the 3-month bill. Thus he could sell out the 6-month bill after 3 months at a rate 40 basis points above the rate at which he bought it, that is, at 8.30, and still earn as many *dollars* on his investment as he would have if he had bought and matured the 3-month bill (Table 1). Therefore the rate on the 3-month bill 3

Table 1
Dollar Calculations of Return in Example of Riding the Yield Curve

I. Buy $1 million of 90-day bills at 7.50% and hold to maturity.

Face value	$1,000,000	Discount at purchase	$18,750
−Purchase price	981,250	−Discount at maturity	0
Return	$ 18,750	Return	$18,750

II. Buy $1 million of 180-day bills at 7.90% and sell at breakeven yield of 8.30%.

Sale price	$979,250	Discount at purchase	$39,500
−Purchase price	960,500	−Discount at sale	20,750
Return	$ 18,750	Return	$18,750

III. Buy $1 million of 180-day bills at 7.90% and sell at 7.50%.

Sale price	$981,250	Discount at purchase	$39,500
−Purchase price	960,500	−Discount at sale	18,750
Return	$ 20,750	Return	$20,750

months hence would have to rise above 8.30 before holding the 6-month bill for 3 months would pay out fewer dollars than buying and maturing the 3-month bill.

How likely is this to occur? Note that because of the slope of the yield curve (a 40-basis-point drop between the 6-month and 3-month bill rates), the rate at which the 3-month bill trades 3 months hence would be 7.50 if no change occurred in interest rates, 80 basis points below the break-even rate of 8.30. Thus the investor has 80 basis points of protection, and the question he has to ask in making his choice is: How likely is it that the Fed will tighten in the next 3 months so sharply that the 3-month bill will rise 80 basis points, from 7.50 to 8.30? If his answer is that it

---

[4] The formula using the notation adopted in the previous chapter is:

$$D = \left(\frac{d \times t_{sm}}{360}\right) (\$1,000,000)$$

The calculation is as follows:

$$\left(\frac{0.001 \times 90}{360}\right) (\$1,000,000) = \$25$$

is highly unlikely, then he would buy the 6-month bill and ride the yield curve.

Note that if the investor buys the 3-month bill and matures it, he will earn $18,750 on each $1 million of bills he buys (see Table 1). If, alternatively, he opts to ride the yield curve and does so successfully (i.e., buys the 6-month bill and is able, because the Fed does not tighten, to sell out at 7.50), he will earn $20,750, which exceeds $18,750 by $2,000. This $2,000 equals the extra 80 90-day basis points he earns; 40 because the 6-month bill is bought at a 40-basis-point spread to the 3-month bill and 40 because he is able to sell it 3 months later at a rate 40 basis points below the rate at which he bought it.

Actually the investor riding the yield curve in our example has more protection than we indicated. The reason is that, when he buys the six-month bill, he invests fewer dollars than when he buys the three-month bill. So on a *simple interest basis,* he would earn an annualized return of 7.75 if he bought and matured the 3-month bill, whereas if he bought the 6-month bill at 7.90 and sold it as the break-even level of 8.30, he would earn an annualized return, again on a simple interest, 365-day-year basis, of 7.92, which is greater.[5] To earn an annualized return of only 7.75 on the funds invested in the 6-month bill, the investor would have to sell it out after 3 months at a discount of 8.46, which is 96 basis points above 7.50. The first break-even calculation we made on a dollar-return basis is easier to make, but this second more refined calculation is the one the investor who wants to maximize yield should make.

Another Maturity Decision   Here's a second example of how a conscious prediction of interest rates over the investor's time horizon can help an investor increase yield. The example is dated, but the point it illustrates still holds. When it appears that the Fed might tighten, the reaction of many portfolio managers is to retreat in panic to the base of the yield curve. Whether doing so is wise depends on the opportunities available and on how fast and how far the Fed is likely to tighten.

In April 1977, it was felt that the Fed was tightening. Funds were trading at 4¾ and no one was sure where that rate was going. It was the feeling in the market that a ¾ point move was needed and that 5½ would probably be the top side, but some in the market suggested 5¾. Just prior to this period, six-month

---

[5] The formula is:

$$\begin{pmatrix} \text{Annualized return on a} \\ \text{simple interest basis} \end{pmatrix} = \begin{pmatrix} \dfrac{\text{Dollar return}}{\text{Principal invested}} \end{pmatrix} \begin{pmatrix} \dfrac{365}{\text{Days held}} \end{pmatrix}$$

BAs had risen in yield from 5.20 to 5.85 because of a lack of demand on the part of investors; the yield on three-month BAs was 5.45. At this point a portfolio manager with three-month money to invest faced a choice.

Stability of Return

As one good portfolio manager after another will note, "Real money is to be made by positioning correctly along the maturity spectrum—by making conscious market judgments and acting on them."

Such positioning does not, however, guarantee *steady* high return. One reason is that sometimes the portfolio manager will be wrong in his rate predictions. A second reason is well described by one manager, "If you can invest out to two years and you feel strongly that rates are going to fall, you might choose to have an average nine- or twelve-month maturity—not everything out in the longer spectrum. If you are correct and the market rallies, the proper response is to shorten the portfolio—not just to sit there and hold this apparent book yield, but to recognize it. The reason you sell is that the market eventually gets to a point where you think it has reached a peak and might go lower. If after you sell you decide that you were wrong and believe—on the basis of a new rate forecast—that rates are likely to go still lower, you buy in again long term."

It's hard to produce a stable income pattern with that sort of portfolio management, and thus it would be criticized by some. But the basic assumption is that the firm is a going concern. Therefore, the portfolio manager's primary goal should be long-term profitability, not stability of income.

Time Horizon and Maturity of Securities Purchased

In the example we gave of why the return on a managed portfolio is likely to fluctuate from month to month, the portfolio manager—believing that rates were likely to fall—might well have extended maturity into the two-year area. In this respect it's important to note that such an extension does not imply that either the portfolio manager's planning horizon or his interest-rate forecast extends anywhere near two years. It simply implies that he is confident that rates will fall during some much shorter period and that he is willing to sell and realize his gain once this occurs.

Good managers of short-term portfolios, who have wide parameters, frequently buy Treasury notes and other longer-term instruments in the hope of realizing short-term gains. Said an ex-portfolio manager, "If I liked the market, I'd buy a 10-year bond even if I needed the money tomorrow." That's an extreme example, but this portfolio manager had the inborn instincts of a good street trader, which he eventually became.

Changing Relative Value

The search for relative value is not a one-time affair. The money market is dynamic; changes in demand, supply, expectations, and external events—announcements of the latest money supply figures, changes in tax laws, the souring of country loans, or the failure of a dealer—are constantly having an impact on it. And as they do, yield spreads and rates change. Thus relative value may reside in one sector today, in another tomorrow.

A good portfolio manager must reassess his position each day, asking not only whether his expectations with respect to interest rates have changed but whether transistory anomalies have arisen in spreads or distortions in rates from which he could profit.

One cause of transitory rate distortions is overreactions by investors. Said one portfolio manager, "When I saw the huge money supply figures last Friday [$2.7 billion for M1, $13 billion for M2], I started buying knowing that in a few days the market would come back. This sort of overreaction has been much more common since '74, in part because there are so many more players in the market today."

Here's an example of another transitory rate situation from which a corporate portfolio manager could benefit. Capital gains are taxed as ordinary income for banks at the capital gains rate for corporations. Thus a longer-term municipal note selling at a discount from par offers a double-barreled tax advantage to a corporation but not to a bank.[6] Banks, however, are such big investors in this market that at times discount muni notes are priced to the bank market rather than to the corporate market. When they are, a corporation can earn a much higher after-tax return on such notes than it could from taxable securities of comparable maturity and risk.

Tracking changes in relative value takes time and effort, but as a portfolio manager gains experience, it becomes almost second nature. Also, a portfolio manager can rely on the dealers for help. Once a portfolio manager recognizes that a change in relative value has occurred between instruments or maturity sectors, his response should be to *swap* or *arbitrage*.

---

[6] This assumes that the corporation is in a position to benefit from tax-exempt income.

As one portfolio manager with wide parameters observed, "Arbitraging a portfolio is one way to make money, whether it's a complete arbitrage or a swapping arbitrage between sectors of the market. Money market instruments oscillate in relative value for very good reasons; and as you get experienced, you can with not too much time keep asking why one sector of the market is out of line with where it should be—the latter judgment being more than an extrapolation of a historical average. Once you have convinced yourself that the reason is transistory, then not to own the instrument that is undervalued and be short in the other instrument that is out of line is foolhardy."

Extension Swaps

One very simple swap strategy many portfolio managers use, when markets are calmer than they have been in recent years, is to do *extension swaps.* They pick a maturity sector of the market they like, say two- or three-year governments, and then, for example, adopt the strategy of *extending* (lengthening maturity) a few months whenever they can pick up five basis points and of *backing up* (shortening maturity) a few months whenever that costs only three basis points. If market conditions are such that many such swaps can be done, a portfolio manager can pick up basis points this way. Note that, whereas a 90-day basis point is worth only $25 per $1 million, a 3-year basis point is worth $300.[7]

A similar practice used by some investors in bills to pick up basis points is to roll the current three-month or six-month bill each week when new bills are auctioned. If conditions are such that new bill issues, which the market has to absorb, are priced in the auction cheap relative to surrounding issues, then by rolling his bills the investor may be able to pick up each week two or three $25 or $50 basis points by doing this. A second advantage of this strategy is that it keeps the investor in current bills, which are more liquid than off-the-run issues.

In swapping and trading generally, "it's important," as one portfolio manager noted, "to know what dealer will deal in what and who will make the best markets. Say a bank has a big writing program and uses the dealer community—Becker, Sali, and Goldman. The bank sells the dealers 70 million, and they resell them to retail. If I have some of that bank's CDs, I would not go to Goldman, since I know their customers are stocked up

---

[7] The calculation is:

$$3(0.0001)(\$1,000,000) = \$300$$

on those CDs. Instead, I would go to some fourth dealer whose customers are light in that bank's CDs."

Leverage

A portfolio manager can enter into a repurchase agreement with the securities he owns.[8] If the portfolio is that of a corporation that does not have direct contact with suppliers of repo money, the portfolio manager can always RP his securities with the dealers, who will in turn hang them out on the other side.

The ability to repo securities can be used by a portfolio manager in various ways. If an unanticipated short-term need for cash arises at a time when the portfolio manager has established a position he wants to maintain, he can bridge that gap by RPing his securities instead of selling them. Said one corporate portfolio manager, "We never fund to dates. We fund to market expectancy—what we think is going to happen to interest rates. We can repo the portfolio so we never have problems raising money for short periods. If we have to raise money for a long period to meet a portfolio embarrassment [securities in the portfolio can only be sold at a loss], that means we made an error and had better face up to it."

Another way a portfolio manager with wide parameters can use the RP market imaginatively is to buy a security, finance the first part of its life with term RP, and thereby create an attractive future security.

Still another way a portfolio manager can use the RP market is to out and out lever his portfolio—buy securities at one rate, turn around and RP them at a lower rate, and then use the funds borrowed to buy more securities. Or the portfolio manager can simply buy securities for which he has no money by doing a repo against them at the time of purchase. A portfolio manager who uses this technique commented, "I repo the portfolio as an arbitrage technique everyday and probably run the biggest matched sale book in American industry. We RP anything we can, even corporates. In doing RP, I am either financing something I have or buying something I don't have any money for. We take the RPs off for quarter ends because they might comprise the aesthetics of our statement." Avoiding repos across quarter ends is common among those corporations that use re-

---

[8] Jargon in this area is confusing. Dealers talk about "doing repos" when they are financing their position and about "doing reverses" when they are borrowing securities. Some portfolio managers who use repurchase agreements—just as dealers do—to lever, talk about doing repo, others talk about doing a reverse (i.e., reversing out securities). We have opted to use the word *repo* when the initiative comes from the side wanting to borrow money, and *reverse* when the initiative comes for the side wanting to borrow securities.

pos, so it is impossible from looking at financial statements to determine whether a corporation uses repos to borrow.

To the corporate portfolio manager who can use repos, it is, in the words of one, "the most flexible instrument in the money market. You can finance with repo, you can borrow using it, and you can ride the yield curve using it—buy a 2-month bill, put it out on repo for a month, and then sell it or do a 30-day repo again. And you can use repo to create instruments: put a six-month bill out on a two-month repo, and you have created a four-month bill two months out."

Despite the many and reasonable ways in which the ability to borrow in the repo market can be used, it is rare for a corporate short-term portfolio manager to be able to hang out any of his portfolio on repo.

Caveat   When nothing calamitous has happened of late in the repo market, there is a tendency for lenders and borrowers in this market to regard repos and reverses as riskless. In fact such transactions expose both parties to a credit risk, as the failures of Financial Corporation, Drysdale, and Lombard-Wall well illustrate.

Because of credit risk, no portfolio manager should do repos or reverses with a dealer or broker before carefully checking the latter's creditworthiness. Also, he should set dollar limits on the exposure he will take to any one dealer or broker, with the limit depending in part on that institution's capital. The New York State Dormitory Authority, which had invested over $300 million of its own spare cash and of that of other state agencies with Lombard-Wall, is a good example of an institution that got into trouble by putting a lot of eggs in one basket: in this case a smallish dealer that had inadequate capital to support the risks it was taking.

Use of the Futures Markets

Portfolio managers who may use futures and options are currently in the distinct minority, but to those who may, these contracts offer an array of opportunities to lock in yields, to arbitrage, to hedge, and to speculate. A few portfolio managers use futures contracts extensively as one more tool of portfolio management. We discuss that in Chapter 13, which focuses on futures contracts for and options on fixed-income securities.

Shorting Securities

It's unusual for the manager of a corporate portfolio to be authorized to sell securities short but less rare than it used to be. The ability to short securities can be useful to a portfolio manager in several ways. For one thing, it permits him to arbitrage—going long in an undervalued security and short in a overvalued security—as a speculation on a yield spread. A few corporate portfolio managers do this quite actively.

As one portfolio manager noted, there are also tax reasons for shorting, "Say you have ballooned maturities in part of your portfolio out to 10 years. You were right on the market and have only 30 days to go to get a long-term capital gain. But you think the market might back up and you want to take some of the risk out of your position. To do so is easy—you short something similar. In the corporate tax environment, the tax on long-term capital gains is 28 percent, while the tax on ordinary income is 46 percent. With that sort of 18-point advantage, you have to be badly wrong on the short not to come out ahead shorting." For banks there is no incentive to short for tax purposes because their long-term capital gains are taxed as ordinary income.

Still another reason a corporate portfolio manager might want to short is because borrowing through a short seems less expensive than selling an attractive investment. Said one portfolio manager, "If we decided, yes, the market is in here [in a given maturity sector], then we would look for the cheapest thing [the instrument with most relative value] on a spread basis—CDs, BAs, or bills—and buy that. Even though bills might yield less than, say, Euro CDs, we might buy them because the spread on Euros into bills was too tight. We'd decide whether to buy or not and then buy the cheapest thing. When we decided to sell, we would sell the most expensive thing. But we could not short so we were sort of up against it at times when we had to sell. I had already bought the cheapest thing around, so generally I had to sell something cheap. It bothered me a lot not to be able to short when we needed cash, but it might have raised questions with stockholders."

Investing when Rates Are High and Highly Volatile

A number of the portfolio strategies we have described make sense in "normal" markets when rates display some stability and predictability and when the yield curve slopes upward. In the period October 1979 to at least mid-1982, investors were playing in a very different ball park. Rates were historically high, historically volatile, and cyclically unpredictable; also, much of the time the yield was negatively sloped.

Noted one portfolio manager in the fall of 1981, "Riding the yield curve and tails are no longer interesting. One had better forget them. I have resisted the temptation to extend maturities, and I have been amazed when I compare my rate of return to what it would have been had I attempted to extend and either hold to maturity or ride the yield curve. During periods of intense rate volatility, what you must do is to make the proper maturity decision because the impact of that decision on total return dwarfs that of all others; right now the correct decision is to opt for the shortest maturity you can. If you can live with day-to-day rollovers, you should do it even though you may have to accept lower rates on Wednesdays."

Compounding   Until recently, neither investors nor borrowers thought much about the impact of frequent rolling of investments or borrowings on the return earned or the cost incurred. To fail to do so in a period of high rates can be an expensive mistake since the impact of compounding on a rate earned or paid increases not only the more often compounding occurs but the higher the rate being compounded is.

To illustrate, suppose, for example, that the yield curve is flat at 14 percent from overnight to six months. If an investor opts to buy a 6-month CD and roll it once, his total return over the year will be 14.49 percent assuming no change in interest rates. If, alternatively, he rolls overnight funds on the 255 business days that typically occur during a year, he will—again assuming no change in rates—earn a total return of 15.02 percent, 53 basis points more than by rolling a 6-month CD. On a $20 million investment, this would amount to $106,000 of extra earnings over a year.

Our simple example is not meant to suggest that interest rates, when they reach 14 percent, are likely to stay there for a year and that a portfolio manager should act accordingly. Rather, our intent is to illustrate the power of compounding to raise total return when rates are high and to suggest that, during such periods, the portfolio manager, in making maturity choices, start by making benchmark calculations of the sort illustrated by our example to get a feel for how compounding would affect his total return under different rate and maturity-choice scenarios.

If a portfolio manager opts to roll overnight funds, from a rate point of view the most attractive place for him to invest is typically the Euromarket. Banks do not go out of their way to ensure that a money manager will get daily compounding on short-term funds deposited at, say, its Caribbean shell. To get daily compounding, the investor in effect must mature his investment each day and then reinvest. This can be easily done if the task is approached systematically. Describing his procedure, one portfolio manager said, "If we put money overnight in Morgan, Cayman, we instruct them at the time the investment is started where to repay the money. A reliable bank should not have to be reinstructed. We check the next day with Chase, our clearing bank, to see that the money has in fact come in, and then we reinvest it at the most attractive rate quoted."

Trading   Volatile markets offer the portfolio manager opportunities for making huge profits if he guesses right on rates. They may thus tempt him to trade his portfolio. Noted the same portfolio manager quoted above, "To trade in volatile markets, you must be very nimble; psychologically prepared to buy at one moment and, if necessary to protect yourself, to unload your position the next moment. Recent fluctuations in interest rates have been mind-boggling. Imagine that on a position in short-term paper you could take a 3 percent capital loss in three weeks. The trading game has become so dangerous in terms of the money you can lose that you must be very attentive to the market and a very skillful trader to take positions on the long side and make money. In an environment like the current one, most corporations ought not to trade. We are not staffed to nor expected to trade securities as dealers are. And even dealers today often do nothing in effect but broker securities. They are scared to death and have reduced their trading positions to the lowest levels possible. It has been quite a market, as we again go up the side of the mountain!"

Money Market Funds

Although money market funds were initially designed to offer individual investors a way to invest indirectly in money market securities, they can also be extremely useful to a corporation running a small short-term portfolio because the small portfolio manager labors under several disadvantages.

First, since minimum denominations are high in many sectors of the money market (the marketability of a negotiable CD suffers if its face value is less than $1 million), it is difficult for a person managing $10 million or less to diversify adequately; he has only limited ability to reduce credit risk by holding a mix of names and to reduce market risk by investing in different types and maturities of instruments.

Also, the net yield earned on a small portfolio is reduced much more by transactions costs than is the net yield earned on a large portfolio. If a bank imposes a $25 fee on an overnight repo, that fee will, on a $250,000 repo, reduce a gross yield of 8 percent to 4.35 percent. Moreover, if the portfolio manager must, in addition, pay a fee to wire his money into and out of the borrowing bank, his net yield will be still lower.

Another problem for the small portfolio manager is that he will inevitably end up buying and selling securities at rates that are less favorable than those big investors can obtain by buying in round-lot amounts from dealers. The problem is particularly acute for the portfolio manager who directs his investments to regional banks rather than to the national money market. An old example of a game still played is an Ohio bank that, at a time when top Chicago banks were paying 4.6 percent for one-month CD money, was offering local corporations 4 percent for one-month money and 4.2 percent if they ran their money through a Euro time deposit in the Caribbean.

Still another problem with a small portfolio is that it typically suffers from unprofessional management. The reason is that the gains to be had from managing a small portfolio are so small in absolute terms that hiring a skilled portfolio manager would not be cost-justified.

Because it is difficult to manage small short-term balances effectively, it would make sense for many institutions holding money of this sort to invest it in an institutions-only money fund instead of investing it directly in money market instruments.

The money fund charges for its expenses, which typically amount to ½ of 1 percent, plus a management fee that runs another 50 basis points or so. These charges, however, are likely to be largely or fully offset by the fact that the fund, because it is professionally managing a big pool of short-term funds, can earn a significantly higher *gross* return than can the small portfolio manager.

There are other advantages to be gleaned by an institution that uses a money fund. Because history suggests that outflows of money from such a fund will be largely offset by inflows, a money fund can extend further out on the yield curve with less risk than a small portfolio manager could. As a result, a corporation investing in a money fund may be able to get a 90-day or longer rate on 30-day, 15-day, or even overnight money, with no market risk. This aspect of a money fund is particularly important to a corporation that has difficulty predicting cash flows that, if it did not invest in a money fund, would consequently feel constrained to roll overnight repo or to invest in very short-dated commercial paper to minimize market risk.

An institution investing in a money fund may also find that its balances with the fund can be used in part as an interest-bearing substitute for checking account balances it formerly maintained.

Most money funds will permit investors to write large checks directly against a zero-balance checking account maintained at a bank associated with the fund. An institution that writes checks against a money fund saves an amount equal to the charges the bank would have imposed for clearing these checks. It also continues automatically to earn interest on its balance with the fund until the checks it has written clear, which often takes several days. Taking advantage of float can significantly increase the yield earned on balances invested short term in a money fund. This is particularly true if the money withdrawn from the fund by writing checks is wired into the fund, so that float operates on only one end of the transaction, the one that increases yield to the investor. Still another advantage of writing checks against a money fund is that a firm which does so need not track daily when these checks clear as it would have to if it wrote checks against a bank account that it was attempting to keep at the minimum level its bank required to compensate for services provided.

Despite the fact that a firm with small short-term balances to manage could often do better using a money fund that invests directly in money market instruments, business usage of money funds is still small. There are several reasons. First, many corporations think of mutual funds as a vehicle for individuals who can't invest efficiently, which supposedly a corporate treasurer can do. Second, there is the ego problem. The person who is in the best position to perceive the benefits of switching to a money fund is the portfolio manager, who if he advises such a switch, will eliminate part or all of his own job. Finally, there is the familiar friend, unmeasured opportunity cost. The typical small firm doesn't track the return it earns on its portfolio and then ask: What cost, if any, did we incur in terms of foregone earnings by doing it ourselves instead of using a money fund?

Perhaps one way to drive home the point of how many more firms and other institutions should be using a money fund rather than investing on their own is to quote a portfolio manager who has tracked his own costs: "If you want to run any money in-house, it is going to cost you $100 to $125,000 just to play the game; that is what it costs you to see the cards. Obviously you have a lot of leverage on that. The same person who can do $10 million can do multiples of that at no additional fixed cost." Assuming that a good portfolio manager can add 100 basis points of yield, which is the amount a money fund takes off in fees, in-house management will not begin to pay unless an institution has $12.5 million to manage. That sum sounds like a lot, but it is far from enough to make active trading of the portfolio worthwhile. To make real money trading, a portfolio manager must deal in $5 million blocks. This means that he needs to control at least $100 million of funds if he is going to be conservative and not put more than 5 percent of his assets in one name.

For many corporations, who do or should consider using money funds, convenience and cost savings are important considerations. In the early 1970s, many banks set up *short-term investment funds* (STIFS) in their trust departments to invest in a pool cash held short-term for one reason or another in accounts they managed. Such banks often found that they could not afford the software and hardware to do the necessary accounting, to track the earnings on and the money flows into and out of separate accounts. Also, they could not recoup these costs with a fee because they were already charging an overall fee for discretionary management of the funds they held in trust.

To get around this problem (prior to 1977 when W. T. Grant got into trouble), many turned to master notes. These provide a stable source of funds to note issuers and provide at no cost to the lender, bank trust departments, and others, subaccounting that precisely fits their needs.

The withdrawal of W. T. Grant from the master note program and its later bankruptcy focused attention on the fact that trust account funds invested in a master note—no matter how good the name of the issuer—were exposed to undue credit risk because of the resulting concentration on a single or on several names. Money funds provide trust departments, pension funds, and others running funds for many with the convenience of subaccounting *plus* the comfort of knowing that they are satisfying the prudent man rule for diversification of risk. Currently money funds are replacing many master notes in bank trust departments; they are also being used more widely by others who have similar investment needs.

It is important to consistently monitor the yield earned on a portfolio and to compare that yield with some yardstick. For a small portfolio manager, the natural yardstick is the yield offered by money funds because such funds have the same investment objectives he has: preservation of capital, high liquidity, and high return, in that order.

To make the yield comparison, the portfolio manager should first determine what *net* yield he is earning on the funds he invests, when all transactions costs and all internal costs—part or all of his own salary, clerical costs, and an appropriate amount of overhead—are subtracted from the gross dollars earned on the portfolio. This net yield should then be compared with the net yield offered by money funds.

Also, the opportunity for a firm with an account at a money fund to use that account as a partial substitute for holding demand deposit balances should be taken into account. Money funds offer the business firm a chance to get paid for *having* a checking account instead of *paying* for it; and this opportunity to increase return should be taken into account in the profitability calculation.

The firm that finds it can do better by investing in a money fund than by investing on its own should adopt the philosophy: If you can't beat them, join them.

Marking to Market

In well-run short-term portfolios, it is common practice to mark the whole portfolio to market each day. The objective of running a portfolio is to maximize over time not interest accrued, but *total financial return*—interest earned plus capital gains realized minus capital losses realized. A portfolio manager who has this objective will, if he buys a two-year note with a 9 percent coupon and then finds that yields on the two-year have risen to 10 percent, view his decision to have bought the 9 percent coupon as a serious mistake. Moreover, if he anticipates that rates will rise still further, he will sell that security at a loss (convert his paper loss into a realized loss) and wait to recommit long term until he thinks rates have stabilized.

The use of this tactic in portfolio management calls for a willingness to book capital losses, and that willingness is a hallmark of every good portfolio manager. Realizing losses is, however, difficult to do psychologically; it is something a trader must discipline himself to do. One advantage of marking a portfolio to market each day is that it helps get the focus of those who buy and sell for the portfolio off book value. As one portfolio manager noted, "If market value declines today and you book to market, tomorrow you start at that market value. And your gain or loss will be a function of whether tomorrow's price is better than today's." Said another, "If you mark to market, the past is gone. You've made a mistake, and the point now is not to make another one."

Tracking Performance

Active management can substantially increase yield on a short-term portfolio. "You can as much as double yield on a short-term portfolio," said one practitioner of the art, "by arbitraging sectors and by changing maturities in response to interest-rate forecasts."

In an institution where the short-term portfolio is actively managed, there are always people in top management who understand the credit market and who are therefore comfortable with creative management of the corporation's portfolio. It is also the case that the focal point in management of the portfolio is on yield earned rather than on when money is needed. In other words, the portfolio manager's main concern in investing is with where relative value lies not with when he needs cash; specifically he does not *fund to dates*—buy three-month bills because he needs money three months hence.

Performance in every liquidity portfolio managed to maximize return is carefully tracked. A key element in this tracking is marking the portfolio to market so that the return-earned calculation incorporates not only realized but unrealized capital gains and losses.

Once performance is tracked, it is compared against a variety of yardsticks. A portfolio manager might, for example, compare his performance with what he could have achieved had he followed any one of several naive strategies: rolling overnight funds, rolling three-month bills, or rolling six-month bills. If the portfolio invests longer-term funds, the yardstick might be the yield on two- or three-year notes.

Another standard often used is the performance achieved by various money funds, each of which runs in effect a large-liquidity portfolio. Comparing the performance of two portfolios is, however, difficult. One has to ask about the differences in the parameters: in maturity restrictions, in percentage restrictions, and in name restrictions. Also differences in the time flow of funds through two portfolios may affect their relative performance.

Still another approach used in evaluating performance achieved is to compare actual results with the optimal results that could have been achieved. In other words, to ask: How high was the return we earned compared with what we could have earned if our market judgments had always been correct?

Tracking performance and comparing it against various yardsticks are important not only because they give the portfolio manager a feel for how well he is doing but because they give management some standard against which to evaluate his performance. As one portfolio manager noted, "I'm a money market specialist working for an industrial concern so it's hard for management to evaluate what I do unless I give them some frame of reference."

In a few rare cases, the portfolio manager is not only judged, but paid, according to how well he performs. That sort of arrangement is typically found in selected corporations that have large short-term portfolios and have recognized that, to get professional management, they must hire street-oriented persons who will never do anything but run money or work at a related job.

THE WAY IT'S DONE

We have discussed so far how an elite minority of portfolio managers who have wide latitude in what they may do and who possess the skill and judgment to make good use of that latitude manage their portfolios.[9]

Most liquidity portfolios owned by corporations, are managed with little sophistication; perhaps it would be more correct to say they are barely managed at all. The problem is often that top management has never focused on what portfolio management is all about and how it should be done. Management will often adopt the attitude: We're in the business of manufacturing widgets, not investing. Having done that, they fail to apply to managing of their short-term portfolio the principles they daily apply to managing the whole corporation.

Restrictive Guidelines

The failure of top management to be interested in and to have knowledge of what managing a liquidity portfolio involves almost invariably results in the establishment of extremely tight guidelines on what the portfolio manager may do, guidelines that reflect, as one portfolio manager noted, "the attempt of a bunch of guys who know nothing about securities to be prudent."

Tight guidelines make it impossible for a portfolio manager to use almost any of the strategies of portfolio management discussed earlier in this chapter. In particular, tight maturity guidelines can create a situation in which a portfolio manager has almost no leeway to raise yield by basing his investments on market judgments. For example, one giant U.S. corporation, which has volatile cash flows, will not permit its portfolio manager to extend further than 30 days; that still leaves him some room to make choices, but none are going to be very remunera-

---

[9] One observer in a position to know puts the number of really well-managed liquidity portfolios in corporate America at half a dozen. If people on the street (Wall Street, that is) were asked to compile their lists of those six corporations, no one would fail to mention Ford, which has portfolios universally viewed as being aggressively and astutely managed. Another portfolio that consistently gets kudos from the street is that of the World Bank.

tive because he is working at best with $8 basis points.[10] Not atypically, there is no one in his corporation who cares and no one who tracks his performance.

Another problem with tight guidelines is that they are sometimes written in terms of amounts rather than percentages. This can make a large portfolio difficult to manage and may lead to false diversification. An extreme example of such guidelines is provided by a corporation that went so far as to limit the amount of bills its portfolio could hold.

The Accounting Hang-Up

The failure of top management to understand or interest itself in the management of the liquidity portfolio also results in what might be called the *accounting hang-up*. Specifically, it has created a situation in which the majority of portfolio managers, all of whom would describe themselves as *conservative*, believe that the correct way to manage a portfolio is to reduce their accounting risk to *zero*. In other words, they attempt to run the portfolio in such a way that they will *never* produce a book loss.

This means that they can take no market risk: They can't do swaps that would produce a book loss regardless of how relative value shifts; when they need cash, they can't decide what to sell on the basis of relative value; they can't arbitrage; in fact, they are literally reduced to rolling overnight money and buying securities they intend to mature.

To fully appreciate how the decision never to take a loss restricts a portfolio manager, it is necessary to understand that when a portfolio acquires a discount security, such as bills or BAs, each day the accountant accrues interest income on that security at the discount rate at which it was purchased, so when the security is redeemed at maturity for full face value, all of the difference between the purchase price and the face value (i.e., the discount at purchase) will have been accrued as interest. This seems reasonable, but it means, for example, that if a portfolio manager buys six-month bills at 7.90 and resells them three months later at 8.30, that is, at a rate *above* that at which he bought the bills, *he will have incurred a capital loss even though in dollar terms he has earned money*. Table 2 spells out the mathematics of this. Note that by buying $1 million of the 6-month bill at 7.90 and holding it for 90 days, the portfolio has earned $18,750

---

[10] The calculation:

$$(0.0001)\left(\frac{30}{360}\right)(\$1,000,000) = \$8.33$$

Table 2
Accounting Treatment of $1 Million of 6-Month
Bills Bought at 7.90 and Sold 3 Months Later at
8.30

Book value at purchase	$960,500
+Interest accrued over 90 days	19,750
Book value at sale	$980,250
Price at sale	$979,250
−Book value at sale	980,250
Accounting capital gain (loss)	(1,000)
Price at sale	$979,250
Price at purchase	960,500
Actual gain	$ 18,750

and the $1,000 capital loss occurs only because the accountant has accrued $19,750 of interest over the holding period.

The yields and maturities in this example were purposely chosen so that they are identical with the yields and maturities used in the example of riding the yield curve presented earlier in this chapter (see Table 1). Once these numbers are seen in the context of that example, it is clear that the unwillingness to take an accounting loss (to expose the portfolio to an accounting risk) rules out even the most basic investment strategy based on market judgment; namely, riding the yield curve. In this respect, note that in our example the portfolio manager who rode the yield curve stood to gain—if interest rates did not rise—an extra $2,000 of return, *and* he had a lot of protection against losing in terms of dollars earned but *not* against incurring an accounting loss.

Portfolio managers preoccupied with accounting losses and gains are encountered by dealers frequently. Said one, "It cracks me up when someone comes to me with BAs or bills and says, 'What's your bid?' and I say, '7.60,' and he says, 'I can't sell because I bought at 7.50 and I can't take a loss.' It makes no sense if he has held the instrument for awhile, but I do not question people any more. I figure they just don't understand the concept. Still it's crazy, if you have to generate cash, to say that you cannot sell the instrument it is best to sell because you cannot take a 10-basis-point loss." Said another dealer, "I talk to portfolio managers about this problem and encounter nothing but resistance. They do not care if they could earn more money, they are just not going to take a loss. It's an organizational not a rational constraint."

The whole accounting problem applies not only to discount securities but to CDs and other interest-bearing securities, because the accountant accrues interest on them just as he does on discount securities; in addition, he amortizes over the time to maturity the premium on coupons purchased at a price above par and accretes the discount over the time to maturity on coupons purchased at a discount from par.

A Negative Sum Game

The aversion to book losses and the failure to track performance that are characteristic of many corporations create a negative sum game for the portfolio manager. If he invests on the basis of market judgment, he ends up in a position where, if his judgment is wrong, the resulting losses—even if they are losses only by accounting standards—will be highly visible and criticized, whereas if his judgment is correct, the resulting gains will not be perceived by senior management.

The obvious response of the portfolio manager put in this position is to make no attempt to predict interest rates and to invest so as to avoid all market risk. If such a portfolio manager reaches for yield at all, he does so by buying P-2 paper or Euro CDs because they offer relatively high yields without ever asking whether they have *relative value*. Such portfolio managers think of themselves as sophisticated because they know a lot about many different markets, *but* when they need cash three months hence, they buy a three-month instrument instead of making a conscious market decision.

Opportunity Cost

The typical "conservative" portfolio manager thinks of himself as never having lost a penny or at least as not having lost very many, and his accountant will confirm this. But in fact an institution with a portfolio run on the principle that it funds to dates and never takes a market risk incurs a large *opportunity cost,* namely, the earnings forgone because the responsibility to manage funds in the portfolio has been abnegated. An example is provided by the example of riding the yield curve given earlier in this chapter. The portfolio manager who rides the yield curve with a lot of basis points of protection built into his gamble need not be right more than half the time to noticeably increase yield. Thus, to refuse to do so to avoid the risk of an accounting loss implies a cost, one no less real because it goes unperceived by most institutions.

There is also a more subtle aspect to opportunity cost. As one portfolio manager commented, "Most people you talk to will buy a six-month bill and hold it to maturity and say that they are taking no risk because they know what they are going to earn. That is farcical. They *are* taking a risk, one that is not measured by the accounting system but is measured in terms of opportunity cost. And the institution may in reality be affected by this risk. If rates rise sharply and the money invested could have been used elsewhere, there is a cost to having bought those securities. Either the institution has to finance them somehow or it may be forced into other business decisions that are suboptimal."

Many common portfolio practices can be pursued only at a considerable opportunity cost. One is to say that, if money is needed in 30 days, cash on hand should be invested in a 30-day instrument even though predictable cash flows will more than suffice to cover that need. Another is to invest a large sum of money in short-term instruments when it is clear that most of that money will not be needed in the short run or even in the long run. A corporation that pursues such a strategy, as some triple-A credits do, pays a large premium year in and year out to ensure that it can survive even a severe credit crunch without mild discomfort.

With respect to the opportunity cost associated with the latter policy, one sales manager noted, "If stockholders realized what was going on in some corporations with cash holdings that are large relative to their total assets, what amount of money it is costing the company to not manage money, you might have some stockholders suits. I found one company that could go no longer than 90 days; they had a roughly $500 million portfolio; and the average life of their investments was 60 days. They could never buy and sell, never swap. I figured that in 1976 the fact they could not extend to the 1-year area probably cost them 1½ to 2 percent in yield. On half a billion that could add significantly to the bottom line [$10 million if the increase in yield was 2 percent]. And there was *no* call for the funds."

It is sometimes suggested that the reason some large corporations do not manage their portfolios is that they have too much money; that is, it is impossible within the confines of the money market to actively manage $3 or $4 billion. Sums of that magnitude are, however, actively managed; the World Bank's $6 billion portfolio is a prime example. So, too, are the actively traded portfolios of some multibillion-dollar money funds.

As noted, there is an opportunity cost to not managing money. The counterpart is that it costs money to have someone manage a portfolio, consequently there is some level below which benign neglect—rolling commercial paper or investing surplus cash in a money market fund—is the preferable alternative. That cutoff point is hard to pinpoint; estimates put it anywhere from $20 to $40 million. Somewhere up from that, between $100 and $150 million, there are solid benefits to be reaped from having someone watch the market daily.

For the firm at the opposite pole, one with hundreds of millions to be managed in one or a number of portfolios, the optimal solution may be one that a few corporations in this position have adopted—namely, to hire a professional, give him wide guidelines, monitor his performance, and pay him on an incentive basis so that making market judgments is for him a positive sum game. A side benefit of doing so is that the same individual can be used, as is done in many corporations, to manage the parent's or its financing sub's commercial paper operations. Anyone who can manage a short-term portfolio well can manage a commercial paper operation equally well, since the latter is nothing but a *negative* portfolio.

Ignorance of opportunity cost and extreme risk aversion are not the only reasons why many large corporations have failed to opt for professional management of their portfolios. Another is that they would have to pay a professional money manager in toto what a senior executive earns. A third reason is that corporations, especially if they are headquartered in outlying places, have difficulty attracting and holding street-oriented people.

For a large corporation that wants to aggressively manage its portfolio, the commonly practiced alternative tactic of having one fast-track rookie do the job for awhile and then train another to do it does not always work out. Said a portfolio manager who traveled that route, "Trading is an art form which I could not succeed in teaching my peers who had come through the system as I did. I would have done better to take on some kid hustling on the streets of Marrakesh."

13

Using Futures and Options in Corporate Short-Term Portfolio Management

Marcia Stigum, Ph.D.
Stigum & Associates

Frank J. Fabozzi, Ph.D., C.F.A.
Walter E. Hanson/Peat, Marwick,
Mitchell Professor of Business
and Finance
Lafayette College

With the advent of interest-rate futures and options on both fixed-income instruments and interest-rate futures, the manager of a corporate short-term portfolio gained new degrees of freedom. He or she can now economically and quickly alter a portfolio's market risk profile. Moreover, these new contracts offer managers risk and return patterns that were previously unavailable. In this chapter we will discuss how these contracts may be used. In particular, we shall focus on contracts in which the underlying instrument is a Treasury bill.

FUTURES CONTRACTS

Forward transactions are common in many areas of economic activity, including the markets for commodities. *In a forward transaction a seller agrees to deliver goods to a buyer at some future date at some fixed price.* For example, a farmer growing onions might, before the harvest, sell some portion of his crop to a buyer at a fixed price for delivery at harvest. For the farmer, this transaction reduces risk. To grow onions, the farmer incurs various costs; by selling his onions forward, he guarantees the revenue he will receive for his onions at harvest, and he thus locks in a profit on his operations. That profit may be more or less than what he would have earned if he had waited to sell his crop at harvest for whatever price was then prevailing in the *cash market* (market for immediate delivery) for onions.

A *futures contract,* like a forward contract, specifies that the seller of the contract will deliver whatever item the contract is for to the buyer at some future date at some fixed price. Futures contracts differ, however, from forward contracts in several respects. First, *futures contracts are standardized agreements made and traded on exchanges that are chartered, designated, and licensed to serve as a trading arena in specific futures contracts.* Second, whereas forward contracts are normally custom-tailored contracts made with the intent that delivery shall be made, *delivery is rarely made in connection with futures contracts.* Instead, a buyer of a futures contract will typically close out his position before the contract matures by making an offsetting sale of the same contract, a seller by making an offsetting purchase.

The reason delivery is not made is that people enter into futures contracts not to buy or sell commodities, but either (1) *to offset risk on a long or short position in a commodity, that is, to hedge that position by taking an equal and offsetting position in futures,* or (2) *to speculate on a change in the price of the commodity or a change in price spreads.* The hedger attempts to put himself in a position where any unanticipated losses he incurs on his cash position in the commodity (e.g., he is long and the price in the cash market drops) will be offset by an equal gain on his futures position. As shown in the examples presented below, he can accomplish this by establishing a position in futures and later closing it out. The speculator, who neither owns nor desires to own the underlying commodity, can also realize whatever gain or loss he makes on his speculation simply by closing out the position he has established in futures.

For a hedger a transaction in the futures market is a temporary substitute for a transaction in the cash or spot market. The hedger transacts in futures because, at the moment he wants to trade, the futures market offers greater liquidity than the spot market. For example, a grain company that contracts to sell wheat forward to Turkey incurs a price risk, which it could cover by immediately buying grain from farmers. The spot market in wheat, however, may be thin and illiquid at the time the forward sale is made; if so, the grain company would have to offer farmers a high premium to get them to sell, and the cheapest and most efficient way for the company to cover its price risk would be to go into the more liquid futures market and buy futures contracts. Later, as grain became available in the spot market, the grain merchant would piece out its purchase of grain, buying 10,000 bushels here, 20,000 bushels there, and simultaneously selling off a comparable amount of futures contracts.

Another difference between futures and forward contracts is that futures contracts are "marked to market" at the end of each trading day while forward contracts are not. Consequently, there are interim cash flow effects with futures contracts as additional margin may be required as a result of adverse price movements or cash withdrawn as a result of favorable price movements. There are no interim cash flow effects with forward contracts because no variation margin is required.

At the time of this writing, there are three futures contracts that are traded in which the underlying instrument is a short-term debt obligation. The three futures contracts, all traded on the International Monetary Market, are 90-day Treasury bill futures, 90-day domestic certificate of deposit futures and Eurodollar time deposit futures. At the longer end of the maturity spectrum, there are futures contracts currently traded on GNMAs, Treasury bonds and 10-year Treasury notes. These contracts are traded on the Chicago Board of Trade (CBT). In the summer of 1984, the Securities and Exchange Commission was expected to consider a proposal by the CBT to trade a futures contract based on a municipal bond index. As proposed, the index would be composed of 50 municipal bonds. The quotes for the bonds in the index would be supplied by five brokers feeding information to *The Bond Buyer*. Since the proposed contract would be based on an index, it would require cash settlement.

Treasury Bill Futures

In January 1976, the International Monetary Market (IMM), now part of the Chicago Mercantile Exchange (CME), opened trading in futures contracts for three-month Treasury bills. The initial reception of the bill futures contract by the street was marked by uncertainty and coolness. The dealers looking at the new market all groped for the "right numbers"; they asked what the relationship between spot and futures prices should be and how they could profit from trading in the new market. Many investors were confused about the nature of the contract and uncertain as to how they might or should use it. Also, some felt that a contract traded by "commodities speculators" next to the pork belly pit was suspect.

Nonetheless, the volume of contracts traded in the bill futures market rose rapidly and dramatically; in fact, the market in bill futures came to be used more widely and more rapidly than any futures market ever had been. By the fall of 1982, daily volume in the bill futures market averaged $25 to $28 billion; in contrast, the volume of bills traded daily in the cash market by all recognized and reporting dealers in governments averaged only $20 to $22 billion. This comparison is impressive for a futures market that was only six years old.

Price Quotes   Bills trade and are quoted in the *cash market* on a yield basis, and consequently, because of this, the bid always exceeds the offer. Also, when yield rises, price falls, and vice versa. This seems reasonable to a person accustomed to trading money market instruments, but it confuses a person who is accustomed to trading commodities or stocks. The IMM therefore decided not to quote bill contracts directly in terms of yield. Instead it developed an *index* system in which a bill is quoted at a "price" equal to 100.00 minus yield; a bill yield of 8.50 would thus be quoted on the IMM at 91.50. Note that in this system, when yield goes down, the index price rises; and the trader with a long position in futures profits. This conforms to the relationship that prevails in other commodity futures markets, where long positions profit when prices rise and short positions profit when prices fall.

Price Fluctuations   Price fluctuations on bill futures are in multiples of an 01, one basis point. Because the contract is for delivery of 90-day bills, each 01 is worth $25.

The maximum price fluctuation permitted in any one day is 60 basis points above or below the preceding day's settling price.[1] However, if on two successive days a contract closes at the normal daily limit in the same direction (not necessarily the same contract month on both days), an expanded daily price limit goes into effect: On the third day the daily price limit on all contract months goes to 150 percent of the normal daily limit. If on that day any contract month closes at its expanded daily price limit and in the same direction as the preceding daily limit price change, the daily price limit expands to 200 percent of the normal daily price limit and remains there as long as any contract month closes at this expanded daily price limit.

Clearing Function of the IMM   Whenever a trade occurs on the IMM, there must be a buyer and an offsetting seller. Each trader's contractual obligation, however, is not to his counterpart in the trade but to the IMM. The IMM stands between the principals in a trade; it is the opposite side of every trade effected on the exchange, even though it never itself assumes any net posi-

---

[1] The *settling price* is the average of the highest and lowest prices at which trades occur during the last minute of trading.

tion long or short in bill futures. The IMM's purpose in acting as what might be called a supervisory *clearinghouse* is to guarantee the fiscal integrity of every trade made on the exchange.

Margin An important part of the IMM's job is to oversee the enforcement of margin requirements and the monetary transfers they require. When a trader buys a contract on the IMM, he does not pay for it immediately, and if he sells a contract, he does not receive payment immediately. Both the buyer and the seller, however, must put up *margin*. Currently the minimum *initial margin* required by the IMM is $1,000 per bill contract on an outright position. On a special position it is less. (A brokerage house through which an individual trader deals may require more.)

When a trader assumes a long or short position, he will incur gains and losses each day thereafter as price fluctuates. The amount of each day's gain (loss) is added to (subtracted from) his margin account at the end of the day. This process is called "marking to market." For example, if a trader bought a contract at 92.50 and the settling price at the end of the day on that contract were 92.20, he would have incurred a loss equal to $750 (30 basis points times $25), and that money would be subtracted by his broker from his margin account. Some other trader would necessarily have made an equal and offsetting gain, and money equal to the amount of that gain would be added to his margin account. This adding and subtracting is done through the IMM, which collects money from brokers whose clients have incurred losses and transfers it to brokers whose clients have earned profits. Because margin balances are adjusted through the IMM at the end of each business day, a trader starts each day having realized, through additions to or deductions from his margin account, the net gain or loss he has made on his position since he established it. The IMM margin system converts on a daily basis what would be *paper* gains and losses into *realized* gains and losses.

If the balance in a trader's margin account falls below the current *maintenance margin* of $700 per contract, which is less than the initial margin, he must immediately deposit additional funds in this account to bring it back to $1,000. If he fails to do so, his broker is required to close out his position. If, alternatively, a trader has earned profits and his margin account has therefore risen above $1,000 he may withdraw the excess margin.

The IMM's requirements with respect to margin maintenance guarantee that a trader's losses on a given day are unlikely to significantly exceed the amount in his margin account and thus make it improbable that any investor would end up in a position of being unable to honor a contract he had made either by liquidating his position through an offsetting trade or by making or taking delivery of securities.

Collateral in the form of securities may be used as initial margin so that the effective cost of putting up initial margin can be reduced to close to zero.

End of Trading   Trading in a bill futures contract terminates in the week of the delivery month on the second business day following the weekly auction of the three-month bill, which is a reopening of the old year bill. This would normally be a Wednesday. Settlement of futures contracts outstanding at the time trading is terminated is made on the following day, Thursday. This is also the day on which settlement is made on the three-month cash bill just auctioned. Thus there are always new three-month bills available for delivery on the day an outstanding futures contract is settled.

Although buyers of futures contracts do not normally take delivery, it can be done.[2] The buyer who wants to take delivery instructs the IMM that he wants delivery to be made at a particular Chicago bank. The IMM then instructs the seller's bank to make delivery there, and delivery is affected against payment in Fed funds.

Commissions   There used to be a minimum commission on a purchase or sale of bill futures. This was phased out with the switch to negotiated commissions, and the rates charged now vary from one brokerage house to another. Currently commissions charged are much higher on small trades than on large trades.

HEDGING WITH FUTURES

A portfolio manager who sells bill futures to limit the risk on a long position in bills and a portfolio manager who buys bill futures to lock in a rate at which he can invest an anticipated cash inflow are both managing risk by *hedging. To hedge using financial futures is to assume a position in futures equal and opposite to an existing or anticipated position, which may be short or long, in cash or cash securities.*

---

[2] During 1981 the total open interest (contracts outstanding) in all bill futures contracts fluctuated from a single-day low of 28,001 to a single-day high of 49,065. Over the year 5,631,290 contracts were traded but delivery was made on only 5,183 contracts.

Delivery

An important point to note about hedging through the purchase or sale of either commodity or financial futures contracts is that delivery need not be and usually is not made or taken in connection with a hedge. Normally, hedges and speculative positions as well are closed out by making an offsetting trade in the same contract. Some newer futures contracts (Euro and stock index contracts) do away with delivery by specifying cash settlement.

The hedger attempts to put himself in a position where any unanticipated loss he incurs on his cash position in the commodity (e.g., he is long and price in the cash market drops) will be offset by an equal gain on his futures position. He may be able to do this by establishing a position in futures and later closing it out. The speculator who neither owns nor desires to own the underlying commodity can also realize whatever gain or loss he makes on his speculation simply by closing out his futures position.

If a hedger, speculator, or other futures market participant wants to make or take delivery, he is, in most markets, free to do so. A trader who maintains an open position in such a market at the expiration of a futures contract must settle by making or taking delivery.

A Perfect Hedge

Consider an investor who has money to invest for three months and is unwilling to assume market risk. He can (1) buy a three-month bill and allow it to mature or (2) buy a six-month bill and sell a bill futures contract expiring three months hence. If he does the latter, i.e., buys the six-month bill and hedges his resulting future long position in a three-month bill, he will have succeeded in eliminating *all* market risk from his position in the six-month bill, even though he will hold it for only three months. A hedge established using a futures contract whose expiration date precisely fits the hedger's time horizon and on which the deliverable instrument corresponds to the instrument being hedged is a *perfect hedge*.

Imperfect Hedges

In practice, *hedges are common but perfect hedges are rare.* The reason is that the standardization of futures contracts required for them to be actively traded and to have liquidity is such that the hedger is normally unable to find a futures position that will give him a perfect offset to his position in the cash market. He has to settle, if you will, for a ready-made rather than a tailor-made suit, and he willingly does so for good reasons: the ability to strike a trade, the liquidity of the position he assumes, and the protection against risk of default that the futures contract offers him.

Typically, a hedger using financial futures will find that the hedge he establishes is *imperfect* for one or both of two reasons: (1) the contract's expiration date does not precisely match the time horizon in which he anticipates dealing, e.g., he sells bill futures against a position in the deliverable bill which he intends to liquidate before the futures contract expires; or (2) he has or anticipates acquiring a position in some instrument other than the deliverable security, e.g., he sells T bill futures to hedge an intended sale of three-month CDs or an anticipated short-term borrowing need. Hedging a cash position in one security by assuming a futures position in a different but similar security is known as a *cross hedge*.

Whenever a market participant undertakes a cross hedge to control risk in a speculative position—long or short—in cash or cash securities, the precise outcome of that hedge is uncertain. How closely his gain (loss) on his futures position will track his loss (gain) on his position in cash or the cash security will depend on how the *spread* (*basis* in commodity jargon) between the rate on the futures contract and that on the cash instrument hedged changes from the time he puts on the hedge until he takes it off.

A Perfect Long Hedge

To illustrate hedging, we will consider a few examples. First, a *perfect long hedge*. Suppose that a treasurer's cash-flow projections tell him that he will have a lot of cash to invest short term in the future; that is, he is going to be *long* investable cash. He can wait to invest until he gets the cash and take the then prevailing rate, or as soon as his projections tell him how much cash he will have, he can lock in a lending rate by buying bill futures.

Table 1 illustrates this. We assume that the treasurer knows in June that he will have $10 million of three-month money to invest in September and that when September arrives he will invest that money in bills. In June, the September bill contract is trading at 10.50. If the treasurer buys 10 of these contracts, he will earn 10.50 on the money he invests in September, regardless of the rate at which the cash three-month bill is then trading.

Table 1
A Long Hedge in T Bill Futures for Bills with a $10 Million Face Value

Step 1 (Thursday, third week of June): Purchase 10 September bill contracts at 10.50.
  Put up security deposit.
  Pay roundturn commission.
Step 2 (Wednesday, third week of September): Sell 10 futures contracts; buy cash bills.

Outcome 1: Cash 91-day bill trading at 10.20.	
Sell September contracts at 10.20.	
Delivery value of futures at sale	$ 9,745,000
− Delivery value of futures at purchase	9,737,500
Profit on futures transactions	$ 7,500
Buy 91-day cash bills at 10.20	
Purchase price of cash bills	$ 9,742,167
− Profit on futures transactions	7,500
Effective price of 91-day bills	$ 9,734,667
Calculate effective discount at which bills are purchased:	
Face value	$10,000,000
− Effective purchase price	9,734,667
Discount at purchase	$ 265,333

Calculate effective discount rate, d, at which cash bills are purchased

$$d = \frac{\text{Discount} \times (360)}{\text{Face} \times (91)} = \frac{\$265,333 \times (360)}{\$10,000,000 \times (91)}$$
$$= 0.1050$$
$$= 10.50\%$$

Outcome 2: Cash 91-day bill trading at 10.80.	
Sell September contracts at 10.80.	
Delivery value of futures at sale	$ 9,730,000
− Delivery value of futures at purchase	9,737,500
Loss on futures transaction	$ (7,500)
Buy 91-day cash bills at 10.80.	
Purchase price of cash bills	$ 9,727,000
+ Loss on futures transaction	7,500
Effective price of 91-day bills	$ 9,734,500
Calculate effective discount at which bills are purchased:	
Face value	$10,000,000
− Effective purchase price	9,734,500
Discount at purchase	$ 265,500

Calculate effective discount rate d at which cash bills are purchased.

$$d = \frac{\text{Discount} \times (360)}{\text{Face} \times (91)} = \frac{\$265,500 \times (360)}{\$10,000,000 \times (91)}$$
$$= 0.1050$$
$$= 10.50\%$$

One way he could get the 10.50 rate would be to take delivery in September of the bills he purchased at 10.50. But to see the nature of the hedge, we assume that, in September when his cash comes in, he closes out his futures position and buys cash bills.

As the September contract approaches maturity, it must trade at a yield close to and eventually equal to the rate at which the three-month cash bill is trading. If a divergence existed between these two rates as trading in the contract terminated, potential for a profitable arbitrage would exist. For example, if, a few days before the September bill contract matured, it was trading at a much higher yield than the cash bill, traders would buy the contract, sell cash bills on a *when issued* basis (i.e., after the bill auction but before settlement), take delivery in Chicago to cover their short position in the cash bill, and profit on the transaction.[3]

In Outcome 1 (Table 1), we assume that, as the September contract matures, the 91-day cash bill trades at 10.20 and the futures contract consequently also trades at 10.20. At this time, the treasurer sells his September contracts and buys the cash three-month bill. He purchases his futures contracts at 10.50 and sells them at 10.20, a lower rate. Since the delivery value of the contracts is higher the lower the yield at which they trade, the treasurer makes (Table 1) a $7,500 profit on his futures transaction.

When his profit on futures is deduced from the price at which he buys cash bills, he ends up paying an effective price for these bills that is $7,500 less than the actual price he pays. And this lower effective price implies that the yield he will earn on his investment is not 10.20, the rate at which he buys *cash bills*, but 10.50, the rate at which he bought bill futures.

Because the prevailing yield at which the cash three-month bill was trading in September was lower than the rate at which the treasurer bought bill futures in June, he made money by engaging in a long hedge; that is, he earned a higher yield than he would have had he not hedged.

There is, however, a counterpart to this. As Outcome 2 in Table 1 shows, if in September the cash three-month bill were trading at 10.80, the treasurer would have lost so many dollars on his hedge that he would have earned only 10.50 on the money he invested.

---

[3] In practice, a maturing bill futures contract will trade during the last few days of its life at a yield a few basis points higher than the deliverable cash bill. The difference reflects the extra commission and other transaction costs that an investor would incur if he bought bill futures and took delivery instead of purchasing 3-month bills in the cash market.

Calculating in Basis Points It is instructive to work out a hedge example in dollars and cents. However, it is quicker to do it in terms of basis points earned and lost. In our example, the treasurer buys September contracts at 10.50 and, according to Outcome 1, sells them at 10.20. On this transaction, he earns on each contract for $1 million of bills 30 90-day basis points. By buying the three-month bill at 10.20 and maturing it, he earns 1020 90-day *basis points* per $1 million of bills purchased. So *net* he earns 1050 90-day basis points per $1 million of bills purchased, a yield of 10.50 over 90 days.

Actually, the basis points earned on the cash bill are 91-day basis points, and those earned on the futures contract are 90-day basis points. This difference, however, is not reflected in the numbers in Table 1 because it affects yield earned only beyond the third decimal point.

The example we presented was a *perfect hedge* because the treasurer bought a futures contract for precisely the instrument and precisely the maturity in which he planned to invest. In the case of a perfect hedge, the investor eliminates *all* risk.

Speculating on spread variation Most investors who use bill futures to hedge an anticipated long position in cash will find that the hedge they establish is *imperfect* for one or both of two reasons:

1. No futures contract or series of contracts precisely matches their projected investment period.
2. They anticipate investing in some money market instrument other than a Treasury bill, e.g., commercial paper or bankers' acceptances.

When a hedge is imperfect, the hedger does not eliminate *all* risk. Instead, he shifts the nature of his speculation from *rate level* speculation to speculation on *spread variation*. A commodities trader would call the latter *basis risk*.

To illustrate, we return to our example and now suppose that the treasurer's cash inflow will occur one month *before* the September contract expires and that, in closing out his hedge, he will sell the September contract one month before it expires and simultaneously buy the new cash bill. At the time the treasurer sells his futures contract, he will be selling the right to take delivery one month hence of the then four-month bill, while he will be buying a three-month bill.

We shall assume that, at the time the treasurer enters his hedge, the yield curve is upward sloping and the spread between the 3- and 4-month bills is 10 basis points. Assuming that

(1) there is no change in that spread and (2) the futures contract trades one month before expiration at a rate equal to the rate on the 4-month bill, the rate our investor will actually earn as a result of his hedge will be 10.40: the 10.50 rate at which he bought the futures contract *minus* the 10 basis point spread between the rate at which he sold it and the rate on the new 3-month bill. Also, so long as our two spread assumptions hold, this result will occur whether the investor sells his futures contract at a low yield (Outcome 1, Table 1) or at a high yield (Outcome 2, Table 1).

In practice, spreads, like rate levels, are not written in stone; they change. What our investor cares about is what happens to the spread between the rate at which he sells his futures contract and the rate on the new 3-month bill. If this spread *widens* by 10 basis points from the level assumed above, i.e., from 10 to 20 basis points, the yield our investor earns will *decrease* by a like amount from 10.50 to 10.30. If, alternatively, the spread *narrows* by 10 basis points, i.e., from 10 basis points to 0, the yield he earns will rise by a like amount, from 10.50 to 10.60.

To sum up, an investor who hedges a future long position in cash must take spread relationships into account in estimating the yield he will earn as a result of his hedge. These relationships, however, are subject to variation. Therefore, the investor cannot know with certainty what return an imperfect hedge will yield, and it is in that sense that a *hedger shifts his risk from rate level speculation to speculation on spread (or basis) variation.*

Earlier we said that a second reason a long hedge is likely to be imperfect is that the investor who hedges intends to buy an instrument other than a T bill. Suppose the investor in our example intended to buy a 3-month CD and that CDs were trading, at the time he bought his futures contract, at a 30-basis-point spread to bills. Then, in establishing a long hedge, our investor would be exchanging a natural speculative position on rate levels (generated by his anticipated cash inflow) for a speculation on the spread x months hence between either (1) the rates on cash 3-month bills and cash 3-month CDs, or (2) the rates on an unexpired bill futures contract and cash 3-month CDs.

When a short futures position in one instrument (e.g., bills) is used to hedge a long position in some *other* instrument (e.g., CDs), the hedge is called a *cross hedge.*

Short Hedges

The bill futures market can also be used to hedge either a long position in money market securities or a future borrowing need. To illustrate, consider a perfect *short* hedge.

Suppose that an investor who has money to invest for three months is unwilling to accept any market risk. We assume that a 6-month bill yields more than a 3-month bill and that the 6-month bill three months hence will be the 3-month bill deliverable when the nearest futures contract expires. In the absence of a futures market, our investor would have no choice but to buy the 3-month bill and allow it to mature. However, given the futures market, he should investigate the relationship among the rates on the 3-month bill, the 6-month bill, and the nearest futures contract. This relationship may be such that, without incurring market risk, he could earn more by buying the 6-month bill and selling the nearest futures contract than by buying and "maturing" the cash 3-month bill. Note that buying the 6-month bill and selling the nearest futures contract against it converts this bill into a 3-month bill, but the return on that bill will differ from that on the 3-month cash bill.

Most short hedges are *imperfect* for one or both of the same reasons that apply to long hedges: (1) a discrepancy exists between the period over which the hedge is needed and the life of any one or series of futures contracts and (2) the instrument or borrowing need being hedged does not correspond to the instrument traded in the futures market. Thus, the short hedger, like the long hedger, is shifting his risk from rate level speculation to speculation on spread (basis) variation.

Cross Hedges

A futures market participant who engages in a cross hedge *shifts* his risk from a speculation on a rate or price level to a *speculation on a spread*. He does *not* eliminate risk; instead, he *shifts* the nature of the risk he assumes. Normally he also reduces the amount of risk he assumes because *he shifts the focus of his speculation from a highly variable rate or price level to a less variable spread;* as a commodities trader would say, he assumes *basis risk.*

Many would-be hedgers do not grasp this crucial point, in part because hedging is frequently described as a form of insurance, which it is not. A person buying insurance sheds a risk by paying an insurer to accept that risk; the insurer is able to do this because it pools many independent risks, e.g., the risks of Jones, Smith, etc., each dying. Reducing risk through pooling, the principle on which insurance works, has nothing to do with hedging. The hedger eliminates risk arising from a speculative position in cash or cash securities by taking an offsetting position in futures. Moreover, because the fit between his hedge and the position he is hedging is imperfect, by hedging he assumes a new risk; namely, he speculates on the rate spread between the cash and the futures instruments.

Imaginative Hedging Strategies

We have defined hedging as assuming a position in futures equal and opposite to an existing or anticipated position, which may be negative or positive, in cash or cash instruments. As our observation that hedging involves speculation on a spread suggests, this definition does *not* imply that the best way to hedge a cash position is necessarily to sell (buy) a futures contract that most nearly corresponds in maturity to the long (short) position being hedged.

Speculation on Spread Variation

To say that speculation on spread variation arises from "imperfect" hedges suggests that it is unfortunate that there are insufficient numbers and types of futures contracts to eliminate all risk by entering a perfect hedge. This view corresponds with the academic view of hedging, which is that the purpose of hedging is to eliminate price risk, not to create an opportunity to profit from a different sort of speculation. In textbooks, hedging is viewed as a form of insurance which has a cost that, like the electric bill, is part of normal business operating expenses.

For an investor or borrower to hedge a position—negative or positive—in cash does in fact insulate his business activity from price level speculation. However, it also *retains* for him the *opportunity to speculate on spread (basis) variation*. Moreover, as our examples suggest, such speculation can become a source of profit as opposed to a cost. In this respect, two comments are important. First, speculation on spread variation did not arise in the money and bond markets after and as a result of the introduction of trading in financial futures. Quite the contrary; it has long been common. An investor who, in anticipation of a fall in rates, buys a 10-year Treasury bond and simultaneously shorts—to minimize risk—an 8-year issue is doing a *bull market arbitrage* that is nothing more or less than speculating on spread variation. Many other transactions commonly done by dealers and investors are a form of speculation on a spread. What the introduction of futures trading did was to provide a vastly more efficient and less costly mechanism for taking forward positions, long and short, and a liquid market in which such forward positions could be traded.

A second important point is that the use of hedging to minimize price level speculation while simultaneously speculating on spread variation is not an innovation fathered by money market participants. Firms that produce, process, or use commodities for which futures markets exist have long understood that speculation on spread, or basis, is a potential source of profit, and they have sought to profit from it.

Once speculation on spreads is viewed as a potential profit center, it becomes clear that hedging should not be viewed as an automatic and thoughtless operation, e.g., a treasurer has money coming in three months hence so he buys the most nearly corresponding futures contract. Instead, hedging is an intricate activity. To succeed at it, the participant should know what spreads have been historically and what factors cause them to change. In establishing a hedge, he should also try to predict how events are most likely to affect the spreads involved in his hedge. Finally, if the unanticipated occurs, he must be prepared to alter his hedge.

The suggestion that investors should consider hedging as a form of potentially profitable speculation is not inconsistent with the suggestion that hedging should be used as a tool to manage risk. Any corporation that holds a portfolio or anticipates borrowing is inescapably speculating on changes in rate level, since it is impossible to be long or short cash and do otherwise. To hedge and thus speculate on spread variation is to trade one form of speculation (on a *naked* long or short position) for another, typically *less risky*, form.

OPTIONS

An option is a contract in which the writer of the option grants the buyer of the option the right to purchase from or sell to the writer a designated instrument at a specified price within a specified period of time.[4] The writer, also referred to as the seller, grants this right to the buyer for a certain sum of money called the *option premium*. The price at which the designated instrument may be bought or sold is called the *exercise* or *strike price*. The date after which an option is void is called the *expiration date*. When an option grants the buyer the right to purchase the designated instrument from the writer, it is called a *call option*. When the option buyer has the right to sell the designated instrument to the writer (seller), the option is called a *put option*.[5]

---

[4] When the designated instrument is a stock index, the buyer receives cash settlement.

[5] An option on a futures contract gives the buyer the right to buy from or sell to the writer a designated futures contract at a designated price at any time during the life of the option. If the option on a futures contract is a call option, the buyer has the right to purchase one

Notice that, unlike a futures contract, the buyer of an option has the *right* but not the obligation to perform. It is the option seller (writer) that has the obligation to perform. Both the buyer and seller are obligated to perform in the case of a futures contract. In addition, in a futures contract the buyer does not pay the seller to accept the obligation as in the case of an option where the buyer pays the seller the option premium.

At the time of this writing, options on fixed-income securities are traded on the American Stock Exchange and the Chicago Board Options Exchange. The underlying fixed-income securities for the options traded on these two exchanges are U.S. Treasury obligations. The Chicago Board of Trade is the only exchange that currently trades an option on an interest-rate futures contract. The fixed-income instrument underlying the interest-rate futures contract is also a U.S. Treasury security.

At the end of 1984, the IMM plans to trade options on Eurodollar time deposit futures contracts. This will be the first exchange-traded option on an interest rate futures contract in which the underlying futures is a short-term debt obligation. There are also over-the-counter options on Treasury notes and bonds, corporate bonds, mortgage-backed securities, and money market instruments. Investment banking firms act as principals as well as brokers for over-the-counter options.

Options on Treasury Bills

Options on 13-week Treasury bills are traded on the American Stock Exchange. These options have a different structure than that of options on Treasury notes and bonds due primarily to the conventions of the Treasury bill cash market. Unlike options on notes and bonds which are for a specific issue, the deliverable 13-week Treasury bill for this option changes from week to week throughout the life of any given option. The principal amount for each option is $1 million, reflecting the fact that this amount is a round lot in the Treasury bill cash market.

Exercise Price A distinctive feature of options on Treasury bills is the manner in which exercise prices are expressed and option premiums are quoted. Since Treasury bills are quoted on

---

designated futures contract at the exercise (strike) price. That is, the buyer has the right to acquire a long futures position in the designated futures contract at the exercise (strike) price. If the call option is exercised by the buyer, the writer (seller) acquires a short position. A put option on a futures contract grants the buyer the right to sell one designated futures contract to the writer at the exercise (strike) price. That is, the buyer has the right to acquire a short futures position in the designated futures contract at the exercise price. If the put option is exercised, the writer acquires a long position in the designated futures contract at the exercise price.

a discount basis in the cash market, the nominal exercise price of an option is found by subtracting the Treasury bill discount rate at which an option is exercisable from 100. For example, an option to buy or sell 13-week Treasury bills at a discount rate of 9.0 percent has a nominal exercise price of 91. However, the nominal exercise price does not reflect the actual dollar settlement price if an option is exercised. The adjusted exercise price in the case of settlement of an exercised option is the same as in the settlement in the cash market.

The procedure is as follows. First, obtain the annualized discount rate from the nominal exercise price by subtracting the latter from 100. Second, compute the actual discount rate for the Treasury bill by adjusting the annualized discount rate to reflect the maturity of the issue. This requires multiplying the annualized rate by a fraction. The numerator of the fraction is the exact number of days to maturity of the Treasury bill and the denominator is 360 days. In the case of 13-week Treasury bills, the numerator is 91 days and the fraction is therefore $91/360$. Third, determine the adjusted exercise price by subtracting the actual discount rate from 100. Finally, multiply the adjusted exercise price (expressed as a percent) by the trading unit of the option which is $1 million. To illustrate the settlement price if an option is exercised, suppose that the nominal exercise price of an option for a 13-week Treasury bill is 91. The annualized discount rate is then 9.0 percent $(100 - 91)$. The actual discount rate is found by multiplying the annualized discount rate by $91/360$. This results in an actual discount rate of 2.275 percent. Subtracting the actual discount rate of 2.275 percent from 100 gives an adjusted exercise price of 97.725 and a settlement price of $977,250 $(0.97725 \times \$1,000,000)$.

Quotation of Option Premiums   Option premiums are quoted in basis points. For $1 million of principal amount, one basis point converts into $25. For purposes of converting a basis point into dollar amounts *it is assumed* that the option matures in 90 days. Consequently, a quote of 0.11 is equal to 11 basis points and an option premium of $275.

Margin Requirements   There are no margin requirements for the buyer of an option once the premium has been paid in full. Because the premium is the maximum amount that the option buyer can lose no matter how adverse the price movement of the underlying instrument, there is no need for margin.

On the other hand, because the writer (seller) of an option has agreed to accept all of the risk (and none of the reward) of the position in the underlying instrument, the writer (seller) is required to put up margin. The margin requirement depends on whether the option is "in-the-money" or "out-of-the-money." The meaning of an "in-the-money" and "out-of-the-money" option is explained in the next section. In the case of an in-the-money option, the margin requirement for options on 13-week Treasury bills is $3,500 plus the premium. For an out-of-the-money option on 13-week Treasury bills the margin requirement is $3,500 plus the premium minus the out-of-the-money amount. However, the minimum margin requirement is the option premium plus $500. For example, if the premium for an out-of-the-money option is $1,800 and the amount by which the option is out-of-the-money is $800, then the minimum margin requirement is $4,500 ($3,500 + $1,800 − $800). If the amount by which the option is out-of-the-money is $4,000, the premium plus $3,500 minus the out-of-the-money amount would be $1,300. Since this amount is less than the premium ($1,800) plus $500, which is $2,300, the minimum margin requirement is $2,300, not $1,300.

Determinants of Option Prices

The cost to the buyer of an option is primarily a reflection of the option's *intrinsic* value and any premium over its intrinsic value. The premium over intrinsic value is called the *time value*. Each is discussed below.

The intrinsic value of a call option is the difference between the current price of the underlying instrument and the exercise price. For example, if the exercise price for a call option is 78 and the current price of the designated instrument is 81, the intrinsic value is 3 (81 − 78). That is, if the option buyer exercised the option and simultaneously sold the underlying instrument, the option buyer would realize 81 from the short position, which would be covered by acquiring an offsetting long position at 78 through exercise of the option—thereby netting 3 points.

When a call option has intrinsic value, it is said to be "in-the-money." When the exercise price of a call option exceeds the current price of the underlying instrument, the call option is said to be "out-of-the-money" and has no intrinsic value. An option for which the exercise price is equal to the current price of the underlying instrument is said to be "at-the-money."

For a put option, the intrinsic value is equal to the amount by which the current price of the underlying instrument is below the exercise price. For example, if the exercise price of a put option is 78 and the current price of the underlying instrument is 71, the intrinsic value is 7. When the put option has intrinsic value, the option is said to be "in-the-money." A put option is "out-of-the-money" when the current price of the underlying instrument exceeds the exercise price.

The premium over intrinsic value or time value is whatever amount buyers are willing to pay over and above any intrinsic value that the option may have. The option buyer hopes that, at some point prior to expiration, changes in the price of the underlying instrument will further increase the value of the rights conveyed by the option. For example, if the option premium (price) for a call option with an exercise price of 78 is 9 when the current price of the underlying instrument is 81, then the time value of this option is 6 (9 − the intrinsic value of 3). If the current price of the underlying instrument is 72 instead of 81, then the time value of this option is 9, since the option has no intrinsic value.

The four factors that affect the option premium for an interest-rate option are (1) the current price of the underlying instrument relative to the exercise price, (2) the time remaining until the expiration of the option, (3) the anticipated volatility of the price of the underlying instrument, and (4) the level of short-term interest rates for borrowing and lending over the life of the option.[6]

1. Current Price of the Underlying Instrument Relative to the Exercise Price.   As we explained earlier, the current price of the underlying instrument relative to the exercise price determines whether the option has intrinsic value. But the relationship is also important for the time value component of the option premium.

All other factors equal, an at-the-money option generally has the greatest time value. For an in-the-money option in which the current price of the underlying instrument differs substantially from the exercise price, the time value is small. One of the reasons is the reduced leverage provided by purchasing the option compared to directly acquiring a position in the underlying instrument. For a substantially out-of-the-money option, the time value is generally small in spite of the substantial leverage afforded by purchasing the option. This is because there is a lower probability that it will be profitable to exercise the option.

---

[6] For a more extensive discussion of pricing, see: Mark Pitts, "An Introduction to the Pricing of Debt Options," chapter 3 in *Winning the Interest Rate Game: A Guide to Debt Options* (ed.) Frank J. Fabozzi (Chicago: Probus Publishing, 1985). For options on coupon securities there is a fifth factor. Coupons tend to decrease the value of call options and increase the value of put options. Consequently, call options on fixed income instruments with high coupons will be less desirable than for call options on lower coupon securities with other factors held constant.

2. Time Remaining to the Expiration of the Option. An option is a "wasting asset." That is, after the expiration date the option has no value. All other factors equal, one would expect that the longer the time to expiration of the option, the greater the option premium. This is because as the time to expiration decreases, less time remains for the price of the underlying instrument to change so as to compensate the option buyer for any time value he has paid. Consequently, as the time remaining until expiration decreases, the option price approaches its intrinsic value.

3. Anticipated Volatility of the Underlying Instrument. All other factors equal, the greater the anticipated volatility of the underlying instrument, the more an investor would be willing to pay for the option and the more an option writer would demand for it. This is because the greater the volatility, the greater the probability that the price of the underlying instrument will move in favor of the option buyer before expiration.

4. Level of Short-Term Interest Rates for Borrowing and Lending over the Life of the Option. Short-term interest rates reflect the cost of carrying a position in a particular underlying instrument or a call option on that underlying instrument. As short-term interest rates rise, the cost of carrying a nondebt instrument such as common stock will rise and the call will be more attractive relative to the underlying instrument. Consequently, for call options on common stock (and also stock indexes), as the level of short-term interest rates rise, the call option premium will increase. On the other hand, for debt instruments any rise in short-term interest rates will have an adverse impact on the price of the debt instrument which will dominate the impact on the cost of carry. Consequently, for call options on debt instruments, a rise in short-term interest rates will cause option premiums to increase. Put options, however, will decrease in value as short-term interest rates rise.[7]

We have limited our discussion to the factors that influence option prices. Evaluation of options is beyond the scope of this chapter,[8] but any portfolio manager using options should be

---

[7] For options or futures contracts there is no cost of carry. For options on interest rate futures that cannot be exercised prior to the expiration date ("European" options), an increase in short-term interest rates will decrease the value of call options as well as put options.

[8] The most commonly used option evaluation model is that developed by Fischer Black and Myron Scholes ("The Pricing of Options and Corporate Liabilities," *Journal of Political Economy*, May–June 1973, pp. 637–54). For a discussion of various common stock option evaluation models, see: Gary L. Gastineau, *The Stock Options Manual* (New York: McGraw-Hill, 1979), pp. 214–63.

certain that he or she has a thorough understanding of the principles of option evaluation. There is no reason why every portfolio manager should understand the mechanics of an option evaluation model or be prepared to develop detailed volatility estimates for the underlying instrument. A portfolio manager planning to employ options in a portfolio strategy should, however, understand that the principal decision variable in the process of option evaluation is the price volatility of the underlying instrument. When planning to adopt the values furnished by vendors of a commercial option evaluation model, the portfolio manager should question how the volatility estimate is being used in the model and how it was developed.

Risks and Rewards of Basic Option Positions

For a *buyer*, options offer one big advantage over futures: *limited downside risk*. A buyer of a put or call option can lose no more than the price he paid for his option, which is precisely what he will lose if he holds the option to expiration and if, at expiration, the option has no intrinsic value and is therefore worthless. A buyer of futures, in contrast to a buyer of options, has unlimited downside risk; should the price of the underlying security drop sharply, he will lose through margin calls an amount equal to the total decline in the market value of the securities he has contracted—by buying a futures contract—to purchase. As disciples of the dismal science, economics, are wont to point out, there is no free lunch. In a bull market the buyer of a futures contract participates fully in any rise in the value of the underlying security, whereas a buyer of an option profits only to the extent that the price of the underlying security rises more than the time value premium he has paid for his option. The amount by which payment of a premium over intrinsic value for an option reduces the profit earned by the option buyer in a rising market is the price the buyer pays for the limited downside risk to which the option exposes him.

Selling a call or put option, as opposed to buying one, exposes the option seller to *unlimited risk* of loss. A seller of options can, however, hedge that risk by taking an offsetting position in either the cash market or the futures market for the security underlying the option. For example, a common strategy among portfolio managers is to *write covered calls;* that is, to write calls against securities that they hold in their portfolios. This strategy will be discussed later. An alternative way to hedge the sale of a call (put) option would be to buy (sell) a futures contract for an equal amount of the underlying security.

HEDGING WITH OPTIONS

When a portfolio manager uses interest-rate futures to reduce downside risk, he sacrifices upside potential. Options on debt instruments also can be used to provide downside risk protection; however, the cost of this protection is known and leaves any remaining upside potential intact.

The purchase of put options provides protection against adverse interest-rate movements for a long position. When interest rates are expected to rise and debt instrument prices fall, the purchase of a put would be appropriate because it locks in a price (yield) at which a debt instrument can be sold. The locked-in price is the exercise price of the put. On the other hand, when rates are expected to fall and the portfolio manager seeks protection against such a situation, the purchase of a call option would be an appropriate strategy. This is because the buyer locks in the price (yield) at which he could purchase a debt instrument. Once again, the locked-in price is the exercise price of the option. The cost of ensuring a minimum price in the case of a put and a maximum price in the case of a call is the option premium. Since the portfolio manager usually has options with several exercise prices available, he can establish the amount he is willing to pay to protect against adverse interest rate movements.

COVERED CALL WRITE STRATEGY

Stock options have long been used as part of a host of often complicated strategies for speculating, arbitraging, and hedging. Traders of fixed-income securities will undoubtedly think of all sorts of strategies they can implement that will involve the use of options. By late 1982, street traders and portfolio managers had just begun to explore the possibilities that options on fixed-income securities offered them.

To illustrate one of the many ways in which an investor might profit through the use of options, we have chosen the example of a covered call write described in Table 2. We assume that in early December 1982 a treasurer had money he wanted to invest until mid-March 1983. If he had bought the cash bill maturing on 3/24/83, he would have earned a return on a simple interest rate, 360-day basis of 8.48 (Choice A, Table 2). Alternatively, if he had been bullish, which people were in early December 1982, he could have bought the 6/23/83 bill at 8.50 and sold against it the out-of-the-money call that was closest to the cash market; this was a call option having a strike price of 92 and selling at a 38 basis-point premium. As the calculations under Choice B in Ta-

Table 2
A Covered Option Write on a T Bill

Choice A:	Buy for settlement on 12/9/82, $1 million of the 3/24/83 bill at 8.28 and hold 105 days to maturity. Earn rate of return, i, on a simple interest, 360-day basis of:

$$i = \frac{(.0828)(360)}{360 - (.0828)(105)} (100) = 8.48$$

Choice B:	Do a covered option write with the bullish expectation that the call sold will be exercised.

Trade put on:	1. Buy, for settlement on 12/9/82, $1 million of T bills maturing on 6/23/83 at 8.50.

$$\text{Gross purchase price} = (\$1,000,000)(.0850)(^{196}\!/_{360})$$
$$= \$953,722.30$$

2. Sell five March 92 calls, each for $200,000 of bills at a 38 basis-point premium. Since a basis point on $1 million of bills is worth $25, a basis point on an option for $200,000 of 90-day bills is worth one fifth of that amount, or $5. Therefore,

$$\text{Proceeds from call sale} = (38)(\$5)(5)$$
$$= \$950.00$$

3. The call sale reduces the net purchase price to:

$$\text{Net purchase price} = \$953,722.30 - \$950.00$$
$$= \$952,772.50$$

Call exercised at option expiration:	1. Deliver 6/23/83 bill on 3/24/83 at a price of 92, i.e., at a yield of 8.00.

$$\text{Sale price} = (\$1,000,000)(.0800)(^{91}\!/_{360})$$
$$= \$979,777.80$$

Compute return earned:

$$\begin{pmatrix} \text{Rate of return,} \\ \text{a 360-day basis} \end{pmatrix} = \left(\frac{\text{Sale price} - \text{Net purchase price}}{\text{Net purchase price}}\right)\left(\frac{360}{105}\right)(100)$$

$$= \left(\frac{\$979,777.80 - \$952,772.30}{\$952,772.30}\right)\left(\frac{360}{105}\right)(100)$$

$$= 9.72$$

ble 2 show, if the market had in fact traded up and if the treasurer's bills were consequently called from him at expiration of the option, he would have earned, over the 105-day holding period, 9.72; that is, 124 more basis points than he would have earned by buying and maturing the 3/24/83 bill.

To get the return rate of 9.76, we had to make several assumptions. One was that the bills were not called from the treasurer until expiration of the option. In fact an option, put or call, may be exercised *at any time* during its life. Our second assumption was that the market rallied sufficiently so that the bills were called from the treasurer. Had the market instead declined, the treasurer would have had on his trade a substantial built-in margin of protection against a market decline because the option sale generated a premium and because the 6/23/83 bill was trading two basis points above the 3/24/83 bill. Specifically he could have sold the 6/23/83 bill on 3/24/83 at a rate as high as 9.46 and still have earned over the holding period the 8.48 return that Choice A would have yielded him.

As the bill option contract is now written, the example we have just worked out turns out to be not a covered write, but a naked write. As we explained earlier, the bill option contract, unlike either the note or bond option contracts, is not for a specific underlying security but rather for the 91-day bill that is current upon exercise of the option. Thus a manager of a corporate short-term portfolio who, as in our example, bought in December 82 a June 83 bill and sold March 83 calls against that bill would in effect be writing—until the call had almost expired—a *naked* option against which he would have to put up *margin*.

CREATING ALTERNATIVE INVESTMENTS WITH FUTURES AND OPTIONS

Futures and options can be used to create alternative synthetic investments that may offer enhanced returns. For example, by purchasing a Treasury obligation that is deliverable under a futures contract and selling that contract, a portfolio manager can effectively shorten the maturity of the Treasury obligation. The maturity of the synthetic short-term instrument is the delivery date of the futures contract. The redemption value of the synthetic short-term instrument is the futures price. Based on the maturity and redemption value of the synthetic short-term instrument, a return can be computed and compared to prevailing returns on short-term money market instruments of the same maturity to determine if there is a yield advantage after transaction costs for the synthetic short-term instrument.[9]

---

[9] A simulation of how futures and options could have been used to create a synthetic short-term tax-exempt portfolio over the period January 1971 to September 1982 can be found in: Gary L. Gastineau, "The Impact of Options and Financial Futures on Municipal Bond Portfolio Management," Chapter 35 in *The Municipal Bond Handbook: Volume I*, ed. F. J. Fabozzi, S. G. Feldstein, I. M. Pollack, and F. G. Zarb (Homewood, Ill.: Dow Jones-Irwin, 1983).

Call options offer several interesting strategies for creating alternative investments. For example, a portfolio manager can purchase a call as an alternative to investing in an equivalent par amount in the long-term sector, using the excess funds to invest in short-term obligations. In our discussion of options, we explained how call options are beneficial when bond prices rise (i.e., interest rates fall). However, the synthetic investment created by this strategy generates a surprising result. This strategy actually provides an option on higher yields.[10]

SUMMARY

Futures and options provide greater flexibility in managing a corporate short-term portfolio. The manager can quickly alter the market risk exposure of a portfolio and create a risk-return pattern that would otherwise not be available. Although the focus in this chapter has been on futures and options on Treasury bills, the principles are applicable to any option on a debt instrument.

---

[10] For an analysis of this strategy, see: Robert W. Kopprasch, *Exchange Traded Options on Fixed-Income Securities*, pp. 10–14.

SECTION V

International Cash
Management

14

Cross-Border International Cash Management

Helen N. Martin
Vice President, Global Cash
Management Consulting
Citibank, N.A.

Until recently, U.S. companies concentrated on improving the efficiency of their domestic treasury operations. However, as international trade has continued to expand, a growing number of large and small companies with international activities have been shifting their focus to the international aspect of cash management in an attempt to also achieve internationally what they have accomplished domestically.

The purpose of this chapter is to provide a basic understanding of international cash management as it relates to managing cross-border third-party and intercompany flows. The intent is to illustrate the wide range of issues and elements which confront the exporter, importer, and company with a global presence that can impact the flow of funds. Specific information regarding practices, principles, and techniques used to manage the global movement of funds efficiently is provided. This chapter describes common problems in international money mobilization and offers a means by which the financial executive can evaluate specific situations in a broad context. Topics covered are international considerations in cash management, international money mobilization, terms of sale, and specialized treasury management techniques and vehicles such as multilateral netting systems, reinvoicing centers, and offshore finance companies.

INTERNATIONAL CONSIDERATIONS

The primary goal of international cash management is to optimize the return on the global assets of the company. The company operating globally must accomplish this in an environment comprised of numerous variables and use techniques which have no relevance to domestic cash management. For example, while the domestic cash manager is striving to accelerate the availability of funds by one or two days or even several hours, his international counterpart is often attempting to increase the availability of funds to the company by several days, weeks, and sometimes even months!

The company dealing internationally must protect and manage its global resources from the impact of exchange rate changes as well as from a wide range of potential problems caused by commercial, legal, political, and cultural differences. The international environment is a complex one, comprised of different elements which vary from country to country and can affect the flow of funds. The factors to be coped with include various

- Payment systems.
- Banking conventions and commercial practices.
- Foreign exchange and capital control regulations.
- Investment vehicles.
- Tax rates.
- Political risks.
- Time zones.

Thus, to manage international cash effectively, one must have a working knowledge of these various factors, constantly review them, and determine the optimal strategies in light of continual changes in exchange rates.

Banking Conventions

In mobilizing funds globally, the exporter, importer, and multinational company must contend with the local banking conventions of each of the countries with which they are involved. These banking practices have no domestic counterpart; vary by country, method, of payment and client; and involve a cost (direct and/or indirect) to the company. For example, to effect an international transfer by cable, in addition to the transfer or handling charges (which typically range from $10–$20 per cable), a company will normally incur other expenses due to

- Float resulting from value dating practices.
- Foreign exchange commissions (in addition to the foreign exchange spread).
- Transfer commissions and possibly other miscellaneous banking charges.

These selected international banking practices and their cash
management implications are described below. Practical recommendations to deal with these phenomena effectively are also
offered.

Value Dating

It is common practice among banks to take one day's value on
either side for collections and disbursements, which are either
domestic or foreign transfers. Therefore, if a German importer
pays a French exporter by cable, both parties lose availability
and the banks involved gain use of the funds. On an intercompany transfer, where a company is involved on both ends of the
transaction, two to three days of float can easily be lost to the
banking system.

Value dating practices vary by country, instrument, and client
and are often negotiable. The value date indicates when a given
transaction becomes effective for interest calculation purposes.
Companies should examine the value dating they are receiving
by reviewing their bank statements which reflect two dates, the
ledger date and the value date. The former indicates when a
transaction passes over the books of the bank, while the latter shows when the funds actually become "available" to the
company.

As a general rule, value dates should always be specified
where cross-border payments are involved. For example, the
exporter should specify a value date (i.e., when he expects to
receive good funds, not when the customer initiates payment)
on all invoices issued to customers. Other information which
the exporter should state on the invoice to ensure timely payment by the importer includes

- The method of payment to be used (cable, bank draft, or
  company check).
- Location where payment is to be directed (bank, company,
  or agent).
- An invoice or reference number.

When making an international payment by cable, the importer, as part of the instructions given to his bank, should also
provide a specific value date on which the transaction is to be
effected with which the bank can comply. Sample instructions
which can be included on the invoice and provided to the remitter's bank are as follows:

Value _____ (settlement date) please pay
this _____ (currency) invoice by cable (telex transfer)
to Bank XYZ, _____ (beneficiary's bank and location)
favor Company ABC Account No. _____ Reference
_____ (invoice number).

If this information is not provided, the banks will assign their
own value dates. In addition, when effecting payment by cable
transfer, companies should insist that the debit entry be made
on the value date and not before. This is especially important on
international transfers involving foreign exchange contracts.

For example, assume that on a Monday a French importer
effects a spot foreign exchange contract to purchase sterling to
pay an exporter in the United Kingdom. The spot contract will
settle in two days (on Wednesday). However, it is not unusual
for the bank to debit the account on Monday but backvalue the
transaction by one day, a common practice in France and in
many other countries. Because of the "weekend effect," the
company can lose availability as of the previous Friday, although the contract will not settle until the following Wednesday! Moreover, the transfer will probably be effected on the day
after settlement date, or Thursday, as no value date was specified. Thus, the company can avoid losing five days use of the
funds by providing a value date along with the transfer instructions and negotiating with its bank so that both the debit and the
transfer are made for value Wednesday (on the contract settlement date).

Same-Day Value Transfers

International telex transfers can be made on a same-day value
basis although this will not typically happen unless negotiated
or specified by the company in its instructions to the bank. In
the previous example, assuming that the French importer had
initiated the transfer by providing the proper instructions to his
bank, the beneficiary could have had his account credited that
same day but not have had use of the funds until the following
day because of the value dating conditions he receives from his
bank. With a same-day value transfer, the remitter's account is
debited and the beneficiary's account is credited on the same
day with good value given, depending on the time zones involved.

To effect such transfers, at least one day's notice should be
given to the remitting bank by the company. In general, advance notice of payment will not result in earlier value dating of

the debit. When possible, the receiving bank should also be pre-advised of the receipt of the funds by the remitting bank via tested telex. It should be noted that, as processing delays can occur and each bank has its own deadlines, good value may not be received on the incoming funds if the credit occurs after the beneficiary bank's cutoff time for same-day value. Therefore, it is recommended that companies familiarize themselves with their respective banks' deadlines for providing same day value on receipts and disbursements made by telex transfer by currency.

Many of the major international banks with global branch networks offer specialized money transfer services which include same-day value transfers. This service is most frequently used for intercompany money transfers as it eliminates float on transfers between related companies, thus allowing the funds to remain available to the overall institution. Moreover, as the payments are routed through the same bank, the remittance channel is simplified and the possibility of delays occurring is reduced.

Transfer Commissions

There are certain banking or handling charges involved in making international payments, such as the per item cost of a telex transfer or a foreign currency draft. A company can also incur transfer commissions to move the funds across borders, thereby increasing the expense of the cross-border payment. Again, these banking costs vary by country, amount, method of payment, and client. In countries where government-imposed transfer charges are mandatory or strong banking cartel agreements on international money transfers exist, such as in Belgium and Holland, they cannot be waived. Moreover, transfer commissions can be levied on both incoming and outgoing cross-border payments (depending on the country) as in Belgium, Holland and Germany. Therefore, while a U.S. company can effect an international payment of several million dollars for the cost of a telex (about $15), its counterpart overseas can pay several hundred or even thousand dollars in transfer commissions to remit and/or receive a cross-border payment of a similar amount. A standard fee schedule is applied to the appropriate amount.

Foreign Exchange Commissions

Typically, international payments involve a foreign exchange conversion executed either by the remitter or the receiver. In addition to the cost of the foreign exchange contract which is included in the price quoted, some countries such as Brazil, France, and Greece also require the banks to charge foreign exchange commissions where there is currency conversion.

In general, the transfer and foreign exchange commission schedules are either on a flat rate or percentage basis, according to amount, and tend to become smaller as the size of the transaction increases. These charges can be minimized by batching transactions or implementing a multilateral netting system if appropriate. (Multilateral netting is discussed in detail later in this chapter.)

INTERNATIONAL MONEY MOBILIZATION

Unlike the United States, there are many countries, such as Brazil, France, Spain, and the Philippines, with stringent exchange control regulations which prohibit the free flow of funds into or out of the country without proper documentation and/or prior approval by the appropriate local regulatory authority. Thus, to avoid delays in collecting or disbursing funds, the international cash manager should be familiar with the exchange control requirements of the countries with which his company is involved for moving funds cross-border. Both local and international banks can provide specific information on how to comply with them. It is recommended that companies ask their banks to advise them of the estimated amount of "lead time" needed to review the documentation corresponding to the international payment to help ensure compliance and the timely execution of the transaction.

Methods of Payment

The four most common methods of payment used for international transactions are: cable (telex transfer), mail transfer, bank draft, and company check. Each of these methods is discussed.

Cable In most instances, the fastest and most efficient way to transfer funds internationally is by cable or telex transfer. However, this method of payment can be costly. Therefore, the company must evaluate the benefit derived from funds acceleration against the cost of the cable to determine if this method should be used for a particular transaction.

Exhibit 1 is a break-even chart which illustrates the float savings versus the cable cost for several transactions. For example, a $6,000 transfer (Point A on the chart) accelerated six days

Exhibit 1
Float Saving versus Cable Cost (When Is It Cheaper to Transfer by Cable?)
(Break-Even Analysis)

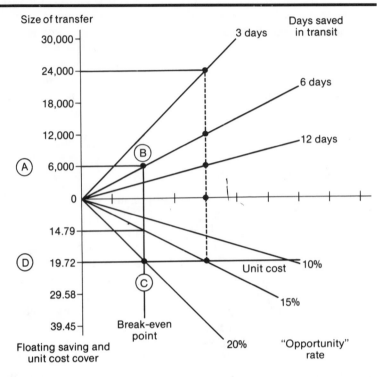

(Point B) at an opportunity cost for funds of 20 percent (Point C) will cover a $19.72 cable charge (Point D). A smaller transfer, a lesser time saving, or a lower opportunity rate would not reach the break-even point. Therefore, it would be cost-justified to use this method of payment for transactions greater than $6,000, assuming all other variables remain constant because of the acceleration of funds. In fact, when appropriate, many exporting companies absorb the cable charges (i.e., the cable charge will be deducted from the amount by the remitting bank) to obtain availability sooner. Exhibit 1 can be read in any direction.

Although telex transfers are the most efficient method of payment, delays can and do occur due to the bank processing cycle. For example, let's examine what occurs when a German company settles by cable a deutsche mark intercompany trade payable due to its Swiss sister company. Assuming that the German company's bank in Frankfurt and the Swiss company's bank in Geneva have reciprocal accounts with each other, outlined below are the steps typically involved in making a telex transfer.

- The German subsidiary mails the payment instructions to the money transfer department of its bank.
- The bank receives and sorts the mail and then delivers the instructions to the money transfer department.
- The money transfer department verifies the signatures on the instructions and also determines if there are sufficient funds in the German company's account before processing the transaction.
- The telex payment text is prepared, as are the corresponding debit and credit tickets.
- The telex is then forwarded to the test key department where a unique code is added as a security measure. (The code will allow the receiving bank to verify the authenticity, source, and instructions stated.)
- The telex department will then transmit the telex along with other messages and telexes in sequence.
- The receiving bank will process the telex using similar procedures but in reverse order.

While a payment can be sent, received, and processed on the same day, it is highly unlikely that this will occur if there is a delay in the cycle. This can easily cause a company to lose one day's value on the funds being transferred. Moreover, if the German and the Swiss banks in the example do not have a relationship with each other, further delays would probably occur, as the payment will have to be routed through a mutual correspondent bank. Thus, many companies are not aware of the processing float which is associated with telex transfers. In following up on late payments, the accounts receivable departments of many companies which export cannot understand it when their foreign customers advise them that they initiated payment by cable several days earlier, yet the funds have not yet been credited to their account. To the extent that a telex transfer goes astray as a result of bank error, the beneficiary should seek compensation from the bank for the number of days lost.

A growing number of corporations are utilizing the electronic banking systems offered by several major U.S. international banks to effect U.S. dollar and foreign currency cable transfers electronically. Some of these systems have evolved from providing multicurrency ledger balances only, to offering detailed information on a real-time basis on account activity, investments and borrowings, foreign exchange contracts, and also allowing the multinational corporation to execute transfers on-line via computer terminal. This transaction initiation capability therefore allows the international cash manager to better monitor, control, and dispose of the funds in a timely manner. As of this writing, one bank's system also offers companies the ability to project their liquidity position based upon the value dated incoming and outgoing transfers that have been entered into the system. Given the growth of electronic banking worldwide, companies will be able to mobilize funds across the borders from an increasing number of overseas locations, regardless of time zones, more efficiently and expeditiously.

Mail Transfer   A less efficient method of payment is the mail transfer. The processing cycle of a mail transfer is similar to that of an international telex transfer, but usually takes longer. The distinction between the two, as the name implies, is that the bank mails versus telexes the payment instructions from one country to another.

A mail transfer is subject to mail float which can take three to five days within Europe and longer to and from countries such as Brazil or Italy. Further delays can occur if there are postal strikes, a common phenomenon outside of the United States. In addition, as the money transfer department does not treat such transfers as priority items, float due to bank processing is increased.

Bank Draft   Another frequently used method of payment is the bank draft. A bank draft is a check drawn either on the company itself for local currency payment, or drawn on a foreign branch or a correspondent bank if the payment is to be made in a foreign currency. It is often used to make foreign currency payments in countries where local regulations prohibit the holding of foreign currencies.

The loss of availability a company suffers will depend on the amount of time which it takes for it to request its beneficiary bank to present and collect payment from the remitting bank. Several options to collect good funds exist. For example, consider the case of a U.K. subsidiary of a U.S. company which receives a U.S. dollar draft drawn on a New York bank. The U.K. subsidiary's local bank could:

- Credit the customer's U.S. dollar account in London with a fixed agreed forward value.
- Purchase the draft from the customer at a rate of exchange which incorporates the time it takes to clear the item and receive payment.
- Send the draft for collection and credit the customer's account with either the local currency or U.S. dollars when the proceeds are available.

Companies purchasing a bank draft denominated in a foreign currency incur a per item cost (between $10 and $20) in addition to the cost of the foreign exchange. The foreign exchange rate quoted by a bank is determined daily, fixed, and negotiable only on sizable amounts. To expedite the availability of funds, the exporter should request that a bank draft denominated in the currency of the seller be drawn on a bank in the seller's country. The item will therefore clear locally.

Company Check   Another method of payment which is used, but not as extensively as in the United States, is the company check. This instrument is issued and mailed by the company and is typically used for third-party versus intercompany payments. Some countries permit only local currency checking accounts. Other countries, such as Switzerland and the United Kingdom allow multicurrency (in various currencies) checking accounts which can even be drawn against the local currency.

The use of a company check provides the remitter with the disbursement float, which can be excessive. On the other hand, when payment is made by telex transfer, mail transfer, or bank draft, the remitter's account is debited immediately by the remitting bank and the banking system has the use of the funds. The collection of foreign checks is a lengthy, cumbersome, and costly process. It can easily take several weeks (10–30 days on average) and in some instances several months for the beneficiary to obtain good value. This is due to inefficient mail systems and bank delays, as the checks are typically returned to the bank on which they are drawn (i.e., "sent for collection") to obtain payment.

As foreign checks often do not have MICR-encoding they cannot be read by the high-speed check processing equipment used by U.S. banks and must therefore be processed manually. Moreover, if correspondent banks are involved, then each institution will charge a fee, thus reducing the amount of funds the beneficiary will ultimately receive. As a result, to compensate for the inconvenience and loss of availability, the exporter will often increase his prices to the importer who insists on paying by a company check (or bank draft) drawn on a foreign bank. (Payment by check is discussed in further detail in the section "International Payment Mechanics—Importer's Currency.)

Some companies which receive numerous checks drawn on foreign banks use courier services to speed the collection process and thereby obtain availability sooner. For example, one Hong Kong subsidiary of a U.S. oil service company made arrangements to have U.S. dollar checks drawn on U.S. banks delivered and deposited at a California bank on a regular basis by a private courier service. Other companies often use the pouch services offered by various banks.

Although frequently used in the United States to speed up the collection of checks, lockboxes are not widely employed overseas. There are several reasons for this. Most banks are either unwilling to handle the extensive paper processing or local regulations (such as in Australia) prohibit banks from having post-office boxes. Additionally, it is impractical to use lockboxes in those countries where the mail service is poor, especially in Latin America. In fact, in some countries where this is the case (Brazil, the Philippines), collection agents are often used. Nevertheless, companies have had some success in countries where lockboxes can exist. Other variations on this technique include having foreign currency checks (1) directed to a foreign subsidiary which in turn deposits them on behalf of the company to a collection account at a local bank or (2) intercepted by a correspondent bank in the country of the currency so that these checks can be collected and cleared locally. The local currency or U.S. dollar proceeds can then be transferred by telex to the company.

INTERNATIONAL PAYMENT MECHANICS

The currency of invoice will determine how and where a transaction is settled. Invoices can be denominated in the exporter's currency, the importer's currency, or in a third currency (i.e., a Dutch exporter selling in the United Kingdom and billing in U.S. dollars). When cross-border payments are made, the funds do not flow across the border. Rather, information moves across borders through a series of debits and credits to various banks' accounts. Regardless of the currency of payment, the remittance channel used by the bank to route the payment will determine how quickly the beneficiary will be credited. Three invoice payments are described and traced to provide the reader with a better understanding of what is involved and why payment delays occur.

Exporter's Currency

When an importer is billed in the exporter's currency, he usually purchases the foreign exchange if he does not have it on hand to effect the trade payment.

Delays can occur if

• The importer's correspondent does not have a relationship with the exporter's bank.

- The importer's bank mails the instructions to effect a cable transfer to the exporter.
- The importer's correspondent pays the exporter or the exporter's bank by draft.

Moreover, if another bank is added to the chain, additional banking charges will be incurred which may be charged to the importer, deducted from the final amount the exporter receives or both. As mentioned earlier, countries with strict exchange controls can be the source of other delays. Many countries require a company to submit supporting documentation to its local bank to justify the transaction and possibly obtain prior approval from the appropriate local regulatory authority before permitting any cross-border transfers to be made into or out of the country.

Exhibit 2 illustrates the steps involved in making a cable transfer paid in the exporter's currency.

Exhibit 2
Export Sales Invoiced in Exporter's Currency (Example: U.S. exporter invoices its German buyer in U.S. dollars resulting in a U.S. dollar transfer from Germany to the U.S.)

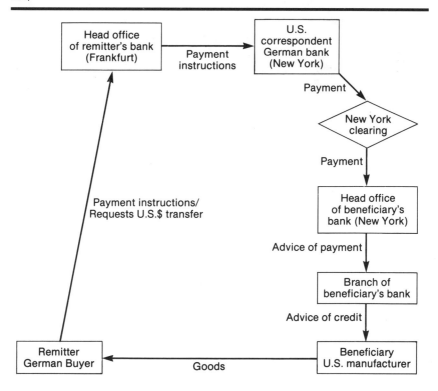

Where the importer and exporter are related, the branch network of a multinational bank should be used. If not, the exporter should open up a concentration account to collect the export receipts with a bank which has a wide correspondent bank network that will include most of the importer's banks. Therefore, to avoid delays and minimize banking charges, the exporter should evaluate the correspondent banking channels of his collecting bank. Otherwise customer payments will be channeled through two or three banks before reaching their destination, as illustrated in Exhibit 2.

If the importer pays by check drawn on a bank in the country of the exporter, then it is cleared locally. As previously stated, checks or drafts drawn on the importer, the importer's bank, or a third country must be presented by the exporter's bank to the bank on which it is drawn. Other options include having the check purchased at a discount by the exporter's bank or couriered to its correspondent bank in the country of the currency.

Importer's Currency

If the importer pays by bank cable or mail transfer in his local currency, then he must instruct his bank to effect a domestic transfer to the branch or correspondent of the exporter's bank. Once the customer is advised of the receipt of payment, he will either keep or sell the foreign exchange. Exhibit 3 illustrates the processing cycle of a cable transfer in the importer's currency.

The exporter could easily experience a loss of funds for several weeks if payment is made by a bank draft or check in local currency, drawn on a local bank. Exhibit 4 outlines the steps involved in collecting a check or draft issued in the importer's currency.

Delays can be avoided if

- The check/draft can be collected and cleared locally by a subsidiary acting as agent.
- A courier (private or bank) is used to intercept the items and deposit the funds locally.
- The exporter instructs the importer to deliver the check to a correspondent of his bank.

Third-Currency Payment

Some exporters invoice in a third currency (i.e., a German company selling to Japan and invoicing in U.S. dollars). To collect bank and mail transfers, the German company can allow the

Exhibit 3
Export Sales Invoiced in Importer's Currency (Example: French exporter invoices its U.K. buyer in sterling resulting in a sterling transfer from the U.K. to France.)

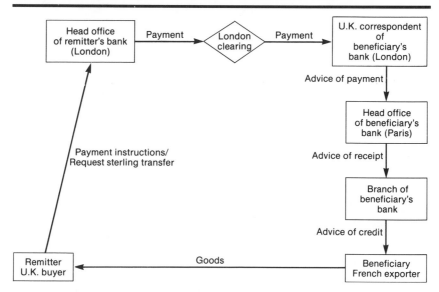

importer's correspondent bank to effect the transfer. An example of this is illustrated in Exhibit 5.

A second option is for the exporter to open up an account in the country of the third currency to collect the payments. As a third option, assuming exchange control regulations permit, the exporter may want to maintain locally an account in the foreign currency. For example, a U.K. exporter selling in deutsche marks may want to have a deutsche mark "hold account" at his U.K. bank. This is simply a foreign currency denominated bank account which is used to maintain short-term inflows and outflows in the same currency. It serves to reduce the foreign exchange costs and risk, as the need to sell and later purchase the same currency, possibly at a higher price, is reduced. However, the exchange control regulations regarding foreign currency hold accounts should be evaluated.

TERMS OF SALE

There are several forms of common terms of sale used in international trade. These are: open account, documentary collection, and letter of credit. These trade terms and their cash management implications are discussed below.

Exhibit 4
Collection of Check/Draft in the Importer's Currency

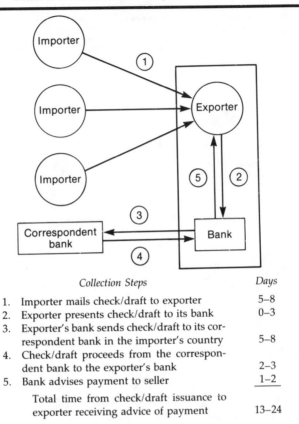

Collection Steps	Days
1. Importer mails check/draft to exporter	5–8
2. Exporter presents check/draft to its bank	0–3
3. Exporter's bank sends check/draft to its correspondent bank in the importer's country	5–8
4. Check/draft proceeds from the correspondent bank to the exporter's bank	2–3
5. Bank advises payment to seller	1–2
Total time from check/draft issuance to exporter receiving advice of payment	13–24

Open Account

The most common terms of sale used worldwide are open accounts terms. However, these terms offer the exporter the least amount of protection as the seller trusts the buyer to make payment. Moreover, such terms leave the timing of the payment up to the discretion of the importer. This makes it difficult for the cash manager to forecast cash receipts. The key to efficient collection of open account sales requires the use of proper payment instruments, precise wording of transfer instructions (which includes a specific value date), and an effective receiving bank. Many exporters impose penalty charges on delinquent invoices where permitted. Open account terms are typically used in trading with stable environments such as Europe.

Exhibit 5
Export Sales Invoiced in a Third Currency (Example: Japanese exporter invoices its West German buyer in U.S. dollars resulting in a U.S. dollar transfer from West Germany to Japan.)

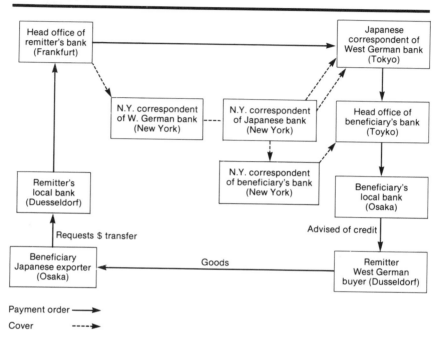

Documentary Collection

Another common method of settlement of payment is through documentary collections. This method provides greater security to the exporter than open account terms as a bank acts as a collection intermediary for the seller. Typically the bill of exchange/draft is the payment instrument used. The bill of exchange is a document written by the exporter requesting the importer to pay a specified amount at a specified date. The usual trade documents included are the bill of lading or warehouse receipt and are kept by the bank until payment or acceptance of the draft.

The advantages of these terms to the exporter are that a bank collects payment and a due date is known. The collecting bank advises the exporter of nonpayment. While this facilitates accounts receivable management, it does not guarantee or enforce payment. Trade drafts can be discounted, thereby providing short-term working capital to the multinational company. The title to the goods passes to the importer on payment or acceptance of the draft.

Exporters should select a bank which is a direct correspondent of the importer's bank. This will reduce the number of banks which must transfer the funds and the associated banking charges. In addition, payment by cable should be included in the payment instructions. Use of a service called "direct collections" offered by many banks will expedite the movement of funds between the remitting bank and the exporter. Typically, the beneficiary bank provides the exporter with a series of pre-numbered forms on bank stationary which are sent directly with the documents to the buyer's bank. As a result, mail float is reduced, as the documents are sent directly to the collecting bank, and payment is accelerated.

Letter of Credit

When the exporter has limited credit knowledge of the buyer, the letter of credit is used, whereby the bank substitutes its credit for that of the purchaser. A letter of credit is an instrument issued by a bank (the issuer) at the request of the importer, in which the bank guarantees to pay the exporter against prescribed documents. The letter of credit specifies the amount and time of payment. Payment by cable should be specified by the exporter to avoid receipt of a bank draft.

There are various types of letters of credit. Under a simple letter of credit, a bank is not committed to pay. On the other hand, under a confirmed letter of credit, assuming all of the documents are in order and are approved by the correspondent of the importer's bank, payment will be made immediately. Thus, the exporter is guaranteed payment and the importer is assured of receiving the appropriate documents. These terms of trade minimize the risk of nonpayment. They are typically used on exports to less-developed countries.

SPECIALIZED TECHNIQUES AND VEHICLES

Many multinational companies with expanding worldwide operations have implemented various specialized techniques and vehicles to centralize the management of their international treasury operations. This trend has been accelerating in the last few years due to record worldwide inflation and the ensuing borrowing costs experienced during this decade and the advent of Financial Accounting Standards Board (FASB) Statement No. 52 which has made foreign currency transaction losses (and gains) more visible in the income statement. The use of bilateral netting, the establishment of multilateral netting systems, reinvoicing centers, and finance companies has lead to numerous quantitative and qualitative benefits due to improved treasury coordination, control, and management of global corporate assets. Each of these is described briefly.

Bilateral Netting

Where local exchange control regulations permit, many multinational companies with subsidiaries which have reciprocal trade flows practice bilateral netting. Simply stated, they settle their accounts on a net basis. As an example, let's assume that two units, a Canadian subsidiary and a German subsidiary are buying from one another and billing each other in their respective currencies. As Exhibit 6 indicates, in the absence of any offset-

Exhibit 6
Sample of Bilateral Netting (Payment in Currency of Seller*)

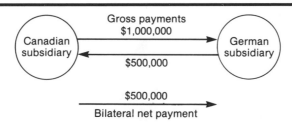

* Shown in U.S. dollar equivalents.

ting, the Canadian unit would have to purchase and remit $1 million worth of deutsche marks to settle its obligation to the German unit. In turn, the German unit would have to purchase and remit $500,000 worth of Canadian dollars to discharge its obligation. In total, therefore, $1.5 million worth of foreign exchange would be purchased and an equivalent amount of funds would be transferred.

With the use of offsetting on a bilateral basis, however, the Canadian unit, which is a net importer of $500,000, would only purchase $500,000 of deutsche marks, the net amount of its obligation to the German unit. Thus, bilateral netting is economical to both subsidiaries as the total amount of foreign exchange purchased and funds remitted cross-border would be only $500,000 instead of the previous $1.5 million.

In addition, the overall company will obtain savings in the following areas through the reduction of

- Foreign exchange conversion expense.
- Float.
- Transfer charges as only one cable is sent.
- Transfer and foreign exchange commissions.

Bilateral netting is frequently used between the parent and its manufacturing operations. While this technique allows the international cash manager to exercise control over the settlement process, a multilateral netting system provides greater control and over more subsidiaries.

Multilateral Netting

Multinational companies that maintain a substantial volume of intercompany trade can often benefit from the use of a multilateral netting system by comparing the intercompany payables and receivables positions of all subsidiaries. Multilateral netting is based on the same concept as bilateral offsetting, except that there are numerous subsidiaries which are located in different countries.

The objectives of a multilateral netting system are to

- Minimize the number of cross-border intercompany payments.
- Centralize the foreign exchange transactions institutionally.
- Minimize the float on transferred funds.
- Achieve streamlining in the settlement routines of intercompany obligations.
- Optimize liquidity management strategies by acting on short-term cash flow information centrally.

Let's examine the flows of a multinational company which have a multilateral nature, i.e., where eight subsidiaries trade among themselves. As in the example used to illustrate bilateral netting, the billing is also assumed to be in the exporter's currency. As Exhibit 7 indicates, without multilateral netting there will be a total of 28 foreign currency cross-border payments made at various times on a monthly basis, probably through different banks. Imagine the foreign exchange spread, fees, and commissions incurred, not to mention the costs due to float, value dating, and bank processing that the company is suffering due to the present method of settling intercompany accounts.

Now let's evaluate the intercompany receivables and payables of each unit as they relate to the rest of the group as a whole. As Exhibit 8 indicates, five of the subsidiaries are net payers, while the other three are net receivers for a total of only eight cross-border transfers per month. The split of the group into net im-

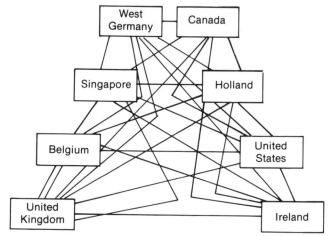

* 8 companies = 28 payment channels
  Foreign exchange costs (i.e., spread, fees, commissions)
  paid on *gross* amount of intercompany payments

Exhibit 8
Multinational Intercompany Trade with Multilateral Netting*

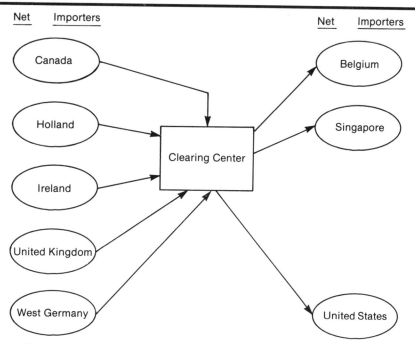

* Eight companies = Eight payment channels: One way only.
  Foreign exchange costs: Paid only on net amount of intercompany payments.

porters and net exporters provides a basis for the settlement process, as intercompany obligations can now be settled on a regular basis (usually monthly).

The international cash manager or multinational bank operating the system as agent for the company requests the net importers to remit the amount of their net obligations into a central pool which is the netting center out of which net exporters are paid. On a predetermined, specified date, the net importers usually remit in their local currency equivalent and the netting center sells these currencies to purchase the currencies of the net exporters to pay them. By having subsidiaries settle their net differences, only net payments are effected. The amount of the actual transfers can often be reduced sharply with a resultant savings of foreign exchange, spreads, fees, and commissions and charges.

It should be noted however that, while the payment and receipt in local currency equivalent facilitates the intercompany settlement process, it does not eliminate the foreign currency transaction exposures which the subsidiaries have by virtue of the fact that they are billed in the currency of the seller. The netting center is simply a cash management vehicle operating a series of resident or nonresident currency accounts, one for each currency in which settlements are to be made. These accounts are typically located in a country which is free from exchange controls. The global cash manager can shift liquidity between subsidiaries by leading (prepaying) and lagging (delaying payment of) intercompany payments where exchange controls permit.

Reinvoicing Center

A specialized financial vehicle used frequently by multinational companies with complex intercompany and third-party cross-border flows is reinvoicing. It is used to facilitate both cash and foreign exchange exposure management on a centralized or regionalized basis. A reinvoicing center is established as a separate legal entity. This subsidiary or reinvoicing company buys goods from a manufacturer in the currency of production and sells or "reinvoices" it to a sales subsidiary in its respective local currency and/or to a third party in another currency. The reinvoicing center acts as an intermediary by taking title to, but not possession of, the goods manufactured. The goods are shipped directly from the exporter to the importer. Exhibit 9 illustrates the reinvoicing center's cash flows.

Reinvoicing centers are typically located in countries which are free from exchange controls, have easy access to the major

Exhibit 9
Reinvoicing Center's Cash Flow

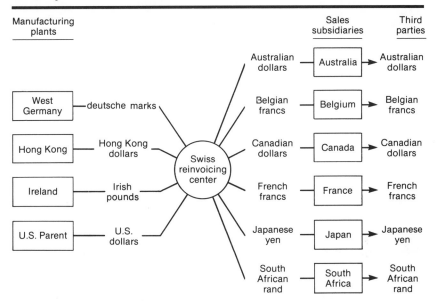

financial markets, and are in tax haven countries such as Switzerland, Panama, and Hong Kong. By concentrating and controlling its cash, foreign exchange exposure, and banking relations from one central location, the company will achieve the following benefits:

- By effecting cross-border transactions centrally, there are numerous opportunities to reduce expenses related to bank fees and commissions on foreign exchange transactions and money transfers.
- Due to the economies of scale available from converting foreign exchange centrally, the reinvoicing center is able to obtain more competitive rates on larger transactions.
- By eliminating third-currency and U.S. dollar items from the books of the subsidiaries, the reinvoicing center relieves them of their foreign exchange risk and thus centralizes foreign currency transaction exposure.
- By placing another subsidiary in the sales or purchase chain, the company can improve its liquidity management on a regional or even global basis.
- The reinvoicing center can be used as a potential source of low-tax foreign source income if the parent has excess foreign tax credits.
- The reinvoicing center can control the collection procedures on third-party exports.

The need to establish a reinvoicing center should be evaluated to ensure that this vehicle will satisfy the company's treasury management needs and objectives in light of the start-up costs and overhead involved.

Finance Company

Another specialized vehicle used by multinational companies to improve international money management by better managing liquidity is the offshore finance company. Some companies have both a reinvoicing center and an offshore finance company. The latter can also be a separate legal entity or a branch of a reinvoicing center whose purpose is to centralize liquidity management. For example, the finance company will borrow both short- and long-term money from financial institutions and lend it to cash-poor sister companies. It also invests excess cash of subsidiaries and generally takes the risks a bank would normally take, the difference being that its clientele is captive. Many companies have revitalized dormant finance companies created as a result of the 1964 passage of the Interest Equalization Tax in the United States to manage borrowings and investments on a centralized basis.

Some of the advantages a finance company offers to a multinational company are listed below.

- Depending on its capitalization and size, the finance company can borrow on a short- and medium-term basis at rates that are often below those available to subsidiaries in their local markets.
- It can gain access to the Euro capital markets for longer-term funds.
- Subsidiaries can lend excess funds to the finance company and often obtain rates of return that are higher than they would otherwise earn locally. The finance company can pool the small amounts, thereby investing larger amounts and obtain higher rates in either the local or Euro money market.
- The finance company can fund subsidiary working capital needs or balance subsidiary foreign exchange exposures through intercompany loans or factoring (i.e., purchasing the receivables from a subsidiary).

Until 1984, the use of this vehicle has allowed U.S. multinational corporations to avoid the 30 percent withholding tax on interest payments which they otherwise would incur through a direct offshore borrowing. An offshore finance company should be located in a country which has tax treaties with the parent country to eliminate the withholding tax on foreign borrowings, has minimal taxes on income or capital, and has an extensive reciprocal tax treaty network with the countries to be involved. The most popular locations have been the Netherlands, the Netherlands Antilles, Switzerland, and Panama.

SUMMARY

The purpose of this chapter was to provide an overview of international cash management on a cross-border basis. Common problems in mobilizing cash globally were discussed and practical suggestions and techniques were described to accelerate the availability of funds and minimize costs to the company.

Given that there are numerous variables to cope with, which often lead to delays, it is imperative that the international cash manager be informed of his/her options; negotiate where possible with banks regarding their practices and charges; provide explicit payment instructions to both banks and customers; and make effective use of a multinational bank with an extensive overseas branch network to expedite the collection and movement of funds globally.

15

In-Country Treasury Management

Andrew D. Kerr
*Vice President, Global Cash
Management Department*
Citibank, N.A.

OVERVIEW

Inflation in the United States in 1983 was 3.6 percent. The trend for the rest of the decade is for interest rates to be below those endured by American corporations in the 1970s. But overseas the picture is quite different: European nations will spend the better part of the 1980s working their rates down into single digits; the Asia-Pacific region varies from low inflation rates, with a fear of increase, to high inflation, with a hope of future improvement; and in Latin America an inflation rate of 100 percent is considered normal. Inflation and interest rates are constantly changing. The lessons of the 1970s are that cash is an asset to be managed and that corporate treasuries can be net revenue generators. The focus even for the multinational corporation, though, has been on domestic operations. Yet, even a cursory review of a multinational's foreign operations will reveal that cash is one of the most expensive commodities an international subsidiary consumes.

As the world continues to grapple with recession, and inflation-battered economies try to recover lost profits, one thing remains certain. Right now, somewhere in the international company, perhaps at an overseas manufacturing or sales location, the consumption of cash is reducing the company's local competitiveness. How effective are the local company's international treasury management practices? How can they be changed? What impact will such changes have on operating policy, product costs, and, most importantly, the all-too-revealing bottom line?

Many of the techniques discussed in the previous chapters are equally relevant to the international scene. There are, though, some notable differences. Certainly the first question facing the multinational is: Why worry about foreign subsidiaries when improvement opportunities remain abundant at the parent level? Increased income, the same justification for automated balance reporting services, lockbox collection systems, and controlled disbursement accounts, is the greatest reason to look beyond one's domestic operation. But troubles can be compounded if some basic understandings are not achieved. Cash management is basically the same set of concerns worldwide. The difference is environmental.

THE INTERNATIONAL ENVIRONMENT

The foreign subsidiary differs from the parent in three major environmental arenas: the foreign subsidiary environment, the country structure environment, and the local treasury environment.

The Company Environment

The first area in which the treasury must alter its approach is in dealing with the financial environment of the specific foreign subsidiary. A subsidiary operating in a country with a low inflation rate will have much less incentive to borrow, knowing the payback will be in relatively expensive money, than the subsidiary operating in a hyperinflationary environment where loan payback can be made with relatively cheap money. A company operating in a country where periodic currency devaluation is the norm must be very careful to minimize the impact of devaluation in its inventory planning of imported raw materials. Companies operating in countries of chronic tight liquidity tend to develop extensive banking networks to ensure fund availability.[1]

The Country Environment

The second environment is unique to each country in the world. Every economy operates within its own idiosyncratic banking, commercial, legal, and political systems. Check-clearing systems, the very use of checks, differ from country to country even when the basic foundations of the banking industry have

---

[1] There are two basic bank network philosophies which will be discussed later in the chapter. Suffice it to say the word "ensure" is used here as reported by actual cases.

the same roots (for example, Canada, England, and Australia). The role of the central bank differs from lender of last resort to actual commercial bank competition. Commercial systems likewise differ. Prompt payment in some countries is 30 days after the month of invoice, resulting in actual terms ranging from 30 to 60 days; in others it could be on or before the due date. To compare one subsidiary's experience to that of the parent or any other subsidiary without adjustment for local payment practices often results in a misinterpretation of what is effective cash management. For example, assume the parent establishes a collection goal of 32 days. If Subsidiary A produces an average of 20 days and Subsidiary B operates with 40 days, Subsidiary A appears to be more efficient. Upon closer inspection, however, if the goal at the parent level is 32 days with a standard of 30, its actual intent is +2 days from standard. If the standard in Country A is 10 and the standard in Country B is 35, then Subsidiary B operating at +5 days is more effective than Subsidiary A at +10 days. Treasurers attempting to reduce days sales outstanding by encouraging local collection managers to squeeze late payers may actually hurt their own cause if they ignore the local customs.

Legal systems are always country-unique. They affect everything from requirements for opening a bank account to procedures to protest a late payer. That politics affects the workings of a company is nothing new. It also affects the treasury; in many countries you need at least one government bank in your lineup for purely political reasons.

The Treasury Environment

The third consideration is the organization of the treasury itself. Rarely, if ever, has a company established a local operation where the treasury was the key component. Treasuries tend to be small and accounting oriented. The personnel are faced with local needs and with reporting their actions to the parent, to say nothing of answering the ever present "emergency telexes." When personnel are added to a subsidiary, they tend to be directed first to marketing (to sell more product) and then to manufacturing (to produce products at a lower cost). Thus, the size of a treasury tends to lag behind the growth of the company, compounding the problem of too few people to efficiently handle the usual treasury evolution of reports, collection volumes, disbursement volumes, and greater funding needs. Non-European treasuries often benefit from low labor rates and clerks in place of automated data equipment. Clerks are very good but very limited. Decision makers are few and very far between. True, there is little time wasted on bureaucratic problems in implementing local decisions, but there are often other alternatives overlooked out of ignorance or the pressure of deadlines. There are too few experts and rarely is there an opportunity to step back and take an objective look at the operation.

COMPONENTS OF TREASURY MANAGEMENT

In in-country cash management, there are three key elements. The first is the actual flow of funds through the company (that is, receipts coming in, disbursements going out, bank balances sitting idle). The second element is the costs of those flows. Those costs take the following forms: (1) the direct cost in terms of fees or balances for services rendered, telex charges, depository fees; (2) the indirect cost of float; and (3) the cost of people. Regardless of how large or small the treasury is, the staff is there in part because of the need to manage these flows, and there is a cost to that staff. When evaluating the cost of the treasury group, all three of those costs should be examined. It may be possible to change a personnel cost that will have a bigger bottom line impact than the change to one bank from another because the telex charge is 20 cents less per item.

The last key element is control. This is generally an area where companies exercise little control over their flows and their actual cost. Portions of the cash cycle are under the treasurer's control, portions are under the control of the financial intermediaries, and portions are under the control of clients or suppliers.

Having established the need to view foreign subsidiary treasury operations in a different light from that of the parent or another subsidiary, the rest of this chapter is devoted to discussing the approach a treasurer may take in helping local operations run as efficient a treasury as possible. Five primary functions of the treasury are reviewed and analyzed. Treasurers must, however, refrain from making a "quick fix" to any one area before the other areas have been reviewed and the implications of any one action on the other functions have been considered.

The foreign company, be it subsidiary or indigenous company, is generally smaller than its parent or U.S. counterpart. Where in the United States is it possible to refine a company's lockbox cash gathering system without tracing the impact of accelerated funds through the rest of the cash management cycle, this is not the case overseas.[2] In a smaller company, especially one facing high inflation and interest rates, every action has a profound effect on the associated functions. One way to visualize the relationship is presented as Exhibit 1.

Exhibit 1
The Cash Management Pentagram

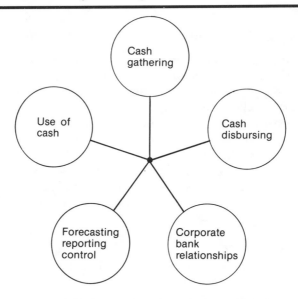

The cash management pentagram demonstrates how each area is linked. For example, a change in the cash gathering system which reduces the inflow, say a sudden delay in customer payments, directly influences what is available to pay down loans or invest overnight. It reduces what is available to disburse to suppliers. It also reduces bank balance inflows and probably the balances as well. It can wreck havoc with any cash projections—worse yet inappropriate internal reporting may not even detect the change. Like a pebble thrown in a pond, the reaction grows until it comes full circle and begins to compound itself. The reduction in cash available to pay suppliers may result in negotiations for a loan or may force the treasurer to choose whom to pay on time and whom to stall (which could

---

[2] Even in the United States, cash gathering impacts the other areas of cash management. The impact, however, is not as dramatic or apparent at the large corporate parent as it is in the smaller subsidiary. In many ways the impact overseas is similar to the impact in the United States of the first lockbox systems in the early 1960s.

alter the mix of suppliers or the terms offered on subsequent purchases). The drop in bank balances could result in a call from the firm's friendly banker reminding the treasurer of agreed-upon compensating balance levels. If operating in a country where credit balances are swept into investment accounts or earn interest on their own, investment income (which the treasurer could be counting on to help pay down loans or provide additional liquidity) will decrease. Certainly the pressure increases on internal reports and forecasts to identify the problem or predict its resolution. Errors in forecasting or reporting may cause the treasurer to take actions which actually worsen the situation. The system is quite dynamic, as shown in Exhibit 2.

Exhibit 2
Managing the Float

In every treasury there are inflows and outflows. The goal of the treasury is quite simple: It needs to accelerate the inflow of cash, slow down its outflow (without injuring supplier relationships), identify the base level of liquidity available, and use excess cash in a manner which minimizes the cost of cash while ensuring sufficient liquidity.

The Cash Gathering Component

A logical starting point is cash gathering. In discussing the cash management of cash gathering it is important to realize that the cycle actually begins with the initial sale of a product. It continues through credit assessment, manufacturing (if appropriate), shipment, invoice production, customer receipt and processing, payment receipt and processing, bank deposit and processing, the actual crediting of the account, and notification of funds availability. Cash management changes can be made throughout the cycle.

In assessing the areas where change will have the greatest positive impact it is best to view the cycle from the standpoint of its component parts and those parts which are under the company's control (see Exhibit 3).

As can be seen in Exhibit 3, there are numerous opportunities for a company to accelerate the cycle prior to the deposit of any

Exhibit 3
Components of the Cash Gathering Cycle

Component Part	Control		
	Company	Customer	Bank
Sale	X	X	
Credit assessment	X		
Production, packaging, etc.	X		
Invoice processing	X		
Shipment and invoicing	X		
Payment processing		X	
Payment		X	
Payment receipt		X	
Payment processing	X		
Bank deposit	X		
Bank clearing			X
Account credit			X
Availability notification	X		X

payments. The first area is sales terms. Are the terms offered by the company consistent with local customs? Often the terms, along with the products, are exported from the parent company in the United States. Thirty days may be normal for the home country but inappropriate elsewhere. The impact of terms, regardless of length, can be further affected by banking practices. Two countries illustrate how the banking system can be used to modify terms. In Brazil, the invoice itself can be discounted at a bank prior to due date. This accelerates cash inflow from sales, but at a significant cost. The cost of discounting is generally higher than other forms of secured or unsecured credit, but there are occasions when the rates are favorable. In Mexico, it is not the invoice a company discounts, but rather a type of check. Most company treasuries are in the Federal District of Mexico City (D.F.), where local checks clear in one day. Companies selling outside the city often receive checks drawn on local banks or local branches of the major banks. These checks, if deposited in the D.F., will not be available in one day but will be assigned an arbitrary float of 5 to 7 days to ensure that the bank has good funds before you draw on them. This float can be reduced to one day by the payment of a $1/10$ percent fee (even this is becoming negotiable).

Value dating, assigning arbitrary availability to either a deposit or withdrawal of funds, is a problem faced internationally that often confuses the U.S. treasurer. In the United States, banks assign availability on a per check basis based either on the Federal Reserve System schedule or a bank's own unique sched-

ule. Value dates are generally assigned based on local convention and can result in a forward value or a back value. Even after
a payment has been received, value dating can stretch effective
payment terms. In some countries such as France, the value
dating is consistent (about two days) and can be factored into a
company's overall cash gathering forecast. On the other hand,
in Italy every item is negotiable and it requires a strong relationship with a collection bank to ensure any sort of predictable
pattern. In general, value dating is a problem faced in countries
with an emphasis on overdraft banking, whereas some form of
assigned availability is more common in countries which prohibit overdrawing of an account. One thing is certain—not
enough attention is paid to the details of terms or the invoices
which reflect terms.

Many countries have adopted some form of direct payment of
invoices, either direct debits and credits or forms of automated
clearings. Where possible, these methods must be spelled out
explicitly on the invoice. A company which is not explicit and
still expects to receive a check in the mail or a direct credit may
be quite surprised to learn the check is being held at the customer's cashier window for pickup.

Another common source of delayed payment originates with
credit approvals. Often treasury procedures will be handed
down by parent organizations to local treasurers with too little
explanation. The general strength of the U.S. dollar as a worldwide reference currency and the use of the "$" sign for local
currency can lead to problems. More than once a sale in countries such as Brazil, Italy, or Japan has been help up pending a
higher level of authority to approve a sale exceeding the stated
policy limits. The need for control and management of risk is
important but it must be made in the context of the local market.
The three countries cited, Brazil, Italy, and Japan, all have currencies which trade at a deep discount to the dollar. A $10,000
limit in the manual, which is incorrectly interpreted as a local
currency amount, can needlessly hold up sales of only a few
hundred U.S. equivalent dollars.

Delivery methods can have a great bearing on ultimate funds
availability. The postal systems of many countries are notori-
ously slow. Yet often these systems are used to deliver invoices
to customers even when payment terms specify the use of services such as direct credit designed to circumvent the postal
system. In such cases the company's sales force may be a more
efficient delivery service, as is the practice of sending the invoice
with the goods themselves.

Payment processing can even be a needless bottleneck. It is

wise to remember the "80/20 rule" here. Quite often attention to the largest payments (rapid posting, same-day deposit, deposits in the drawee bank where possible) will result in a 20 percent effort yet will cover up to 80 percent of the value of cash received. Many bank services which cannot be cost-justified for all payments are relatively inexpensive for these payments. Conversely, in some countries where the cost of labor is extremely low, processing is done by the banks more cheaply than a company could manage with limited volume and staff. The corporate cost of these services is longer float on funds availability. Much of this lost float can be recaptured by isolating the large payments and processing them in-house. It should be remembered that a bank's vested interest in collections is with itself. Banks will not willingly slow the collection of funds, but there may be avoidable delays in crediting an account with good funds. The worldwide proliferation of bank balance reporting services is beginning to reduce this passive source of bank earning assets but elimination will never be realized. In fact it is the "little guys" whose long floats subsidize the major corporations' rapid funds availability. Therefore, complete elimination of such a system-induced inefficiency is actually undesirable from the multinational's perspective.

The Cash Disbursing Component

The second area of our cash management pentagram is cash disbursing. At the foreign subsidiary level, cash disbursing is one of the least exploited and most misunderstood areas of cash management. Part of the problem stems from the tendency of treasuries to be accounting-driven or even mere units of accounting departments. The control and caution prevalent in accounting can mask commonsense opportunities to generate cash savings.

Similarly to cash gathering, it is helpful to focus on those components of cash disbursing over which the treasurer has greatest control (see Exhibit 4). In other words, instead of second-guessing the bank clearing system, much can be gained in areas of direct control such as choosing a payment vehicle. Without injuring supplier relationships or altering terms of a purchase, the company can stretch the payment process through the deliberate choice of a slow payment method such as sending a check through the mail, or writing a check and leaving it with the cashier for supplier pickup, a common method in Latin America. Of course, if the supplier specifies a method, any

Exhibit 4
Components of the Cash Disbursing Cycle

	Control		
Component Part	Company	Supplier	Bank
Payment due date		X	
Choice of disbursement vehicle	X		
Payment processing	X		
Payment release/issuance	X		
Supplier receipt	X	X	
Supplier processing		X	
Supplier deposit		X	
Bank clearing system			X
Accounting debit			X
Account notification	X		X

deviation from that instruction places the relationship at risk and the ultimate cost could easily exceed any one-time float gains. The key to prudent cash management is to operate within the limits of commercial and banking regulations, conventions, and constraints, and not to change the underlying rules of being a good corporate citizen.

That checks are legal documents is one of the underpinnings of their success as payment instruments. That checks are mere pieces of paper is a bonus for prudent cash management. Many controller/treasurers operate under the misguided notion that there must be good funds in an account at the time a check is written or that good funds must be moved into an account to cover checks written. In most countries where overdraft banking is *not* the norm, such understandings are supported by bank regulations and governmental laws. Prudent cash management does not suggest that check kiting is appropriate, desirable, or beneficial. Prudent cash management does, however, recognize that a company's funds are at its disposal until properly debited from its account. The intent of the laws is that companies are not to write checks on funds which are nonexistent. Cash management attempts to more closely match the timing of cash availability and cash need. Consider a check written on an account on Wednesday but not picked up by a supplier until Friday and not deposited in the supplier's bank until Monday. The debit may occur up to six or seven days after the check is written. Must funds remain idle for six or seven days? Many accountants would argue that these payments should be covered immediately because it is not known how long they will be outstanding.

But the use of historical analysis, perhaps the "80/20 rule" again, and common sense argue that payment practices may identify specific supplier or class of payment habits.

Once identified, these habits can be used. Treasuries can even be structured to generate such opportunities. Unless terms explicitly specify a method of payment, it is common in many countries to have payments placed with the cashier for pick up by suppliers. In some Latin American countries the days and hours of the cashiers' windows can be severely limited; they are often open only one or two days a week and/or only after the bank's deposit cutoff for the day. Such tactics are designed to virtually guarantee one, two, or more days of float. Exhibit 5

Exhibit 5
The Payment Time Line

| Check written | Check issued | Check pickup | Check deposit | Check clearing |

presents the float steps involved from check writing to check clearing.

From a legal perspective, the check becomes a legal document when negotiated by the payee. Until the moment of deposit it represents a call on funds but not an absolute store of value (you can stop payment on a check; you cannot do that with currency). Therefore, it is critical to have good funds in the account to cover clearing checks.

A company which tracks checks rather than anticipated clearings may be foregoing substantial income opportunities. It is possible to generate several days of usable float and still fund the account days prior to the anticipated check presentment.

While this explanation of disbursement float should be all too familiar to cash managers, subsidiary controllers and treasury staffs often find it a revelation. Even those companies which claim to use disbursement float through various payment-delaying tactics often overlook the fact that it takes time—controllable time in part—for a check to clear once it has been picked up by a supplier.

Some cynics insist that the use of discounts at foreign subsidiaries is a waste of time. No one pays on time so who would ever pay early? And futhermore, how could offering a discount be justified for on-time payment when that is merely compliance to stated terms? But payment terms must be looked at in a different context. As a customer, early payment results in an implicit funding charge compared to any current practice. To a supplier, normal terms should be included in the gross margin of the product sold. Any delay in payment beyond this results in receivables financing. At what point, therefore, will a customer pay early? At what point is it economical for a supplier to offer a discount?

Suppliers should offer a discount which at least offsets their costs of financing the receivable. A discount of less than the customer's cost of funds rarely offers the customer any advantage over paying late or financing payments in the marketplace. Customers should consider accepting discounts only if there is a net benefit to doing so, as outlined in Exhibit 6.

Exhibit 6
Discount Threshold for Accepting Discounts

I. Gross invoice
− amount of discount
(percentage discount times gross invoice)

  Net payable

II. Net payable
× annual effective rate
÷ 365

  Daily interest on net payable
  × days of financing*

  Cost of discount

III. Amount of discount
− cost of discount

  + Net benefit to company
  − net deficit to company
  ○ Actual indifference threshold

  * For example, Actual payment terms = 35 days
  Normal terms = 2/10 net 30
  Days of financing = 35 − 10 = 25 days

When the final number is positive, the company benefits from the discount; where the remainder is negative, the amount of discount does not even cover the implicit value of the forgone use of funds. When the remainder is zero, the company's costs are just offset and it would be indifferent to the discount.

For example, consider the XYZ company which routinely pays suppliers in 42 days. ABC contractors is now offering a discount of 3 percent for payments made in 7 days with their standard net terms of 30 days. The local economy is experiencing tight liquidity and the overnight investment rate has jumped to an annualized 147 percent. Should XYZ take the discount? What instruction, if any, should XYZ's treasurer give its purchasing manager and payments supervisor regarding negotiating for and taking discounts?

To answer the first question, the formula in Exhibit 6 is applied to the example in Exhibit 7. The net deficit to XYZ is

Exhibit 7
XYZ's Cost of a Discount

Gross invoice	100%	
Discount	3%	
Days of financing	35	(42 − 7)
Opportunity cost	147%	

I. $ 100   Invoice
    −3   Discount amount
    $ 97   Net invoice payable

II. $ 97   Net payable
    ×147%   Annualized opportunity cost
    ÷365
    $13.67   Cost of discount

III. Amount of discount $ 3.00   per $100 invoice
     Cost of taking discount $ 13.67   per $100 invoice
         Net deficit to XYZ $(10.67)

$10.67. In other words it will cost XYZ $13.67 to take advantage of a $3.00 discount. Consequently, XYZ should not change its normal payment practice.

It is important to note two things in this example: (1) The days of financing must be figured from actual practice of XYZ, not ABC's terms and (2) it is assumed that XYZ is following accepted local practices in paying late. In some countries a late payment fee may have been assessed on all or part of the 12 days. This amount should be deducted from the cost of a discount in calculating the net benefit (deficit) to the company since early payment would eliminate this cost. In this example, the cost of taking the discount is the amount the company would have earned had it invested the net payable amount for the 35 days between discount date and actual payment date.

But what information should be distributed within XYZ regarding discount policy? To answer this, it is necessary to find the equilibrium rate where the cost of any discount is offset by the discount amount. The equation that should be used to solve for the equilibrium point is:

$$y = \frac{((p - d)(i/365))}{1 + ((p - d)(i/365))}$$

where

i = cost of funds
p = normal payment period
d = discount payment period
y = equilibrium point

In the case of XYZ company paying ABC, the rate offered, given a 7-day discount period and a cost of funds of 147 percent ($i = 1.47$) would have to rise to 12.35 percent before reaching an indifference point as shown below:

$$y = \frac{((42 - 7)(1.47/365))}{1 + ((42 - 7)(1.47/365))} = 12.35\%$$

For XYZ company, the message to the staff should be in the form of a graph such as Exhibit 8.

Exhibit 8
A Model Indifference Graph for Use in Selecting Discounts

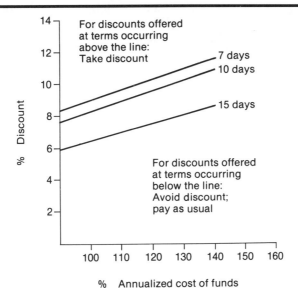

The Banking Component

The third area of our pentagram, corporate banking, is a key area where foreign companies operate at a real disadvantage to their U.S. counterparts. U.S. banks are often mocked by foreign banks wondering why so much information is given to their clients. Make no mistake about it, foreign banks usually know which accounts are profitable. When one reviews the industries operating in a high-inflation economy, rarely, if ever, does banking appear as anything other than a top profit performer. This is not to say that certain services couldn't be improved, only that banks are quite profitable and, being so, have the luxury of not working quite as hard as their clients in becoming more efficient producers.

In most English/overdraft foundation banking systems (United Kingdom, Australia, Canada, Hong Kong, Singapore, among others) it is common for a company to maintain only one major relationship. Elsewhere, and especially in Latin America, the tendency is to develop an ever-increasing roster of banks.

The reason for this difference is the feeling in overdraft countries that cash availability is not a major problem. Therefore, all financial needs can be met by one bank. Other countries do not allow the use of overdrafts and, coupled with chronic inflation, corporations must continually cope with tight liquidity. In Latin America this has been carried to the extreme. Banks have controlled the credit markets for so many decades that companies have abdicated their role in negotiations. The question is no longer what bank should a company use, but how soon can another one be added. The prevalent feeling in Latin America is that a company needs as many banks as possible to ensure access to credit facilities when they are needed, not when they are offered.[3]

In many one-bank countries, the major concern is ensuring that the company is aware of all the services available and that the prices charged (fees and/or balances) for those services are competitive.[4] In multibank countries there are two conflicting philosophies: maintaining the maximum number of banks, as

---

[3] This may result in the use of every commercial bank in a country in order to obtain the necessary cash. Such is the current situation in Colombia where extremely tight liquidity and individual bank-imposed ceilings on loans to any one company effectively require the establishment of credit lines with every commercial bank.

[4] While historical precedent has resulted in a one-bank, one-company environment, bank needs should be evaluated independently. Different commercial banks possess unique expertise owing to their internal capabilities, geographic location and dispersion, and their corporate strategic business philosophy. Upon investigation and solicitation of various bank package offerings, it may prove appropriate to break with tradition and use two or more commercial banks

described, or concentrating relationships in as few banks as necessary. The latter philosophy is preferable for reasons of both internal and external control. It is very difficult to manage more than six to eight banks, it is even more difficult to monitor daily balances and activity in more than eight banks. Yet it is common to find 20 to 30 banks being used often, with more than one account per bank. One company in Brazil used 40 banks, maintaining 238 accounts.[5]

It is far easier to open accounts than to close them, so even accounts dormant for years are not closed out or zero balanced, resulting in pockets of cash which slowly erode in value due to inflation and which are never monitored. One cause of frequent account openings stems from the authority and autonomy of branch managers operating in large countries with nationwide branching. Of necessity these managers must make many decisions without the ability to consult higher authorities. Managers also are capable of establishing unique arrangements for valued customers, such as staying past normal closing time to accept for deposit large but late-arriving checks. They can find local currency when none is available. Therefore, when a branch manager moves on to a new branch or bank, the customer moves on, opening a new account and leaving idle funds behind. Because of the local clout of a branch manager, the concept of bankwide profitability of a relationship is nonexistent. The branch manager is evaluated on the basis of his branch's loan volume, balance levels, and volume of activity. In these situations, the presumed value of a multinational's worldwide size or well-known name is of little value. If the branch manager is forced to allocate credit in times of tight liquidity he will allocate it first to those accounts which generate the most at that branch (and in turn support his bonus). A company maintaining dozens to hundreds of accounts has spread itself so thin in the quest for credit sources[6] that it has undermined its own negotiating ability. A company is in a much stronger position when it is important enough to the bank manager to jeopardize his bonus if the account were to be closed for poor service or credit.

It is important to note, however, that there will generally be two to four bank relationships maintained beyond the core

---

[5] This is not only a problem in multibank countries. A company in Australia, using only one bank, had over 214 accounts.

[6] There are some types of credit allocated by central banks or governments, such as rural credit in Brazil, which force even large companies to maintain many credit relationships. Often the volume of idle balances or noncredit business directed to these additional banks far outweighs the value of the credit provided. In such cases, the account should be reviewed regularly to ensure only the minimum level of balances to ensure that the specific credit is maintained.

group. These accounts are either established for corporate reasons ("This is our major international bank, we maintain accounts with them around the world") or political reasons ("Everyone who does business in this district maintains an account with the district bank" or "If you want to get funds out of this country, you better keep an account at the central bank's commercial bank"). There are other very good business reasons for accounts. Whatever the reason, accounts have a cost. There's a cost to idle balances, a cost to inferior service quality, a cost in the time it takes to decide what bank to use for a particular service on a given day. Extra accounts being maintained for reasons other than direct service usage act as insurance accounts. It is appropriate for a company to determine what price it is willing to pay for its insurance.

Regardless of the number of banks and accounts or the reason for an account, one aspect of banking remains universal. Companies do not adequately communicate with their banks or internally with themselves in their use of banks. Companies, especially those with decentralized treasury operations, often are unaware of the extent of a particular bank relationship. With autonomous nationwide branching, the problem is often compounded by banks that do not know the extent of their relationship with customers. The solution is to hold formal reviews with banks. These reviews should be held a minimum of once a year. The purpose is several-fold.

At the meeting the company has an opportunity to review the prior year's relationship. This includes a review of credit requests, extensions and rates; compensating balance requirements; the volume and price of noncredit services used by the company; and the quality of service rendered by the bank. If the bank is unaware of some of the services the company has used, it cannot be expected to have monitored the quality of its service. But the role of the meeting is not to complain about past service. The goal is to improve the overall relationship which requires an open, two-way dialogue. The bank should be made aware of upcoming plans—Will the company be increasing, decreasing, or maintaining its credit usage? Will the company be changing in any way which would change the type of credit used or noncredit services required? What level of activity will be directed to the bank? Certain information is basic to bank reviews and a proper understanding of the relationship itself. This information includes such items as:

- Age — How old is this relationship?
- Purpose — Why was the relationship initiated? Who was the initiator (company or bank)?

Are the original reasons for existence still viable?
Do any affiliates maintain an account?
Is there a relationship with any of the officers of the company or bank?

- Services   What services are currently used?
Why was this bank chosen for this (these) particular service(s)?

- Delivery   What do the services cost?
How does their quality compare with the company's expectations?
How does their quality compare to their competition?

- Needs   What did the company plan to do with them in the past year?
How does actual experience compare to the plan?
If there is a difference, can it be explained?
What does the company plan to use the bank for in the coming year?

The art of negotiating is understanding that the goal is arriving at a win-win solution beneficial to all parties. In order to receive the best "deal" from the bank, recognizing that it is also a profit oriented institution, it is necessary to know what is required, why it is required, and the potential for business. Only then is the bank in a position to put its best position forward. This is the ultimate benefit of the annual bank review.

In the case of one multinational subsidiary operating in Brazil, banks are primarily selected for their ability to provide short- and long-term financing, accept collector deposits, make collections on behalf of the company, perform disbursement services including check handling and bordereaux[7] processing, and provide payroll services. The emphasis is definitely on the extension of credit.

The company manages its bank relationships in a most uncharacteristically Brazilian way. The objectives are:

- To maintain *several* strong relationships to ensure a high quality of services rendered.
- To ensure convenience and quality service in handling its collection requirements.
- To establish relationships in order to secure competitive financing arrangements.
- To ensure that balances in each account adequately but not excessively compensate the bank for services and float.

---

[7] A Brazilian bank bordereau is a listing of corporate payments by vendor by due date, instructing the bank to debit a particular amount on a particular date and pay the supplier on behalf of the company.

To many these would seem obvious, even basic. But in Brazil, some of these objectives are difficult to achieve due to the constraints of the banking system. These constraints are outlined below.

Banks do not furnish companies with account analyses detailing assigned or achieved funds availability. Consequently, a company must estimate this information.

The nationwide branching system, by its very nature, offers a segregated framework for the evaluation of a particular bank. The capabilities of banks vary on a branch-to-branch basis.

The pricing of services, borrowing, and funds availability is extremely negotiable for prime customers. The lack of explicit information on account activity and actual balance levels places banks in a comparatively advantageous position.

One response to the problems of lack of information and tight liquidity is the adoption of the package plan approach to banking. Again, this is a practice widespread in the United States but not overseas. This approach facilitates the annual review and increases the negotiating position of the company. In the package plan the treasurer considers all aspects of a bank's services in evaluating the relationship and its cost. The company, using these data, will approach its banks with a specific request, generally a credit request, in consideration of which the company will expand and/or adjust current service usage, and in return expect concessions on loan rates, amounts or compensating balance levels. The company prepares itself by establishing its negotiating ranges well ahead of the meeting. Services used for "barter" in these situations include collections (or additional collections), disbursement activity or payroll, foreign exchange, short-term investments, tax financing, insurance, or even idle compensating balances. The negotiations could also include the quality of service rendered such as collection availability, timing of disbursement funding or advance payroll deposits, or even the nominal loan rate/compensating balance mix.

Their goal is to manage both the quality and quantity of services delivered by the bank, and more important, to be able to know when the operations are out of synchronization with the market or the company's budget parameters.

The Information Component

Arriving at the information to convey to the banks at the review meeting is one of the roles of the internal reporting, forecasting, and control function—area four of the cash management penta-gram. This section is the critical link in translating changing systems into bottom line savings; for if a company does not know where its funds are, what the company's cash needs are, or how much cash is available, the resulting decisions will be ineffective.

A sound control system recognizes that the primary issue is the assurance of corporate liquidity at an acceptable cost. Its first efforts, therefore, must be directed at monitoring where funds are and why they are fluctuating. It must also be noted that cash monitoring relies on actual information, concerning cash in-flows and outflows, not on accounting information, based on the receipt of hard copy documentation.

In multibank systems, the form may look like the one in Ex-hibit 9. But regardless of the number of banks used or the estab-lished target balances[8] for the accounts, the form must provide an accurate indication of daily balances and activities. This is a critical factor in bank systems requiring compensating balances. The effective cost of borrowing often is double or even triple the presumed cost through negligent balance monitoring, which results in actual balances climbing to 50 percent or more of the loan. Compensation rates in Brazil, Mexico, and Colombia have even reached the 100 percent levels through negligence or gross miscalculations of float.

As seductive as overdraft banking may be, one must remem-ber that deficit balances cost a company interest expense and credit balances generate no revenue. Companies should there-fore not manage their accounts on the basis of the limit of their overdraft facility but on the basis of a zero balance target. With the plethora of financing and investing options available (to be discussed later), a company may be incurring substantial "pen-alties" by relying on overdrafts. By remaining cognizant of daily cleared balance levels through calls to the bank verified by telex, telex balance reporting, or use of soon-to-be-available auto-mated reporting services, a company can begin to minimize—when desirable—its overdraft level and reduce any credit bal-

---

[8] Target balances are quite different from compensating balances. The primary differ-ences are that compensating balances are requirements of a bank to secure and maintain a credit facility. Target balances are determined, established, and maintained by the company itself. This difference is often lost on local management. The target balance should include any required balance plus balances maintained, if necessary, for services, negotiating incen-tive, disbursement liquidity, or any other corporate identified reason. The company should manage target balances, recognizing that any amount over the minimum requirement results in a cash management cost. The company must therefore determine what cost is appropriate to secure liquidity and services. The cost of inflation on bank earnings world-wide is placing greater emphasis on fee income. As banks move in this direction, excess balances will be even more expensive than they are at present, the company having periodi-cally paid for services in full by fee.

Exhibit 9. Daily Bank Position Form

Category	Explanation of Terms
Beginning balance	Previous day's ending balance
Bank reported balance	Received from banks via telephone call in the morning. Used to adjust beginning balance.
Credits	
Collections—today	Collections expected to be deposited today. Figure supplied by collection manager.
Deposits—others	Other deposits to be made today, plus unanticipated collections deposited yesterday.
Maturing investments	Principal amount of maturing investments.
Investment income	Interest earnings on investments.
Reimbursements due	Any reimbursements (taxes, incentives, etc.) to be received today.
Transfers	Transfers of funds from outlying offices to concentration account(s).
Loan proceeds	Principal amount of loan taken down today.
Other credits	Voided or canceled checks, miscellaneous credits, direct bank credits from customers, etc.
Disbursements	
Supplier payments:	
Telex transfers	Funds transfers to suppliers as of today.
Checks	Checks issued to suppliers as of today.
Payroll funding	Funds disbursed today to meet payroll.
Tax payments	Tax payments made today.
Bank charges and fees	Bank service charges and activity fees. (Notice received late yesterday.)
Investments—short-term	Today's investments—principal only.
Interest payments	Interest payments made today.
Loan principal repayment	Loan principal payments made today.
Other debits	Miscellaneous debits, direct bank debits, other bank charges. (Notice received late yesterday.)
Float adjustments	Accounting for payments not debited today or collections not credited today.
Special disbursement	Disbursed checks that have not cleared. Includes calculated float on today's and previous day's checks.
Other disbursement	Same as above for all other payments.
Bank transfers	Transfers between banks for investment, disbursement and other bank compensation needs.
Collection float	Collected checks that have not cleared. Includes calculated float on today's and prior day's collections.
Estimated bank balance	Beginning balance + Credits − Debits + Net float adjustments.
Target balance	Each bank's established target balance.
Difference	Difference between estimated bank balance and target balance. This figure should be monitored to see if additional changes should be made in bank activity or target balances.

ances. The real value of balance monitoring is realizable when it is used in conjunction with short-term forecasts indicating cash (not accounting) needs and sources.

The most serious problem encountered in this area is the commingling of accounting and cash information which distorts the true flow of cash in and out of the bank. The difference between the recording of a transaction and the actual debit or credit results from two principal factors:

Information Lags   There are delays in the receipt of credit advices for collections. This is especially true if funds are transferred in from geographic (state, provincial, territory, etc.) or branch offices. The bank balance will reflect the credit once the payment has cleared. The company's book balance, however, tends to lag the actual credit due to mail or processing float, delaying the receipt of the credit advice and hence the recognition of the actual credit.

Disbursement Float   Book debits tend to be recorded upon release of checks from the company. Perhaps the debit will be delayed to due date if checks are released early. Some automated check-clearing systems input debit information to the accounting records on the date the check is issued. The basis for this is the operating policy stating that checks are to be signed and released the day they are printed. Practice, though, doesn't often equal policy. These practices result in record balances reflecting debits before the instruments ever enter the bank clearing system, not to mention the actual debiting of the account.

Any balance reporting service, though, is hollow without a corresponding short-term cash forecast. The most common rationalization for not incorporating short-term forecasts into daily treasury operations is that either the company uses its overdraft facilities (if available) to meet any contingency or that the company would like to forecast cash needs and availability but lacks the computer power of the parent organizations. Indigenous companies tend to have a slightly different excuse: The treasury ranks last in priority on the company's computer and simply can't schedule it in.

The multinational subsidiary/branch may further feel that the reports which are sent to the parent after the fact each month suffice as an adequate substitute for a timely cash flow forecast. The local company can take solace in the knowledge that the annual budget incorporates a cash flow statement which is revised each quarter. There are also personal excuses such as "I don't really need to write out a forecast—I've always got the information (in my head)." This is fine so long as job responsibilities don't change, payment practices remain constant, major customers remain consistent in number and in remittance practices, and the individual doesn't leave the company. If any one of these variables changes, the carefully constructed mental pattern built from months or years of experience can crumble in a day.

One company has gone so far as to program a small computer to calculate check clearings on a monthly basis and highlights any deviation from historical averages. While performed only on major suppliers, this has had the effect of increasing the company's use of disbursement float by two days. The reason for the initial analysis was to help the company forecast more accurately, not to "play the float." Another company now requires forecasts of the coming two-week disbursements and anticipated collections at sales offices to be sent to headquarters each Friday. The report is completed day by day. This company has been able to sweep its accounts and greatly increase its net investable cash. The computer isn't ignored and its benefits are recognized but much can be gained from the hand-held calculator and the pencil.

One alternative gaining favor is the big picture calendar, a copy of which appear as Exhibit 10. Companies have experienced varying degrees of success with a pencil, calendar, and

Exhibit 10
A Better Cash Forecast Form

Month					
Monday	Tuesday	Wednesday	Thursday	Friday	Saturday
2	3	4	5	6	7
9	10 100,000	11	12	13	14 (70,500) Tax debit
16	17	18	19	20	21
23	24	25	26	27	28
30	31				

calculator approach. On a large (two foot by three foot) calendar of the month, divided into days, known cash needs or sources are written by one of two methods. The first method calls for data to be entered on a due date basis. For instance, a company knows a tax payment of $70,500 is due on the 10th of the month and so enters −70,500 on the 10th. As it happens, a short-term investment matures on the 10th in the amount of $100,000 and it is so entered. Apart from any unknown flows the company now knows that on the 10th of the coming month at least $29,500 will be available to cover clearing checks.

The second method is the experienced clearing system where data are entered on the calendar, not on due dates but according to historical clearing patterns. Thus, the tax payment due on the 10th is not entered on the 10th but on the 14th as historically the government clearing process provides four days of disbursement float at a minimum.

On the other hand, a maturing investment will be available for use at maturity. Thus this company, net of any other information being entered, has $100,000 at its disposal from the 10th to the 14th with $29,500 available thereafter. This provides an implicit gain of $70,500 for 4 days which at 10 percent is worth $78 in incremental interest income. A small figure? True. But in practice such forecasting yields opportunities amounting from thousands to hundreds of thousands of dollars in incremental pre-tax interest income or reduced interest expense.

A forecast by definition is an estimate of less than 100 percent accuracy. It is only a tool to aid decision making. The need is to identify those cash inflows and outflows by magnitude which will impact the overall availability of cash need to fund the company. Many of these items are easily identified and readily available, such as:

Cash inflows, credits

- Major customer payments which historically are made with a consistent time from invoice generation.
- Periodic inflows for the payment of annual service contracts.
- Proceeds of a local loan.
- Maturing investments with a fixed tenor.
- Infusions of cash from the parent company.

Cash outflows, debits

- Payroll.
- Major suppliers with consistent purchase levels (e.g., utilities).
- Tax payments.

- Insurance payments.
- Union contributions.
- Loan interest repayments.
- Loan repayments of principal.
- Dividends to the parent company.
- Royalty payments.
- Investment principal.

Not only are the due dates and planned payment dates of outflows known in advance, but through an analysis of historic clearing times the company should have a fairly accurate idea of the actual bank debit for these disbursements. Likewise with cash inflows, historic clearing analyses will indicate the average actual credit date of a given inflow.

The Income Component

Unless the company which implements the concepts and techniques of the previous four areas follows through with area five of the pentagram described in Exhibit 1, "the use of funds," all the efforts will have been purely academic. Very often companies come to the last area, relax, and rely on standard answers. Standard answers may prove inappropriate. Companies which claim to invest funds in only one instrument or borrow through only one vehicle without investigating market alternatives are likely to miss sources of potential incremental income.

The previous sections showed how incremental cash inflows could be accelerated, cash outflows stretched, bank balances controlled, and information quality and accuracy improved. At this point the company has identified an enhanced source of earning assets for their banks. To derive the maximum benefit, these cash flows and excess balances must be used to increase investments or decrease borrowings so to generate interest income or savings. Whichever route is chosen, the net impact is a better net income figure than the company currently experiences. Because the information component has allowed the treasurer to better forecast the company's sources of and requirements for funds over the coming 28 to 30 days, the treasurer is obligated to review the local money market. This evaluation is aimed at locating investment or borrowing vehicles which better match the company's cash cycle, without sacrificing either risk or rate. Indeed, this new information power should allow the treasurer to secure both better rates and terms which more closely match its needs.

Many treasurers of foreign subsidiaries are told to stay as short as possible in order to ensure liquidity. This is generally a parent-directed policy based on a lack of understanding of the local environment rather than a reasoned approach to maximizing investment return and minimizing investment risk (credit risk, sovereign risk, devaluation risk). It is well to recognize that the subsidiaries are not there to play in the money market, nor should they take financial risks which jeopardize the profits of the underlying business. The goal is to better cover the risks inherent in the business. In so doing, however, new risks are a possible outcome, such as the massive changes made by the Mexican government in the summer of 1982. Nearly everyone anticipated a large devaluation, but even the most savvy market makers were surprised at the rest of the austerity package, especially the freezing of dollar accounts. On the other hand, based on a continued recession and crippling agricultural losses from drought and fire, a devaluation of the Australian dollar was looming as a possibility in early 1983. The election of a labor prime minister made it a sure bet. Those who live and work in Australia or who regularly deal in the currency were not surprised by the 10 percent devaluation after the election. Those who are only casually in touch were caught off-guard. The point is that it is sometimes appropriate to stay short—more so with investments than with borrowings—but each subsidiary should be treated uniquely. Decisions should reflect not only the policies of the corporation but the local policies embraced by the prudent manager.

If levels of liquidity can be forecasted, the treasurer could, and should, attempt to reduce his costs. For example, a company which only borrows extremely short, perhaps under a week, will be able to reduce its cost of funds by borrowing via unsecured term debt for longer periods, matching the gap in the cash cycle. If secured debt is allowed by the parent, the costs would be further reduced. In another case, the company which habitually borrows via discounted receivables may be able to eliminate the need to do so by a better cash flow. If the funds are still required, either an unsecured line of credit or term debt could be tapped at a lower cost.

The People Factor

Not specifically identified in the cash management pentagram, but underlying each activity are people. People include clerks— which in many countries are quite abundant, supervisors— which can be home-grown or purchased from a somewhat smaller marketplace than clerks, and managers—which in some countries (notably in Latin America) are chronically in woefully short supply.

It's this vital factor which the company must rely on to implement stated policies and any improvements that can be identified and adopted. The treatment of the staff—from the local treasurer on through the ranks—by the parent organization will have a significant impact on their approach to their jobs and their willingness to consider changes. All too often the major decision makers at the parent company (Assistant Treasurer International, Treasurer, CFO, etc.) see the local decision makers of their countries only once a year. And then the visit is far too brief to allow the parent to understand why lockboxes are or are not a viable collection alternative, or how the dynamics of the money market affects the local portfolio. Much has been gained in terms of understanding and increased productivity at those companies where the local management feels that its uniqueness is understood by the parent. This does not mean that everything (such as dire warnings of tight liquidity) reported by the subsidiary is gospel. A healthy skepticism should always be maintained. A dispassionate, objective viewpoint is an appropriate response. Operating within a context of a basic understanding of the local situation, local management may view any skepticism as a challenge and develop creative (yet legal) alternatives of their own.

TREASURY CENTRALIZATION

The rapid escalation of salary and perks required to secure and keep a quality, bilingual treasury manager in places such as Latin America during the early 1980s has been a prime impetus for centralizing foreign subsidiary treasury functions. Coupled with this interest has been the continued merger and acquisition activity by multinationals, resulting in the duplication of many foreign operations. In some cases the acquired companies are in the same field and there is near-complete duplication of activities and functions. In other cases when different businesses combine, the only duplication is at the administrative staff levels, such as treasury.

Companies often find that their relatively small size in a country hinders their borrowing and negotiating power, despite any stature or status of the parent's name. Such companies can regain that economic clout through treasury centralization where all collection, disbursement, bank balance, borrowing, and investing volumes are aggregated. The accounting detail remains at the subsidiary levels, unless the systems are identical and they too can be centralized. With one centralized bank interface, both the quality and price of services rendered the company can be markedly improved over that available for individual subsidiaries. Generally speaking, in bank negotiations, and in negotiations with suppliers concerning their terms—if such negotiation is possible,[9] the economic stature of the combined enterprise will result in more favorable treatment than if each subsidiary negotiated on its own. Such negotiations are testimony to the concept of a whole being greater than the sum of its parts.

In some countries, limits on the size of the money market require such a consolidation to afford the opportunity of accessing the best investment and borrowing vehicles. Such is often the case in developing commercial paper markets.

In all cases the centralization takes one of two forms: a new legal entity or an enhanced position of the strongest contributing part. Where a separate legal structure is not required, time and expense can be saved through using the strongest company to operate as the central treasury. Strong in this case can be defined as best people, largest economic component, largest market position, or best current economic health. It is a partly economic, partly political, and certainly subjective decision.

Where a new legal structure is called for, the company must determine who will manage the structure, where it will be located, and who will ultimately control it. These questions are quite similar to those facing management in its domestic operations, though the language, culture, and customs of the particular country are integral to the decisions.

SUMMARY

In this chapter we have discussed the cash management concepts and techniques facing the multinational treasurer and his subsidiary counterparts. That many of these points bear close resemblance to those problems and situations confronting the U.S. company, domestically, is no mere coincidence. Treasury management is far more similar worldwide than is, for example, accounting management. Every country has its own

---

[9] Even in companies which appear to serve vastly different markets it may be possible to find suppliers common to all. Perhaps different products are purchased from one supplier or different volumes of the same product. Occasionally the same product may be purchased from different suppliers and consolidation is possible. In these cases, central negotiations can result in purchase terms which are better for the company as a whole, even if different units may end up with less attractive terms than before.

accounting, reporting, and disclosure requirements but cash is cash. The fundamental problems remain how to:

- Get your cash from customers more rapidly.
- Pay your cash to suppliers more slowly.
- Know where cash is and how much is there.
- Do something with that cash: profitability.

The rub is that all this should be done in a manner that does not injure customer relationships or jeopardize supplier relationships, that maintains satisfactory bank relationships, and that doesn't require reliance on excessive risk.

Once this primary cash philosophy is exported from the parent it must, to be successful, be tempered with the realities of the dynamics and constraints of the local markets. This can often lead to greater creativity and a better meshing of local needs with local answers. The successful multinationals recognize this need for local knowledge and make the necessary commitment to develop a thorough understanding. Where this has been done, local profits or income contributions support the validity of the investment.

INDEX

This book has been set Quadex 202, in 10 and 9 point Palatino, leaded 2 points. Section numbers and titles are 24 point Univers Medium Condensed. Chapter numbers and titles are 18 point Univers Medium Condensed. The size of the type page is 27 by 47 picas.